CASE CLOSED

V O L U M E   33

CASE FILE:
MURDER

G o s h o   A o y a m a

Case Briefing:

Subject:
Occupation:
Special Skills:
Equipment:

Jimmy Kudo, a.k.a. Conan Edogawa
High School Student/Detective
Analytical thinking and deductive reasoning, Soccer
Bow Tie Voice Transmitter, Super Sneakers,
Homing Glasses, Stretchy Suspenders

The subject is hot on the trail of a pair of suspicious men in black when he is attacked from behind and administered a strange substance which physically transforms him into a first grader. When the subject confides in the eccentric inventor Dr. Agasa, they decide to keep the subject's true identity a secret for the safety of everyone around him. Assuming the new identity of first-grader Conan Edogawa, the subject continues to assist the police force on their most baffling cases. The only problem is that most crime-solving professionals won't take a little kid's advice!

Table of Contents

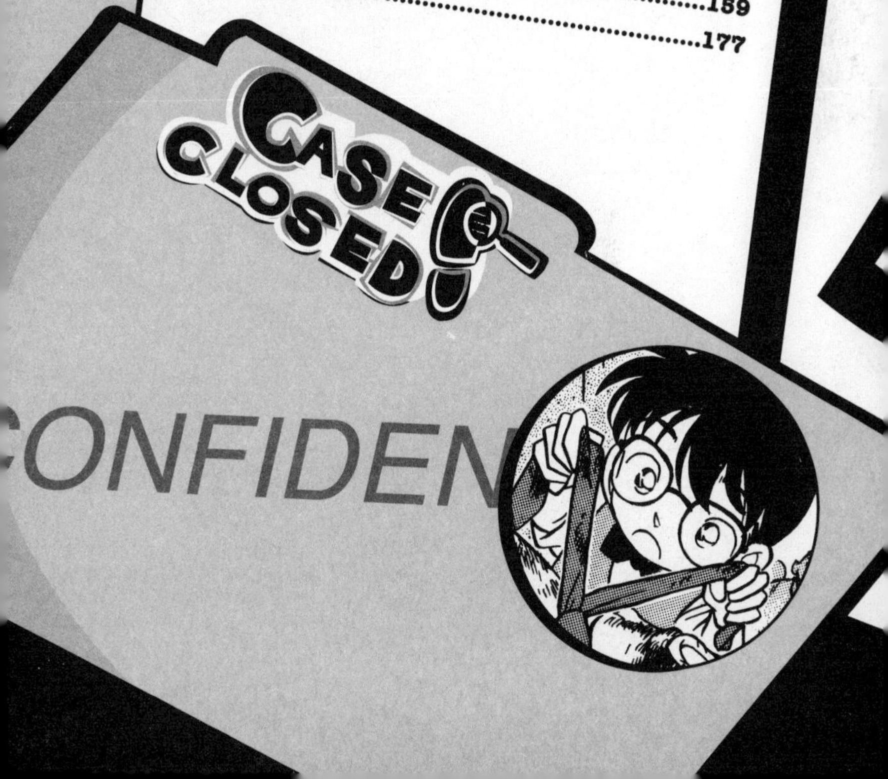

CASE CLOSED
CONFIDEN

CASE CLOSED

Volume 33 • Shonen Sunday Edition

GOSHO AOYAMA

Original Japanese edition "MEITANTEI CONAN" published by SHOGAKUKAN Inc.

Translation
Tetsuichiro Miyaki

Touch-up & Lettering
Freeman Wong

Cover & Graphic Design
Andrea Rice

Editor
Shaenon K. Garrity

Printed in the U.S.A.

Published by VIZ Media, LLC
P.O. Box 77010
San Francisco, CA 94107

10 9 8 7 6 5 4 3 2
First printing, January 2010
Second printing, April 2014

WWW.SHONENSUNDAY.COM

RATED T+ FOR OLDER TEEN
PARENTAL ADVISORY
CASE CLOSED is rated T+ for Older Teen and is recommended for ages 16 and up. This volume contains realistic and graphic violence.
ratings.viz.com

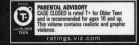

www.viz.com

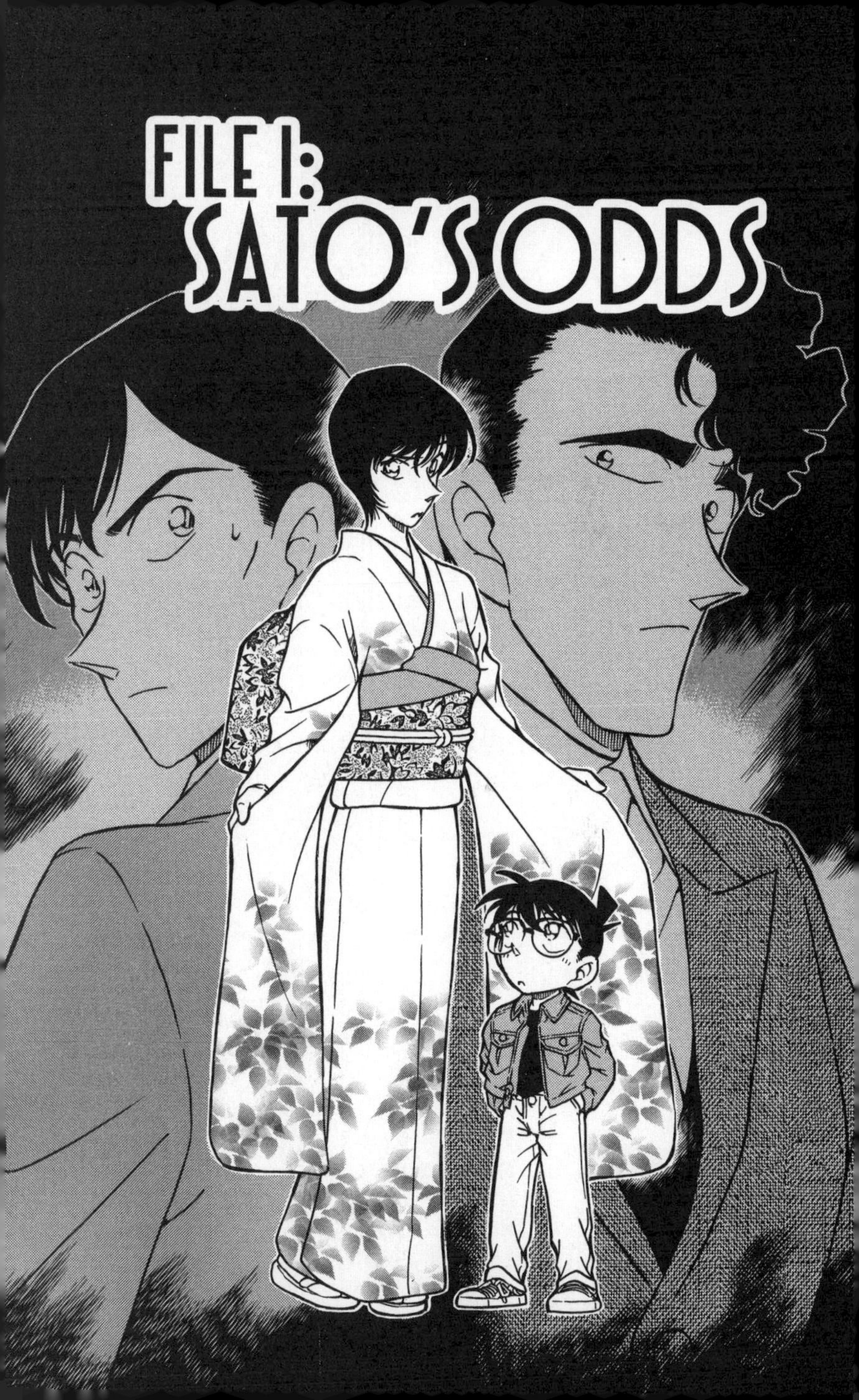
FILE 1:
SATO'S ODDS

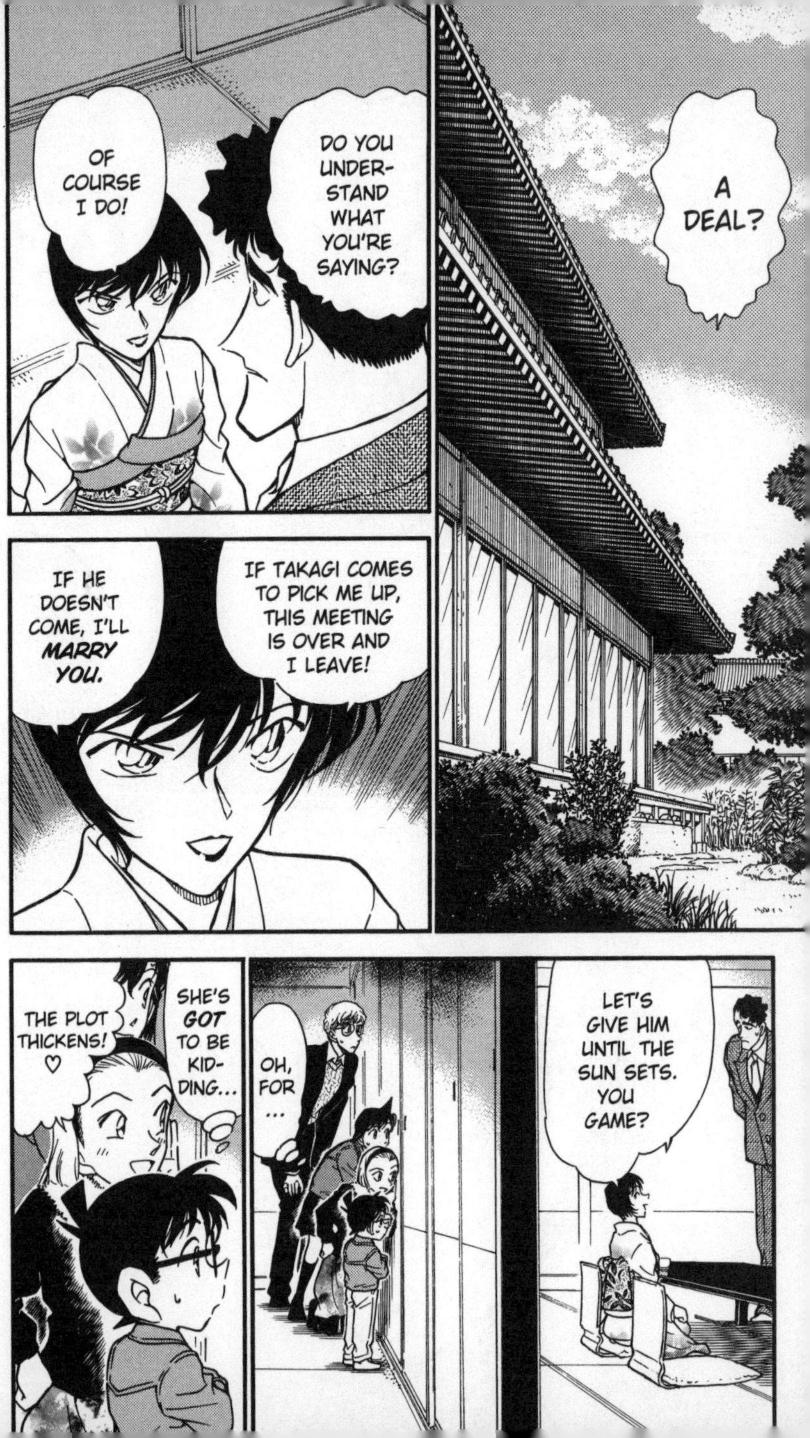
A DEAL?
DO YOU UNDERSTAND WHAT YOU'RE SAYING?
OF COURSE I DO!
IF TAKAGI COMES TO PICK ME UP, THIS MEETING IS OVER AND I LEAVE!
IF HE DOESN'T COME, I'LL ***MARRY YOU.***
LET'S GIVE HIM UNTIL THE SUN SETS. YOU GAME?
OH, FOR ...
SHE'S ***GOT*** TO BE KIDDING...
THE PLOT THICKENS! ♡

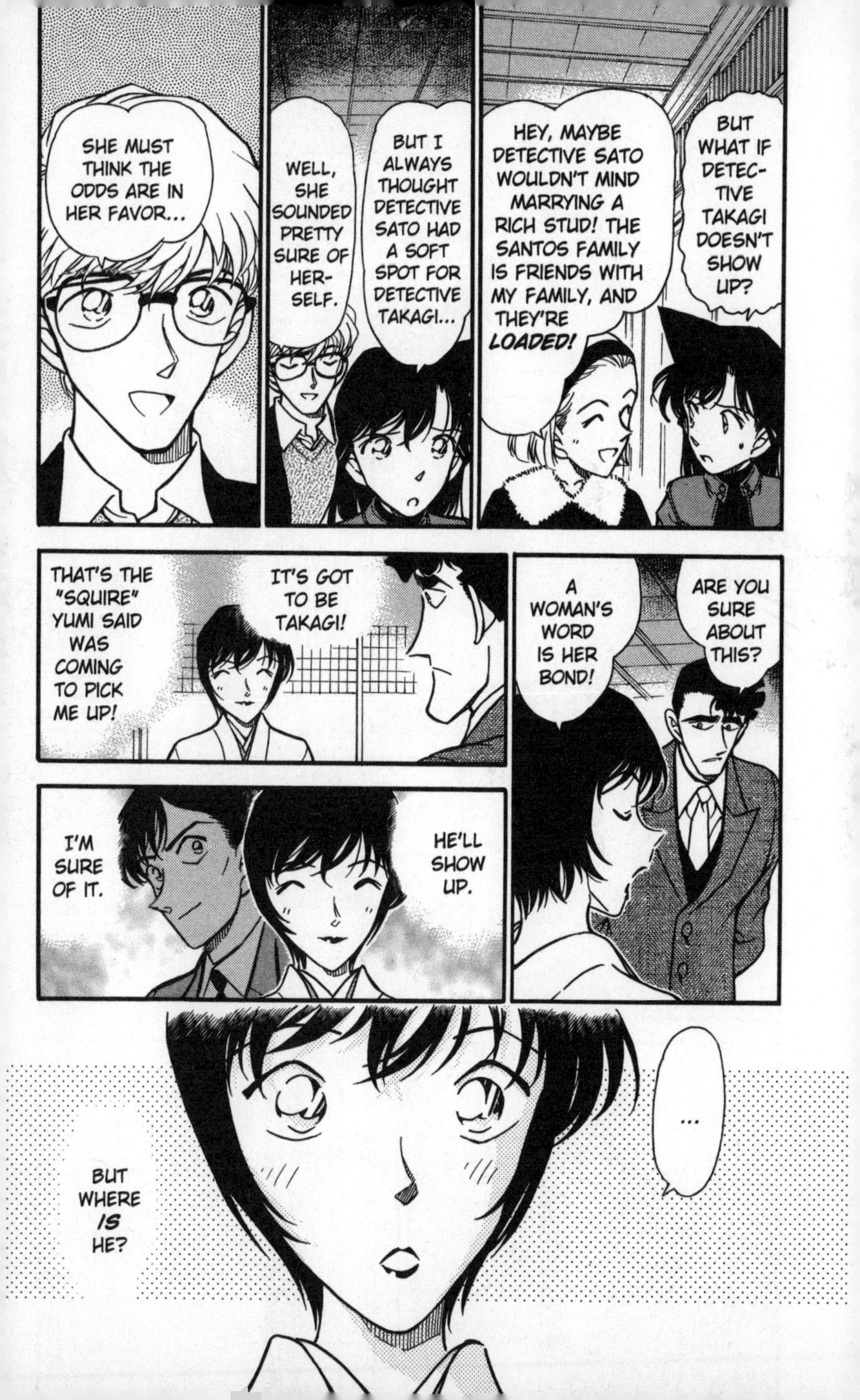
BUT WHAT IF DETECTIVE TAKAGI DOESN'T SHOW UP?
HEY, MAYBE DETECTIVE SATO WOULDN'T MIND MARRYING A RICH STUD! THE SANTOS FAMILY IS FRIENDS WITH MY FAMILY, AND THEY'RE ***LOADED!***
BUT I ALWAYS THOUGHT DETECTIVE SATO HAD A SOFT SPOT FOR DETECTIVE TAKAGI...
WELL, SHE SOUNDED PRETTY SURE OF HERSELF.
SHE MUST THINK THE ODDS ARE IN HER FAVOR...
ARE YOU SURE ABOUT THIS?
A WOMAN'S WORD IS HER BOND!
IT'S GOT TO BE TAKAGI!
THAT'S THE "SQUIRE" YUMI SAID WAS COMING TO PICK ME UP!
HE'LL SHOW UP.
I'M SURE OF IT.
...
BUT WHERE *IS* HE?

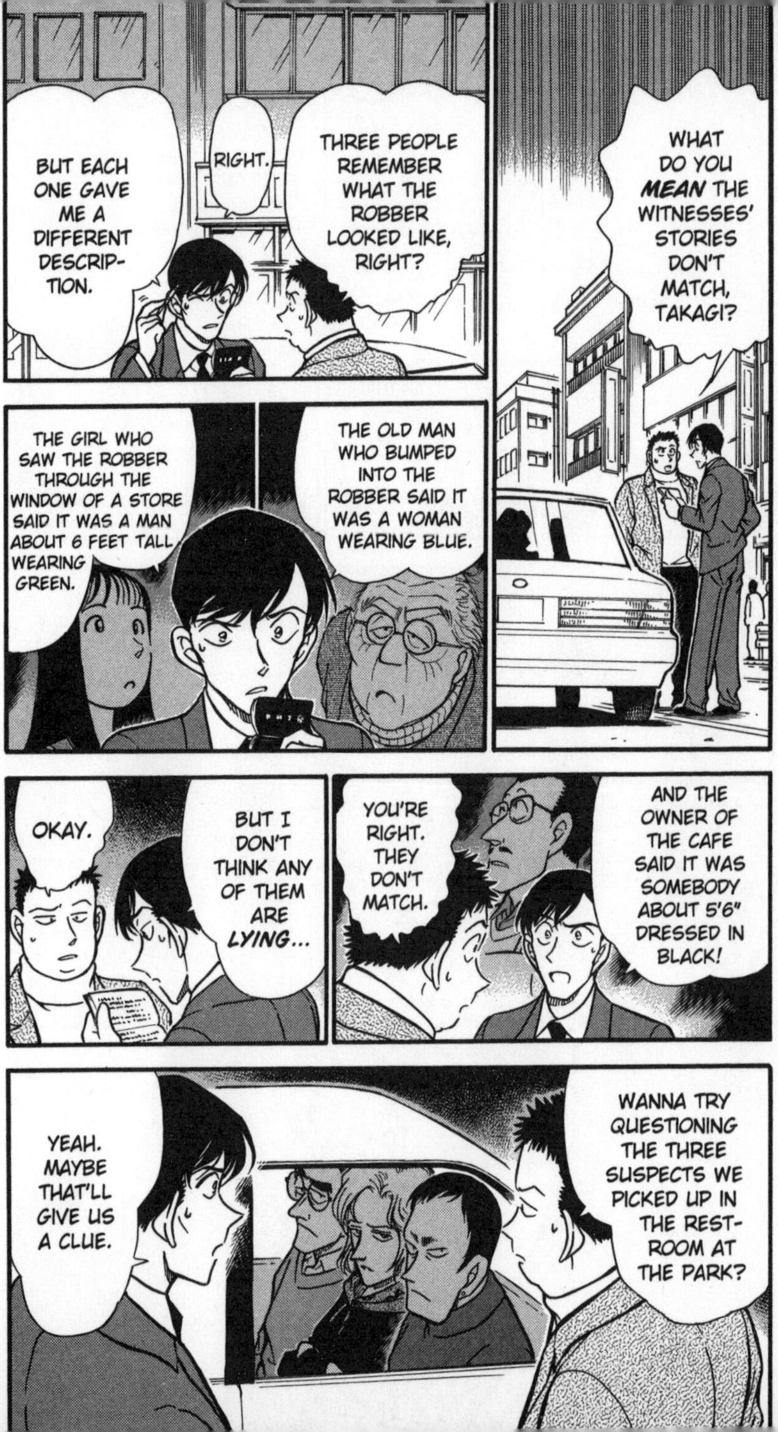
WHAT DO YOU *MEAN* THE WITNESSES' STORIES DON'T MATCH, TAKAGI?
THREE PEOPLE REMEMBER WHAT THE ROBBER LOOKED LIKE, RIGHT?
RIGHT.
BUT EACH ONE GAVE ME A DIFFERENT DESCRIP-TION.
THE OLD MAN WHO BUMPED INTO THE ROBBER SAID IT WAS A WOMAN WEARING BLUE.
THE GIRL WHO SAW THE ROBBER THROUGH THE WINDOW OF A STORE SAID IT WAS A MAN ABOUT 6 FEET TALL WEARING GREEN.
AND THE OWNER OF THE CAFE SAID IT WAS SOMEBODY ABOUT 5'6" DRESSED IN BLACK!
YOU'RE RIGHT. THEY DON'T MATCH.
BUT I DON'T THINK ANY OF THEM ARE *LYING*...
OKAY.
WANNA TRY QUESTIONING THE THREE SUSPECTS WE PICKED UP IN THE REST-ROOM AT THE PARK?
YEAH. MAYBE THAT'LL GIVE US A CLUE.

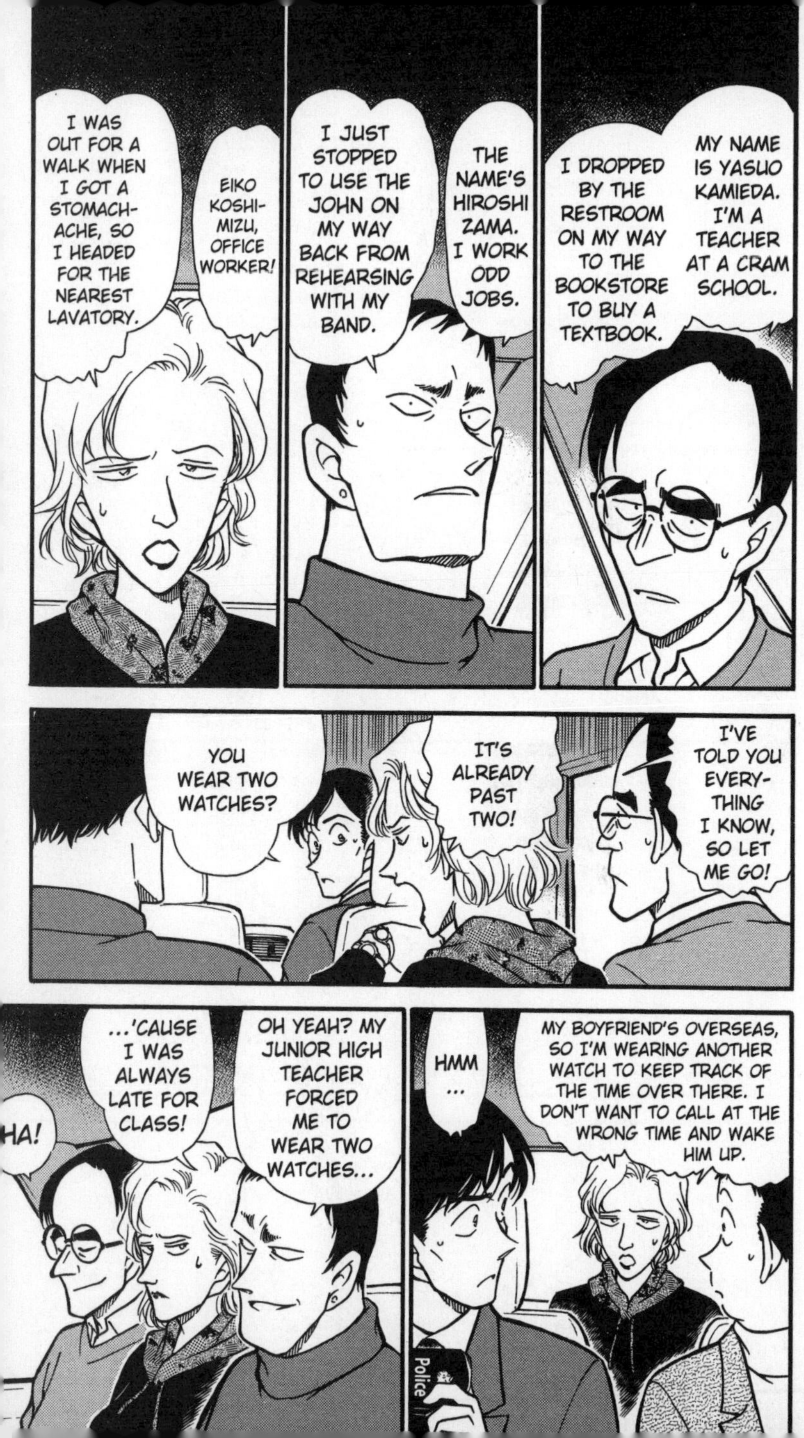
MY NAME IS YASUO KAMIEDA. I'M A TEACHER AT A CRAM SCHOOL.
I DROPPED BY THE RESTROOM ON MY WAY TO THE BOOKSTORE TO BUY A TEXTBOOK.
THE NAME'S HIROSHI ZAMA. I WORK ODD JOBS.
I JUST STOPPED TO USE THE JOHN ON MY WAY BACK FROM REHEARSING WITH MY BAND.
EIKO KOSHIMIZU, OFFICE WORKER!
I WAS OUT FOR A WALK WHEN I GOT A STOMACHACHE, SO I HEADED FOR THE NEAREST LAVATORY.
I'VE TOLD YOU EVERYTHING I KNOW, SO LET ME GO!
IT'S ALREADY PAST TWO!
YOU WEAR TWO WATCHES?
MY BOYFRIEND'S OVERSEAS, SO I'M WEARING ANOTHER WATCH TO KEEP TRACK OF THE TIME OVER THERE. I DON'T WANT TO CALL AT THE WRONG TIME AND WAKE HIM UP.
HMM...
Police
OH YEAH? MY JUNIOR HIGH TEACHER FORCED ME TO WEAR TWO WATCHES...
...'CAUSE I WAS ALWAYS LATE FOR CLASS!
HA!

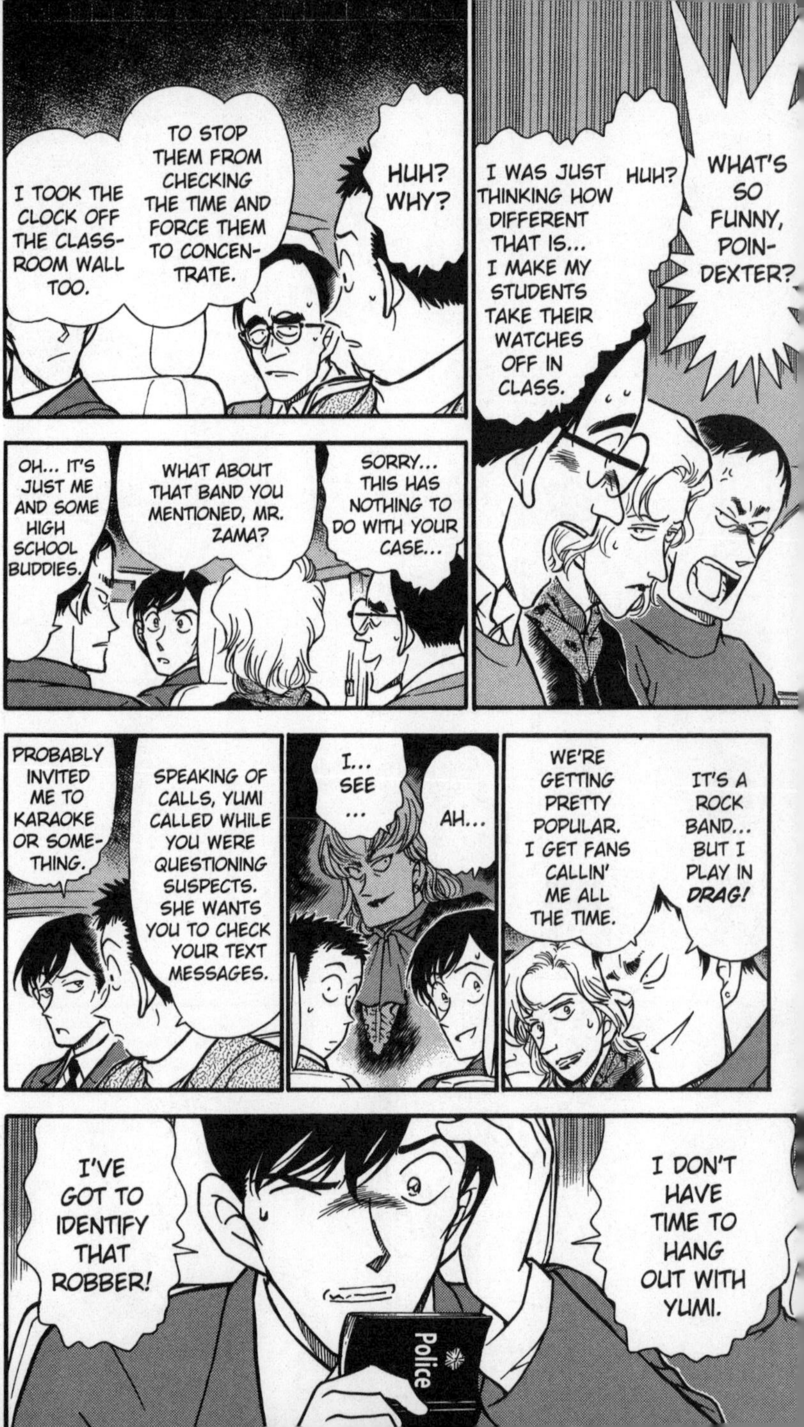
WHAT'S SO FUNNY, POIN-DEXTER?
HUH?
I WAS JUST THINKING HOW DIFFERENT THAT IS... I MAKE MY STUDENTS TAKE THEIR WATCHES OFF IN CLASS.
HUH? WHY?
TO STOP THEM FROM CHECKING THE TIME AND FORCE THEM TO CONCEN-TRATE.
I TOOK THE CLOCK OFF THE CLASS-ROOM WALL TOO.
SORRY... THIS HAS NOTHING TO DO WITH YOUR CASE...
WHAT ABOUT THAT BAND YOU MENTIONED, MR. ZAMA?
OH... IT'S JUST ME AND SOME HIGH SCHOOL BUDDIES.
IT'S A ROCK BAND... BUT I PLAY IN *DRAG!*
WE'RE GETTING PRETTY POPULAR. I GET FANS CALLIN' ME ALL THE TIME.
AH...
I... SEE ...
SPEAKING OF CALLS, YUMI CALLED WHILE YOU WERE QUESTIONING SUSPECTS. SHE WANTS YOU TO CHECK YOUR TEXT MESSAGES.
PROBABLY INVITED ME TO KARAOKE OR SOME-THING.
I DON'T HAVE TIME TO HANG OUT WITH YUMI.
I'VE GOT TO IDENTIFY THAT ROBBER!
Police

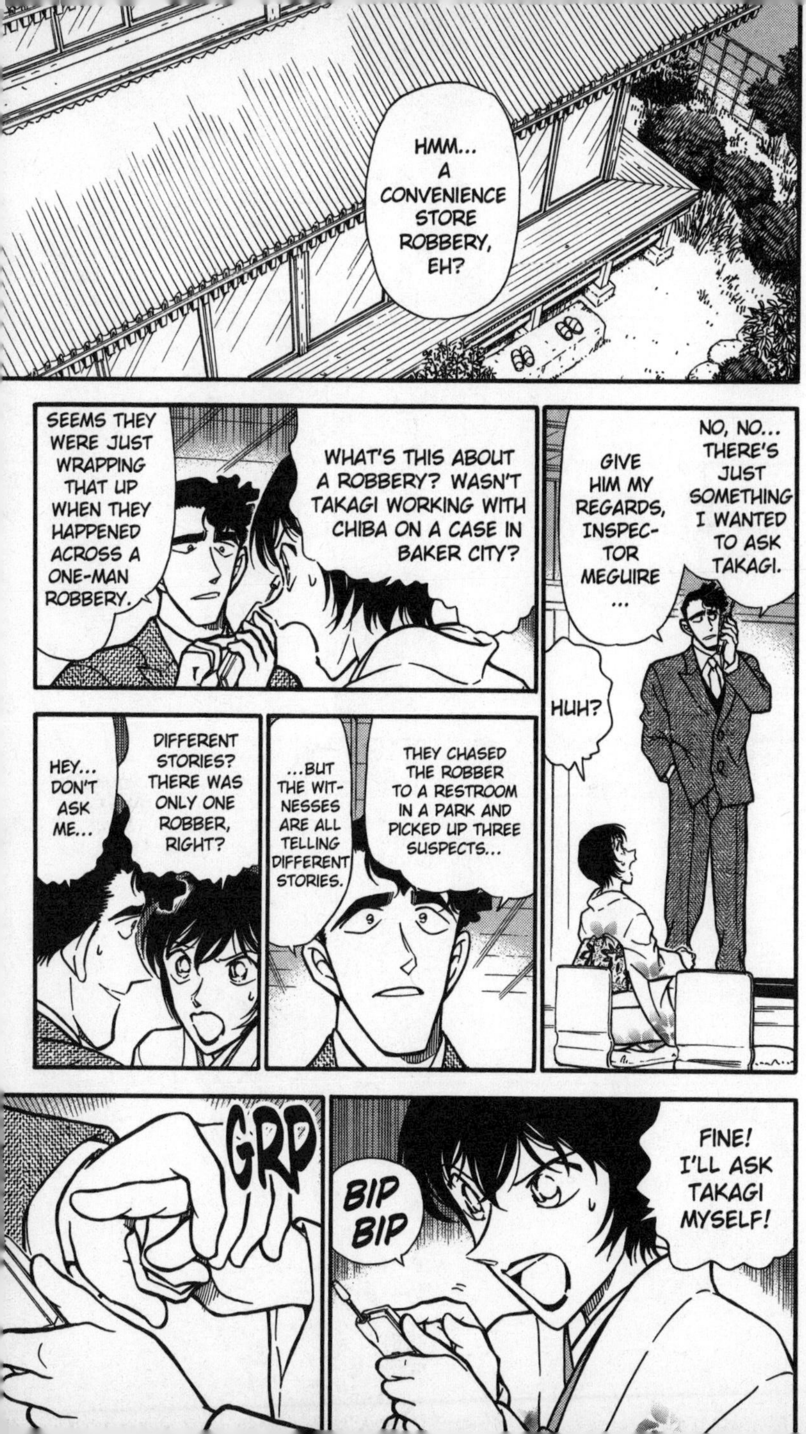
HMM... A CONVENIENCE STORE ROBBERY, EH?
NO, NO... THERE'S JUST SOMETHING I WANTED TO ASK TAKAGI.
GIVE HIM MY REGARDS, INSPECTOR MEGUIRE...
HUH?
WHAT'S THIS ABOUT A ROBBERY? WASN'T TAKAGI WORKING WITH CHIBA ON A CASE IN BAKER CITY?
SEEMS THEY WERE JUST WRAPPING THAT UP WHEN THEY HAPPENED ACROSS A ONE-MAN ROBBERY.
THEY CHASED THE ROBBER TO A RESTROOM IN A PARK AND PICKED UP THREE SUSPECTS...
...BUT THE WITNESSES ARE ALL TELLING DIFFERENT STORIES.
DIFFERENT STORIES? THERE WAS ONLY ONE ROBBER, RIGHT?
HEY... DON'T ASK ME...
FINE! I'LL ASK TAKAGI MYSELF!
BIP BIP
GRP

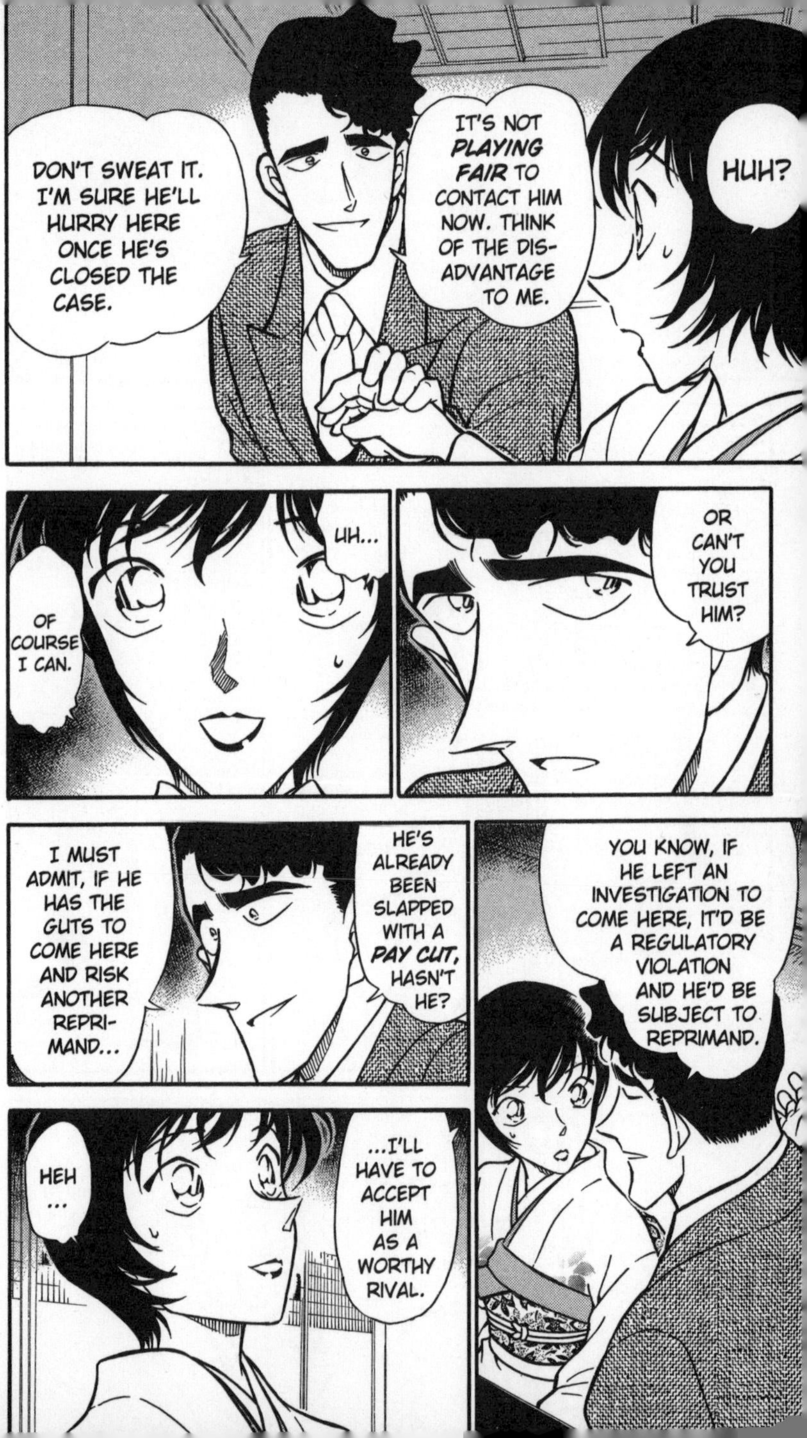
HUH?
IT'S NOT PLAYING FAIR TO CONTACT HIM NOW. THINK OF THE DIS-ADVANTAGE TO ME.
DON'T SWEAT IT. I'M SURE HE'LL HURRY HERE ONCE HE'S CLOSED THE CASE.
OR CAN'T YOU TRUST HIM?
UH...
OF COURSE I CAN.
YOU KNOW, IF HE LEFT AN INVESTIGATION TO COME HERE, IT'D BE A REGULATORY VIOLATION AND HE'D BE SUBJECT TO REPRIMAND.
HE'S ALREADY BEEN SLAPPED WITH A PAY CUT, HASN'T HE?
I MUST ADMIT, IF HE HAS THE GUTS TO COME HERE AND RISK ANOTHER REPRIMAND...
...I'LL HAVE TO ACCEPT HIM AS A WORTHY RIVAL.
HEH ...

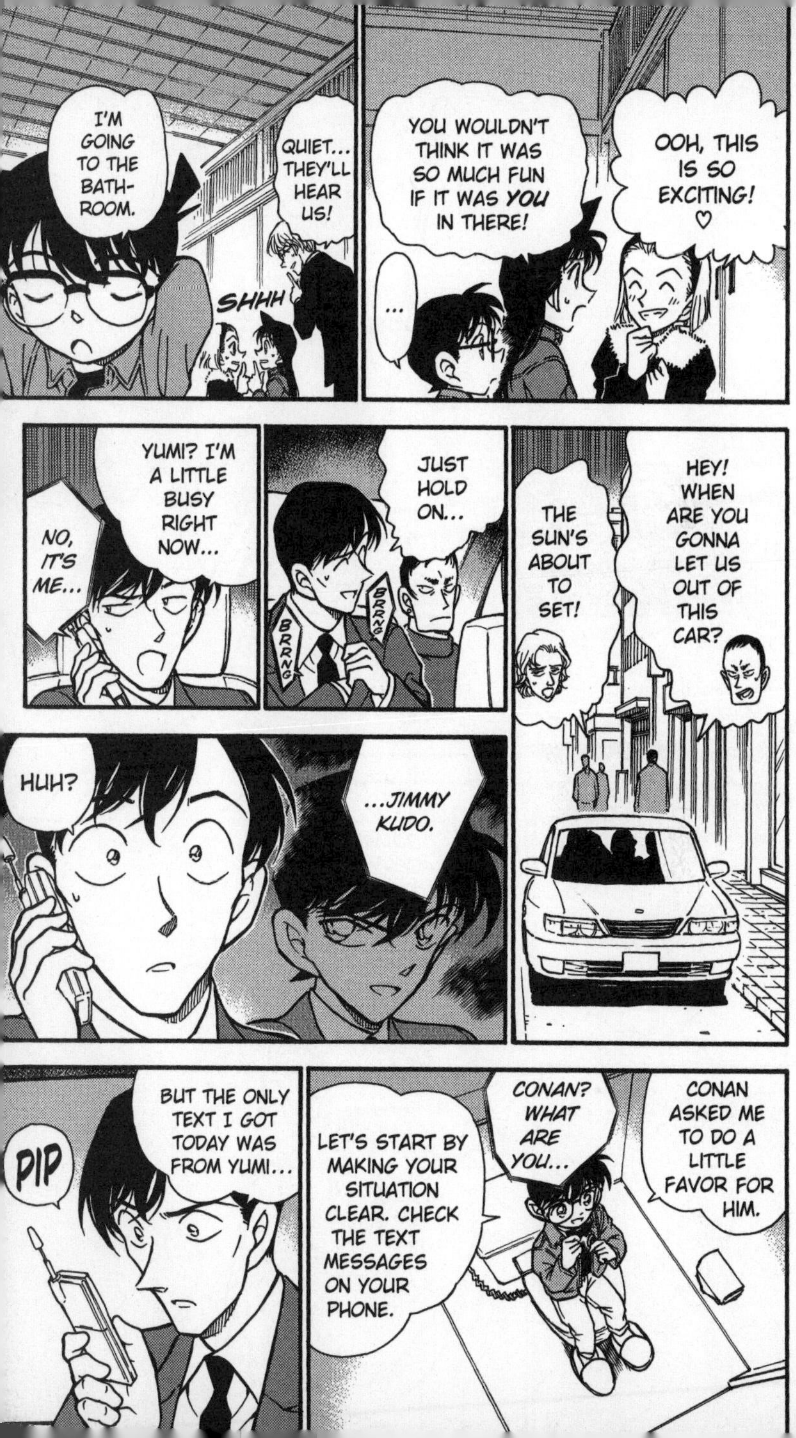
OOH, THIS IS SO EXCITING! ♡
YOU WOULDN'T THINK IT WAS SO MUCH FUN IF IT WAS *YOU* IN THERE!
...
QUIET... THEY'LL HEAR US!
I'M GOING TO THE BATH-ROOM.
SHHH
HEY! WHEN ARE YOU GONNA LET US OUT OF THIS CAR?
THE SUN'S ABOUT TO SET!
JUST HOLD ON...
BRRNG
BRRNG
YUMI? I'M A LITTLE BUSY RIGHT NOW...
NO, IT'S ME...
...JIMMY KUDO.
HUH?
CONAN ASKED ME TO DO A LITTLE FAVOR FOR HIM.
CONAN? WHAT ARE YOU...
LET'S START BY MAKING YOUR SITUATION CLEAR. CHECK THE TEXT MESSAGES ON YOUR PHONE.
BUT THE ONLY TEXT I GOT TODAY WAS FROM YUMI...
PIP

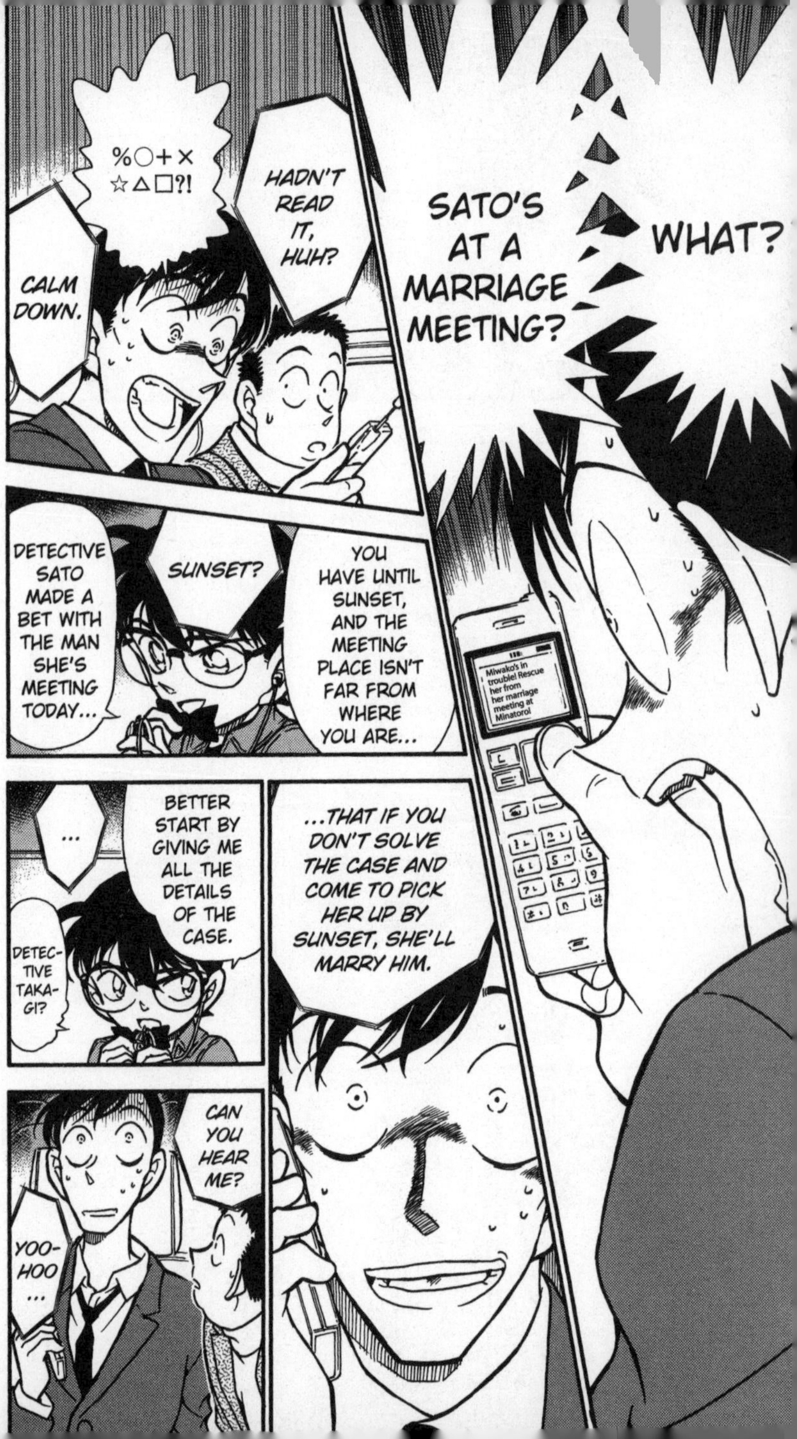

WHAT?
SATO'S AT A MARRIAGE MEETING?
Miwako's in trouble! Rescue her from her marriage meeting at Minatoro!
HADN'T READ IT, HUH?
%○+× ☆△□?!
CALM DOWN.
YOU HAVE UNTIL SUNSET, AND THE MEETING PLACE ISN'T FAR FROM WHERE YOU ARE...
SUNSET?
DETECTIVE SATO MADE A BET WITH THE MAN SHE'S MEETING TODAY...
...THAT IF YOU DON'T SOLVE THE CASE AND COME TO PICK HER UP BY SUNSET, SHE'LL MARRY HIM.
BETTER START BY GIVING ME ALL THE DETAILS OF THE CASE.
...
DETECTIVE TAKAGI?
CAN YOU HEAR ME?
YOO-HOO...

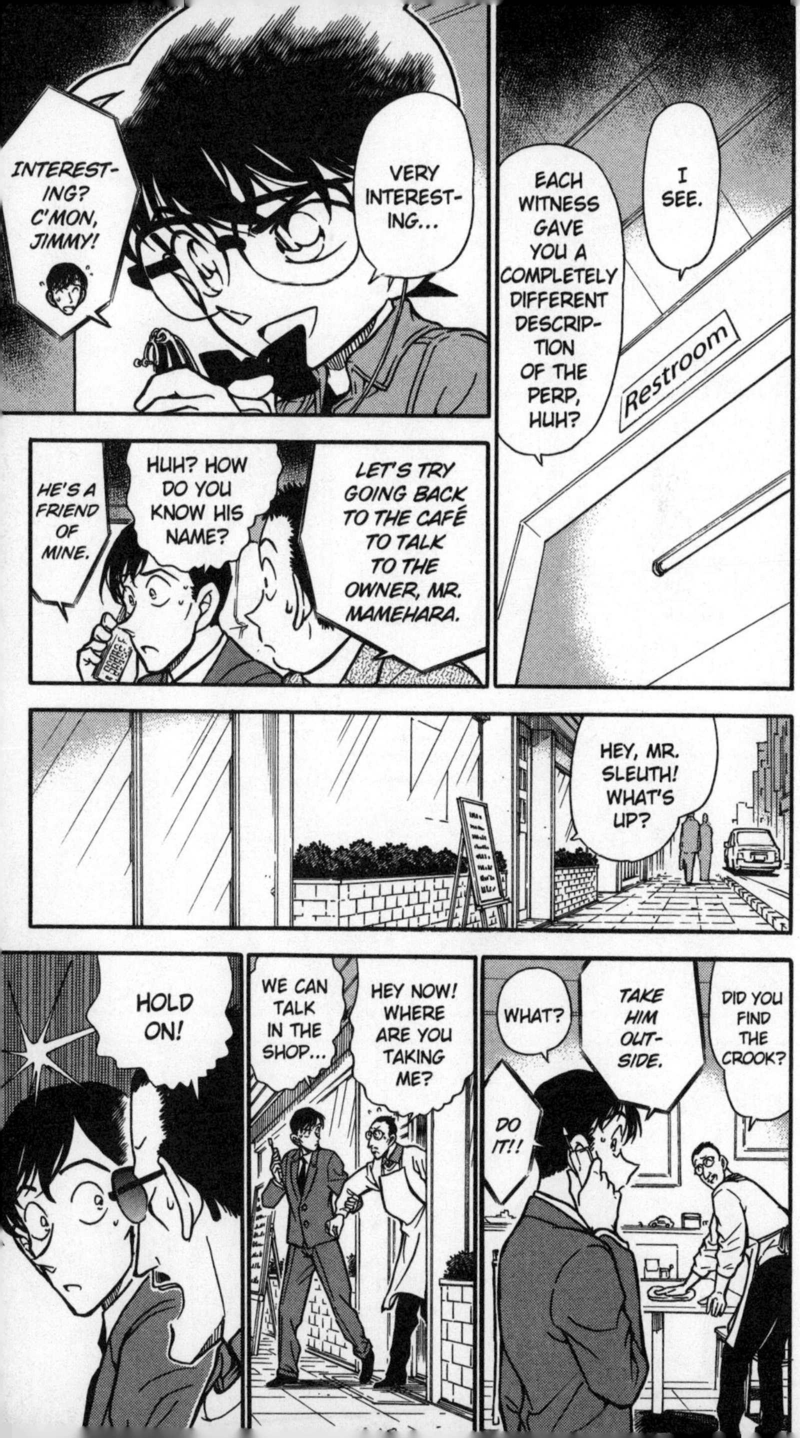
I SEE.
EACH WITNESS GAVE YOU A COMPLETELY DIFFERENT DESCRIPTION OF THE PERP, HUH?
Restroom
VERY INTERESTING...
INTERESTING? C'MON, JIMMY!
LET'S TRY GOING BACK TO THE CAFÉ TO TALK TO THE OWNER, MR. MAMEHARA.
HUH? HOW DO YOU KNOW HIS NAME?
HE'S A FRIEND OF MINE.
HEY, MR. SLEUTH! WHAT'S UP?
DID YOU FIND THE CROOK?
TAKE HIM OUTSIDE.
WHAT?
DO IT!!
HEY NOW! WHERE ARE YOU TAKING ME?
WE CAN TALK IN THE SHOP...
HOLD ON!

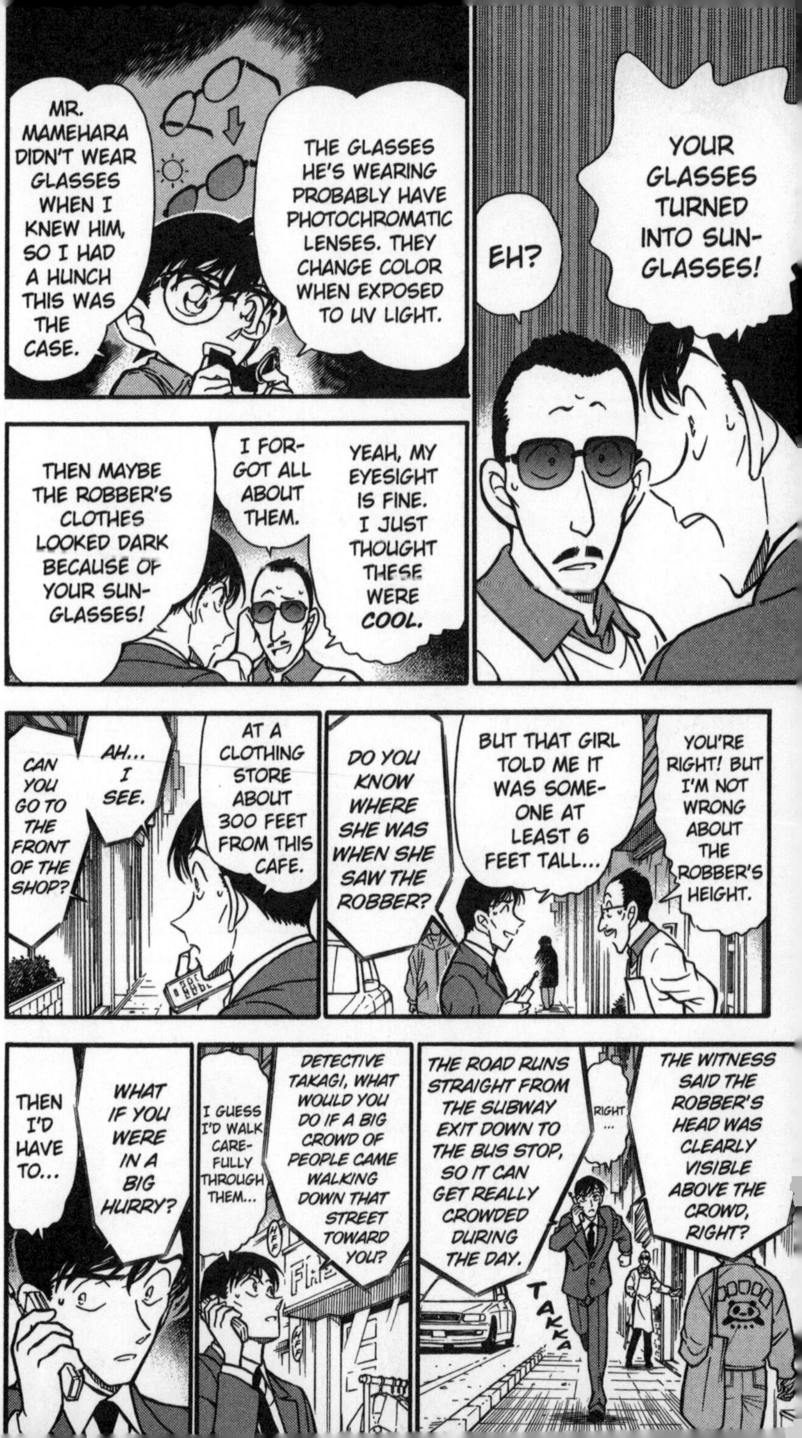
YOUR GLASSES TURNED INTO SUN-GLASSES!
EH?
THE GLASSES HE'S WEARING PROBABLY HAVE PHOTOCHROMATIC LENSES. THEY CHANGE COLOR WHEN EXPOSED TO UV LIGHT.
MR. MAMEHARA DIDN'T WEAR GLASSES WHEN I KNEW HIM, SO I HAD A HUNCH THIS WAS THE CASE.
YEAH, MY EYESIGHT IS FINE. I JUST THOUGHT THESE WERE **COOL.**
I FOR-GOT ALL ABOUT THEM.
THEN MAYBE THE ROBBER'S CLOTHES LOOKED DARK BECAUSE OF YOUR SUN-GLASSES!
YOU'RE RIGHT! BUT I'M NOT WRONG ABOUT THE ROBBER'S HEIGHT.
BUT THAT GIRL TOLD ME IT WAS SOME-ONE AT LEAST 6 FEET TALL...
DO YOU KNOW WHERE SHE WAS WHEN SHE SAW THE ROBBER?
AT A CLOTHING STORE ABOUT 300 FEET FROM THIS CAFE.
AH... I SEE.
CAN YOU GO TO THE FRONT OF THE SHOP?
THE WITNESS SAID THE ROBBER'S HEAD WAS CLEARLY VISIBLE ABOVE THE CROWD, RIGHT?
RIGHT...
THE ROAD RUNS STRAIGHT FROM THE SUBWAY EXIT DOWN TO THE BUS STOP, SO IT CAN GET REALLY CROWDED DURING THE DAY.
TAKKA
DETECTIVE TAKAGI, WHAT WOULD YOU DO IF A BIG CROWD OF PEOPLE CAME WALKING DOWN THAT STREET TOWARD YOU?
I GUESS I'D WALK CARE-FULLY THROUGH THEM...
HFF
HFF
WHAT IF YOU WERE IN A BIG HURRY?
THEN I'D HAVE TO...

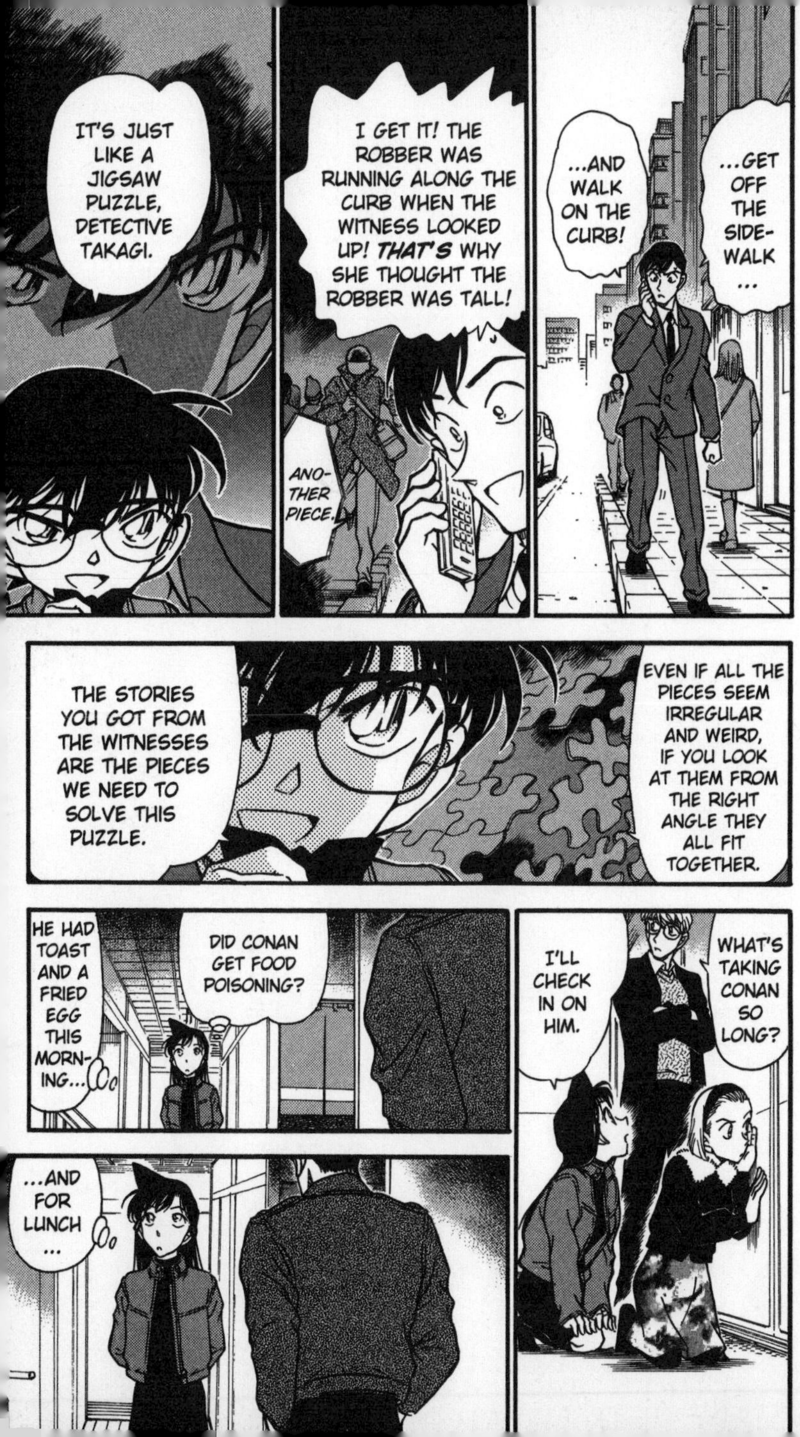
...GET OFF THE SIDE-WALK...
...AND WALK ON THE CURB!
I GET IT! THE ROBBER WAS RUNNING ALONG THE CURB WHEN THE WITNESS LOOKED UP! *THAT'S* WHY SHE THOUGHT THE ROBBER WAS TALL!
ANOTHER PIECE.
IT'S JUST LIKE A JIGSAW PUZZLE, DETECTIVE TAKAGI.
EVEN IF ALL THE PIECES SEEM IRREGULAR AND WEIRD, IF YOU LOOK AT THEM FROM THE RIGHT ANGLE THEY ALL FIT TOGETHER.
THE STORIES YOU GOT FROM THE WITNESSES ARE THE PIECES WE NEED TO SOLVE THIS PUZZLE.
WHAT'S TAKING CONAN SO LONG?
I'LL CHECK IN ON HIM.
DID CONAN GET FOOD POISONING?
HE HAD TOAST AND A FRIED EGG THIS MORNING...
...AND FOR LUNCH...

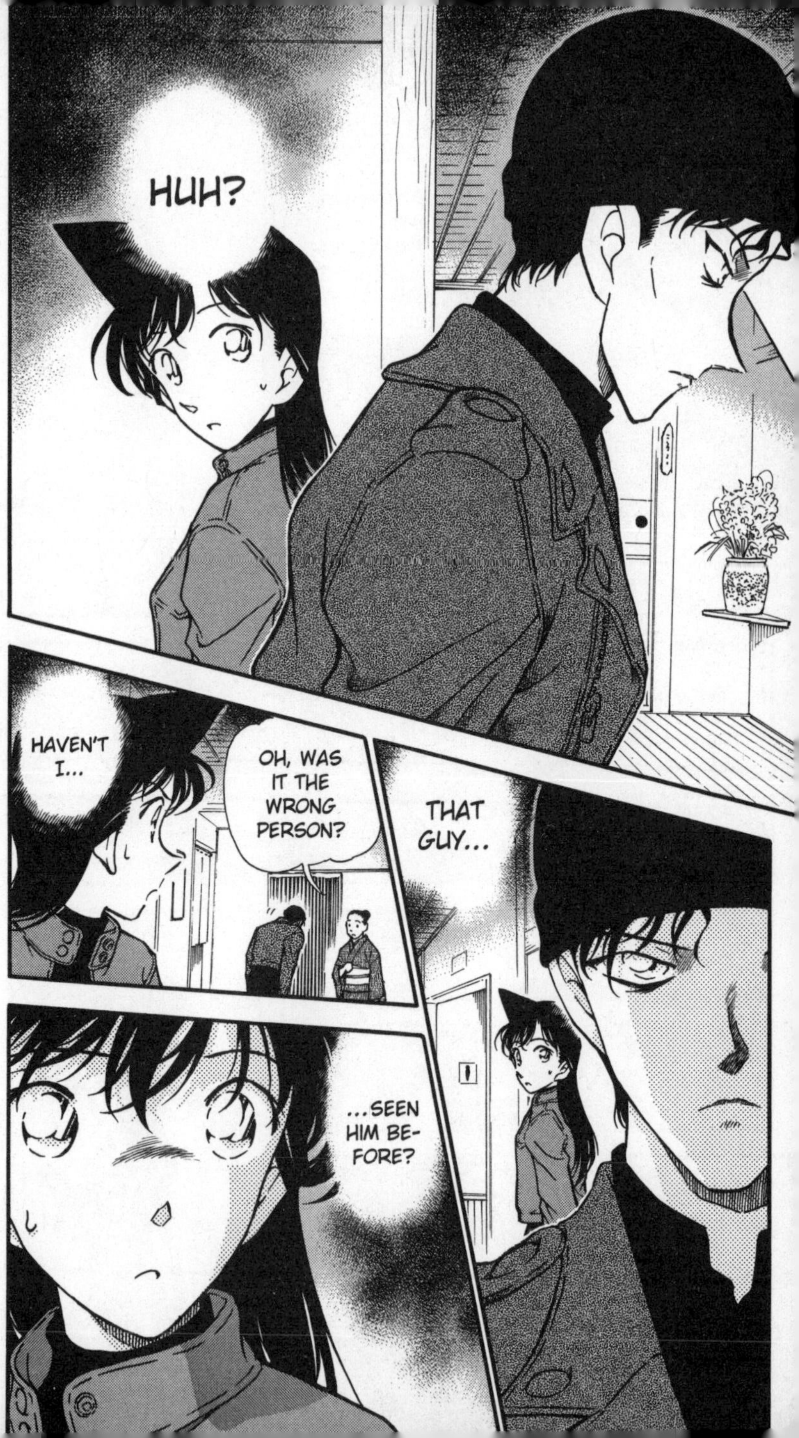
HUH?
THAT GUY...
OH, WAS IT THE WRONG PERSON?
HAVEN'T I...
...SEEN HIM BEFORE?

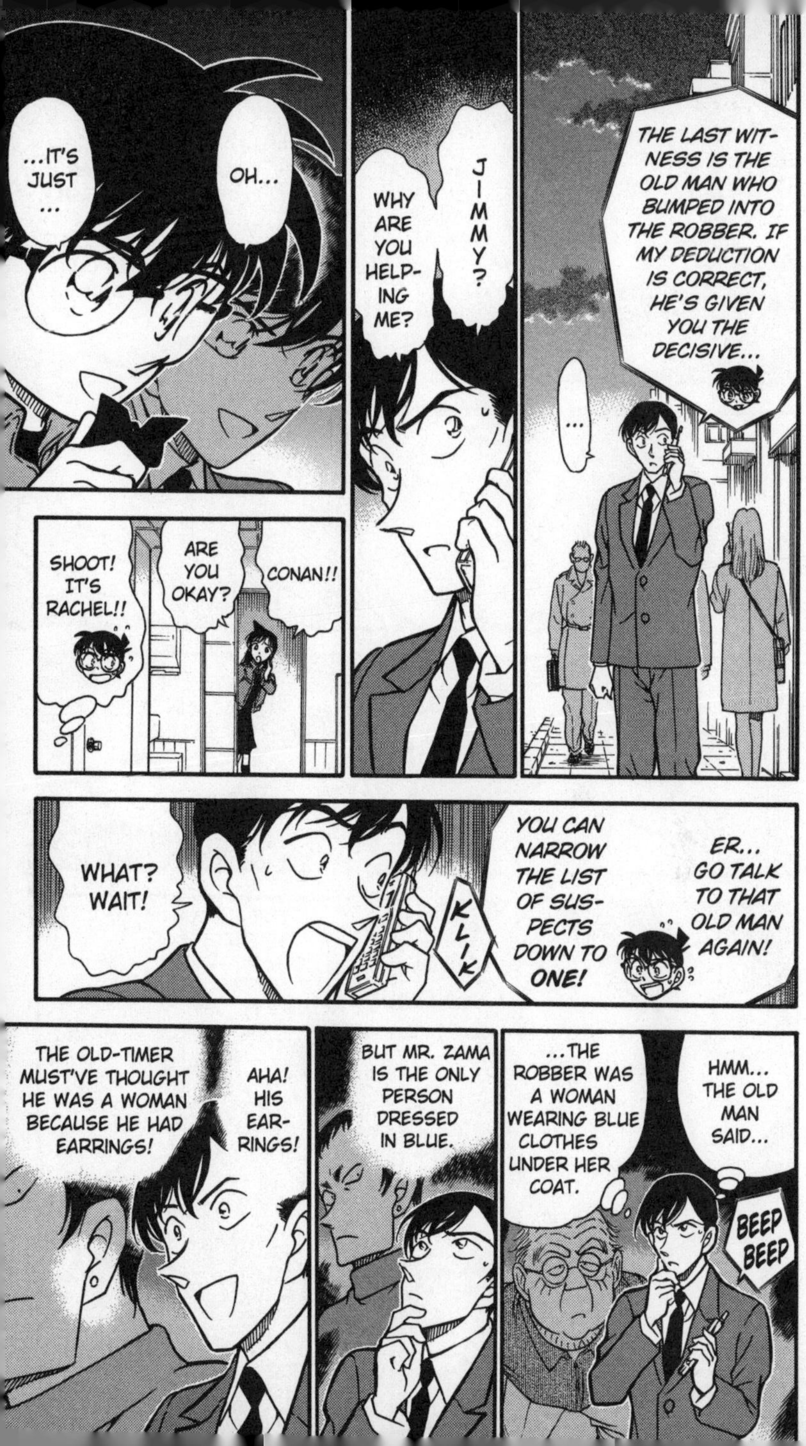
THE LAST WITNESS IS THE OLD MAN WHO BUMPED INTO THE ROBBER. IF MY DEDUCTION IS CORRECT, HE'S GIVEN YOU THE DECISIVE...
...
JIMMY?
WHY ARE YOU HELPING ME?
OH...
...IT'S JUST ...
CONAN!!
ARE YOU OKAY?
SHOOT! IT'S RACHEL!!
ER... GO TALK TO THAT OLD MAN AGAIN!
YOU CAN NARROW THE LIST OF SUSPECTS DOWN TO ONE!
KLIK
WHAT? WAIT!
HMM... THE OLD MAN SAID...
BEEP BEEP
...THE ROBBER WAS A WOMAN WEARING BLUE CLOTHES UNDER HER COAT.
BUT MR. ZAMA IS THE ONLY PERSON DRESSED IN BLUE.
AHA! HIS EARRINGS!
THE OLD-TIMER MUST'VE THOUGHT HE WAS A WOMAN BECAUSE HE HAD EARRINGS!

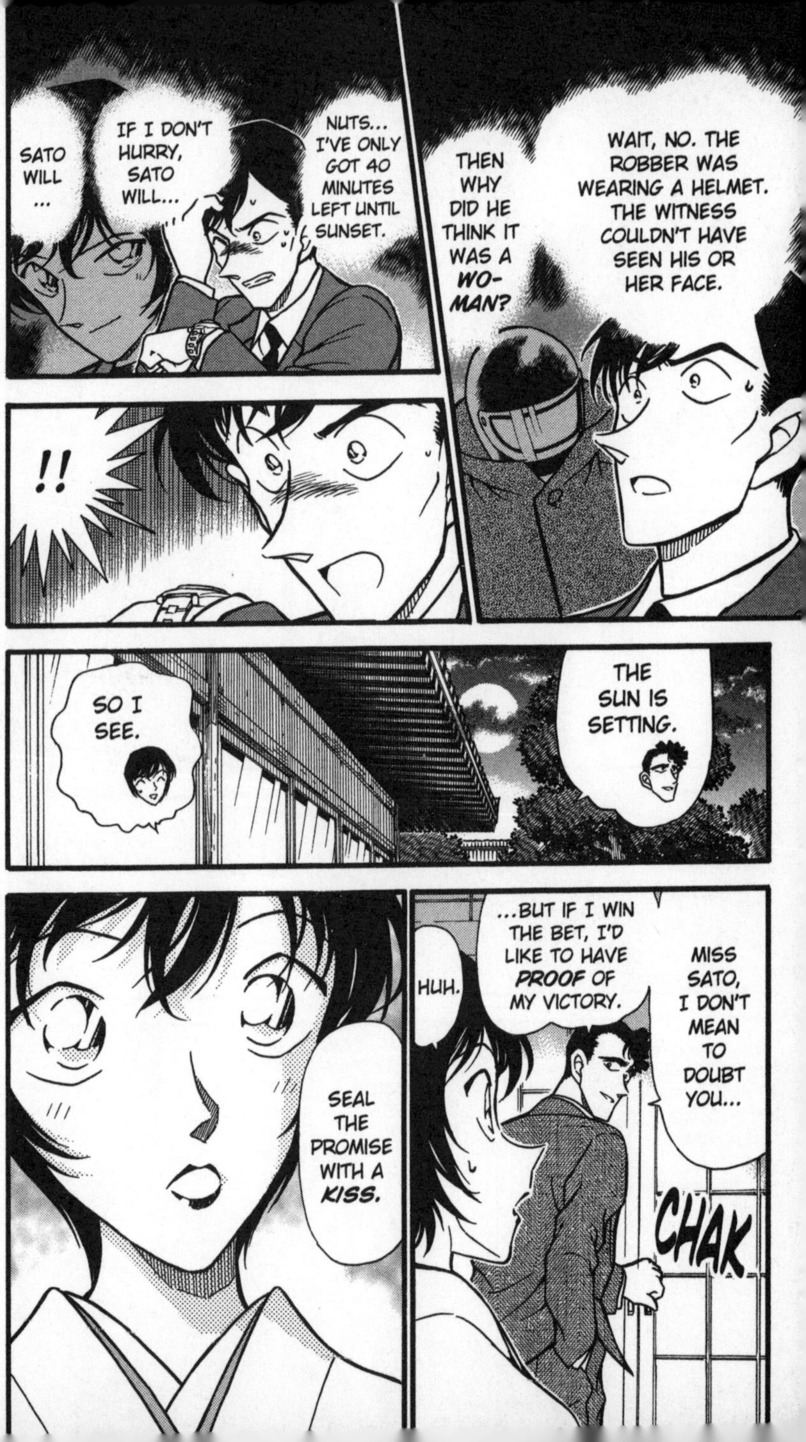
WAIT, NO. THE ROBBER WAS WEARING A HELMET. THE WITNESS COULDN'T HAVE SEEN HIS OR HER FACE.
THEN WHY DID HE THINK IT WAS A *WOMAN?*
NUTS... I'VE ONLY GOT 40 MINUTES LEFT UNTIL SUNSET.
IF I DON'T HURRY, SATO WILL...
SATO WILL ...
!!
THE SUN IS SETTING.
SO I SEE.
MISS SATO, I DON'T MEAN TO DOUBT YOU...
...BUT IF I WIN THE BET, I'D LIKE TO HAVE *PROOF* OF MY VICTORY.
HUH.
CHAK
SEAL THE PROMISE WITH A *KISS.*

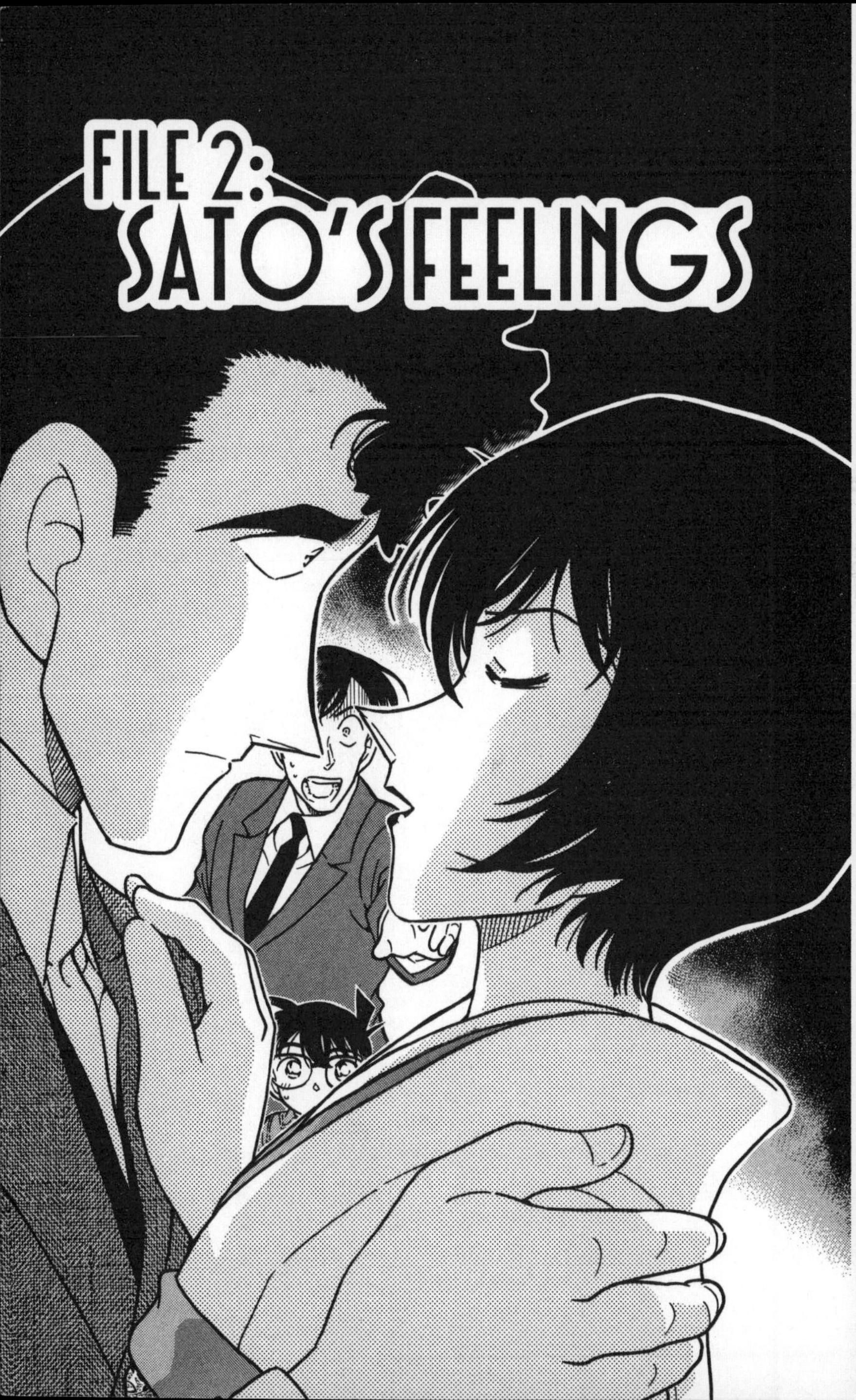
FILE 2:
SATO'S FEELINGS

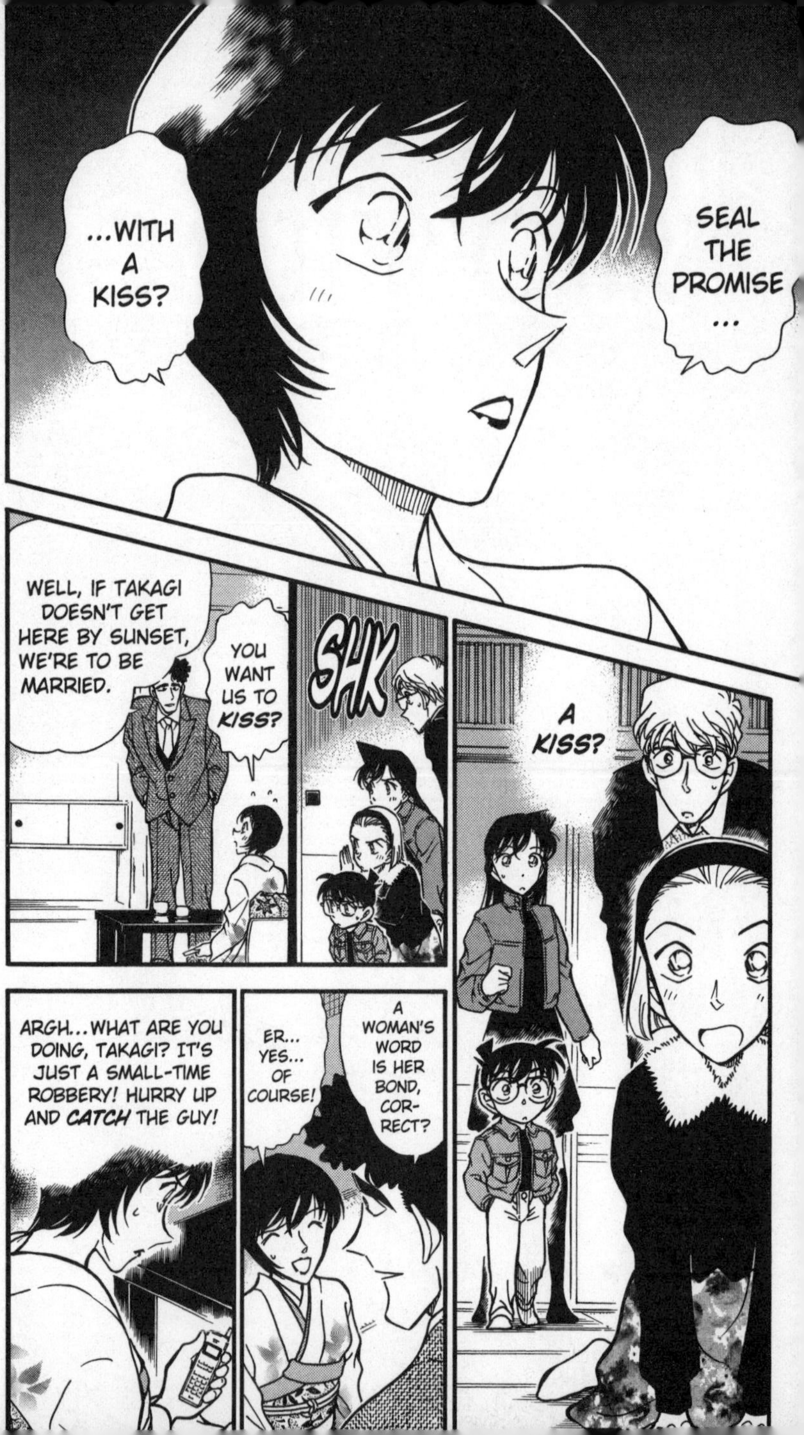
SEAL THE PROMISE ...
...WITH A KISS?
A KISS?
SHK
WELL, IF TAKAGI DOESN'T GET HERE BY SUNSET, WE'RE TO BE MARRIED.
YOU WANT US TO *KISS?*
A WOMAN'S WORD IS HER BOND, COR-RECT?
ER... YES... OF COURSE!
ARGH...WHAT ARE YOU DOING, TAKAGI? IT'S JUST A SMALL-TIME ROBBERY! HURRY UP AND *CATCH* THE GUY!

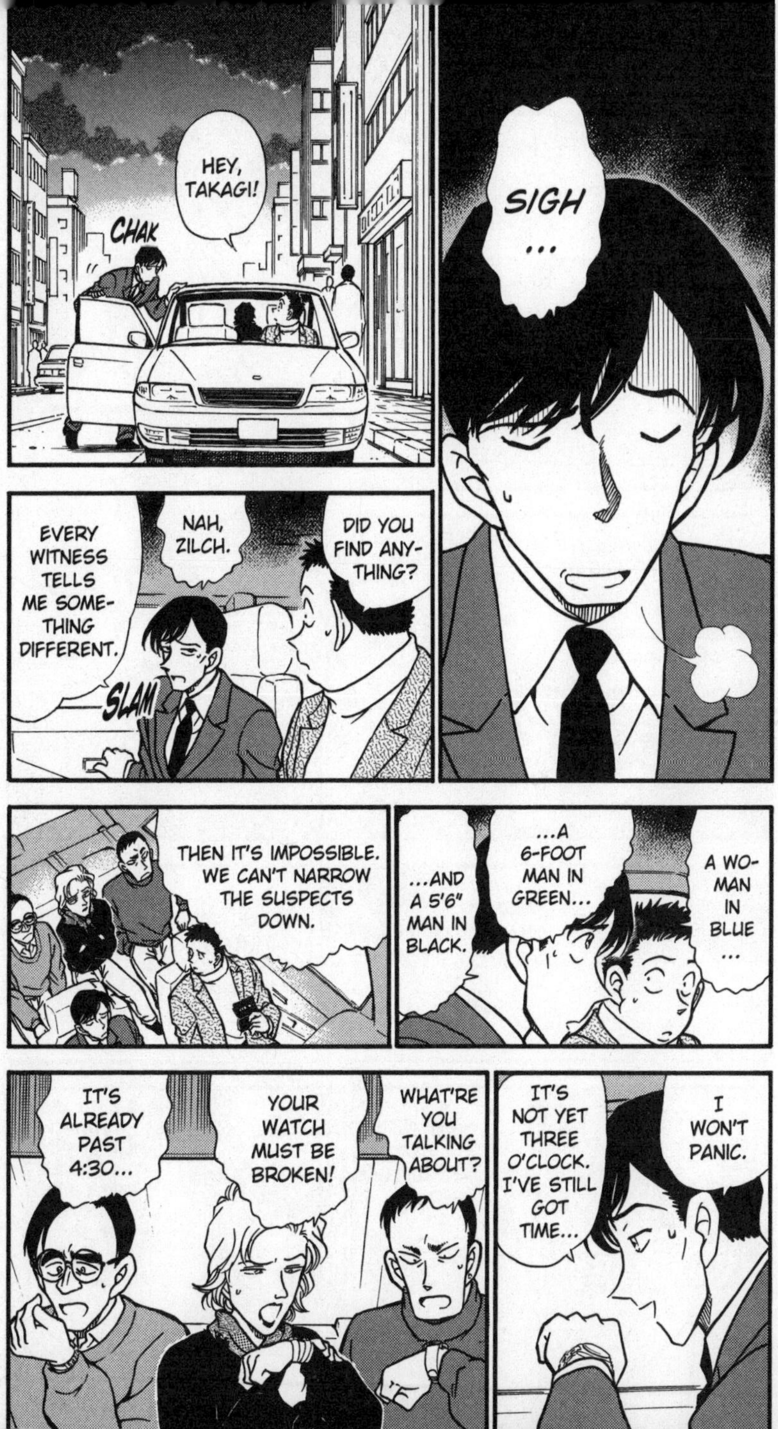
SIGH ...
HEY, TAKAGI!
CHAK
DID YOU FIND ANYTHING?
NAH, ZILCH.
EVERY WITNESS TELLS ME SOMETHING DIFFERENT.
SLAM
A WOMAN IN BLUE ...
...A 6-FOOT MAN IN GREEN...
...AND A 5'6" MAN IN BLACK.
THEN IT'S IMPOSSIBLE. WE CAN'T NARROW THE SUSPECTS DOWN.
I WON'T PANIC.
IT'S NOT YET THREE O'CLOCK. I'VE STILL GOT TIME...
WHAT'RE YOU TALKING ABOUT?
YOUR WATCH MUST BE BROKEN!
IT'S ALREADY PAST 4:30...

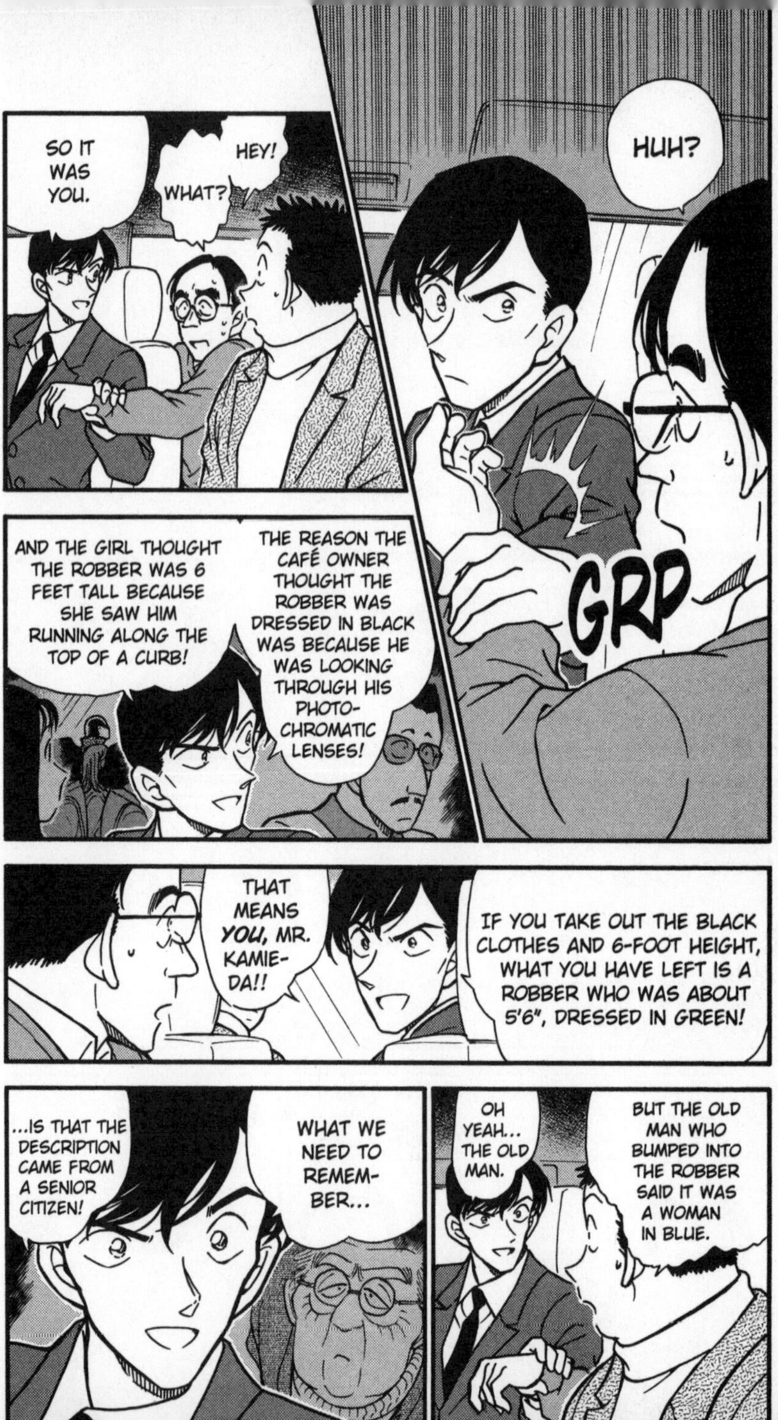
HUH?
GRP
HEY!
WHAT?
SO IT WAS YOU.
THE REASON THE CAFÉ OWNER THOUGHT THE ROBBER WAS DRESSED IN BLACK WAS BECAUSE HE WAS LOOKING THROUGH HIS PHOTO-CHROMATIC LENSES!
AND THE GIRL THOUGHT THE ROBBER WAS 6 FEET TALL BECAUSE SHE SAW HIM RUNNING ALONG THE TOP OF A CURB!
IF YOU TAKE OUT THE BLACK CLOTHES AND 6-FOOT HEIGHT, WHAT YOU HAVE LEFT IS A ROBBER WHO WAS ABOUT 5'6", DRESSED IN GREEN!
THAT MEANS *YOU*, MR. KAMIE-DA!!
BUT THE OLD MAN WHO BUMPED INTO THE ROBBER SAID IT WAS A WOMAN IN BLUE.
OH YEAH... THE OLD MAN.
WHAT WE NEED TO REMEM-BER...
...IS THAT THE DESCRIPTION CAME FROM A SENIOR CITIZEN!

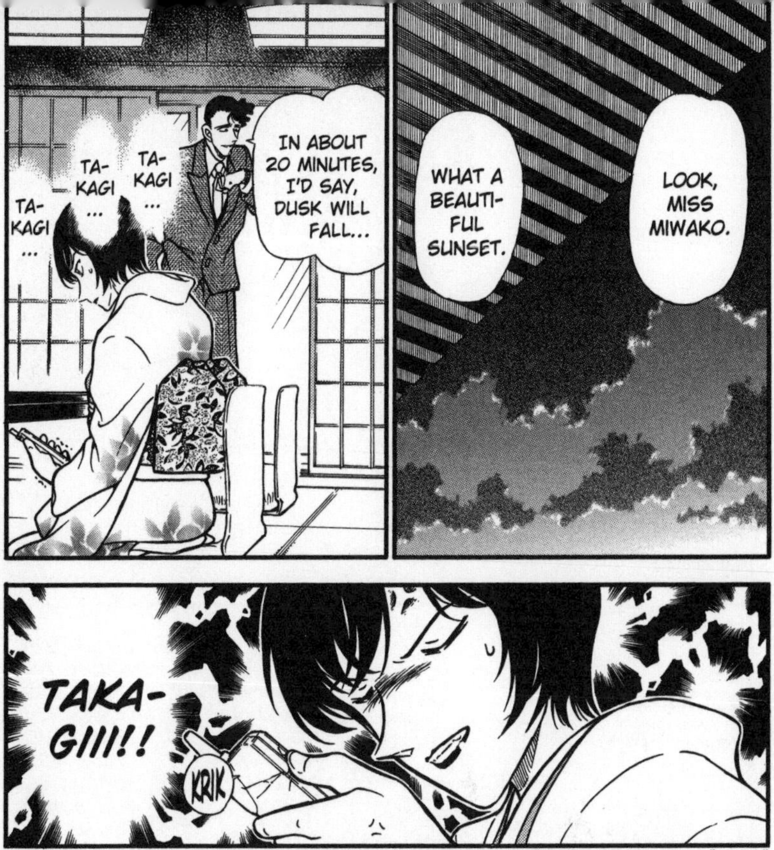
LOOK, MISS MIWAKO.
WHAT A BEAUTIFUL SUNSET.
IN ABOUT 20 MINUTES, I'D SAY, DUSK WILL FALL...
TA-KAGI...
TA-KAGI...
TA-KAGI...
TAKA-GIII!!
KRIK

*The word is *ao*. Nowadays, *ao* usually means "blue" and *midori* means "green."

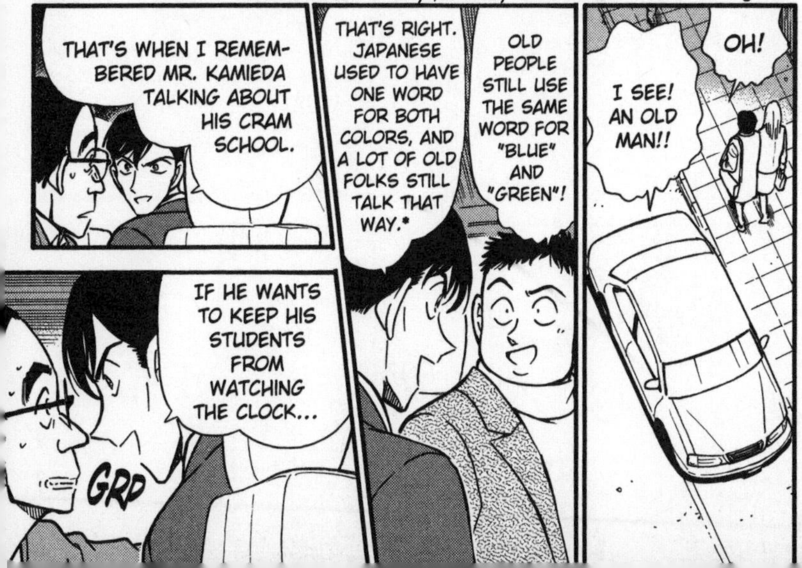
OH!
I SEE! AN OLD MAN!!
OLD PEOPLE STILL USE THE SAME WORD FOR "BLUE" AND "GREEN"!
THAT'S RIGHT. JAPANESE USED TO HAVE ONE WORD FOR BOTH COLORS, AND A LOT OF OLD FOLKS STILL TALK THAT WAY.*
THAT'S WHEN I REMEMBERED MR. KAMIEDA TALKING ABOUT HIS CRAM SCHOOL.
IF HE WANTS TO KEEP HIS STUDENTS FROM WATCHING THE CLOCK...
GRP

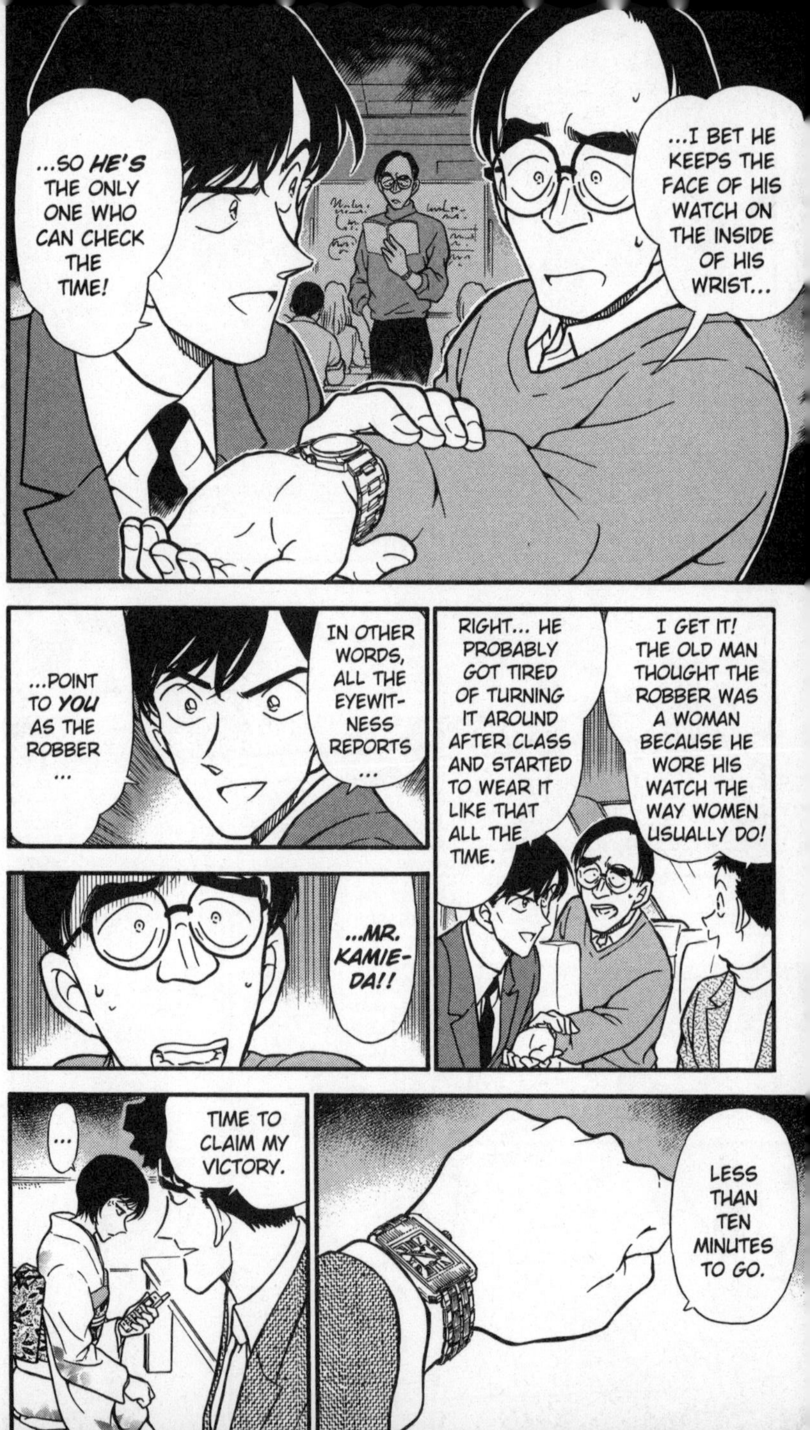
...I BET HE KEEPS THE FACE OF HIS WATCH ON THE INSIDE OF HIS WRIST...
...SO *HE'S* THE ONLY ONE WHO CAN CHECK THE TIME!
I GET IT! THE OLD MAN THOUGHT THE ROBBER WAS A WOMAN BECAUSE HE WORE HIS WATCH THE WAY WOMEN USUALLY DO!
RIGHT... HE PROBABLY GOT TIRED OF TURNING IT AROUND AFTER CLASS AND STARTED TO WEAR IT LIKE THAT ALL THE TIME.
IN OTHER WORDS, ALL THE EYEWITNESS REPORTS ...
...POINT TO *YOU* AS THE ROBBER ...
...MR. KAMIEDA!!
LESS THAN TEN MINUTES TO GO.
TIME TO CLAIM MY VICTORY.
...

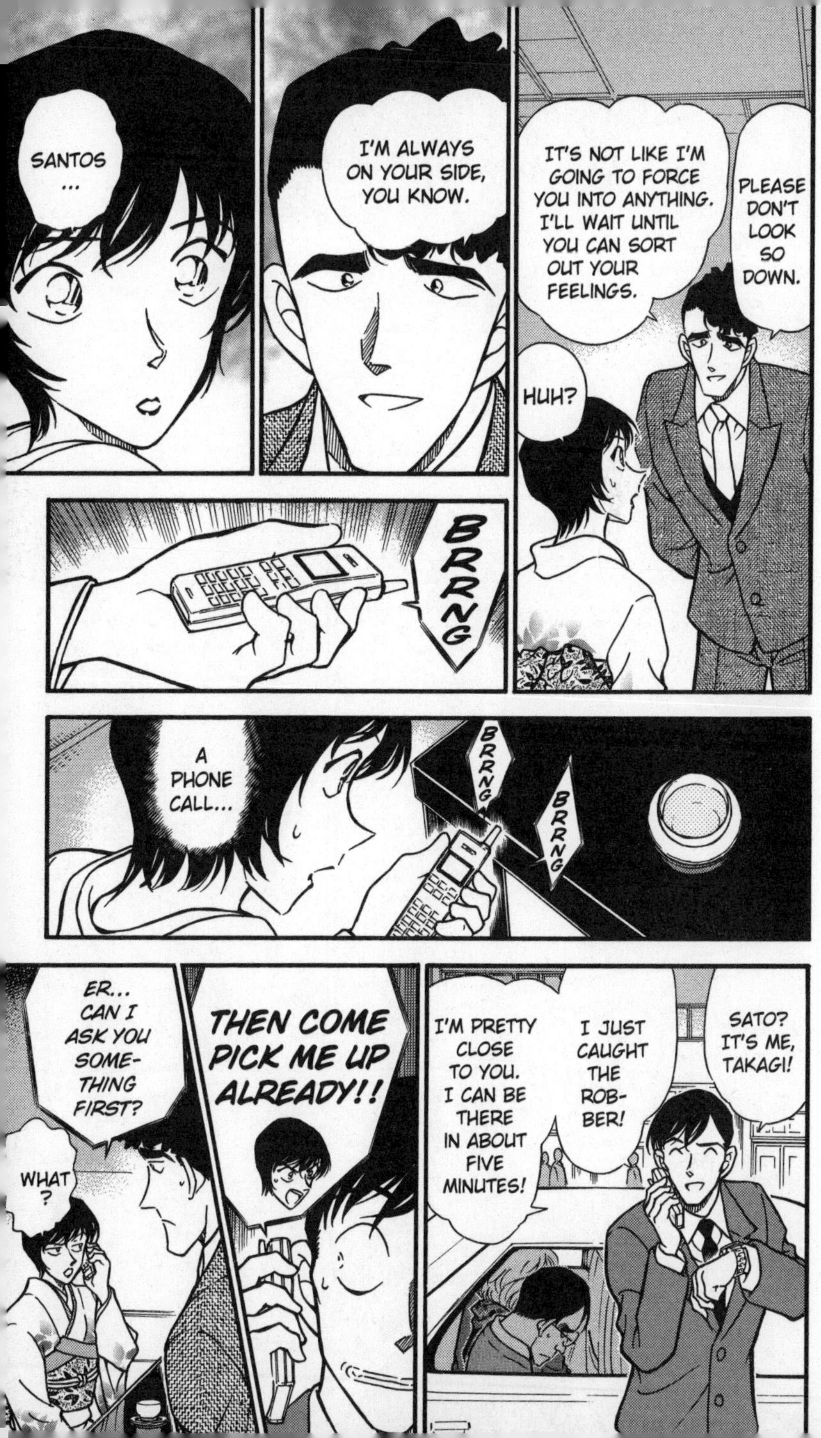
PLEASE DON'T LOOK SO DOWN.
IT'S NOT LIKE I'M GOING TO FORCE YOU INTO ANYTHING. I'LL WAIT UNTIL YOU CAN SORT OUT YOUR FEELINGS.
HUH?
I'M ALWAYS ON YOUR SIDE, YOU KNOW.
SANTOS ...
BRRNG
BRRNG
BRRNG
A PHONE CALL...
SATO? IT'S ME, TAKAGI!
I JUST CAUGHT THE ROB-BER!
I'M PRETTY CLOSE TO YOU. I CAN BE THERE IN ABOUT FIVE MINUTES!
THEN COME PICK ME UP ALREADY!!
ER... CAN I ASK YOU SOME-THING FIRST?
WHAT?

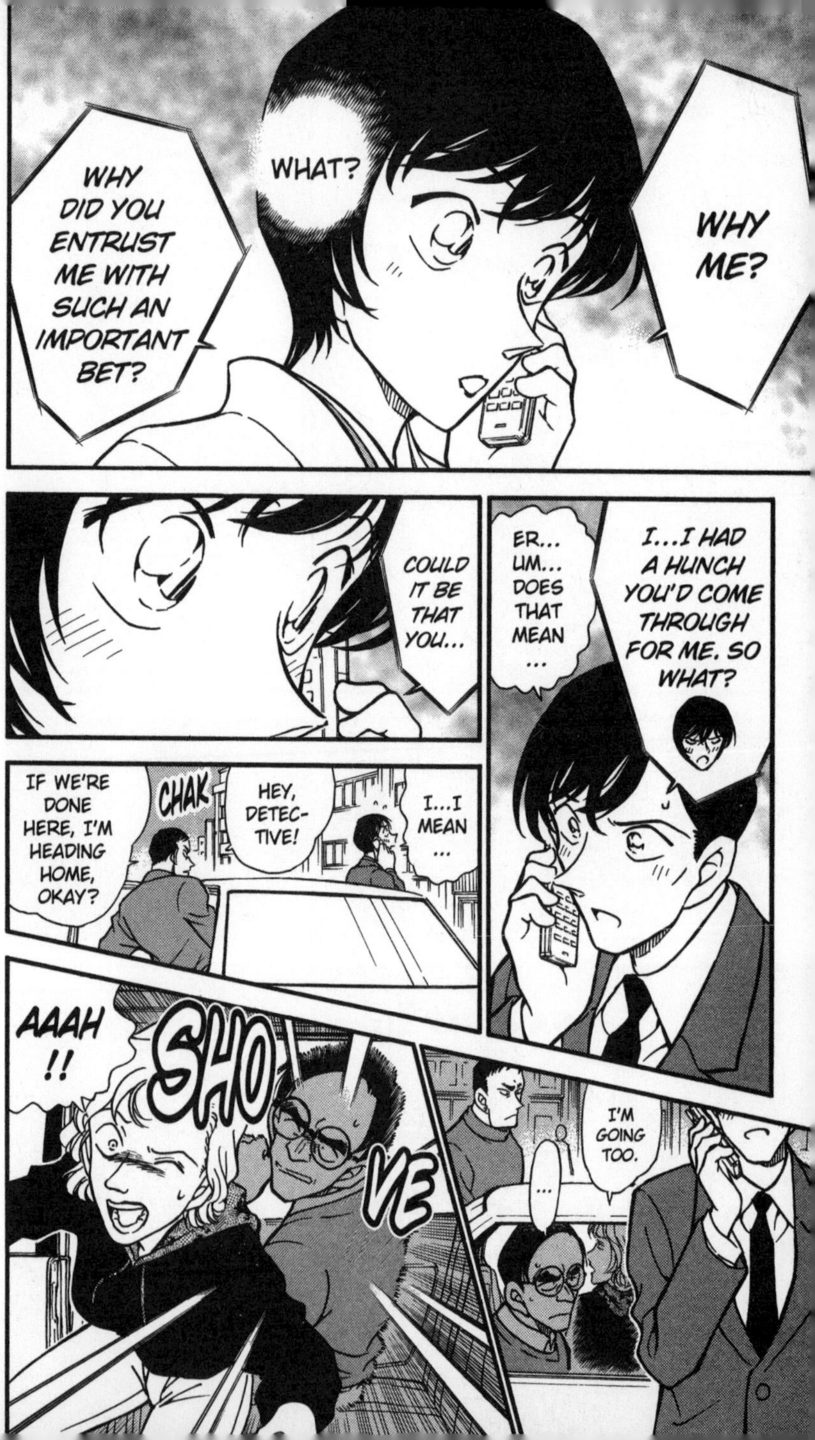
WHY ME?
WHAT?
WHY DID YOU ENTRUST ME WITH SUCH AN IMPORTANT BET?
I...I HAD A HUNCH YOU'D COME THROUGH FOR ME. SO WHAT?
ER... UM... DOES THAT MEAN ...
COULD IT BE THAT YOU...
I...I MEAN ...
HEY, DETECTIVE!
CHAK
IF WE'RE DONE HERE, I'M HEADING HOME, OKAY?
I'M GOING TOO.
...
SHOVE
AAAH !!

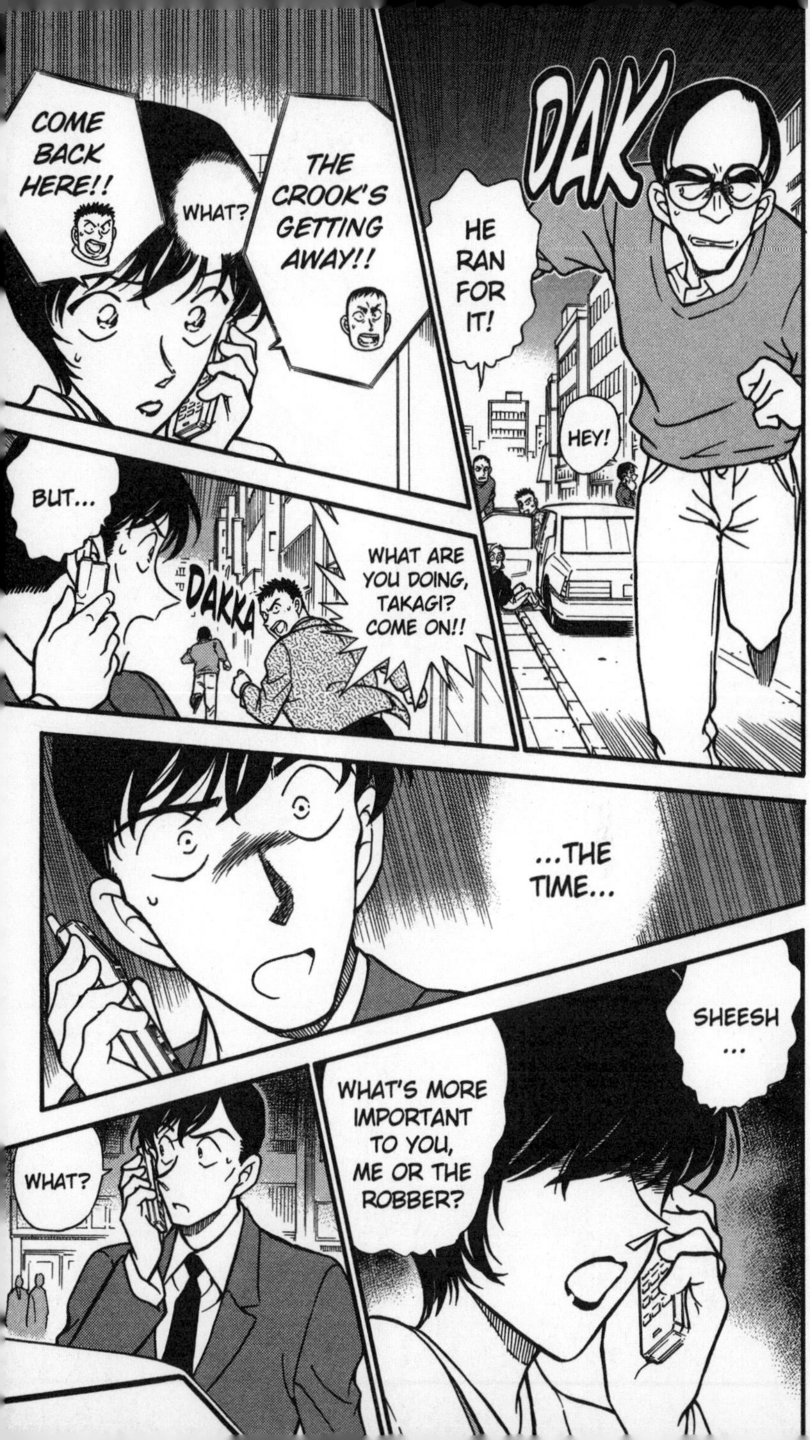
DAK
HE RAN FOR IT!
HEY!
THE CROOK'S GETTING AWAY!!
WHAT?
COME BACK HERE!!
WHAT ARE YOU DOING, TAKAGI? COME ON!!
DAKKA
BUT...
...THE TIME...
SHEESH ...
WHAT'S MORE IMPORTANT TO YOU, ME OR THE ROBBER?
WHAT?

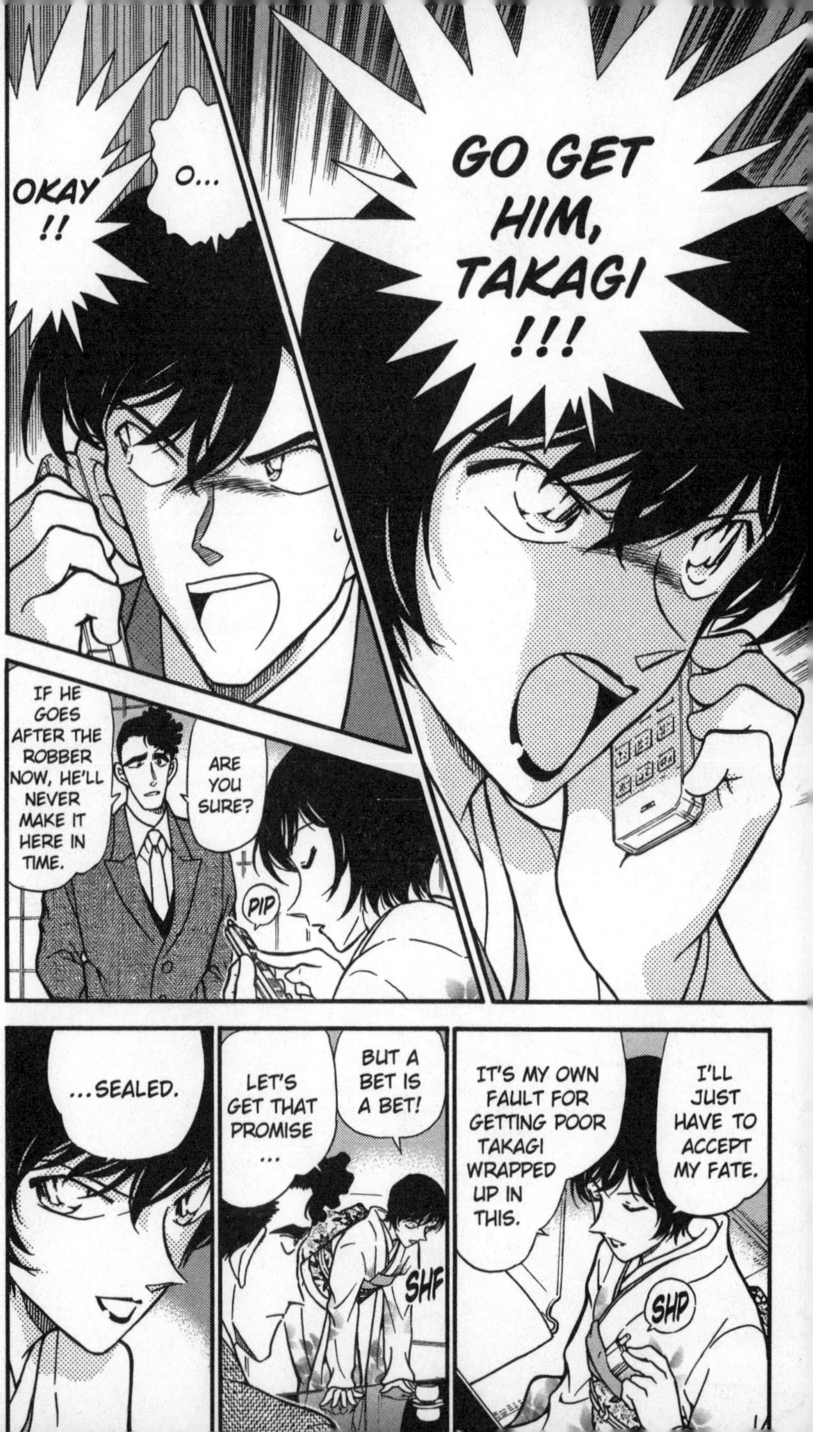
GO GET HIM, TAKAGI!!!
O...
OKAY!!
ARE YOU SURE?
IF HE GOES AFTER THE ROBBER NOW, HE'LL NEVER MAKE IT HERE IN TIME.
PIP
I'LL JUST HAVE TO ACCEPT MY FATE.
IT'S MY OWN FAULT FOR GETTING POOR TAKAGI WRAPPED UP IN THIS.
SHP
BUT A BET IS A BET!
LET'S GET THAT PROMISE...
SHF
...SEALED.

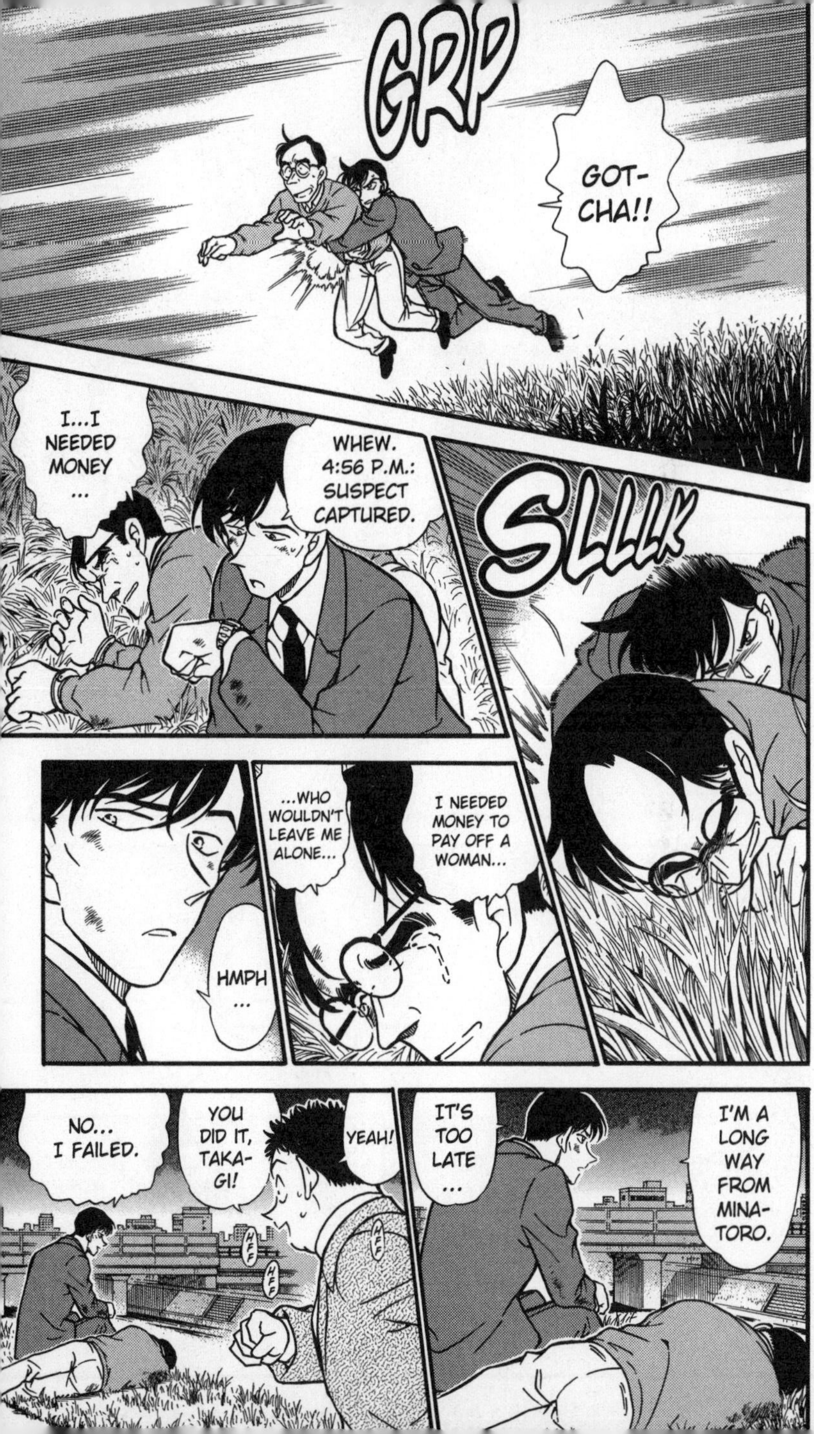
GRP
GOT-CHA!!
SLLLK
WHEW. 4:56 P.M.: SUSPECT CAPTURED.
I...I NEEDED MONEY ...
I NEEDED MONEY TO PAY OFF A WOMAN...
...WHO WOULDN'T LEAVE ME ALONE...
HMPH ...
I'M A LONG WAY FROM MINA-TORO.
IT'S TOO LATE ...
HFF
YEAH!
YOU DID IT, TAKA-GI!
HFF
HFF
NO... I FAILED.

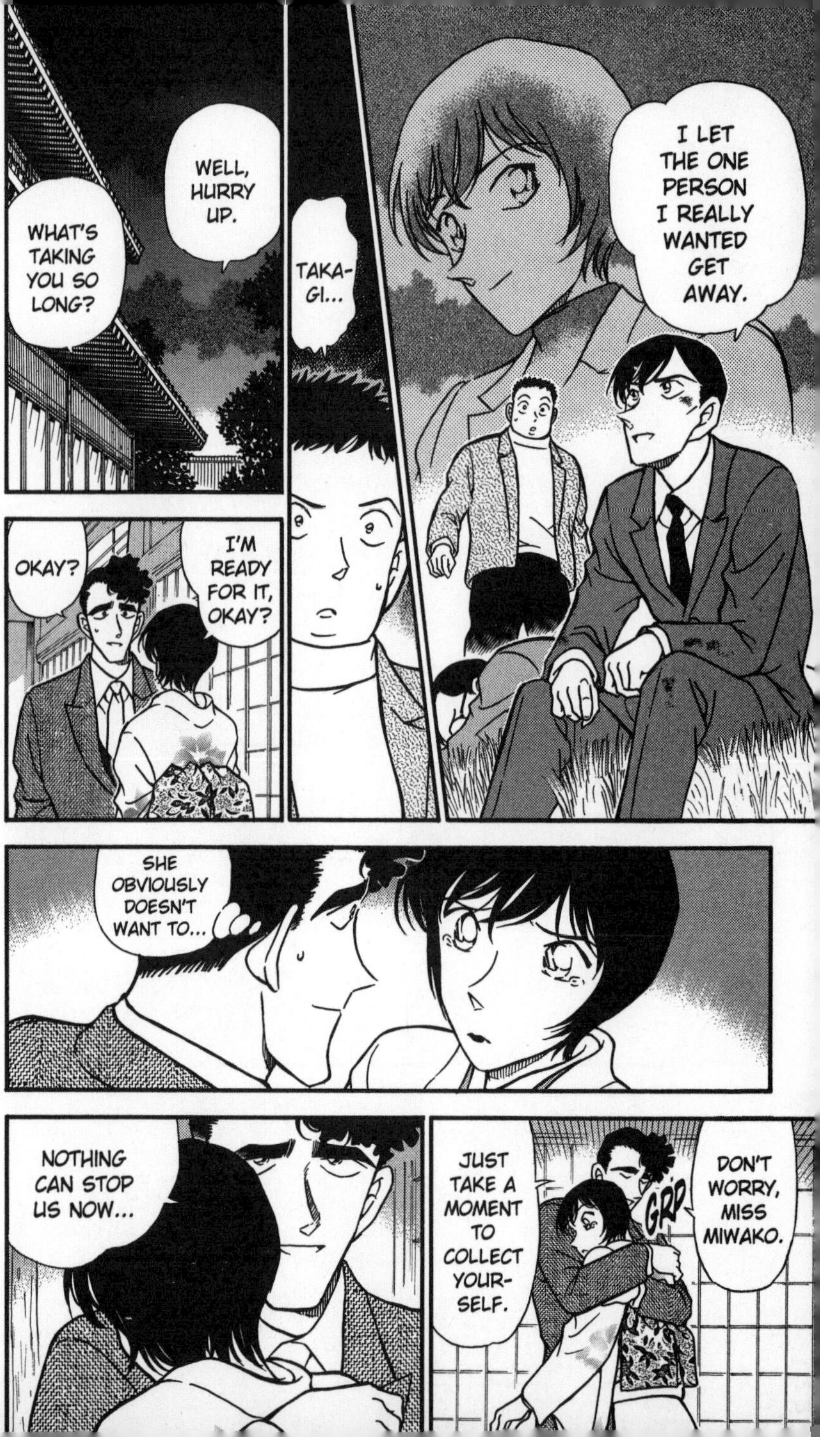
I LET THE ONE PERSON I REALLY WANTED GET AWAY.
TAKAGI...
WELL, HURRY UP.
WHAT'S TAKING YOU SO LONG?
I'M READY FOR IT, OKAY?
OKAY?
SHE OBVIOUSLY DOESN'T WANT TO...
DON'T WORRY, MISS MIWAKO.
GRP
JUST TAKE A MOMENT TO COLLECT YOURSELF.
NOTHING CAN STOP US NOW...

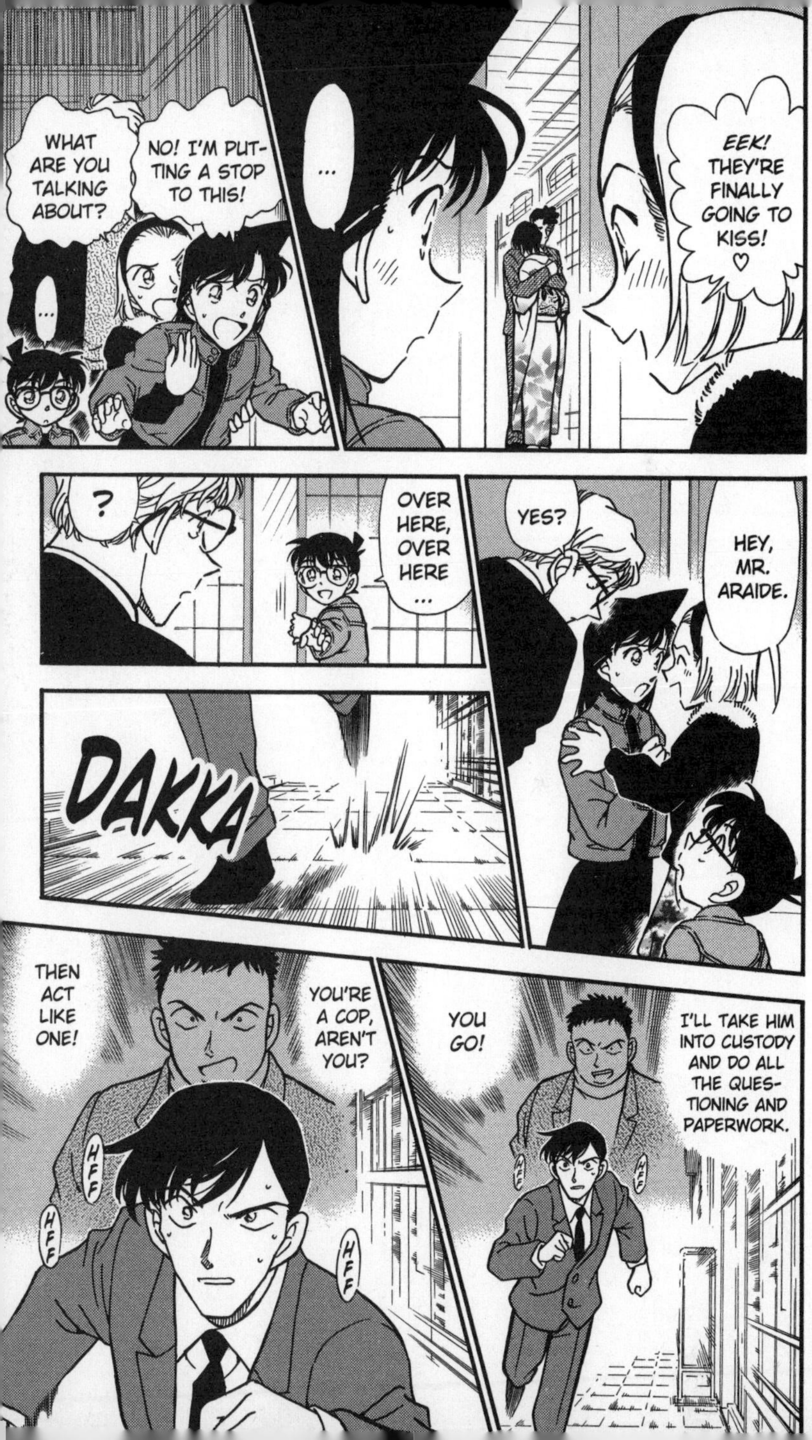
EEK! THEY'RE FINALLY GOING TO KISS! ♡
...
NO! I'M PUTTING A STOP TO THIS!
WHAT ARE YOU TALKING ABOUT?
...
HEY, MR. ARAIDE.
YES?
OVER HERE, OVER HERE ...
?
DAKKA
I'LL TAKE HIM INTO CUSTODY AND DO ALL THE QUESTIONING AND PAPERWORK.
YOU GO!
HFF
HFF
YOU'RE A COP, AREN'T YOU?
THEN ACT LIKE ONE!
HFF
HFF
HFF

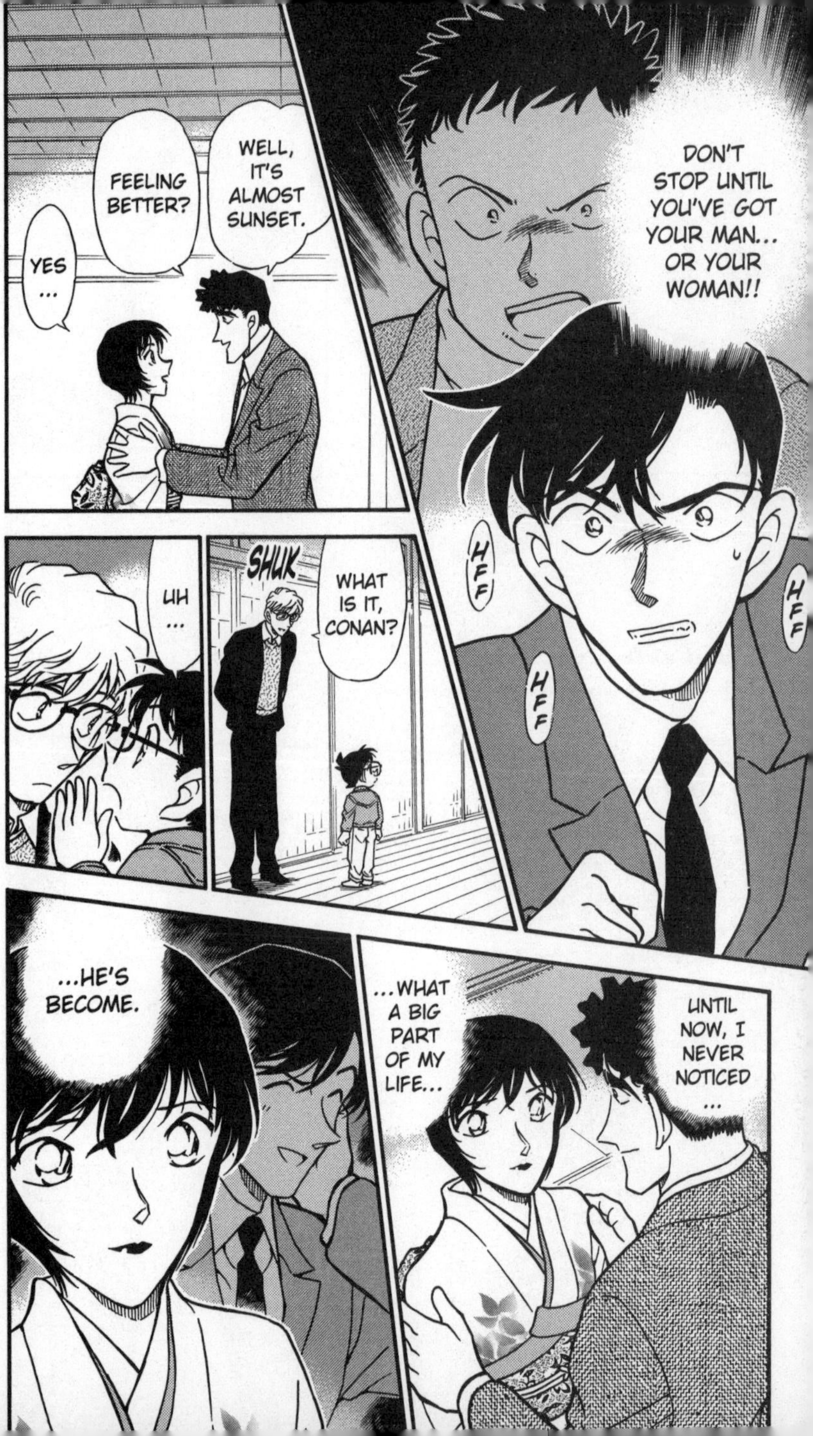
DON'T STOP UNTIL YOU'VE GOT YOUR MAN... OR YOUR WOMAN!!
HFF
HFF
HFF
WELL, IT'S ALMOST SUNSET.
FEELING BETTER?
YES ...
SHUK
WHAT IS IT, CONAN?
UH ...
UNTIL NOW, I NEVER NOTICED ...
...WHAT A BIG PART OF MY LIFE...
...HE'S BECOME.

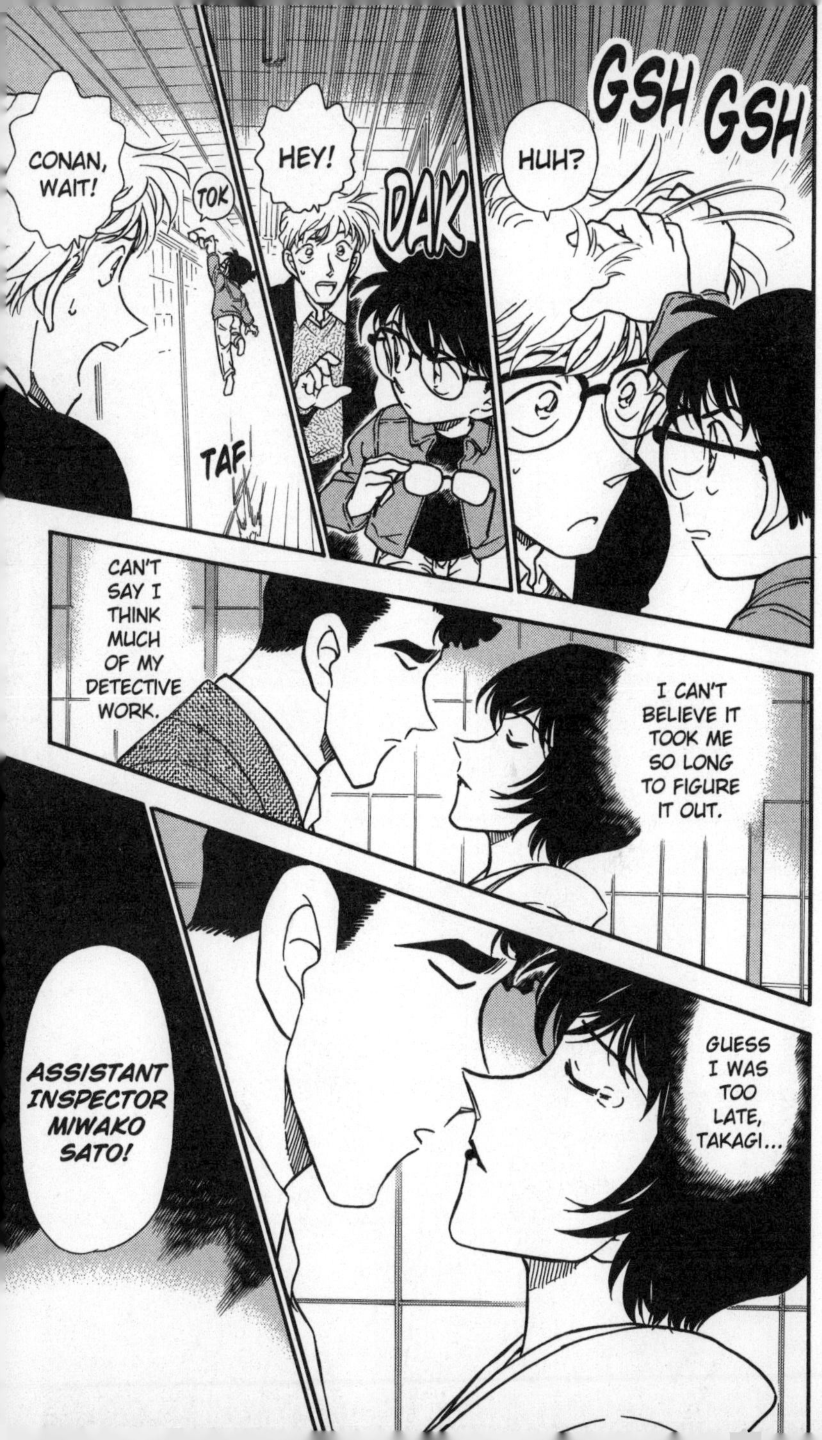
GSH GSH
HUH?
HEY!
DAK
CONAN, WAIT!
TOK
TAF
I CAN'T BELIEVE IT TOOK ME SO LONG TO FIGURE IT OUT.
CAN'T SAY I THINK MUCH OF MY DETECTIVE WORK.
GUESS I WAS TOO LATE, TAKAGI...
ASSISTANT INSPECTOR MIWAKO SATO!

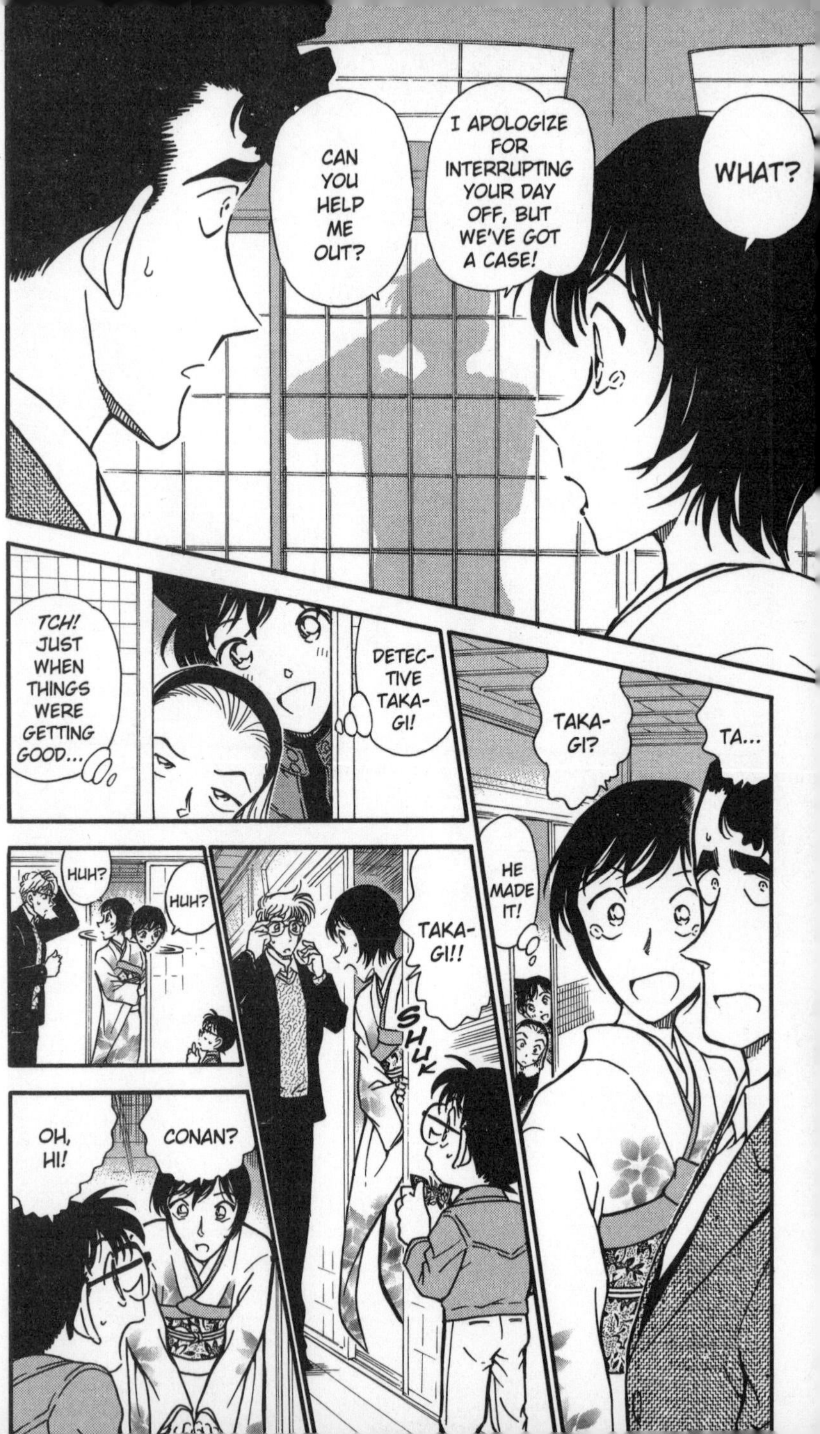
WHAT?
I APOLOGIZE FOR INTERRUPTING YOUR DAY OFF, BUT WE'VE GOT A CASE!
CAN YOU HELP ME OUT?
TA...
TAKA-GI?
HE MADE IT!
DETEC-TIVE TAKA-GI!
TCH! JUST WHEN THINGS WERE GETTING GOOD...
TAKA-GI!!
SHUK
HUH?
HUH?
CONAN?
OH, HI!

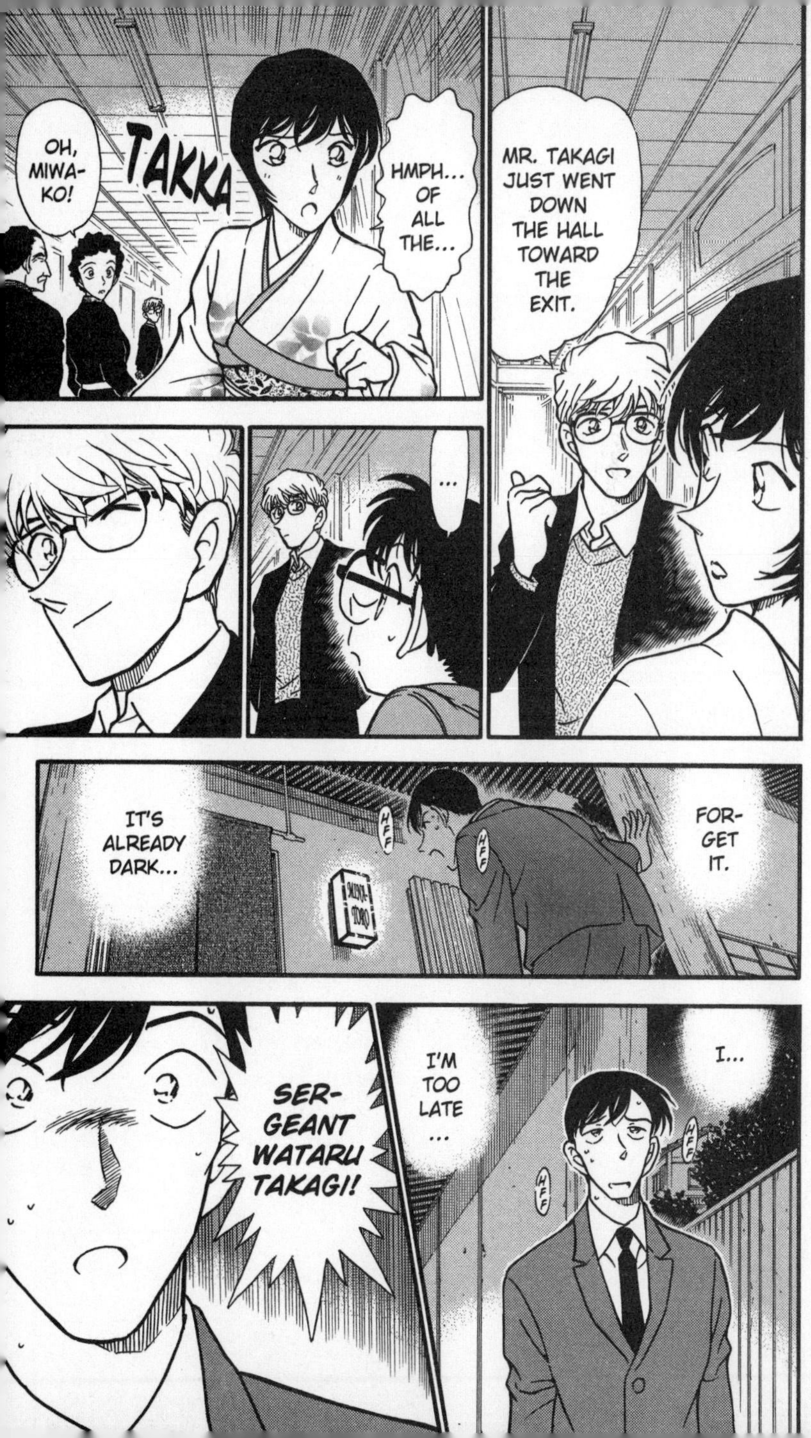
MR. TAKAGI JUST WENT DOWN THE HALL TOWARD THE EXIT.
HMPH... OF ALL THE...
TAKKA
OH, MIWAKO!
...
FOR-GET IT.
HFF
HFF
IT'S ALREADY DARK...
I...
HFF
HFF
I'M TOO LATE ...
SER-GEANT WATARU TAKAGI!

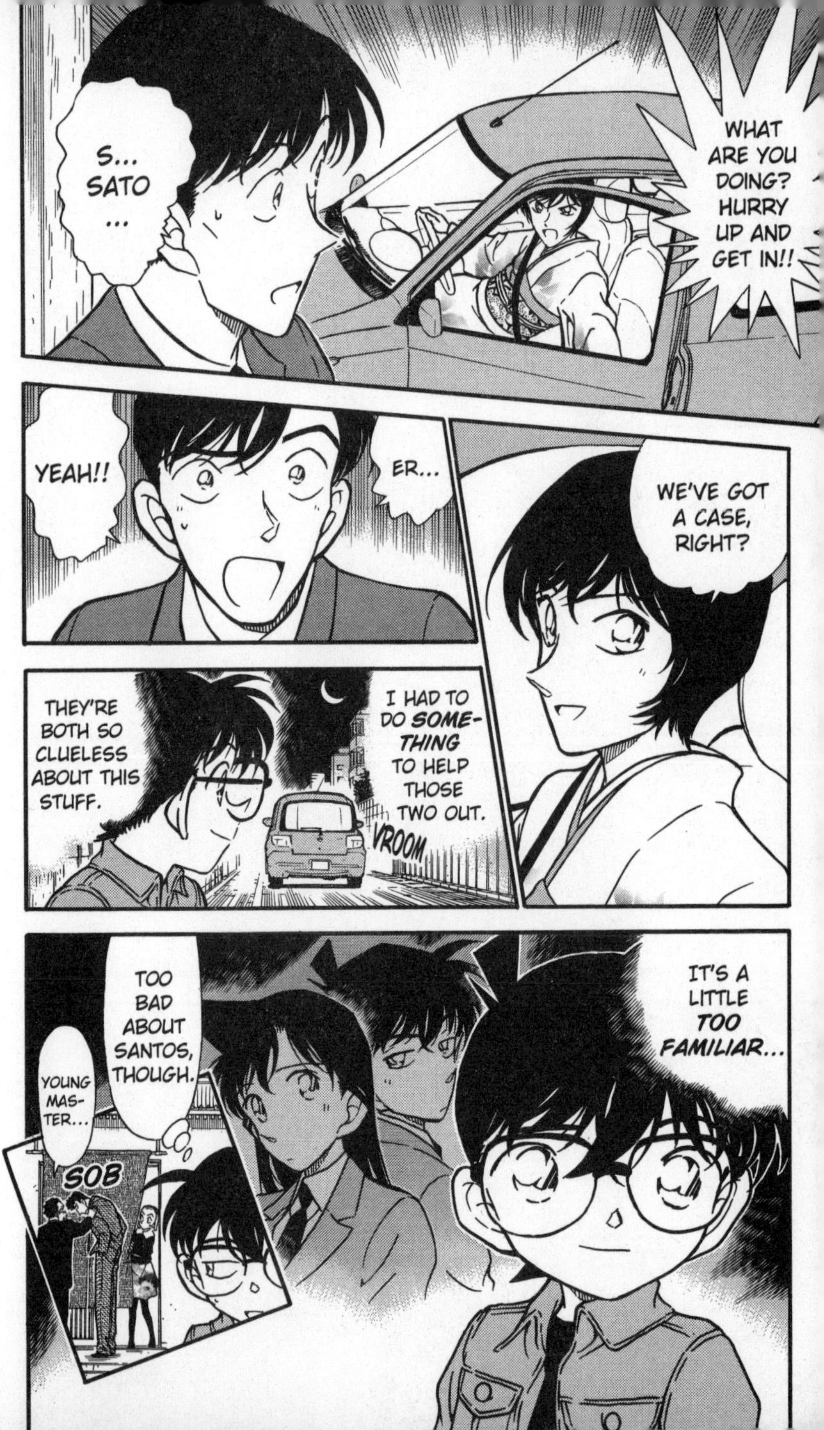
WHAT ARE YOU DOING? HURRY UP AND GET IN!!
S... SATO ...
WE'VE GOT A CASE, RIGHT?
ER...
YEAH!!
I HAD TO DO SOMETHING TO HELP THOSE TWO OUT.
VROOM
THEY'RE BOTH SO CLUELESS ABOUT THIS STUFF.
IT'S A LITTLE TOO FAMILIAR...
TOO BAD ABOUT SANTOS, THOUGH.
YOUNG MASTER...
SOB

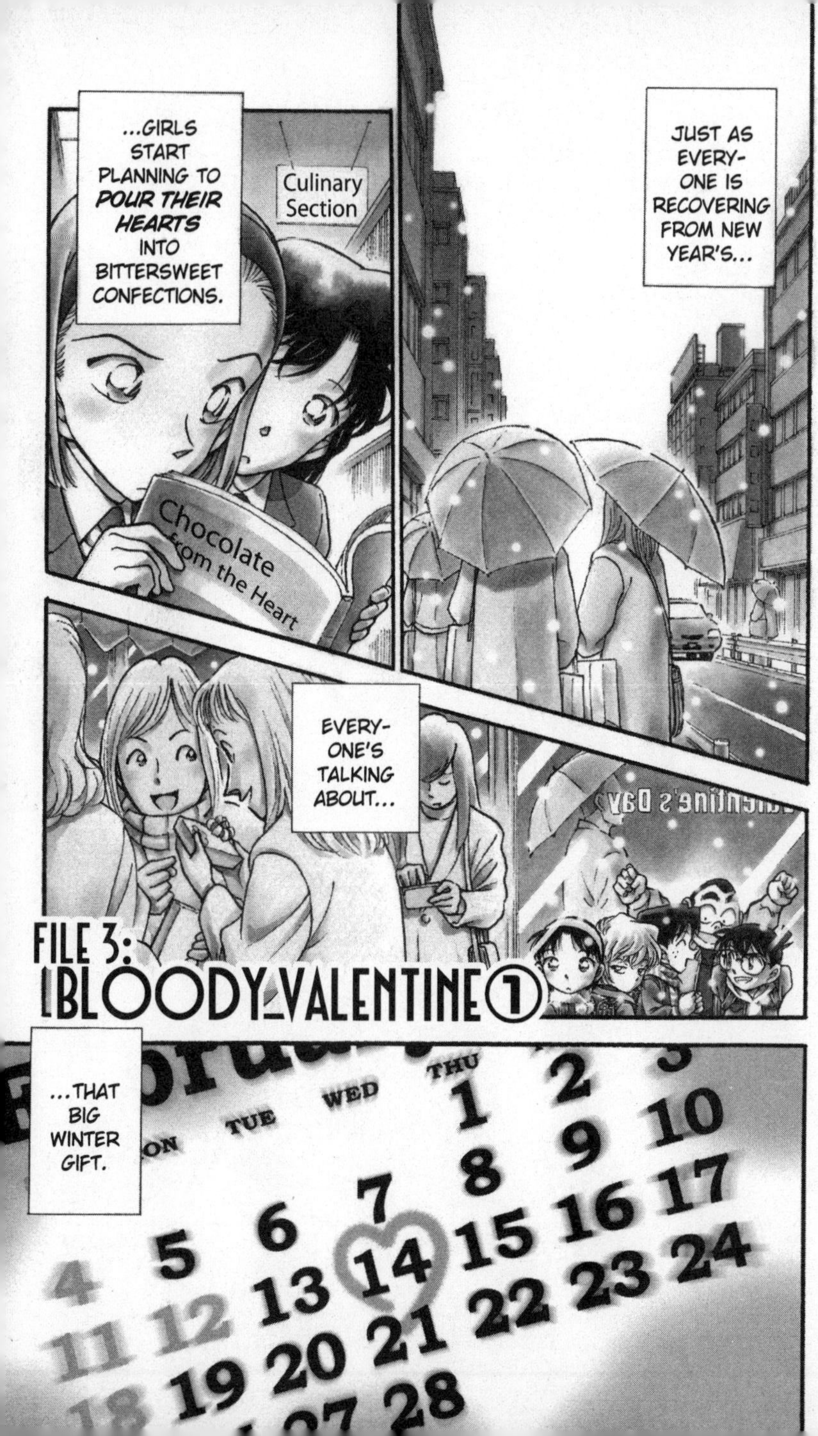
JUST AS EVERY-ONE IS RECOVERING FROM NEW YEAR'S...
...GIRLS START PLANNING TO *POUR THEIR HEARTS* INTO BITTERSWEET CONFECTIONS.
Culinary Section
Chocolate from the Heart
EVERY-ONE'S TALKING ABOUT...
FILE 3: BLOODY VALENTINE ①
...THAT BIG WINTER GIFT.
TUE
WED
THU

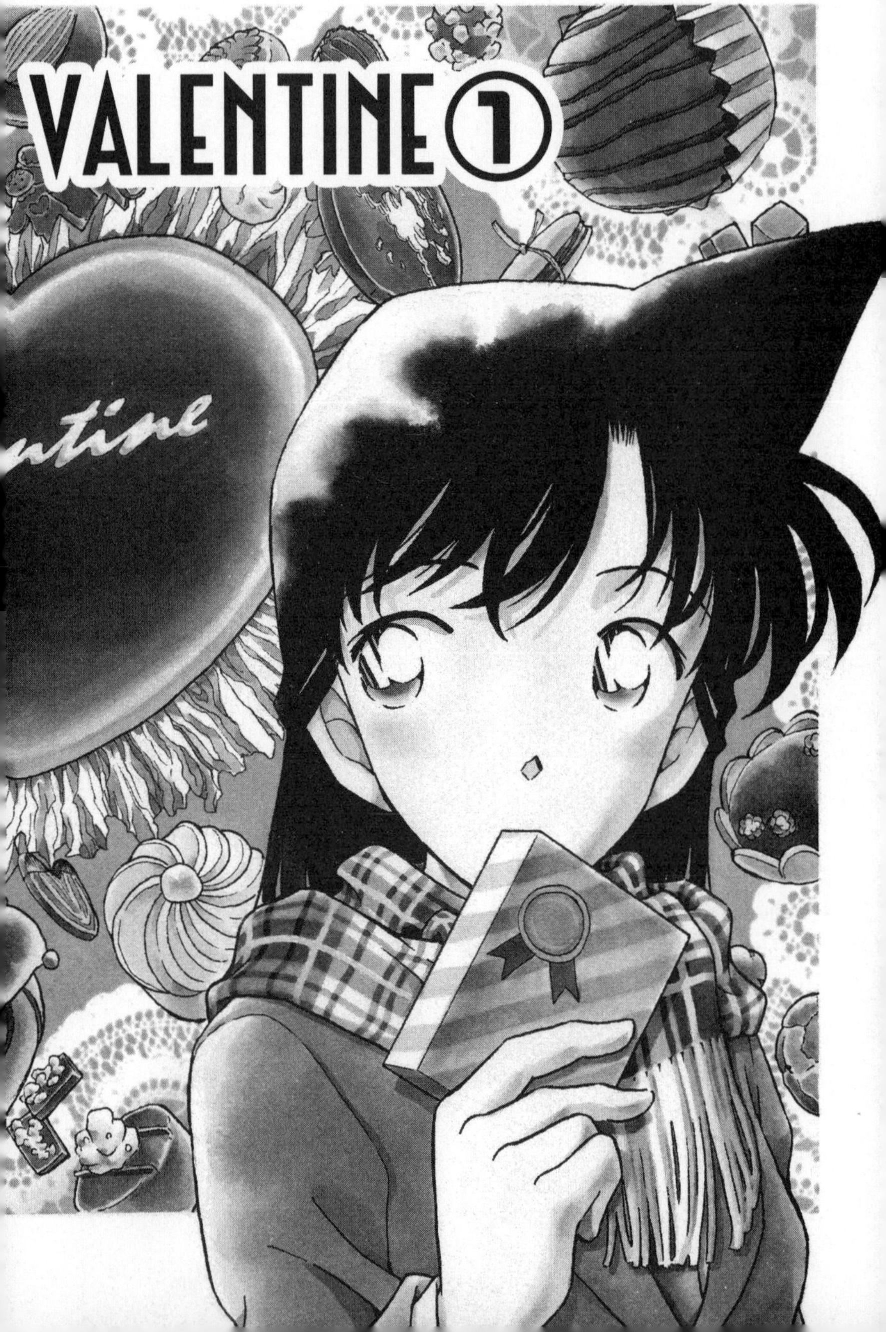
VALENTINE ①
ntine

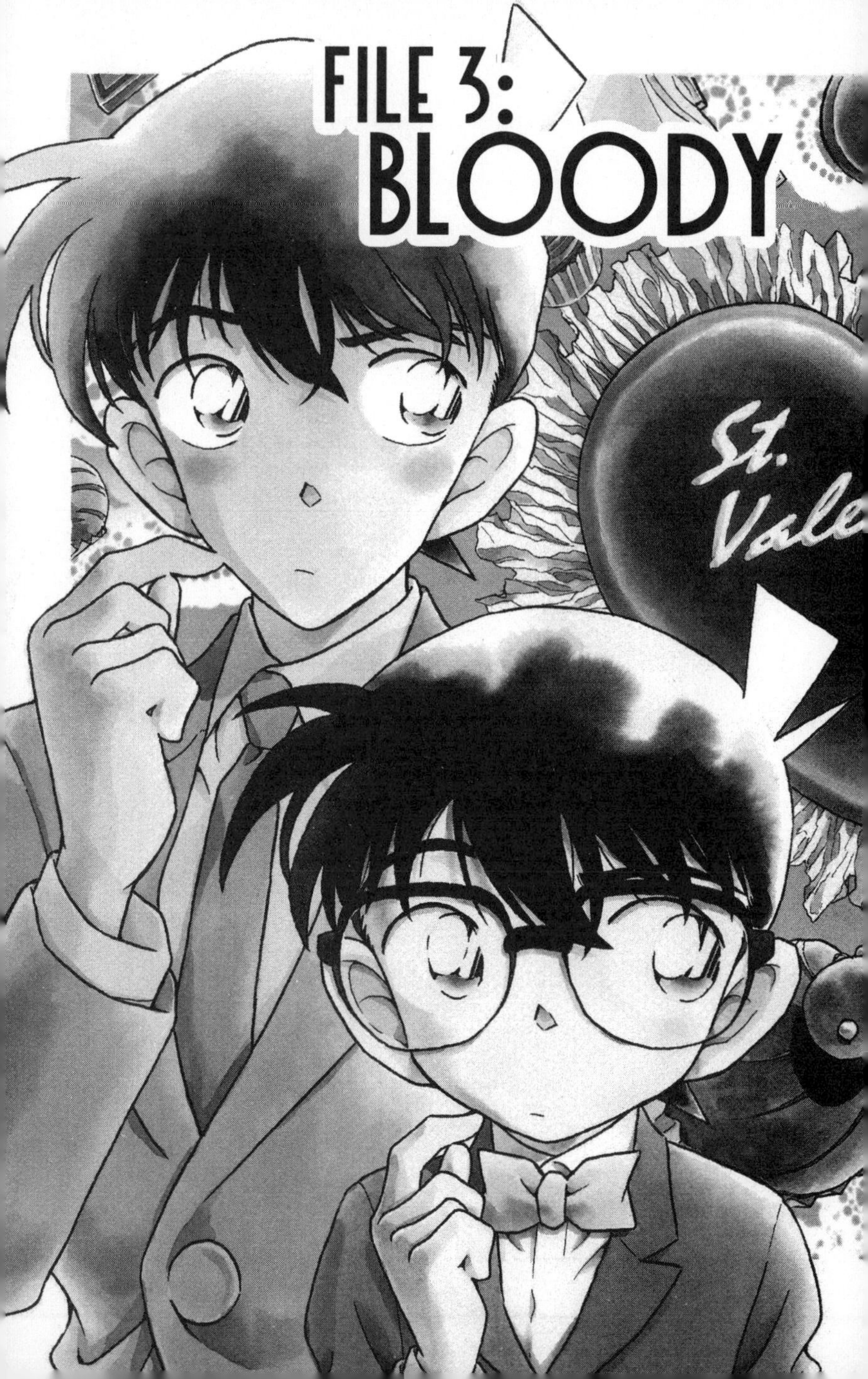
FILE 3:
BLOODY
St.
Vale

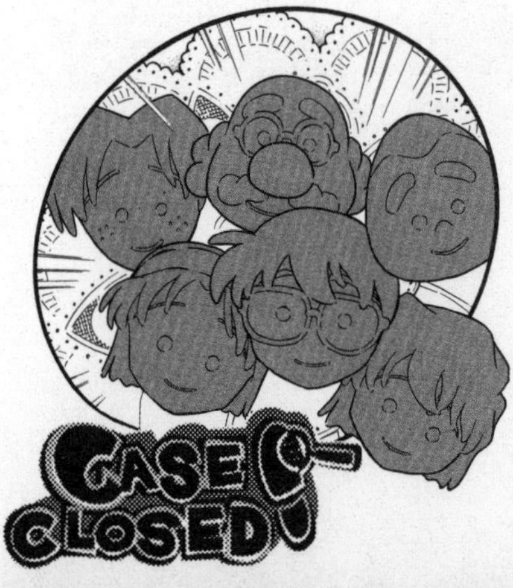
CASE CLOSED

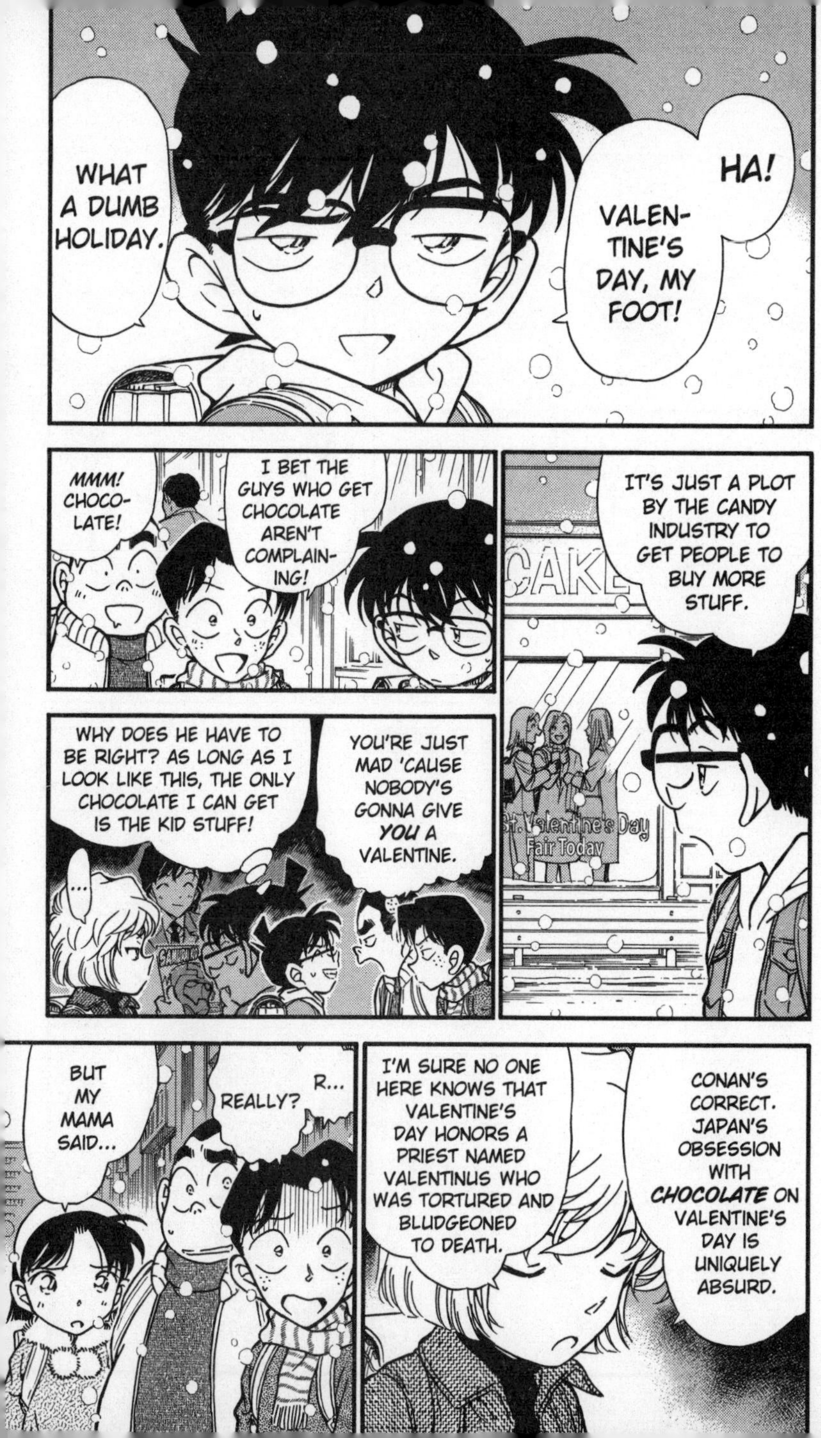
HA!
VALEN-TINE'S DAY, MY FOOT!
WHAT A DUMB HOLIDAY.
IT'S JUST A PLOT BY THE CANDY INDUSTRY TO GET PEOPLE TO BUY MORE STUFF.
CAKE
St. Valentine's Day Fair Today
I BET THE GUYS WHO GET CHOCOLATE AREN'T COMPLAIN-ING!
MMM! CHOCO-LATE!
YOU'RE JUST MAD 'CAUSE NOBODY'S GONNA GIVE *YOU* A VALENTINE.
WHY DOES HE HAVE TO BE RIGHT? AS LONG AS I LOOK LIKE THIS, THE ONLY CHOCOLATE I CAN GET IS THE KID STUFF!
...
CONAN'S CORRECT. JAPAN'S OBSESSION WITH *CHOCOLATE* ON VALENTINE'S DAY IS UNIQUELY ABSURD.
I'M SURE NO ONE HERE KNOWS THAT VALENTINE'S DAY HONORS A PRIEST NAMED VALENTINUS WHO WAS TORTURED AND BLUDGEONED TO DEATH.
R... REALLY?
BUT MY MAMA SAID...

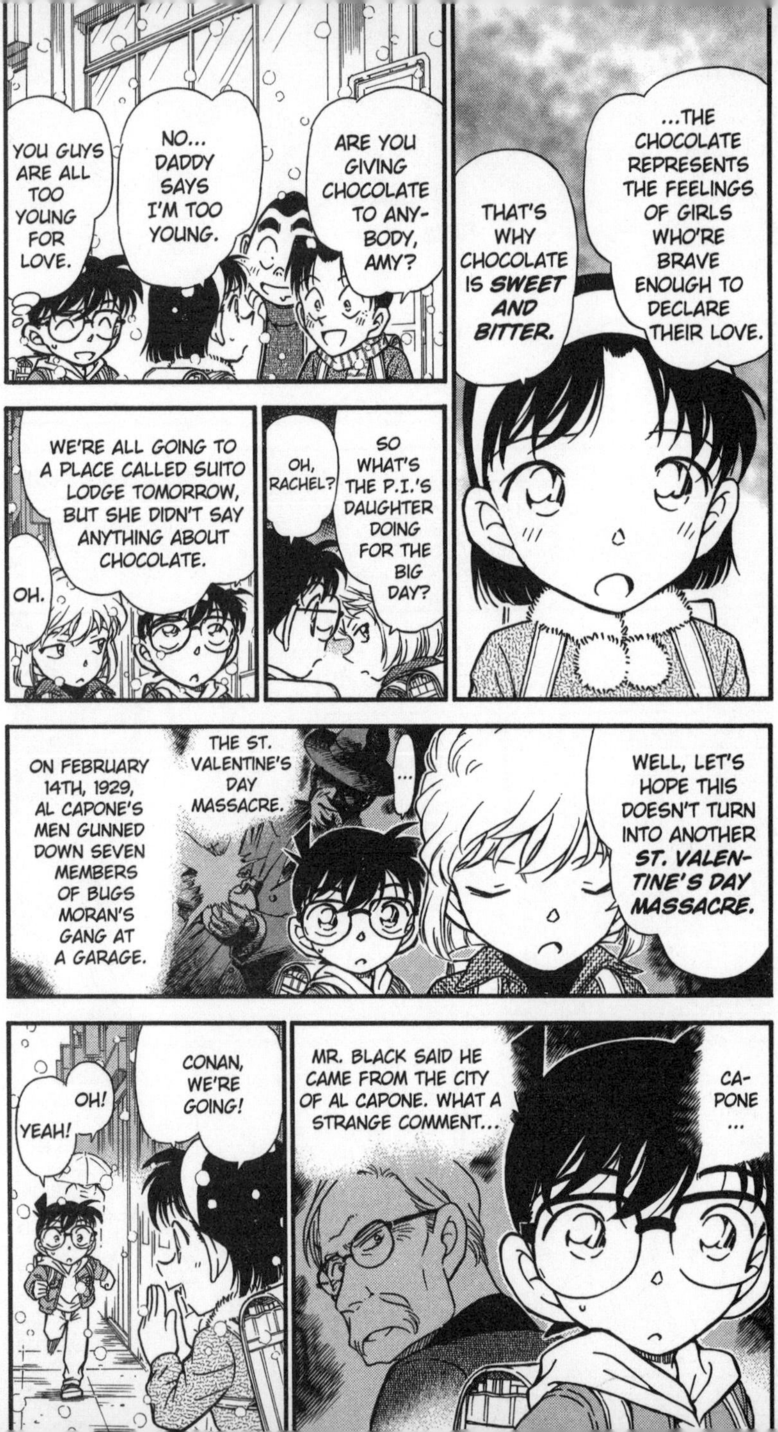
...THE CHOCOLATE REPRESENTS THE FEELINGS OF GIRLS WHO'RE BRAVE ENOUGH TO DECLARE THEIR LOVE.
THAT'S WHY CHOCOLATE IS ***SWEET AND BITTER.***
ARE YOU GIVING CHOCOLATE TO ANY-BODY, AMY?
NO... DADDY SAYS I'M TOO YOUNG.
YOU GUYS ARE ALL TOO YOUNG FOR LOVE.
SO WHAT'S THE P.I.'S DAUGHTER DOING FOR THE BIG DAY?
OH, RACHEL?
WE'RE ALL GOING TO A PLACE CALLED SUITO LODGE TOMORROW, BUT SHE DIDN'T SAY ANYTHING ABOUT CHOCOLATE.
OH.
WELL, LET'S HOPE THIS DOESN'T TURN INTO ANOTHER ***ST. VALEN-TINE'S DAY MASSACRE.***
...
THE ST. VALENTINE'S DAY MASSACRE.
ON FEBRUARY 14TH, 1929, AL CAPONE'S MEN GUNNED DOWN SEVEN MEMBERS OF BUGS MORAN'S GANG AT A GARAGE.
CA-PONE...
MR. BLACK SAID HE CAME FROM THE CITY OF AL CAPONE. WHAT A STRANGE COMMENT...
CONAN, WE'RE GOING!
OH! YEAH!

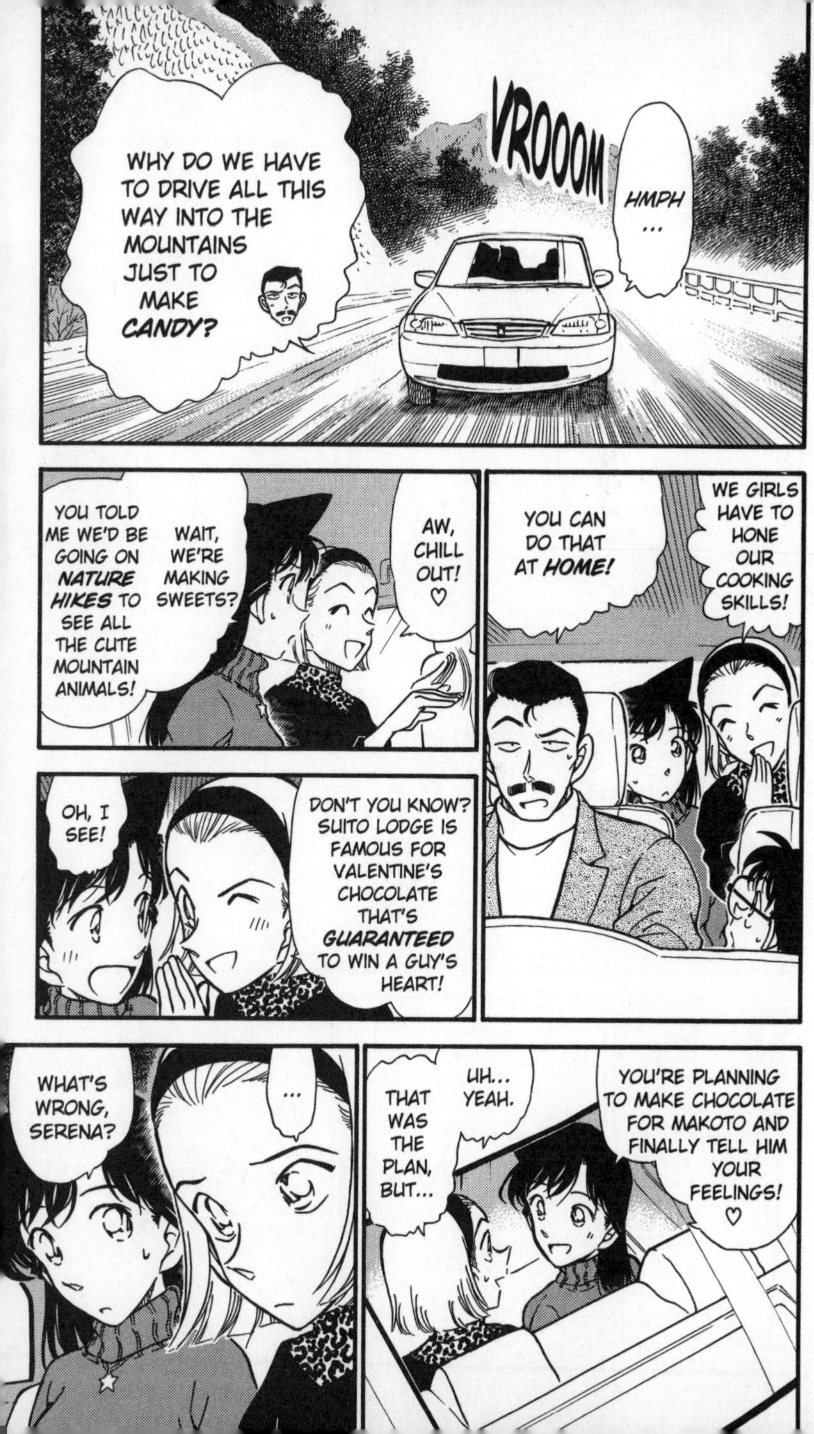
VROOOM
HMPH ...
WHY DO WE HAVE TO DRIVE ALL THIS WAY INTO THE MOUNTAINS JUST TO MAKE CANDY?
WE GIRLS HAVE TO HONE OUR COOKING SKILLS!
YOU CAN DO THAT AT HOME!
WAIT, WE'RE MAKING SWEETS?
YOU TOLD ME WE'D BE GOING ON NATURE HIKES TO SEE ALL THE CUTE MOUNTAIN ANIMALS!
AW, CHILL OUT! ♡
DON'T YOU KNOW? SUITO LODGE IS FAMOUS FOR VALENTINE'S CHOCOLATE THAT'S GUARANTEED TO WIN A GUY'S HEART!
OH, I SEE!
YOU'RE PLANNING TO MAKE CHOCOLATE FOR MAKOTO AND FINALLY TELL HIM YOUR FEELINGS! ♡
UH... YEAH.
THAT WAS THE PLAN, BUT...
...
WHAT'S WRONG, SERENA?

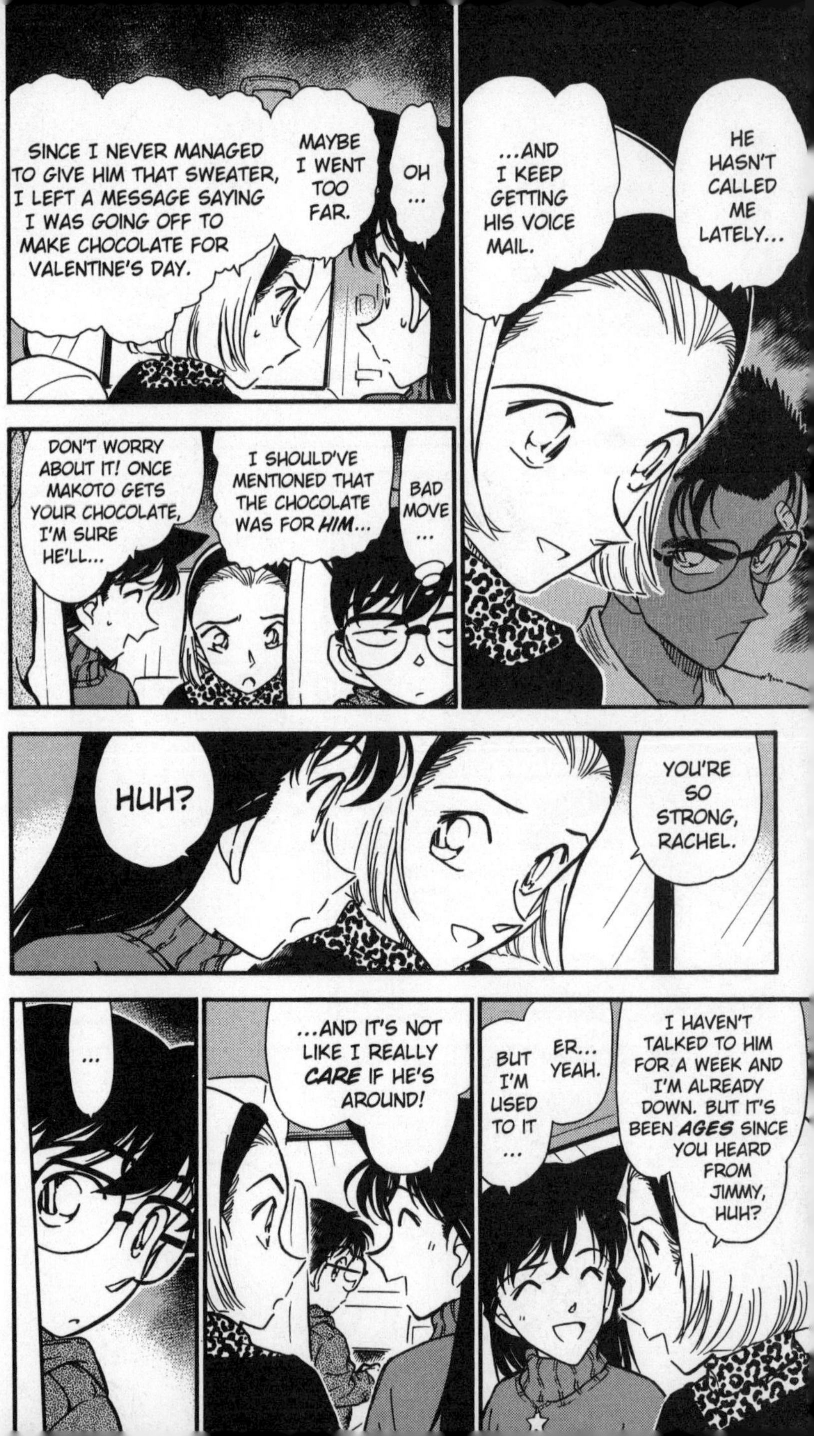
HE HASN'T CALLED ME LATELY...
...AND I KEEP GETTING HIS VOICE MAIL.
OH ...
MAYBE I WENT TOO FAR.
SINCE I NEVER MANAGED TO GIVE HIM THAT SWEATER, I LEFT A MESSAGE SAYING I WAS GOING OFF TO MAKE CHOCOLATE FOR VALENTINE'S DAY.
BAD MOVE ...
I SHOULD'VE MENTIONED THAT THE CHOCOLATE WAS FOR *HIM*...
DON'T WORRY ABOUT IT! ONCE MAKOTO GETS YOUR CHOCOLATE, I'M SURE HE'LL...
YOU'RE SO STRONG, RACHEL.
HUH?
I HAVEN'T TALKED TO HIM FOR A WEEK AND I'M ALREADY DOWN. BUT IT'S BEEN *AGES* SINCE YOU HEARD FROM JIMMY, HUH?
ER... YEAH.
BUT I'M USED TO IT ...
...AND IT'S NOT LIKE I REALLY *CARE* IF HE'S AROUND!
...

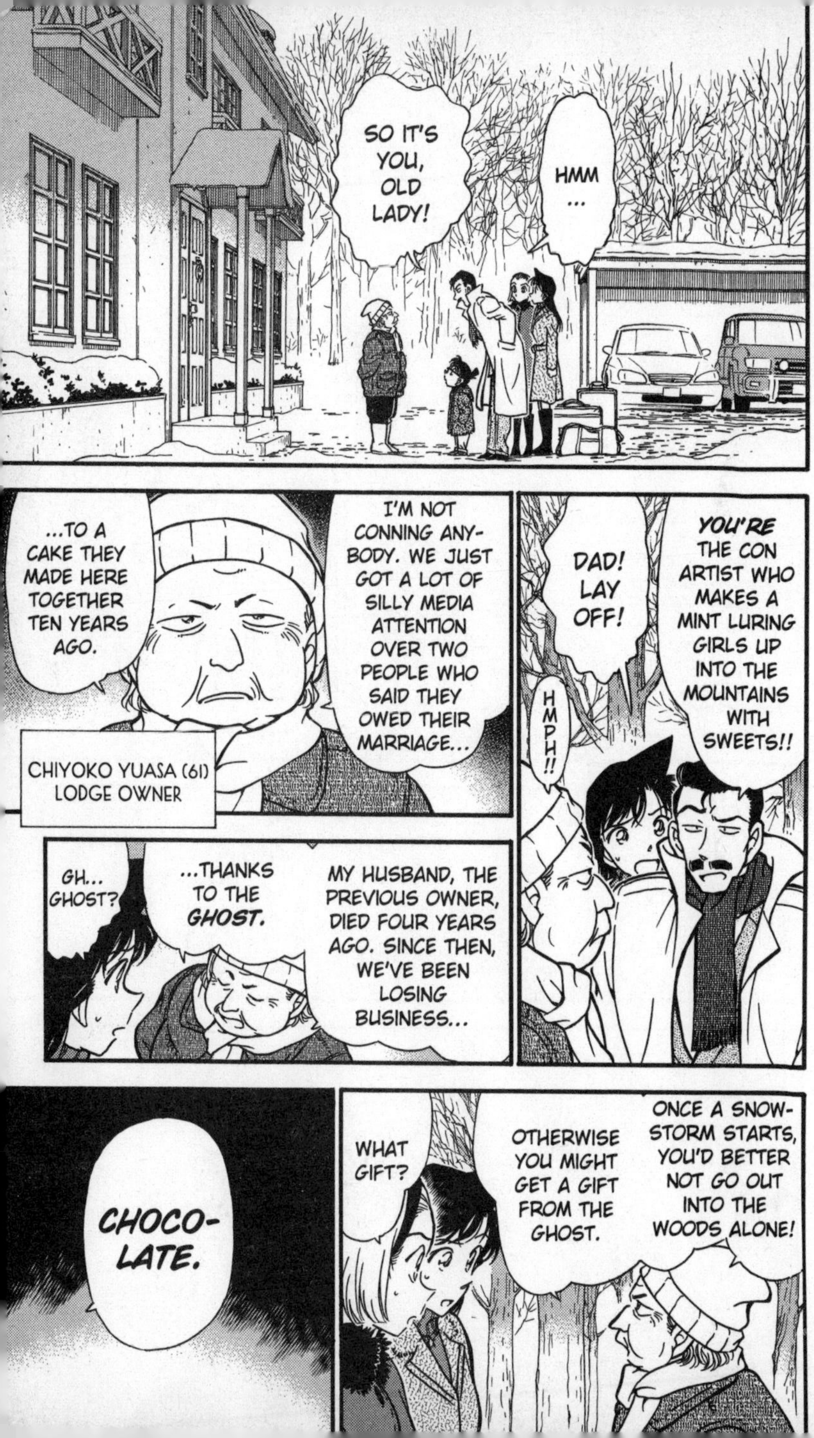
HMM ...
SO IT'S YOU, OLD LADY!
YOU'RE THE CON ARTIST WHO MAKES A MINT LURING GIRLS UP INTO THE MOUNTAINS WITH SWEETS!!
DAD! LAY OFF!
HMPH!!
I'M NOT CONNING ANY-BODY. WE JUST GOT A LOT OF SILLY MEDIA ATTENTION OVER TWO PEOPLE WHO SAID THEY OWED THEIR MARRIAGE...
...TO A CAKE THEY MADE HERE TOGETHER TEN YEARS AGO.
CHIYOKO YUASA (61) LODGE OWNER
MY HUSBAND, THE PREVIOUS OWNER, DIED FOUR YEARS AGO. SINCE THEN, WE'VE BEEN LOSING BUSINESS...
...THANKS TO THE *GHOST.*
GH... GHOST?
ONCE A SNOW-STORM STARTS, YOU'D BETTER NOT GO OUT INTO THE WOODS ALONE!
OTHERWISE YOU MIGHT GET A GIFT FROM THE GHOST.
WHAT GIFT?
CHOCO-LATE.

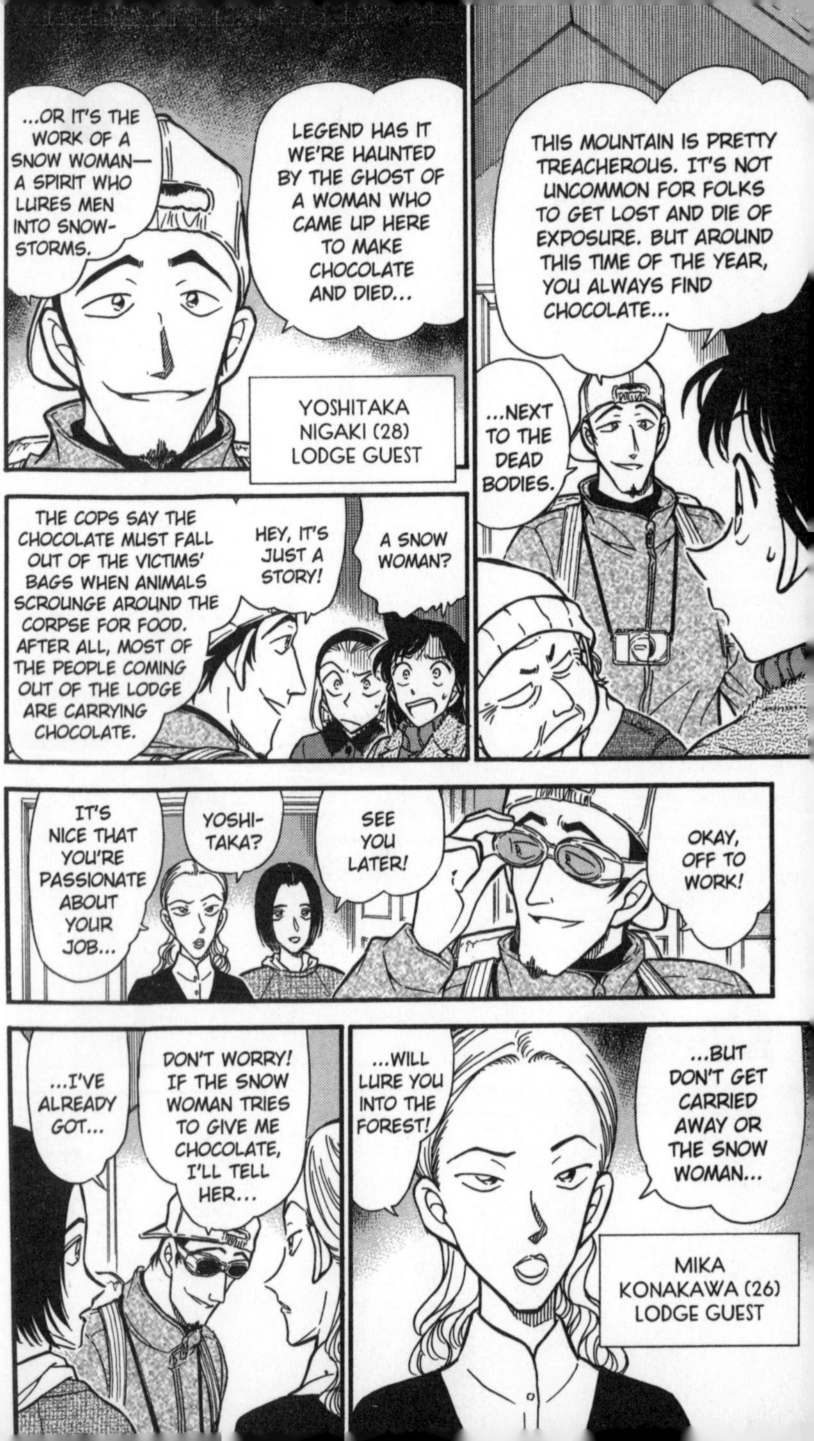
THIS MOUNTAIN IS PRETTY TREACHEROUS. IT'S NOT UNCOMMON FOR FOLKS TO GET LOST AND DIE OF EXPOSURE. BUT AROUND THIS TIME OF THE YEAR, YOU ALWAYS FIND CHOCOLATE...
...NEXT TO THE DEAD BODIES.
LEGEND HAS IT WE'RE HAUNTED BY THE GHOST OF A WOMAN WHO CAME UP HERE TO MAKE CHOCOLATE AND DIED...
...OR IT'S THE WORK OF A SNOW WOMAN—A SPIRIT WHO LURES MEN INTO SNOW-STORMS.
YOSHITAKA NIGAKI (28) LODGE GUEST
A SNOW WOMAN?
HEY, IT'S JUST A STORY!
THE COPS SAY THE CHOCOLATE MUST FALL OUT OF THE VICTIMS' BAGS WHEN ANIMALS SCROUNGE AROUND THE CORPSE FOR FOOD. AFTER ALL, MOST OF THE PEOPLE COMING OUT OF THE LODGE ARE CARRYING CHOCOLATE.
OKAY, OFF TO WORK!
SEE YOU LATER!
YOSHI-TAKA?
IT'S NICE THAT YOU'RE PASSIONATE ABOUT YOUR JOB...
...BUT DON'T GET CARRIED AWAY OR THE SNOW WOMAN...
...WILL LURE YOU INTO THE FOREST!
MIKA KONAKAWA (26) LODGE GUEST
DON'T WORRY! IF THE SNOW WOMAN TRIES TO GIVE ME CHOCOLATE, I'LL TELL HER...
...I'VE ALREADY GOT...

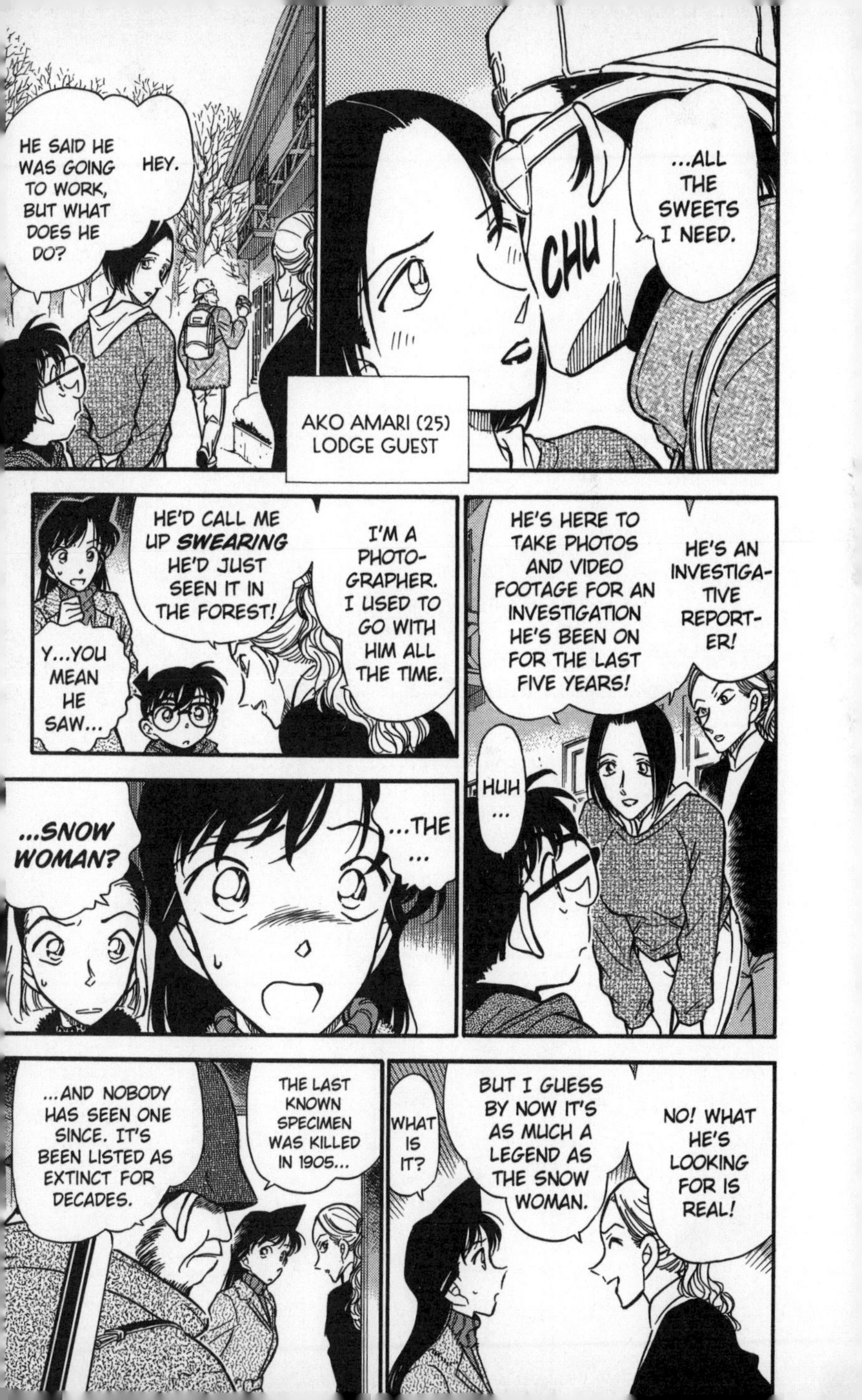
CHU
...ALL THE SWEETS I NEED.
AKO AMARI (25) LODGE GUEST
HEY.
HE SAID HE WAS GOING TO WORK, BUT WHAT DOES HE DO?
HE'S AN INVESTIGATIVE REPORTER!
HE'S HERE TO TAKE PHOTOS AND VIDEO FOOTAGE FOR AN INVESTIGATION HE'S BEEN ON FOR THE LAST FIVE YEARS!
HUH...
I'M A PHOTOGRAPHER. I USED TO GO WITH HIM ALL THE TIME.
HE'D CALL ME UP *SWEARING* HE'D JUST SEEN IT IN THE FOREST!
Y...YOU MEAN HE SAW...
...THE...
...SNOW WOMAN?
NO! WHAT HE'S LOOKING FOR IS REAL!
BUT I GUESS BY NOW IT'S AS MUCH A LEGEND AS THE SNOW WOMAN.
WHAT IS IT?
THE LAST KNOWN SPECIMEN WAS KILLED IN 1905...
...AND NOBODY HAS SEEN ONE SINCE. IT'S BEEN LISTED AS EXTINCT FOR DECADES.

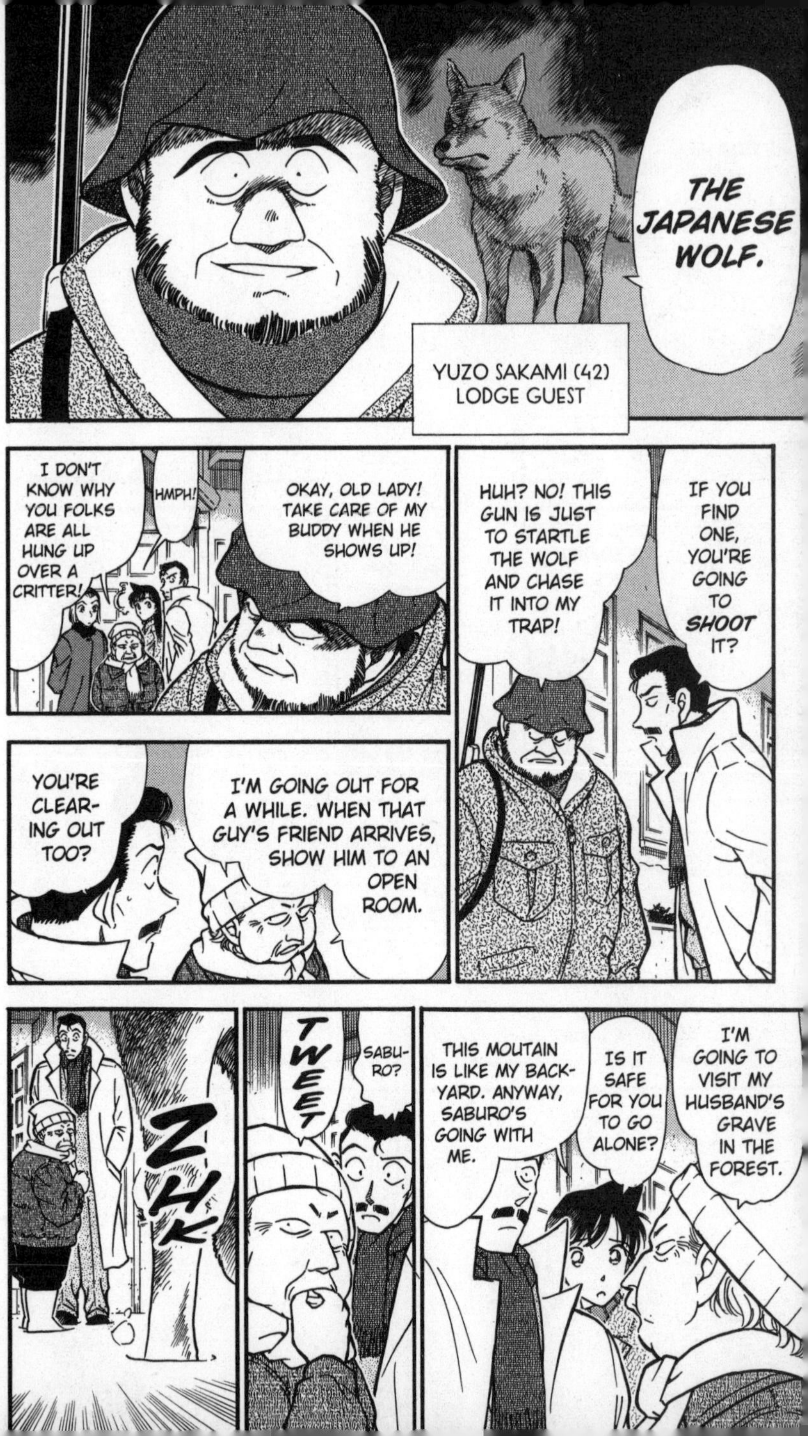
THE JAPANESE WOLF.
YUZO SAKAMI (42)
LODGE GUEST
IF YOU FIND ONE, YOU'RE GOING TO SHOOT IT?
HUH? NO! THIS GUN IS JUST TO STARTLE THE WOLF AND CHASE IT INTO MY TRAP!
OKAY, OLD LADY! TAKE CARE OF MY BUDDY WHEN HE SHOWS UP!
HMPH!
I DON'T KNOW WHY YOU FOLKS ARE ALL HUNG UP OVER A CRITTER!
I'M GOING OUT FOR A WHILE. WHEN THAT GUY'S FRIEND ARRIVES, SHOW HIM TO AN OPEN ROOM.
YOU'RE CLEAR-ING OUT TOO?
I'M GOING TO VISIT MY HUSBAND'S GRAVE IN THE FOREST.
IS IT SAFE FOR YOU TO GO ALONE?
THIS MOUTAIN IS LIKE MY BACK-YARD. ANYWAY, SABURO'S GOING WITH ME.
SABU-RO?
TWEET
ZHK

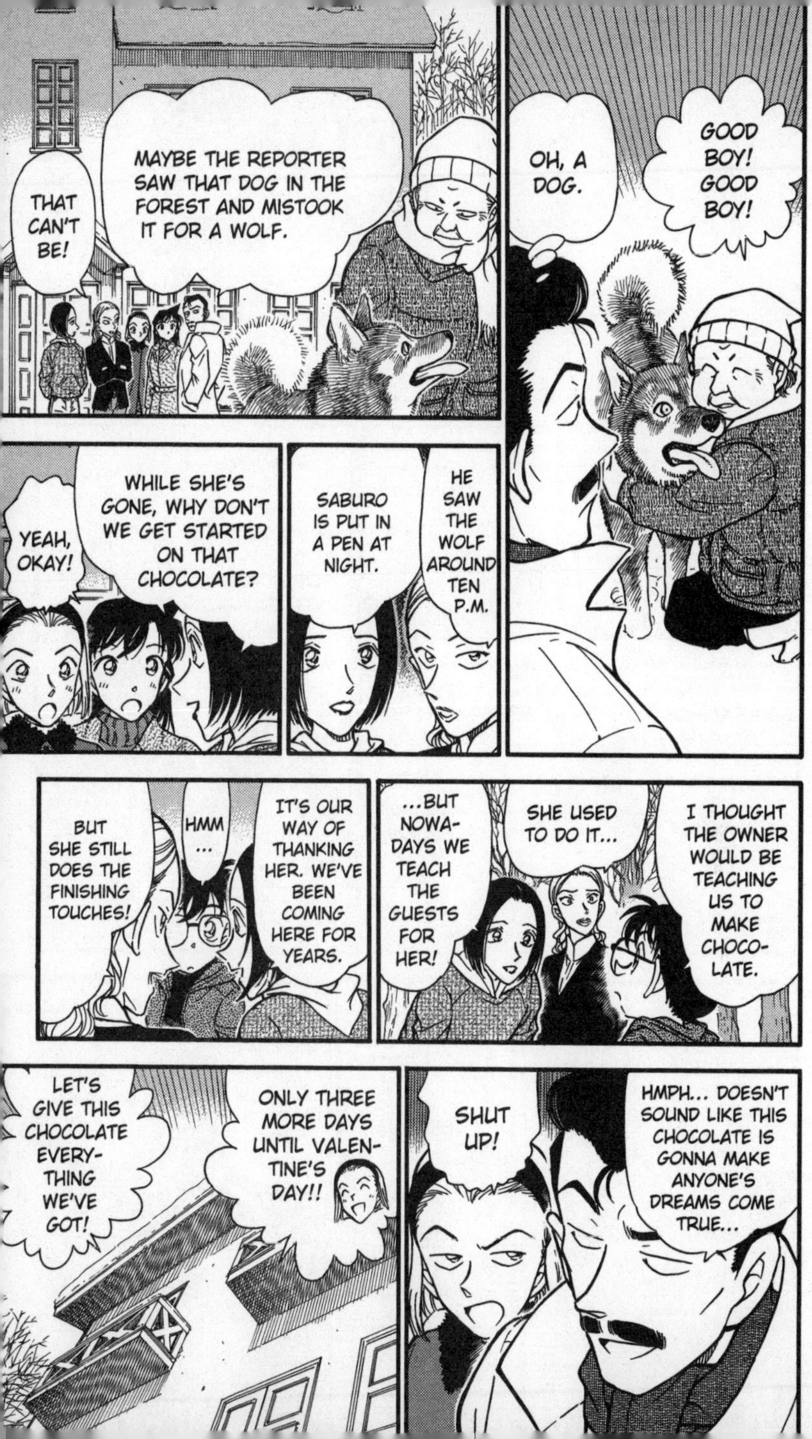
GOOD BOY! GOOD BOY!
OH, A DOG.
MAYBE THE REPORTER SAW THAT DOG IN THE FOREST AND MISTOOK IT FOR A WOLF.
THAT CAN'T BE!
HE SAW THE WOLF AROUND TEN P.M.
SABURO IS PUT IN A PEN AT NIGHT.
WHILE SHE'S GONE, WHY DON'T WE GET STARTED ON THAT CHOCOLATE?
YEAH, OKAY!
I THOUGHT THE OWNER WOULD BE TEACHING US TO MAKE CHOCO-LATE.
SHE USED TO DO IT...
...BUT NOWA-DAYS WE TEACH THE GUESTS FOR HER!
IT'S OUR WAY OF THANKING HER. WE'VE BEEN COMING HERE FOR YEARS.
HMM ...
BUT SHE STILL DOES THE FINISHING TOUCHES!
HMPH... DOESN'T SOUND LIKE THIS CHOCOLATE IS GONNA MAKE ANYONE'S DREAMS COME TRUE...
SHUT UP!
ONLY THREE MORE DAYS UNTIL VALEN-TINE'S DAY!!
LET'S GIVE THIS CHOCOLATE EVERY-THING WE'VE GOT!

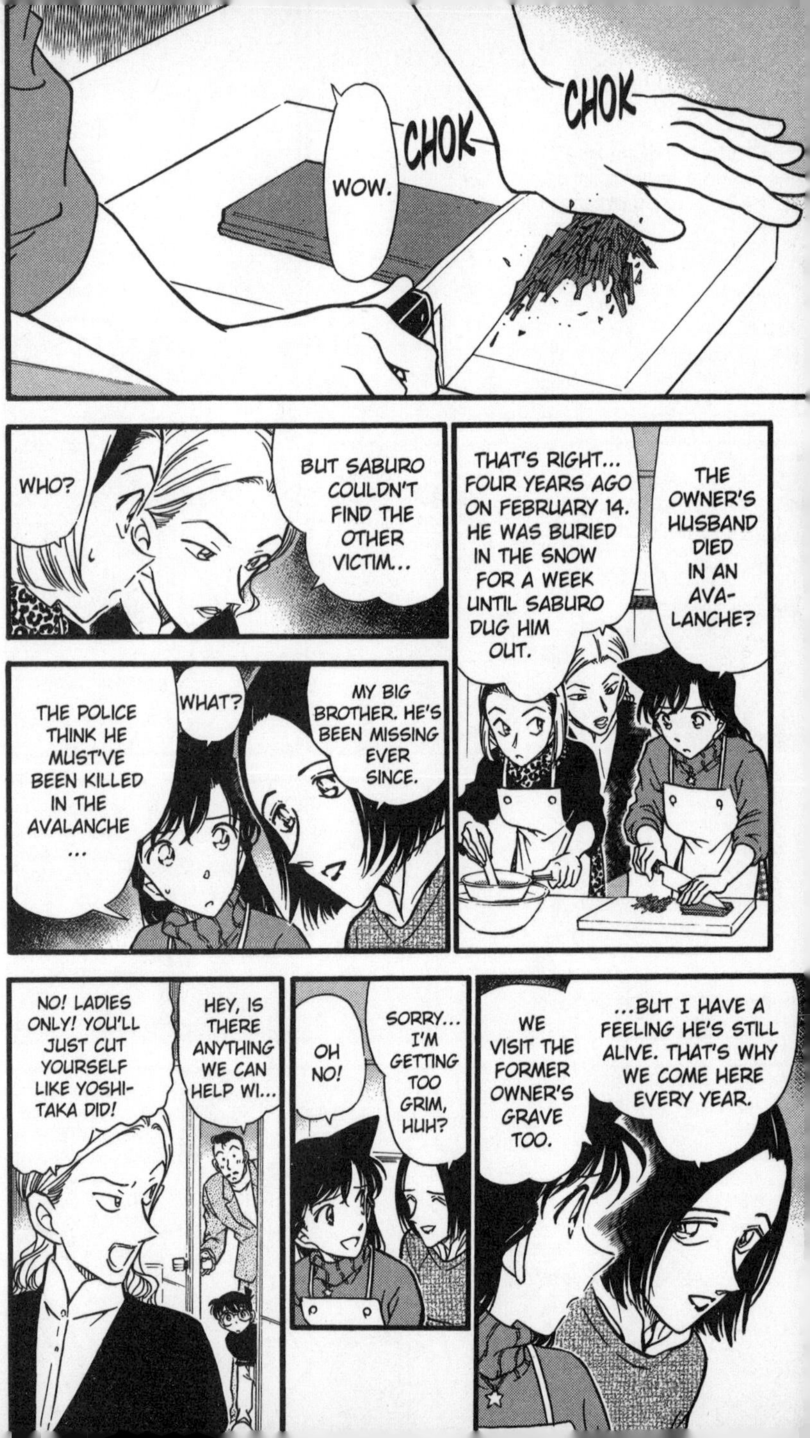
CHOK
CHOK
WOW.
THE OWNER'S HUSBAND DIED IN AN AVALANCHE?
THAT'S RIGHT... FOUR YEARS AGO ON FEBRUARY 14. HE WAS BURIED IN THE SNOW FOR A WEEK UNTIL SABURO DUG HIM OUT.
BUT SABURO COULDN'T FIND THE OTHER VICTIM...
WHO?
MY BIG BROTHER. HE'S BEEN MISSING EVER SINCE.
WHAT?
THE POLICE THINK HE MUST'VE BEEN KILLED IN THE AVALANCHE ...
...BUT I HAVE A FEELING HE'S STILL ALIVE. THAT'S WHY WE COME HERE EVERY YEAR.
WE VISIT THE FORMER OWNER'S GRAVE TOO.
SORRY... I'M GETTING TOO GRIM, HUH?
OH NO!
HEY, IS THERE ANYTHING WE CAN HELP WI...
NO! LADIES ONLY! YOU'LL JUST CUT YOURSELF LIKE YOSHI-TAKA DID!

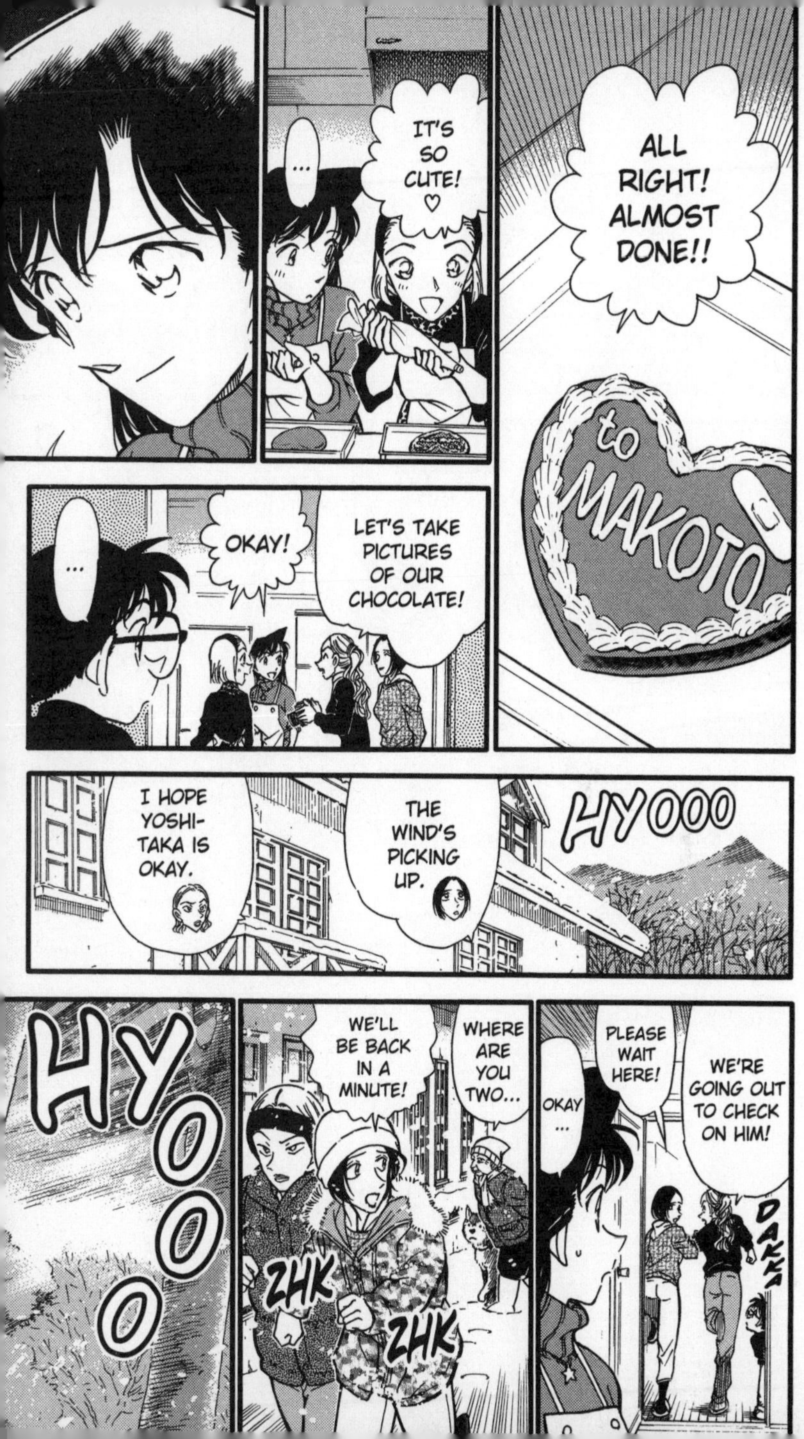
ALL RIGHT! ALMOST DONE!!
to MAKOTO
IT'S SO CUTE! ♡
...
LET'S TAKE PICTURES OF OUR CHOCOLATE!
OKAY!
...
HYOOO
THE WIND'S PICKING UP.
I HOPE YOSHI-TAKA IS OKAY.
WE'RE GOING OUT TO CHECK ON HIM!
PLEASE WAIT HERE!
OKAY...
DAKA
WHERE ARE YOU TWO...
WE'LL BE BACK IN A MINUTE!
ZHK
ZHK
HYOOOO

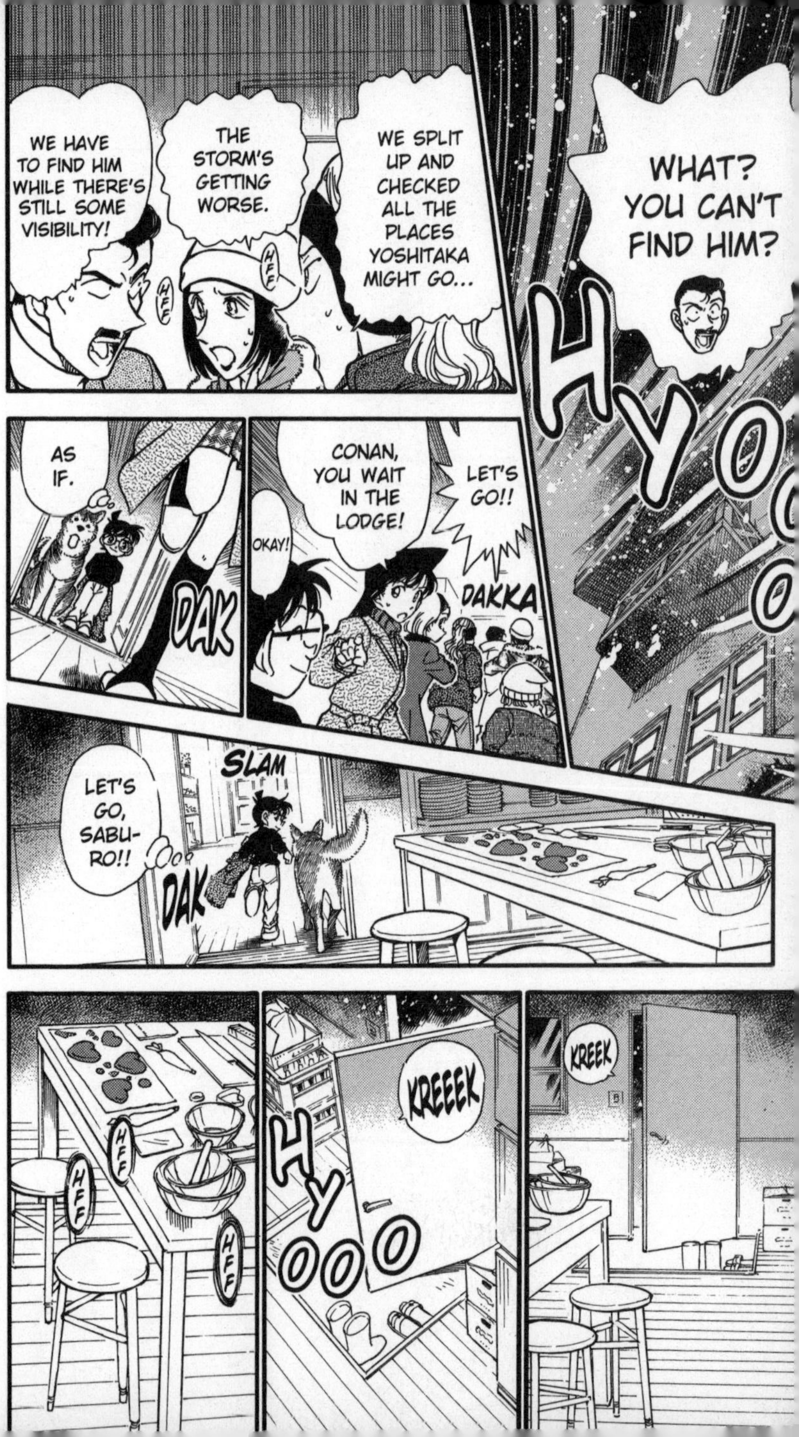
WHAT? YOU CAN'T FIND HIM?
HYOOO
WE SPLIT UP AND CHECKED ALL THE PLACES YOSHITAKA MIGHT GO...
THE STORM'S GETTING WORSE.
HFF
HFF
WE HAVE TO FIND HIM WHILE THERE'S STILL SOME VISIBILITY!
LET'S GO!!
CONAN, YOU WAIT IN THE LODGE!
OKAY!
DAKKA
AS IF.
DAK
SLAM
LET'S GO, SABURO!!
DAK
KREEK
KREEEK
HYOOO
HFF
HFF
HFF

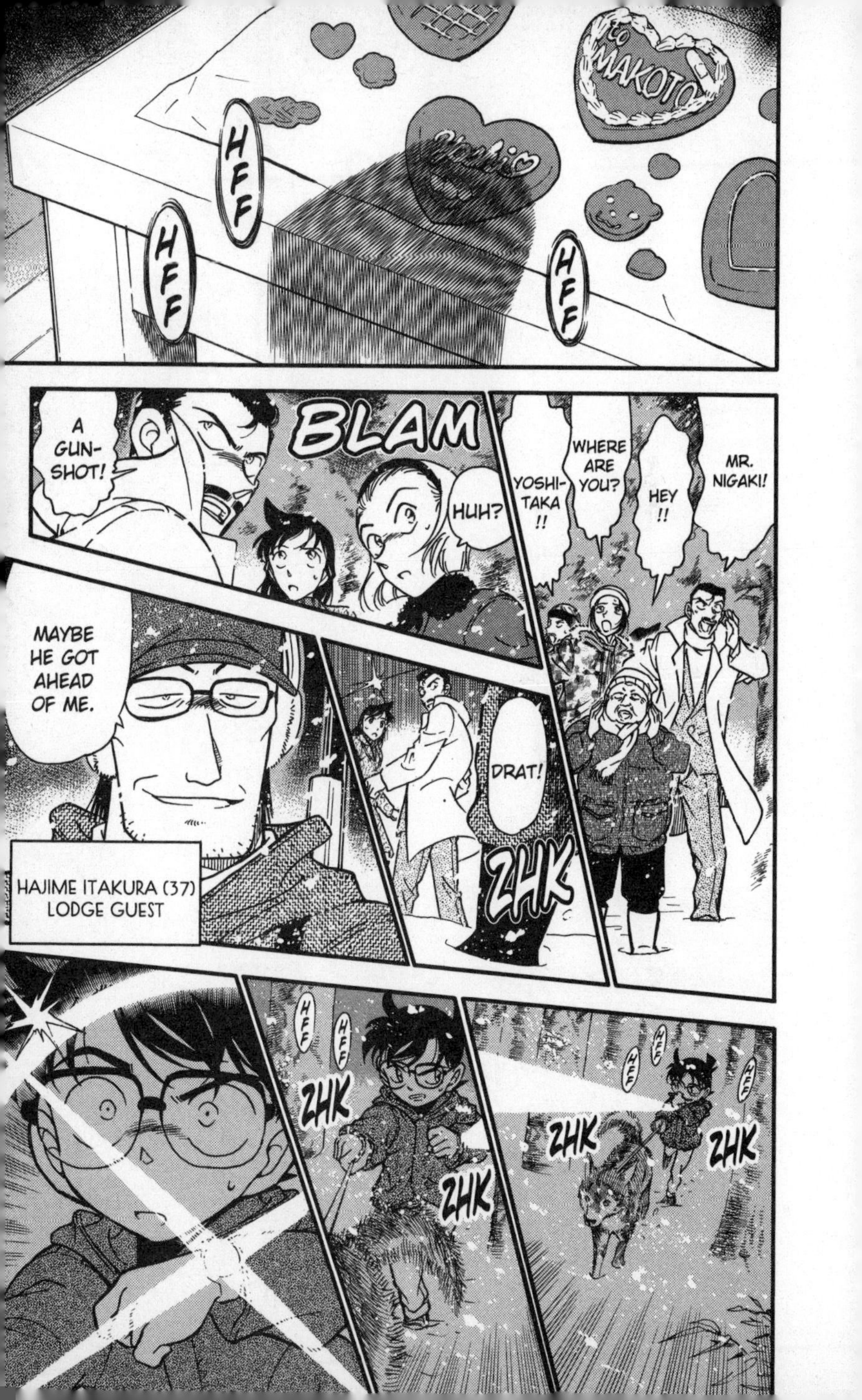
to MAKOTO
HFF
HFF
HFF
MR. NIGAKI!
HEY !!
WHERE ARE YOU?
YOSHI-TAKA !!
BLAM
HUH?
A GUN-SHOT!
DRAT!
ZHK
MAYBE HE GOT AHEAD OF ME.
HAJIME ITAKURA (37) LODGE GUEST
HFF
HFF
HFF
ZHK
ZHK
HFF
HFF
ZHK
ZHK

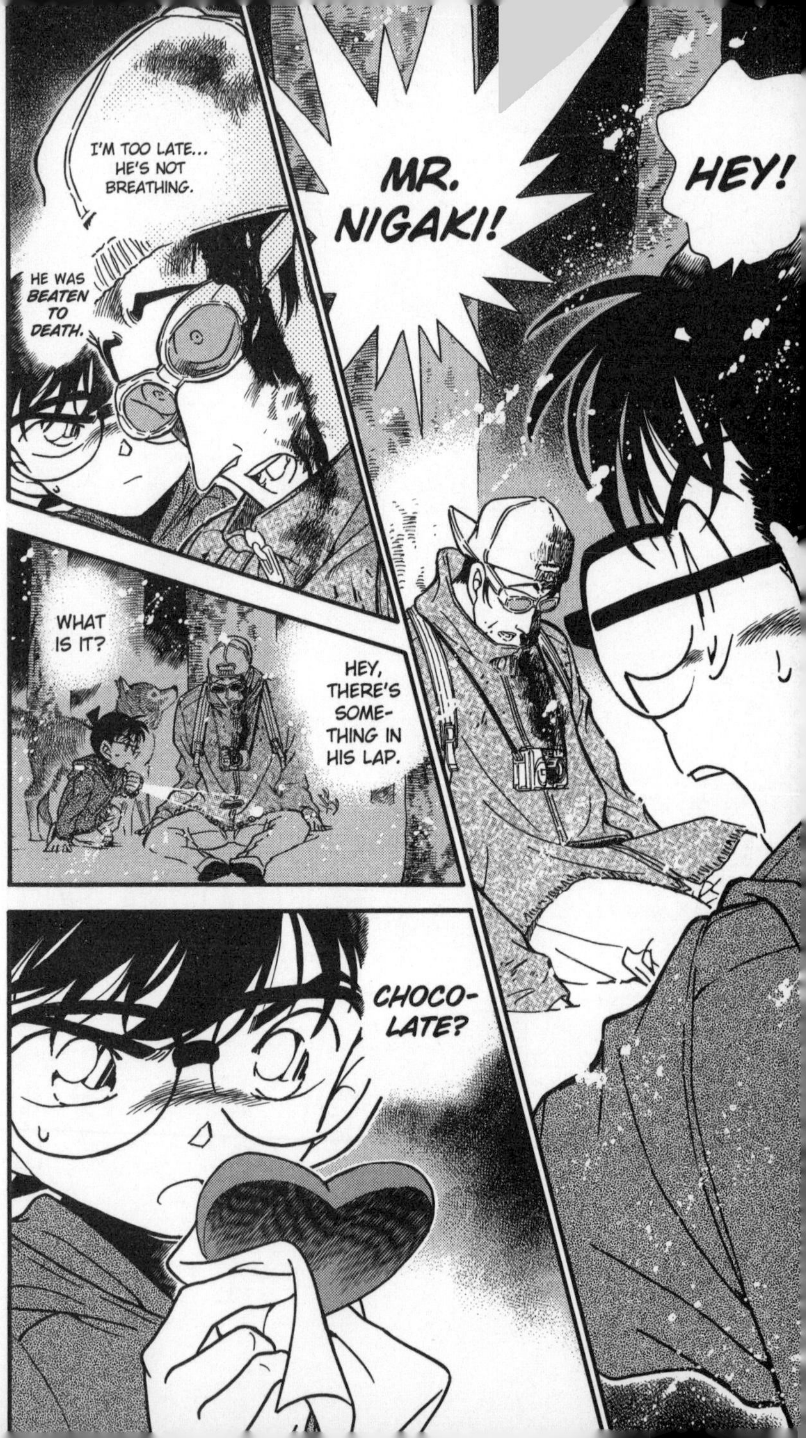
HEY!
MR. NIGAKI!
I'M TOO LATE... HE'S NOT BREATHING.
HE WAS *BEATEN* TO DEATH.
HEY, THERE'S SOME-THING IN HIS LAP.
WHAT IS IT?
CHOCO-LATE?

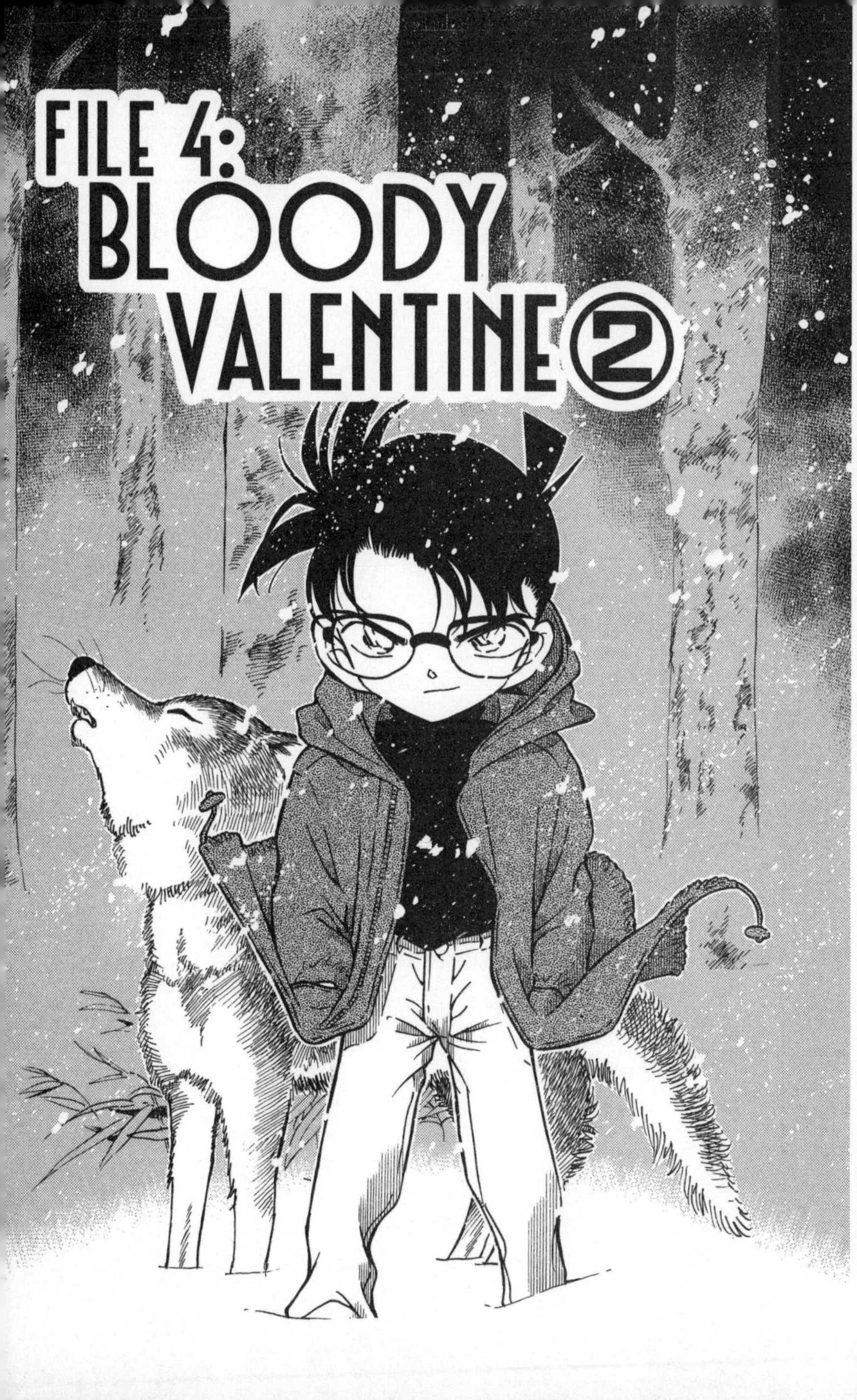
FILE 4:
BLOODY
VALENTINE ②

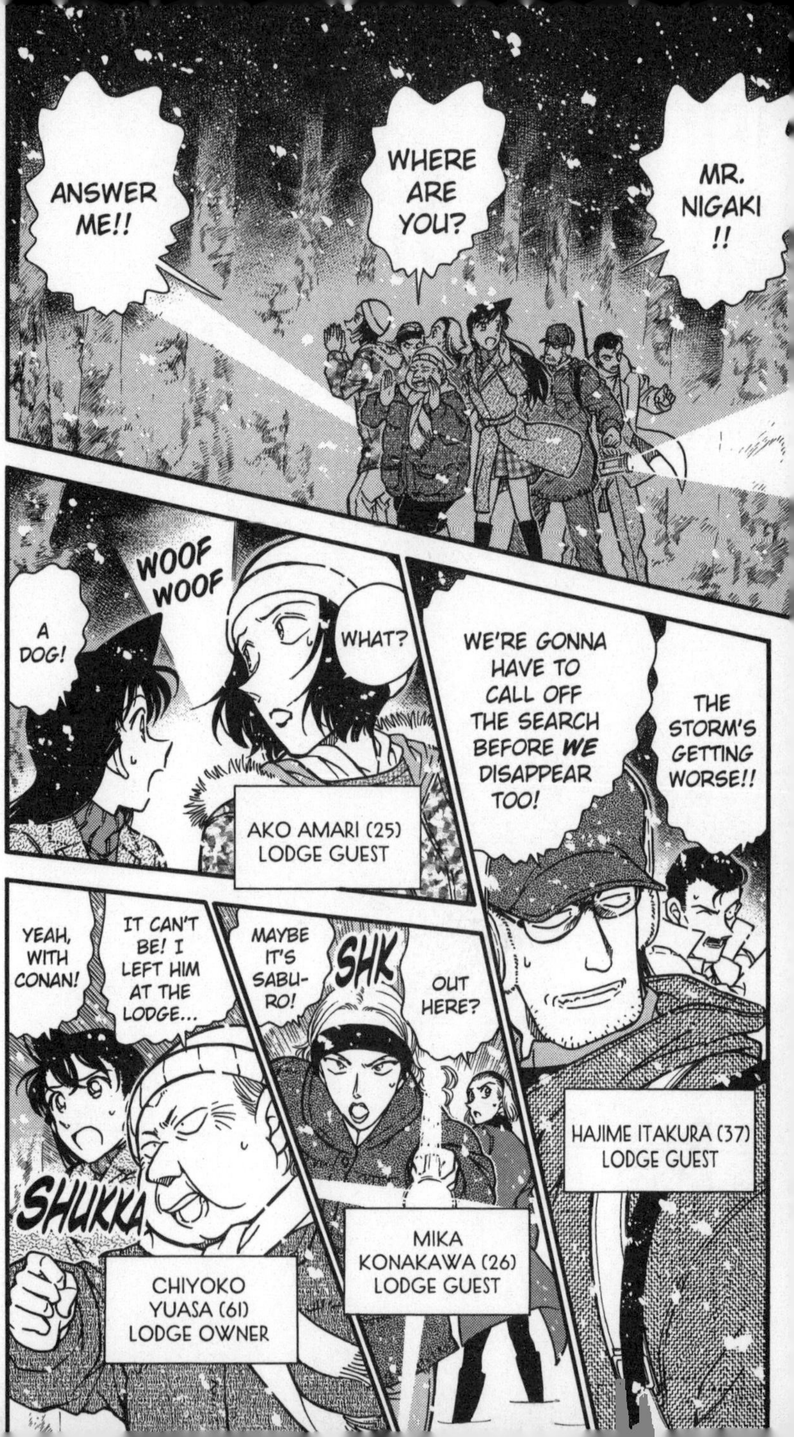

MR. NIGAKI!!
WHERE ARE YOU?
ANSWER ME!!
THE STORM'S GETTING WORSE!!
WE'RE GONNA HAVE TO CALL OFF THE SEARCH BEFORE WE DISAPPEAR TOO!
HAJIME ITAKURA (37) LODGE GUEST
WOOF WOOF
WHAT?
A DOG!
AKO AMARI (25) LODGE GUEST
OUT HERE?
SHK
MAYBE IT'S SABURO!
MIKA KONAKAWA (26) LODGE GUEST
IT CAN'T BE! I LEFT HIM AT THE LODGE...
YEAH, WITH CONAN!
SHUKKA
CHIYOKO YUASA (61) LODGE OWNER

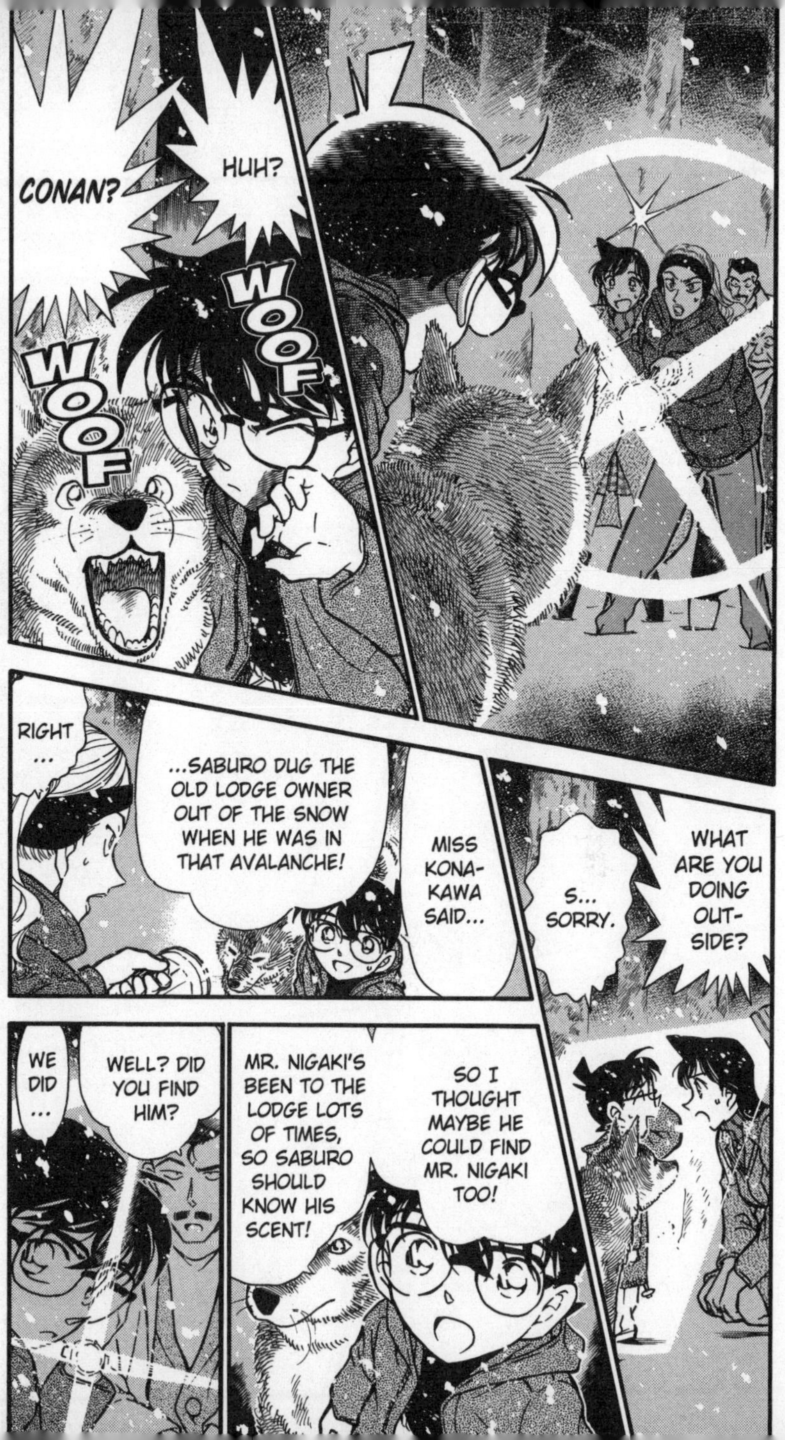
HUH?
CONAN?
WOOF
WOOF
WHAT ARE YOU DOING OUT-SIDE?
S... SORRY.
MISS KONA-KAWA SAID...
...SABURO DUG THE OLD LODGE OWNER OUT OF THE SNOW WHEN HE WAS IN THAT AVALANCHE!
RIGHT ...
MR. NIGAKI'S BEEN TO THE LODGE LOTS OF TIMES, SO SABURO SHOULD KNOW HIS SCENT!
SO I THOUGHT MAYBE HE COULD FIND MR. NIGAKI TOO!
WELL? DID YOU FIND HIM?
WE DID ...

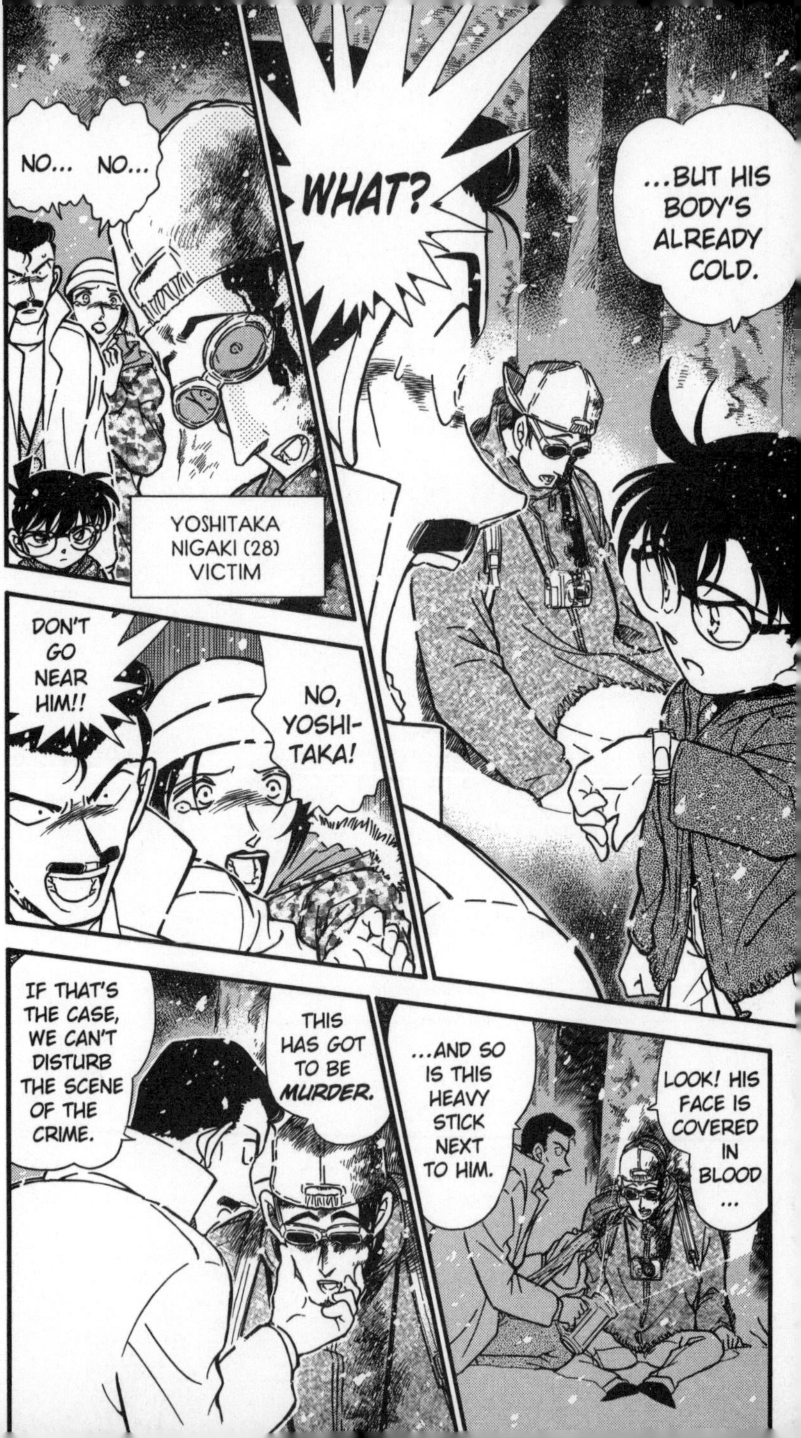
...BUT HIS BODY'S ALREADY COLD.
WHAT?
NO... NO...
YOSHITAKA NIGAKI (28) VICTIM
NO, YOSHI-TAKA!
DON'T GO NEAR HIM!!
LOOK! HIS FACE IS COVERED IN BLOOD ...
...AND SO IS THIS HEAVY STICK NEXT TO HIM.
THIS HAS GOT TO BE MURDER.
IF THAT'S THE CASE, WE CAN'T DISTURB THE SCENE OF THE CRIME.

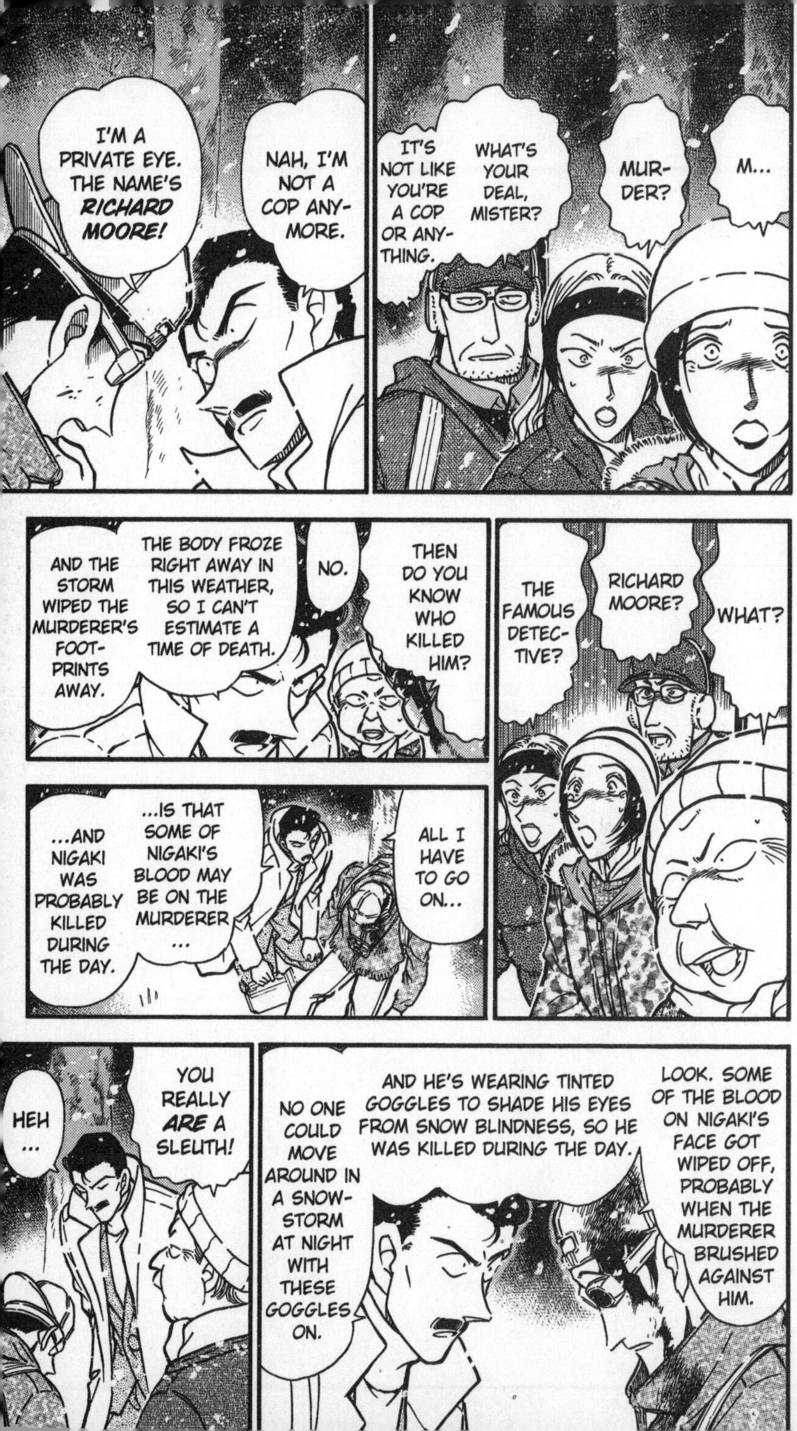
M...
MURDER?
WHAT'S YOUR DEAL, MISTER?
IT'S NOT LIKE YOU'RE A COP OR ANYTHING.
NAH, I'M NOT A COP ANYMORE.
I'M A PRIVATE EYE. THE NAME'S RICHARD MOORE!
WHAT?
RICHARD MOORE?
THE FAMOUS DETECTIVE?
THEN DO YOU KNOW WHO KILLED HIM?
NO.
THE BODY FROZE RIGHT AWAY IN THIS WEATHER, SO I CAN'T ESTIMATE A TIME OF DEATH.
AND THE STORM WIPED THE MURDERER'S FOOTPRINTS AWAY.
ALL I HAVE TO GO ON...
...IS THAT SOME OF NIGAKI'S BLOOD MAY BE ON THE MURDERER...
...AND NIGAKI WAS PROBABLY KILLED DURING THE DAY.
LOOK. SOME OF THE BLOOD ON NIGAKI'S FACE GOT WIPED OFF, PROBABLY WHEN THE MURDERER BRUSHED AGAINST HIM.
AND HE'S WEARING TINTED GOGGLES TO SHADE HIS EYES FROM SNOW BLINDNESS, SO HE WAS KILLED DURING THE DAY.
NO ONE COULD MOVE AROUND IN A SNOWSTORM AT NIGHT WITH THESE GOGGLES ON.
YOU REALLY ARE A SLEUTH!
HEH...

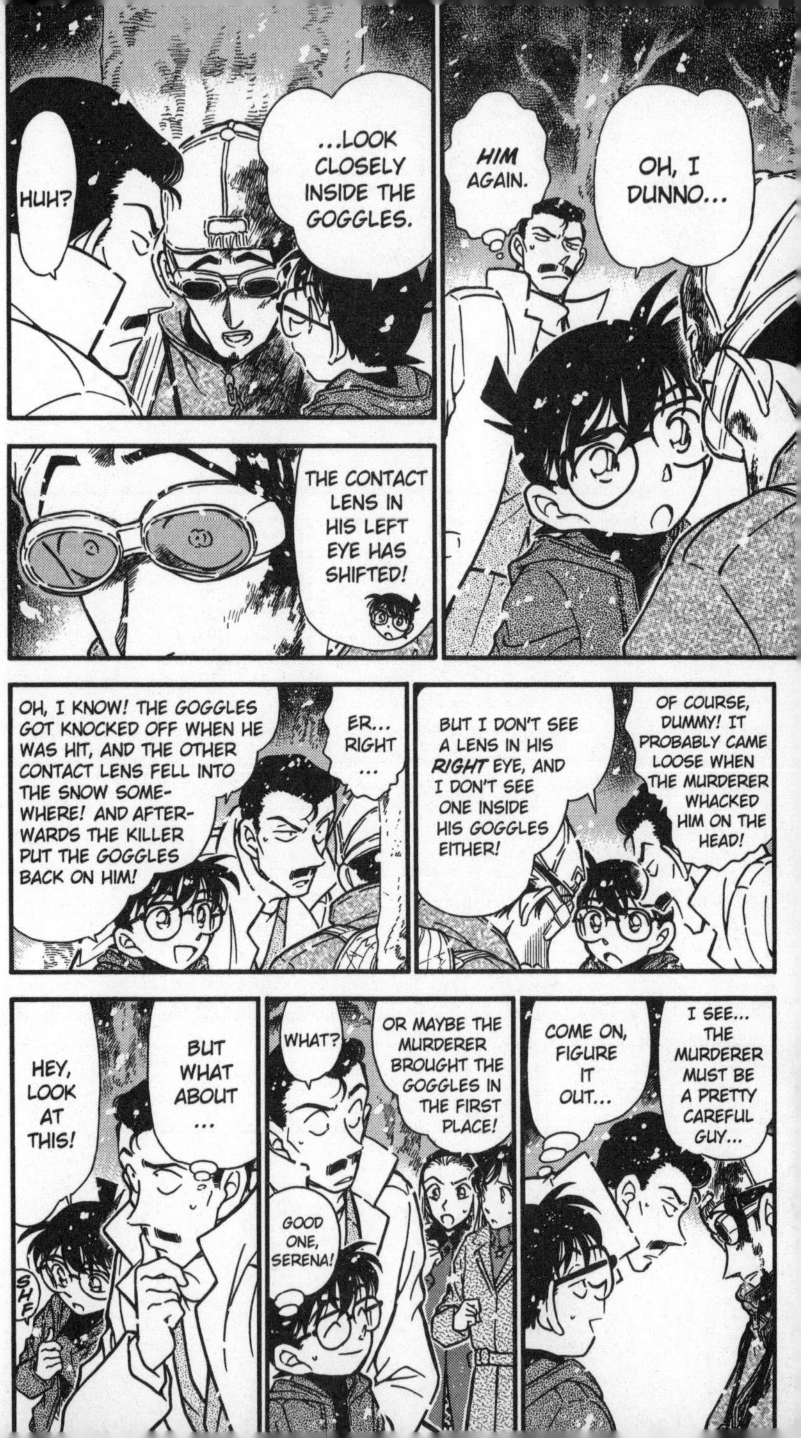
OH, I DUNNO...
HIM AGAIN.
...LOOK CLOSELY INSIDE THE GOGGLES.
HUH?
THE CONTACT LENS IN HIS LEFT EYE HAS SHIFTED!
OF COURSE, DUMMY! IT PROBABLY CAME LOOSE WHEN THE MURDERER WHACKED HIM ON THE HEAD!
BUT I DON'T SEE A LENS IN HIS RIGHT EYE, AND I DON'T SEE ONE INSIDE HIS GOGGLES EITHER!
ER... RIGHT...
OH, I KNOW! THE GOGGLES GOT KNOCKED OFF WHEN HE WAS HIT, AND THE OTHER CONTACT LENS FELL INTO THE SNOW SOMEWHERE! AND AFTERWARDS THE KILLER PUT THE GOGGLES BACK ON HIM!
I SEE... THE MURDERER MUST BE A PRETTY CAREFUL GUY...
COME ON, FIGURE IT OUT...
OR MAYBE THE MURDERER BROUGHT THE GOGGLES IN THE FIRST PLACE!
WHAT?
GOOD ONE, SERENA!
BUT WHAT ABOUT...
HEY, LOOK AT THIS!
SHF

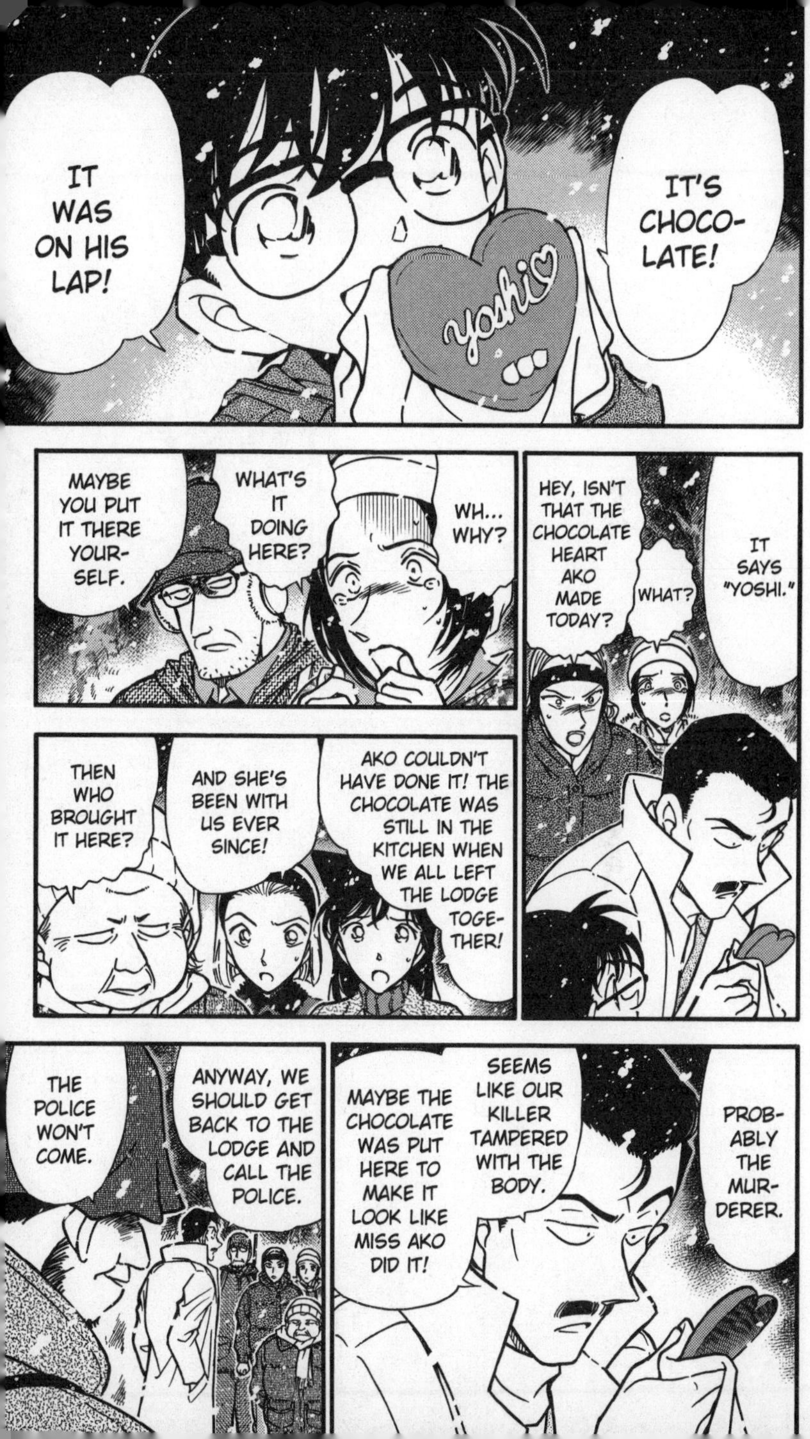
IT'S CHOCOLATE!
yoshi
IT WAS ON HIS LAP!
IT SAYS "YOSHI."
WHAT?
HEY, ISN'T THAT THE CHOCOLATE HEART AKO MADE TODAY?
WH... WHY?
WHAT'S IT DOING HERE?
MAYBE YOU PUT IT THERE YOURSELF.
AKO COULDN'T HAVE DONE IT! THE CHOCOLATE WAS STILL IN THE KITCHEN WHEN WE ALL LEFT THE LODGE TOGETHER!
AND SHE'S BEEN WITH US EVER SINCE!
THEN WHO BROUGHT IT HERE?
PROBABLY THE MURDERER.
SEEMS LIKE OUR KILLER TAMPERED WITH THE BODY.
MAYBE THE CHOCOLATE WAS PUT HERE TO MAKE IT LOOK LIKE MISS AKO DID IT!
ANYWAY, WE SHOULD GET BACK TO THE LODGE AND CALL THE POLICE.
THE POLICE WON'T COME.

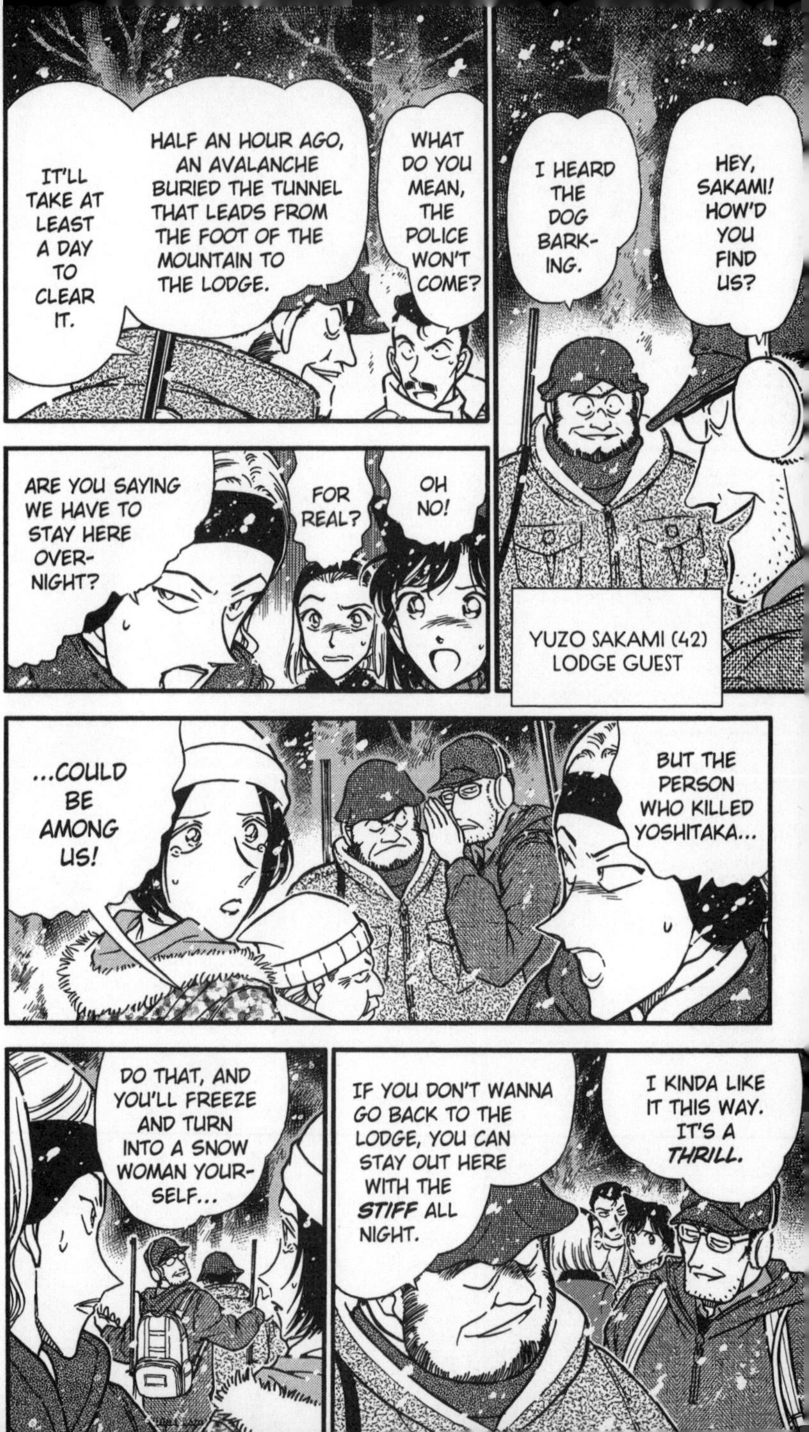
HEY, SAKAMI! HOW'D YOU FIND US?
I HEARD THE DOG BARK-ING.
YUZO SAKAMI (42) LODGE GUEST
WHAT DO YOU MEAN, THE POLICE WON'T COME?
HALF AN HOUR AGO, AN AVALANCHE BURIED THE TUNNEL THAT LEADS FROM THE FOOT OF THE MOUNTAIN TO THE LODGE.
IT'LL TAKE AT LEAST A DAY TO CLEAR IT.
OH NO!
FOR REAL?
ARE YOU SAYING WE HAVE TO STAY HERE OVER-NIGHT?
BUT THE PERSON WHO KILLED YOSHITAKA...
...COULD BE AMONG US!
I KINDA LIKE IT THIS WAY. IT'S A THRILL.
IF YOU DON'T WANNA GO BACK TO THE LODGE, YOU CAN STAY OUT HERE WITH THE STIFF ALL NIGHT.
DO THAT, AND YOU'LL FREEZE AND TURN INTO A SNOW WOMAN YOUR-SELF...

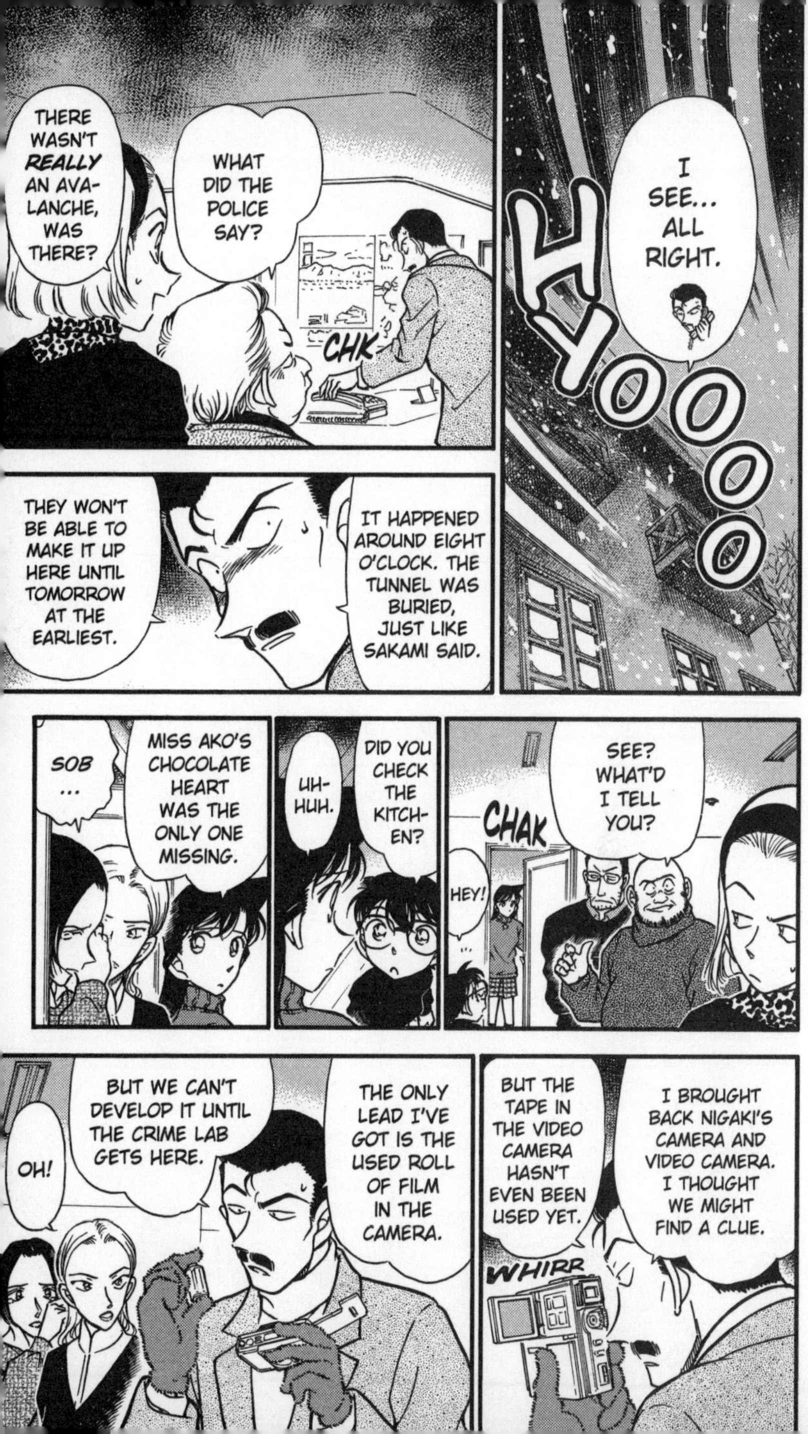
I SEE... ALL RIGHT.
HYOOOOO
WHAT DID THE POLICE SAY?
THERE WASN'T **REALLY** AN AVALANCHE, WAS THERE?
CHK
IT HAPPENED AROUND EIGHT O'CLOCK. THE TUNNEL WAS BURIED, JUST LIKE SAKAMI SAID.
THEY WON'T BE ABLE TO MAKE IT UP HERE UNTIL TOMORROW AT THE EARLIEST.
SEE? WHAT'D I TELL YOU?
CHAK
HEY!
...
DID YOU CHECK THE KITCHEN?
UH-HUH.
MISS AKO'S CHOCOLATE HEART WAS THE ONLY ONE MISSING.
SOB ...
I BROUGHT BACK NIGAKI'S CAMERA AND VIDEO CAMERA. I THOUGHT WE MIGHT FIND A CLUE.
BUT THE TAPE IN THE VIDEO CAMERA HASN'T EVEN BEEN USED YET.
WHIRR
THE ONLY LEAD I'VE GOT IS THE USED ROLL OF FILM IN THE CAMERA.
BUT WE CAN'T DEVELOP IT UNTIL THE CRIME LAB GETS HERE.
OH!

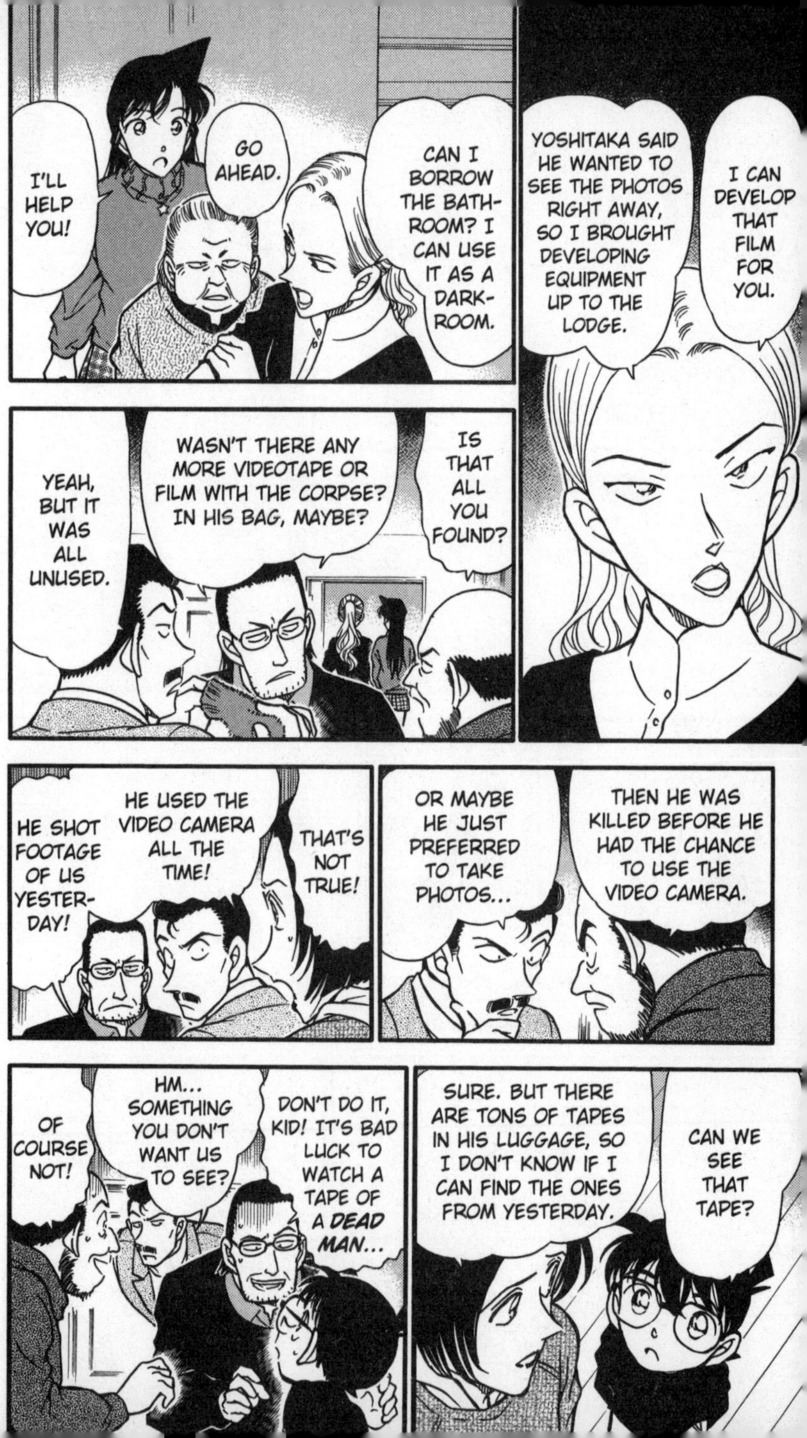
I CAN DEVELOP THAT FILM FOR YOU.
YOSHITAKA SAID HE WANTED TO SEE THE PHOTOS RIGHT AWAY, SO I BROUGHT DEVELOPING EQUIPMENT UP TO THE LODGE.
CAN I BORROW THE BATHROOM? I CAN USE IT AS A DARKROOM.
GO AHEAD.
I'LL HELP YOU!
IS THAT ALL YOU FOUND?
WASN'T THERE ANY MORE VIDEOTAPE OR FILM WITH THE CORPSE? IN HIS BAG, MAYBE?
YEAH, BUT IT WAS ALL UNUSED.
THEN HE WAS KILLED BEFORE HE HAD THE CHANCE TO USE THE VIDEO CAMERA.
OR MAYBE HE JUST PREFERRED TO TAKE PHOTOS...
THAT'S NOT TRUE!
HE USED THE VIDEO CAMERA ALL THE TIME!
HE SHOT FOOTAGE OF US YESTERDAY!
CAN WE SEE THAT TAPE?
SURE. BUT THERE ARE TONS OF TAPES IN HIS LUGGAGE, SO I DON'T KNOW IF I CAN FIND THE ONES FROM YESTERDAY.
DON'T DO IT, KID! IT'S BAD LUCK TO WATCH A TAPE OF A *DEAD MAN*...
HM... SOMETHING YOU DON'T WANT US TO SEE?
OF COURSE NOT!

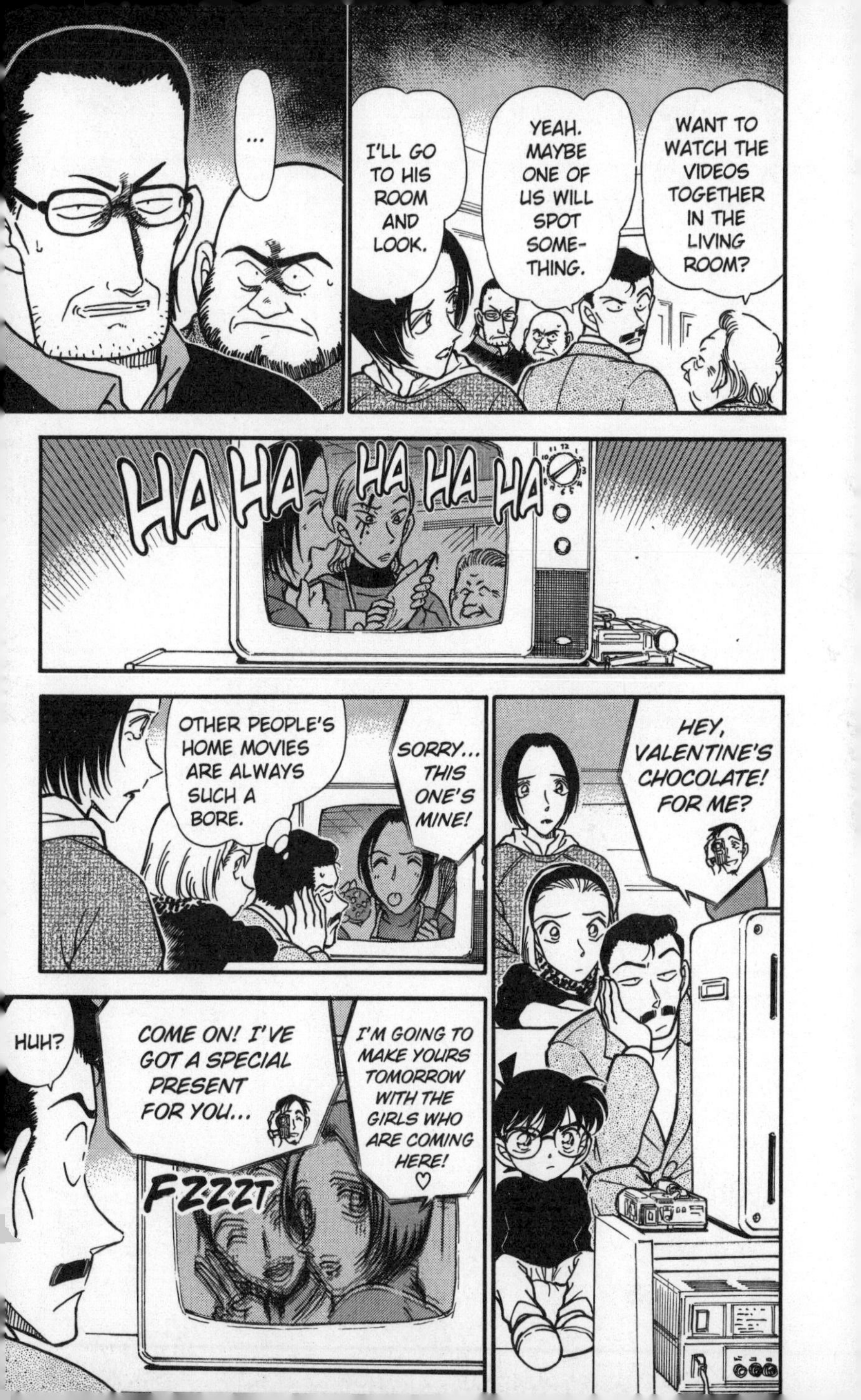
WANT TO WATCH THE VIDEOS TOGETHER IN THE LIVING ROOM?
YEAH. MAYBE ONE OF US WILL SPOT SOMETHING.
I'LL GO TO HIS ROOM AND LOOK.
...
HA HA HA HA HA
HEY, VALENTINE'S CHOCOLATE! FOR ME?
SORRY... THIS ONE'S MINE!
OTHER PEOPLE'S HOME MOVIES ARE ALWAYS SUCH A BORE.
I'M GOING TO MAKE YOURS TOMORROW WITH THE GIRLS WHO ARE COMING HERE! ♥
COME ON! I'VE GOT A SPECIAL PRESENT FOR YOU...
HUH?
FZZZT

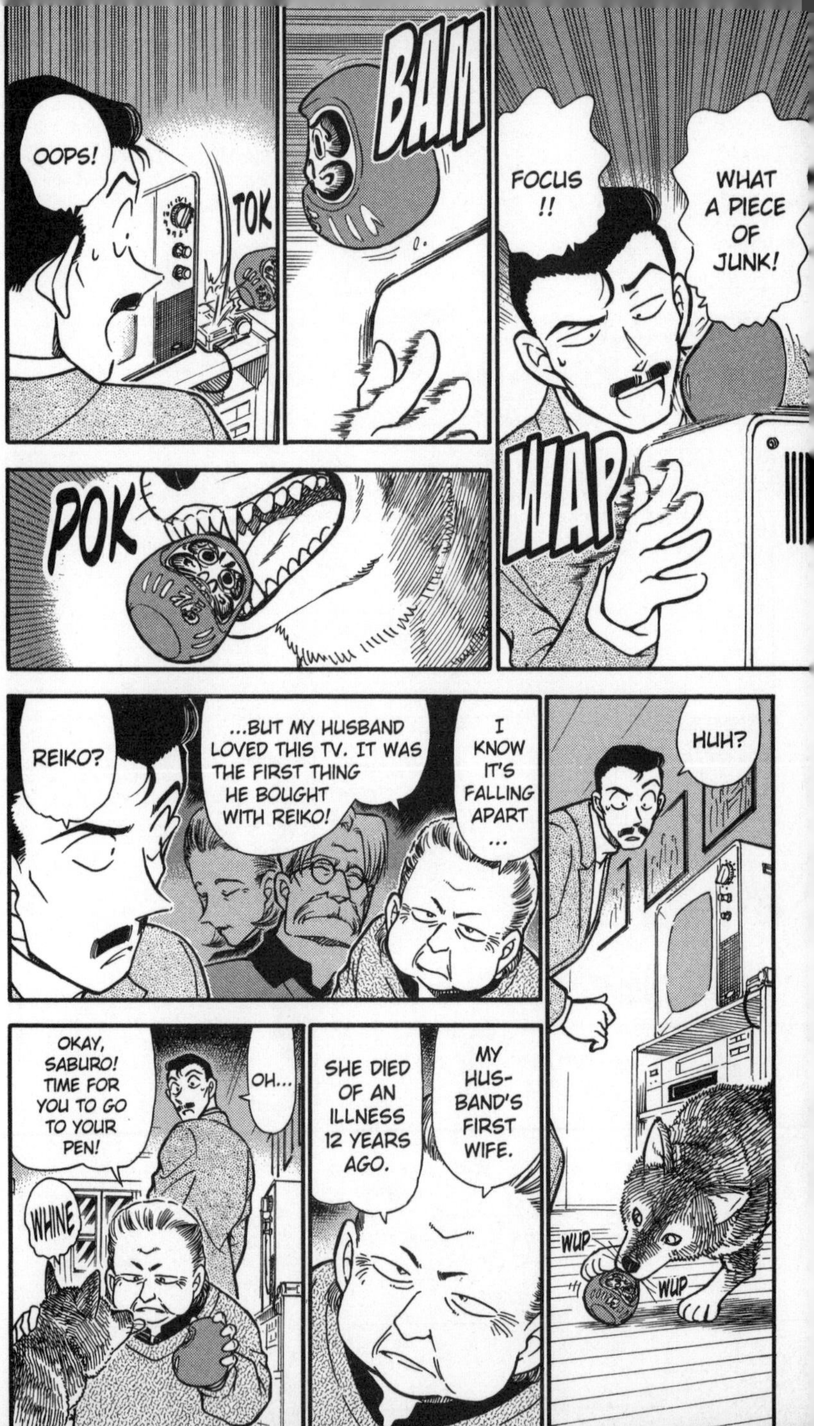
WHAT A PIECE OF JUNK!
FOCUS !!
WAP
BAM
OOPS!
TOK
POK
HUH?
WUP
WUP
I KNOW IT'S FALLING APART ...
...BUT MY HUSBAND LOVED THIS TV. IT WAS THE FIRST THING HE BOUGHT WITH REIKO!
REIKO?
MY HUS-BAND'S FIRST WIFE.
SHE DIED OF AN ILLNESS 12 YEARS AGO.
OH...
OKAY, SABURO! TIME FOR YOU TO GO TO YOUR PEN!
WHINE

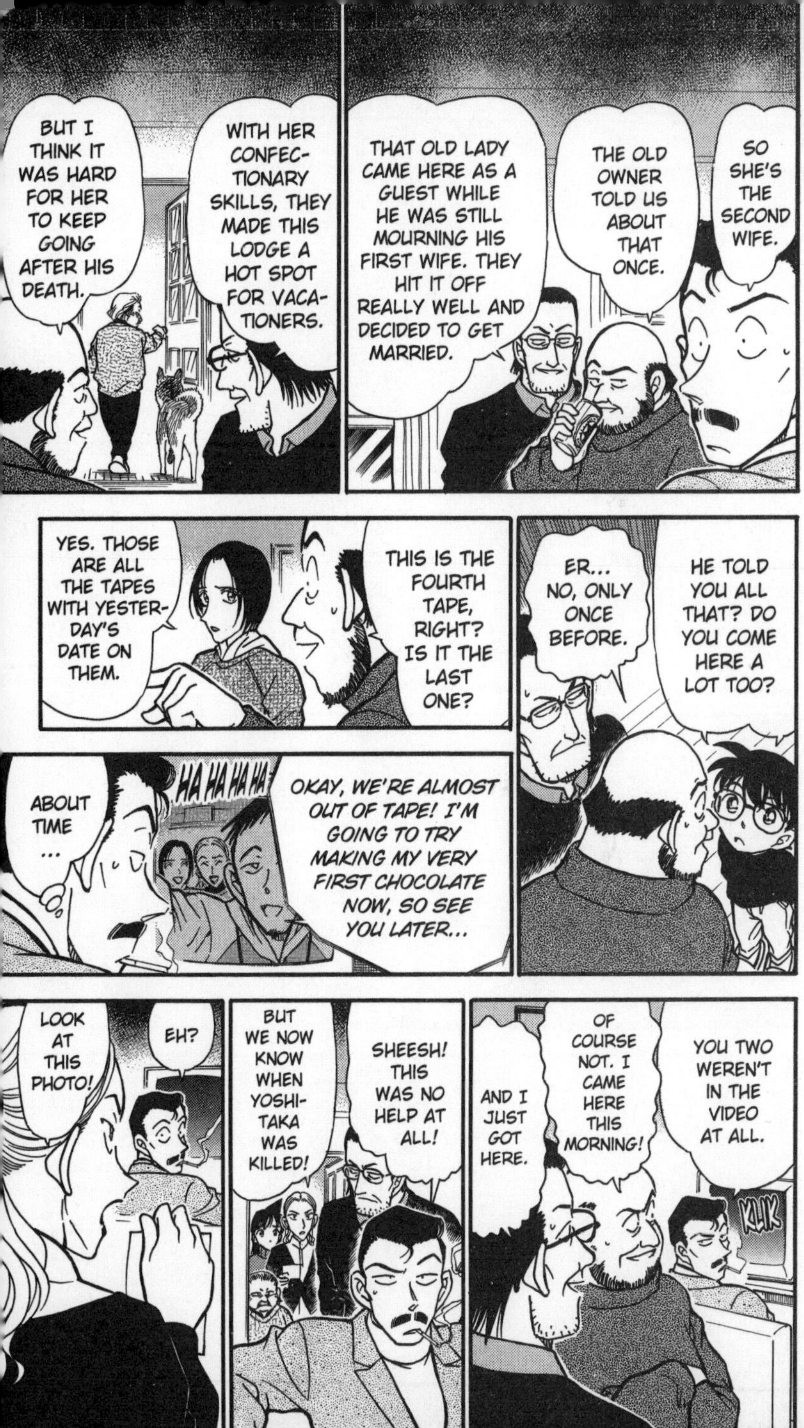
SO SHE'S THE SECOND WIFE.
THE OLD OWNER TOLD US ABOUT THAT ONCE.
THAT OLD LADY CAME HERE AS A GUEST WHILE HE WAS STILL MOURNING HIS FIRST WIFE. THEY HIT IT OFF REALLY WELL AND DECIDED TO GET MARRIED.
WITH HER CONFEC-TIONARY SKILLS, THEY MADE THIS LODGE A HOT SPOT FOR VACA-TIONERS.
BUT I THINK IT WAS HARD FOR HER TO KEEP GOING AFTER HIS DEATH.
HE TOLD YOU ALL THAT? DO YOU COME HERE A LOT TOO?
ER... NO, ONLY ONCE BEFORE.
THIS IS THE FOURTH TAPE, RIGHT? IS IT THE LAST ONE?
YES. THOSE ARE ALL THE TAPES WITH YESTER-DAY'S DATE ON THEM.
HA HA HA HA
OKAY, WE'RE ALMOST OUT OF TAPE! I'M GOING TO TRY MAKING MY VERY FIRST CHOCOLATE NOW, SO SEE YOU LATER...
ABOUT TIME ...
YOU TWO WEREN'T IN THE VIDEO AT ALL.
KLIK
OF COURSE NOT. I CAME HERE THIS MORNING!
AND I JUST GOT HERE.
SHEESH! THIS WAS NO HELP AT ALL!
BUT WE NOW KNOW WHEN YOSHI-TAKA WAS KILLED!
EH?
LOOK AT THIS PHOTO!

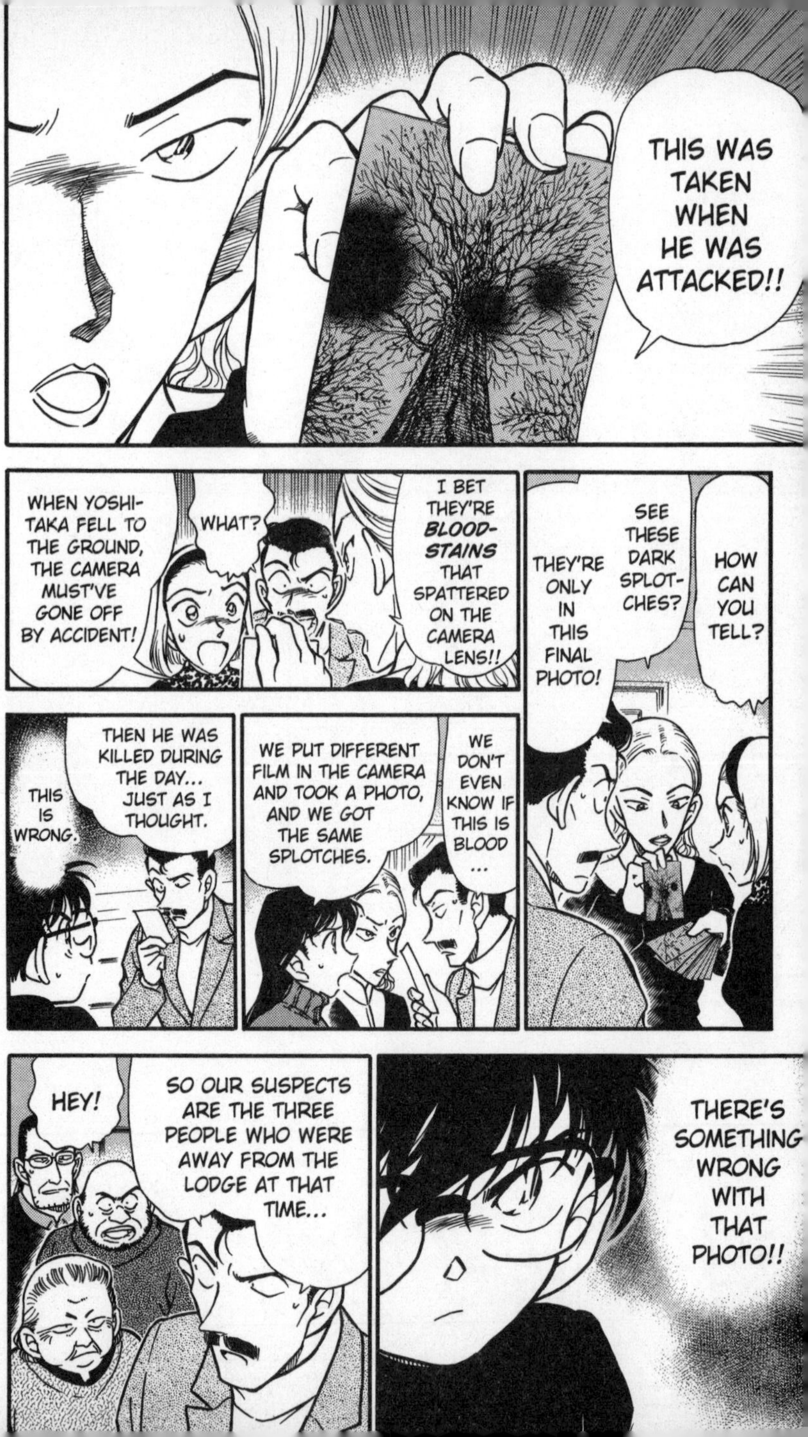
THIS WAS TAKEN WHEN HE WAS ATTACKED!!
HOW CAN YOU TELL?
SEE THESE DARK SPLOTCHES?
THEY'RE ONLY IN THIS FINAL PHOTO!
I BET THEY'RE *BLOOD-STAINS* THAT SPATTERED ON THE CAMERA LENS!!
WHAT?
WHEN YOSHI-TAKA FELL TO THE GROUND, THE CAMERA MUST'VE GONE OFF BY ACCIDENT!
WE DON'T EVEN KNOW IF THIS IS BLOOD...
WE PUT DIFFERENT FILM IN THE CAMERA AND TOOK A PHOTO, AND WE GOT THE SAME SPLOTCHES.
THEN HE WAS KILLED DURING THE DAY... JUST AS I THOUGHT.
THIS IS WRONG.
THERE'S SOMETHING WRONG WITH THAT PHOTO!!
SO OUR SUSPECTS ARE THE THREE PEOPLE WHO WERE AWAY FROM THE LODGE AT THAT TIME...
HEY!

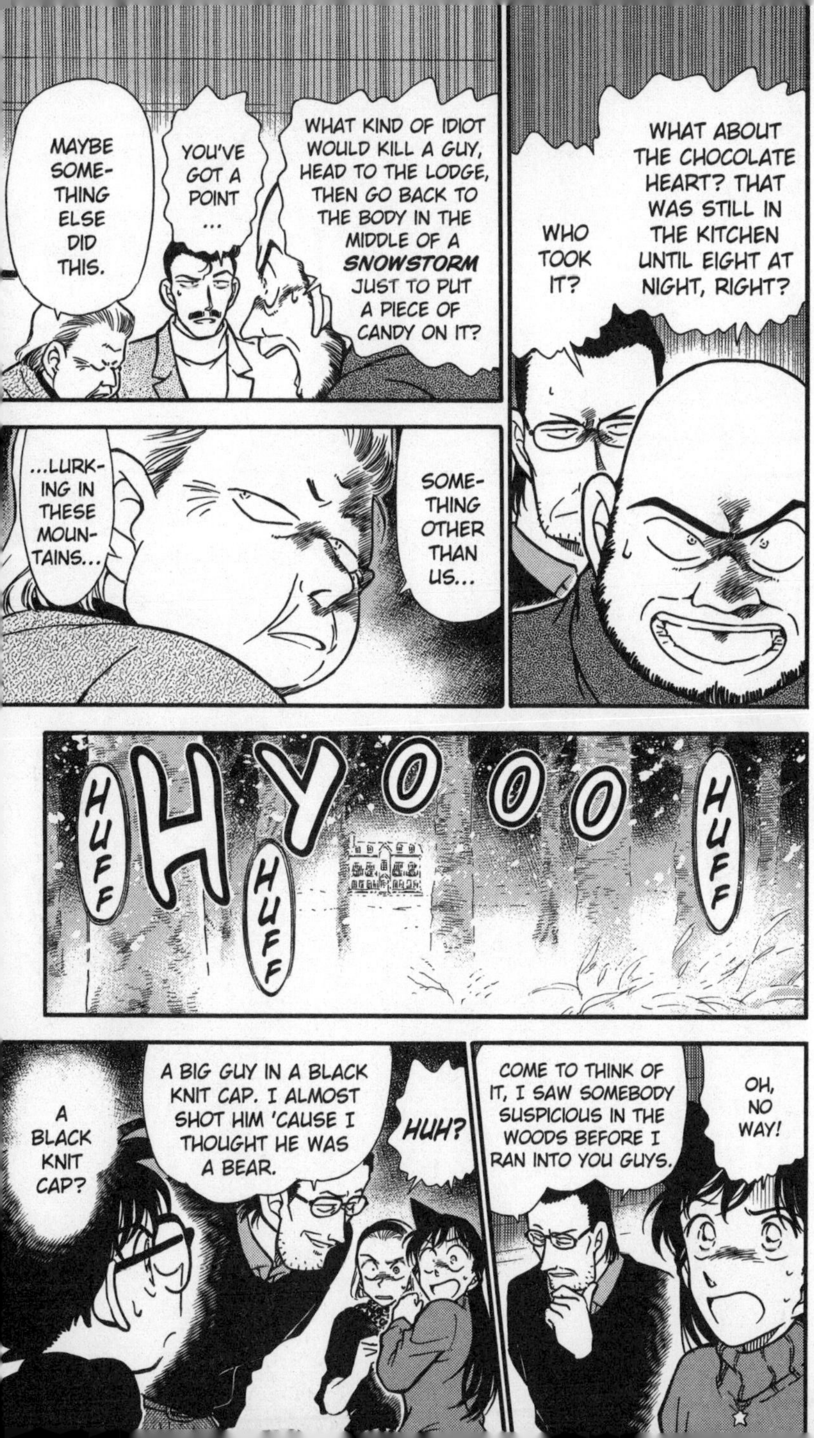
WHAT ABOUT THE CHOCOLATE HEART? THAT WAS STILL IN THE KITCHEN UNTIL EIGHT AT NIGHT, RIGHT?
WHO TOOK IT?
WHAT KIND OF IDIOT WOULD KILL A GUY, HEAD TO THE LODGE, THEN GO BACK TO THE BODY IN THE MIDDLE OF A *SNOWSTORM* JUST TO PUT A PIECE OF CANDY ON IT?
YOU'VE GOT A POINT ...
MAYBE SOME-THING ELSE DID THIS.
SOME-THING OTHER THAN US...
...LURK-ING IN THESE MOUN-TAINS...
HUFF
HYOOO
HUFF
HUFF
OH, NO WAY!
COME TO THINK OF IT, I SAW SOMEBODY SUSPICIOUS IN THE WOODS BEFORE I RAN INTO YOU GUYS.
HUH?
A BIG GUY IN A BLACK KNIT CAP. I ALMOST SHOT HIM 'CAUSE I THOUGHT HE WAS A BEAR.
A BLACK KNIT CAP?

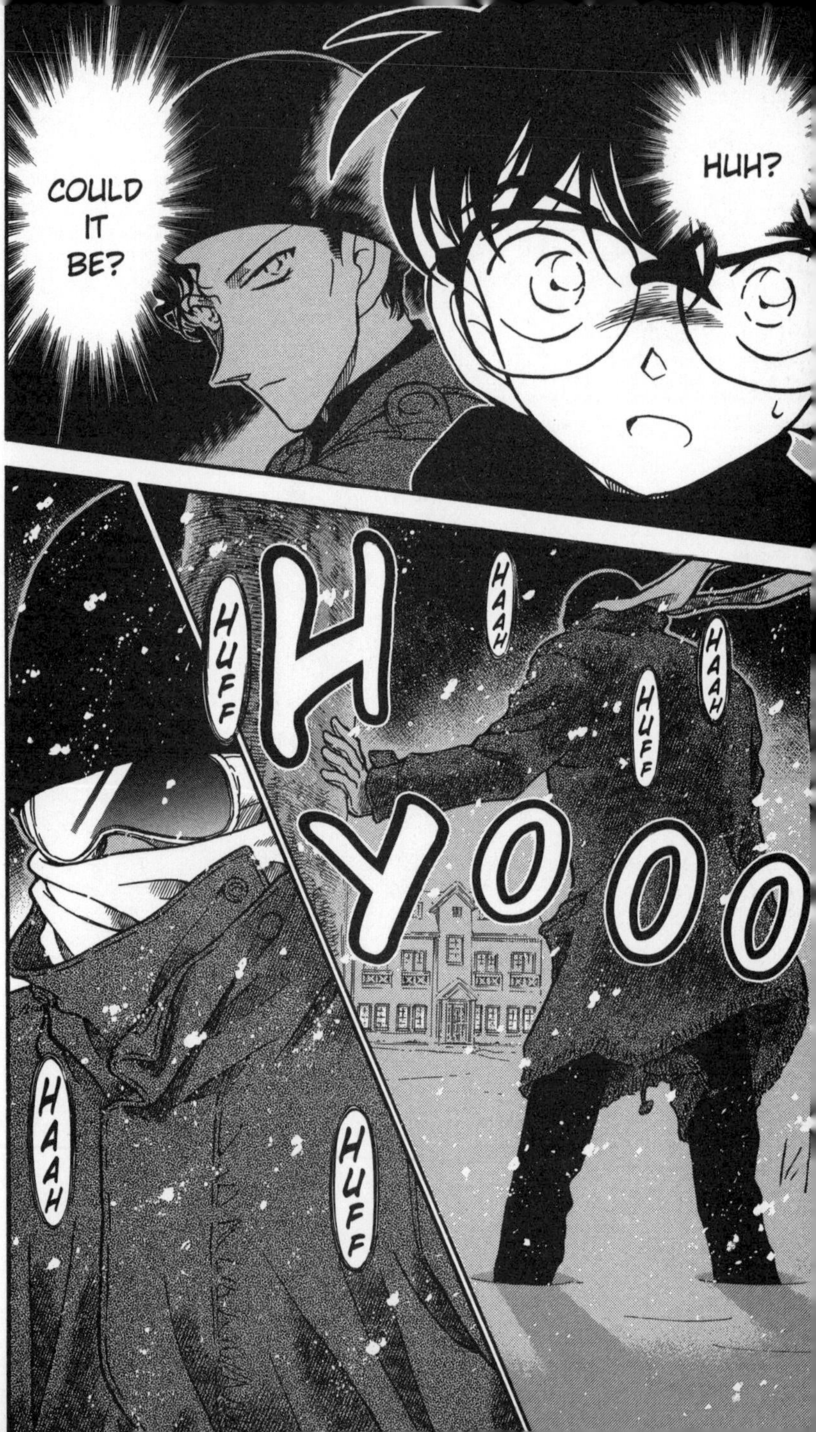
HUH?
COULD IT BE?
HAAH
HUFF
HAAH
HYOOO
HUFF
HUFF
HAAH

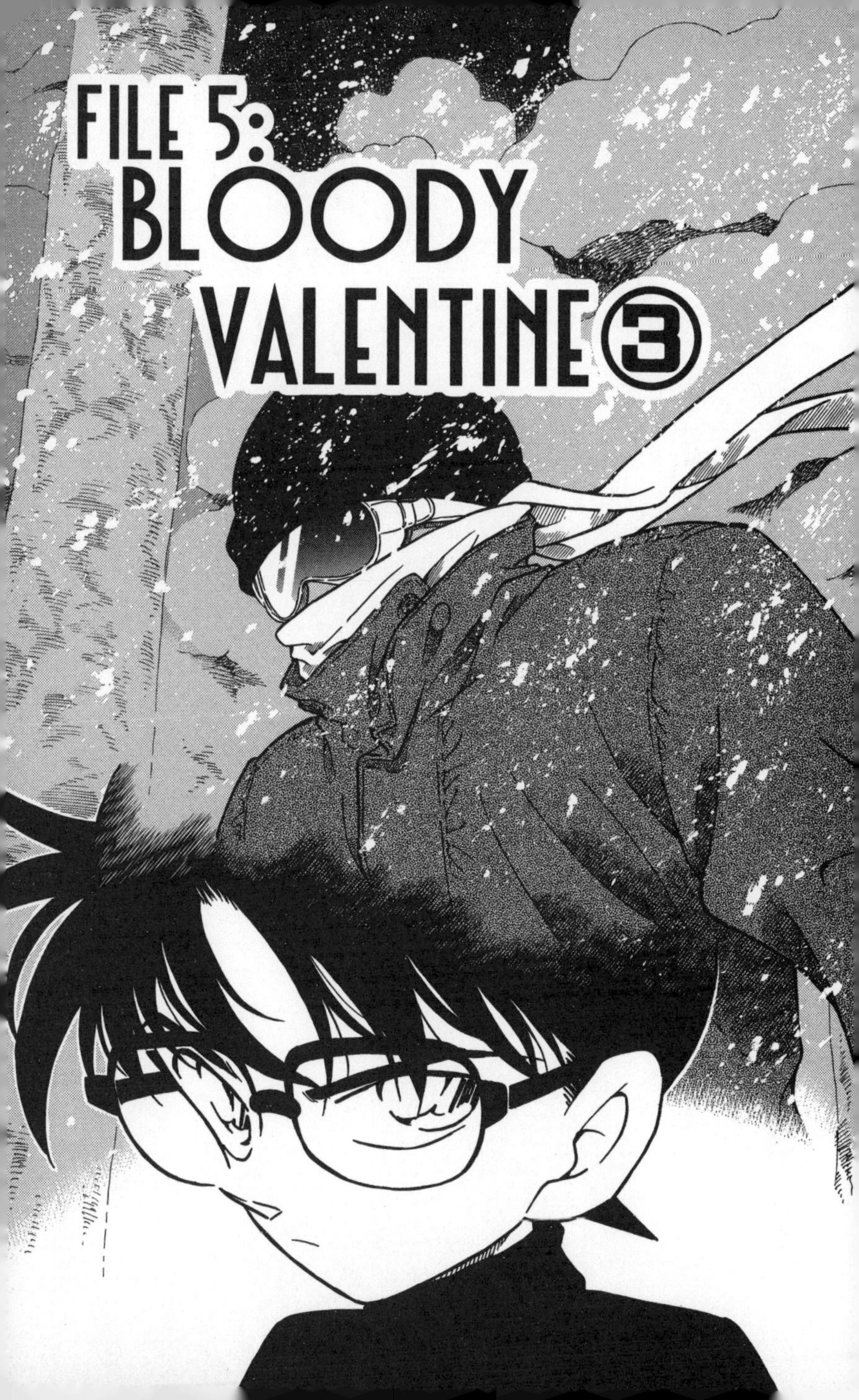
FILE 5:
BLOODY
VALENTINE ③

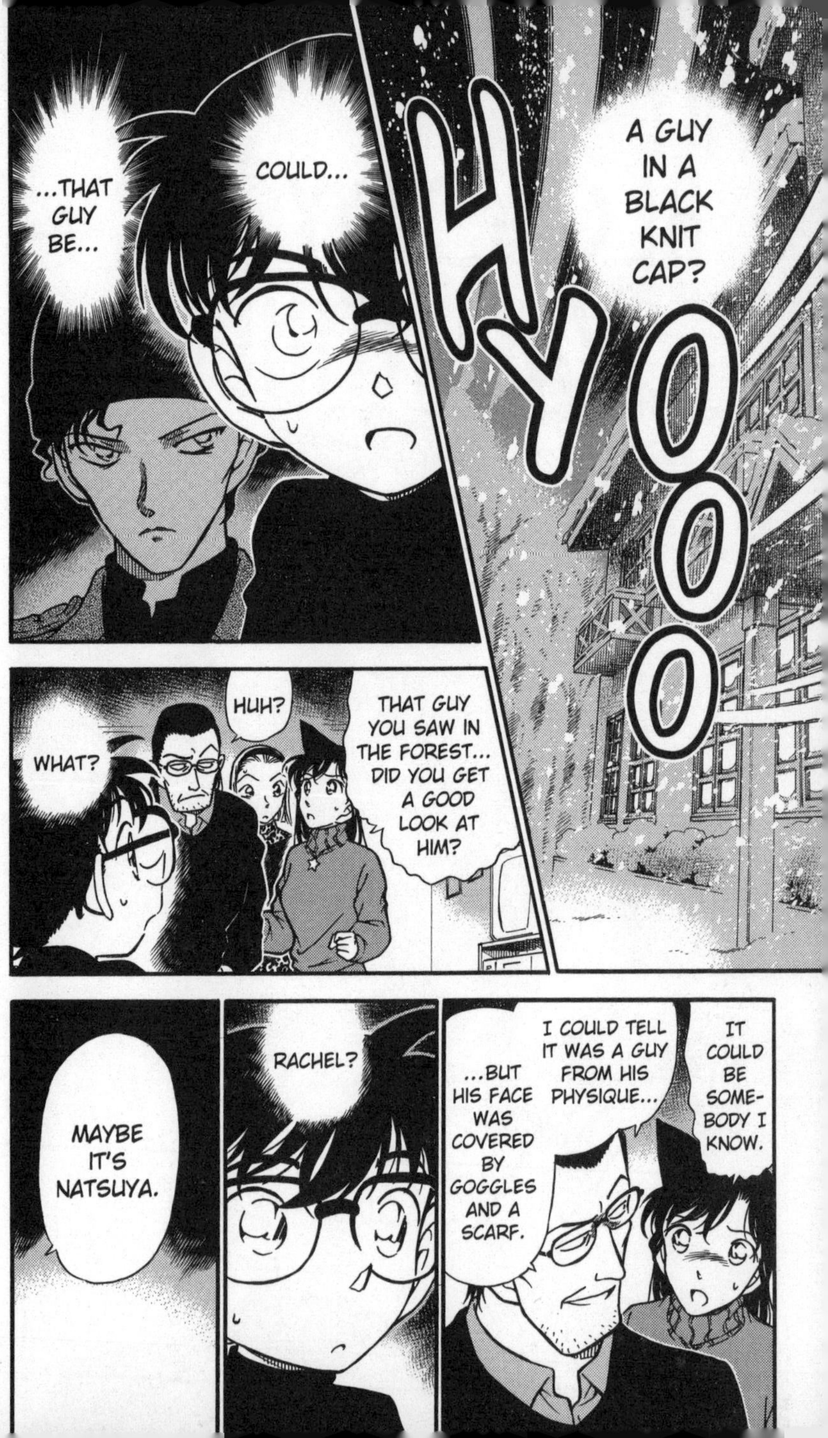
A GUY IN A BLACK KNIT CAP?
HYOOO
COULD...
...THAT GUY BE...
THAT GUY YOU SAW IN THE FOREST... DID YOU GET A GOOD LOOK AT HIM?
HUH?
WHAT?
IT COULD BE SOMEBODY I KNOW.
I COULD TELL IT WAS A GUY FROM HIS PHYSIQUE...
...BUT HIS FACE WAS COVERED BY GOGGLES AND A SCARF.
RACHEL?
MAYBE IT'S NATSUYA.

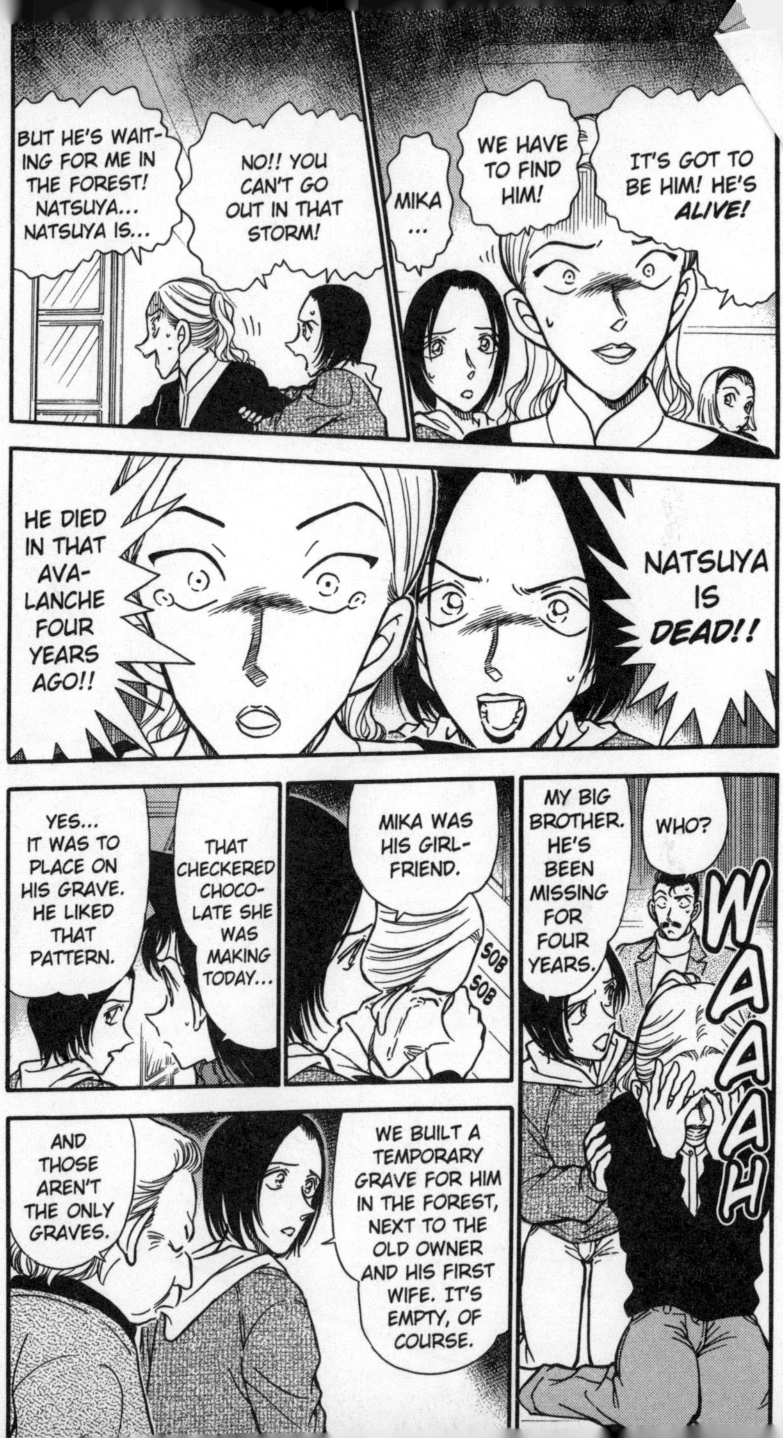
IT'S GOT TO BE HIM! HE'S ALIVE!
WE HAVE TO FIND HIM!
MIKA ...
NO!! YOU CAN'T GO OUT IN THAT STORM!
BUT HE'S WAITING FOR ME IN THE FOREST! NATSUYA... NATSUYA IS...
NATSUYA IS DEAD!!
HE DIED IN THAT AVALANCHE FOUR YEARS AGO!!
WHO?
WAAAAH
MY BIG BROTHER. HE'S BEEN MISSING FOR FOUR YEARS.
MIKA WAS HIS GIRLFRIEND.
SOB SOB
THAT CHECKERED CHOCOLATE SHE WAS MAKING TODAY...
YES... IT WAS TO PLACE ON HIS GRAVE. HE LIKED THAT PATTERN.
WE BUILT A TEMPORARY GRAVE FOR HIM IN THE FOREST, NEXT TO THE OLD OWNER AND HIS FIRST WIFE. IT'S EMPTY, OF COURSE.
AND THOSE AREN'T THE ONLY GRAVES.

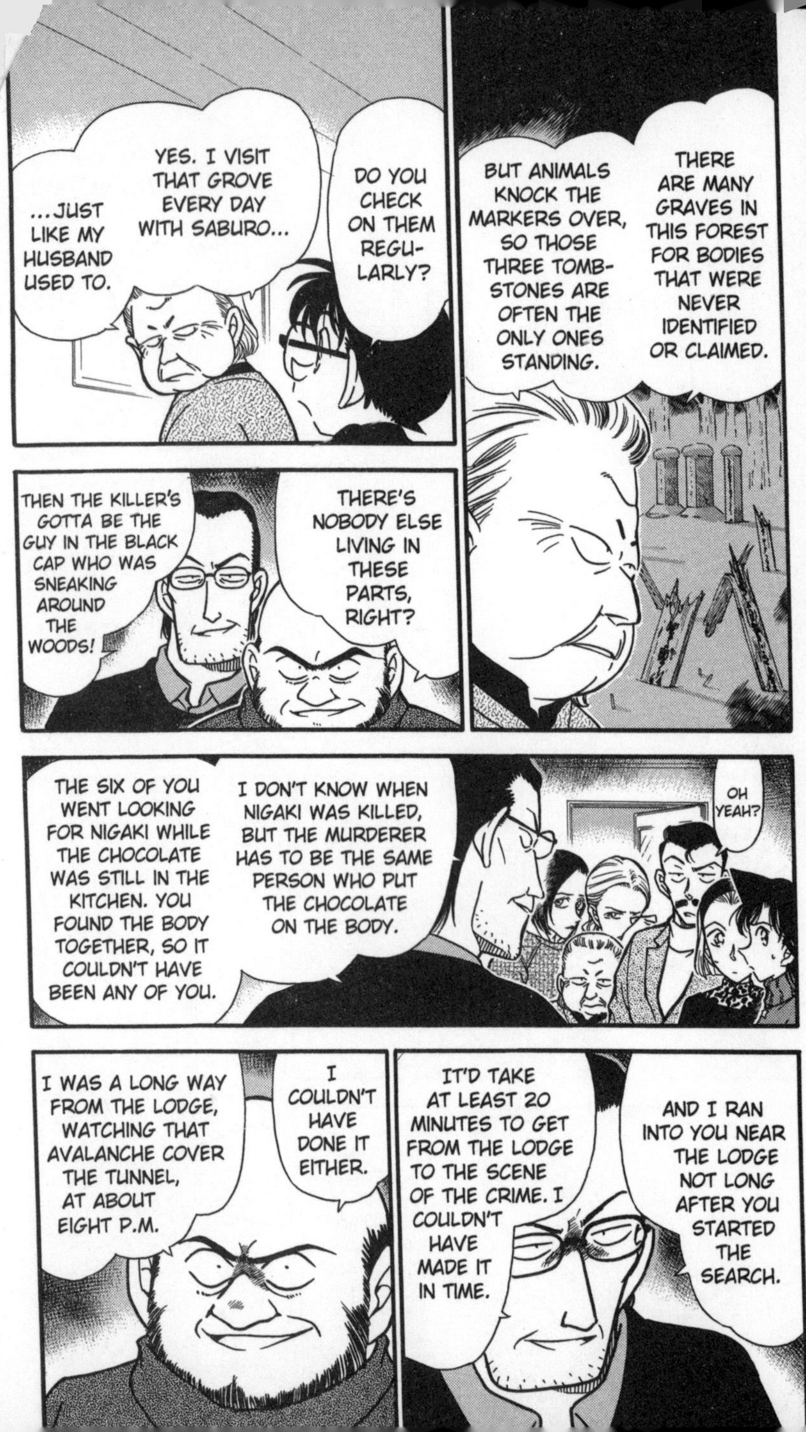
THERE ARE MANY GRAVES IN THIS FOREST FOR BODIES THAT WERE NEVER IDENTIFIED OR CLAIMED.
BUT ANIMALS KNOCK THE MARKERS OVER, SO THOSE THREE TOMB-STONES ARE OFTEN THE ONLY ONES STANDING.
DO YOU CHECK ON THEM REGU-LARLY?
YES. I VISIT THAT GROVE EVERY DAY WITH SABURO...
...JUST LIKE MY HUSBAND USED TO.
THERE'S NOBODY ELSE LIVING IN THESE PARTS, RIGHT?
THEN THE KILLER'S GOTTA BE THE GUY IN THE BLACK CAP WHO WAS SNEAKING AROUND THE WOODS!
OH YEAH?
I DON'T KNOW WHEN NIGAKI WAS KILLED, BUT THE MURDERER HAS TO BE THE SAME PERSON WHO PUT THE CHOCOLATE ON THE BODY.
THE SIX OF YOU WENT LOOKING FOR NIGAKI WHILE THE CHOCOLATE WAS STILL IN THE KITCHEN. YOU FOUND THE BODY TOGETHER, SO IT COULDN'T HAVE BEEN ANY OF YOU.
AND I RAN INTO YOU NEAR THE LODGE NOT LONG AFTER YOU STARTED THE SEARCH.
IT'D TAKE AT LEAST 20 MINUTES TO GET FROM THE LODGE TO THE SCENE OF THE CRIME. I COULDN'T HAVE MADE IT IN TIME.
I COULDN'T HAVE DONE IT EITHER.
I WAS A LONG WAY FROM THE LODGE, WATCHING THAT AVALANCHE COVER THE TUNNEL, AT ABOUT EIGHT P.M.

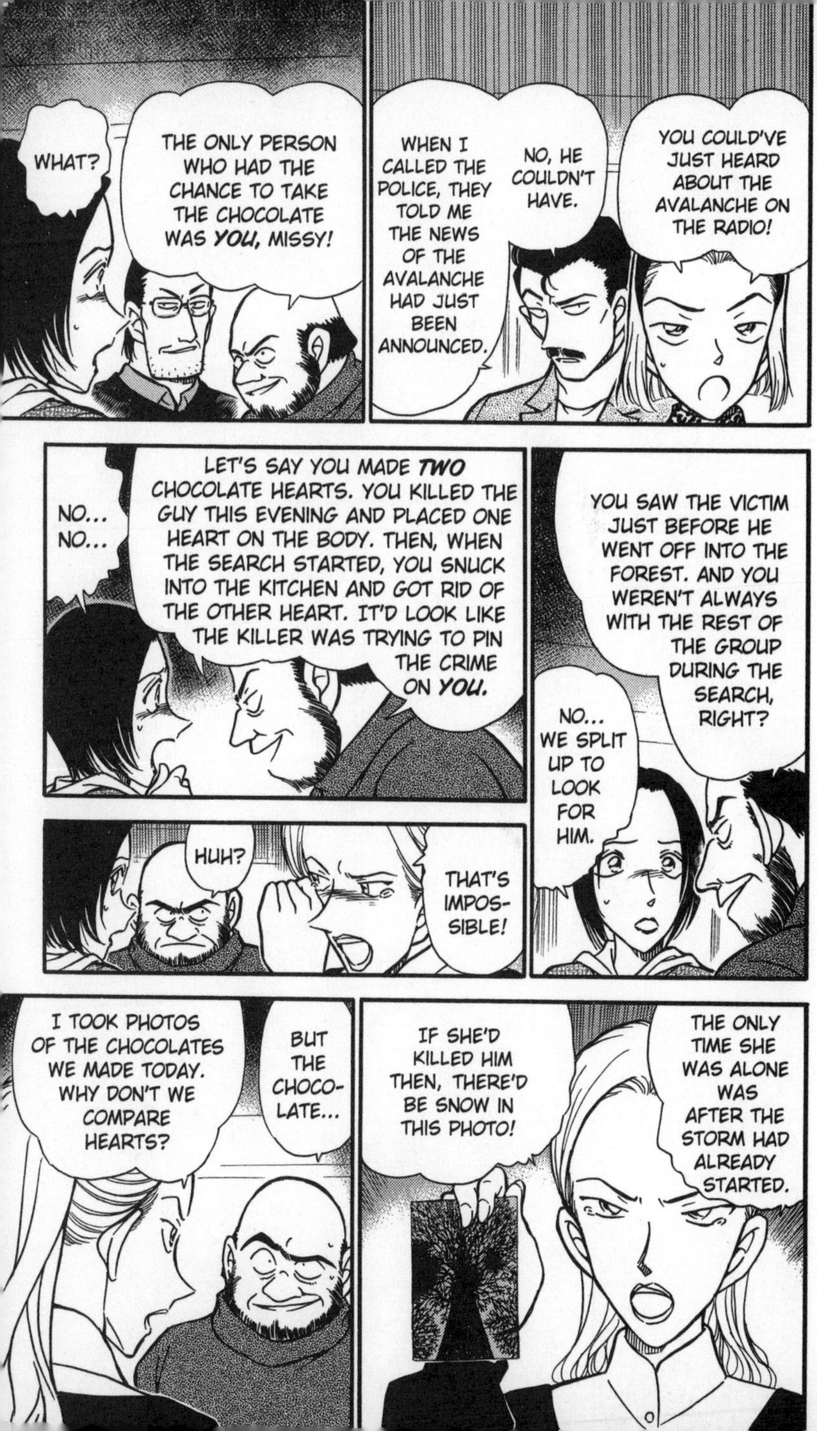
YOU COULD'VE JUST HEARD ABOUT THE AVALANCHE ON THE RADIO!
NO, HE COULDN'T HAVE.
WHEN I CALLED THE POLICE, THEY TOLD ME THE NEWS OF THE AVALANCHE HAD JUST BEEN ANNOUNCED.
THE ONLY PERSON WHO HAD THE CHANCE TO TAKE THE CHOCOLATE WAS *YOU,* MISSY!
WHAT?
YOU SAW THE VICTIM JUST BEFORE HE WENT OFF INTO THE FOREST. AND YOU WEREN'T ALWAYS WITH THE REST OF THE GROUP DURING THE SEARCH, RIGHT?
NO... WE SPLIT UP TO LOOK FOR HIM.
LET'S SAY YOU MADE ***TWO*** CHOCOLATE HEARTS. YOU KILLED THE GUY THIS EVENING AND PLACED ONE HEART ON THE BODY. THEN, WHEN THE SEARCH STARTED, YOU SNUCK INTO THE KITCHEN AND GOT RID OF THE OTHER HEART. IT'D LOOK LIKE THE KILLER WAS TRYING TO PIN THE CRIME ON *YOU.*
NO... NO...
THAT'S IMPOS-SIBLE!
HUH?
THE ONLY TIME SHE WAS ALONE WAS AFTER THE STORM HAD ALREADY STARTED.
IF SHE'D KILLED HIM THEN, THERE'D BE SNOW IN THIS PHOTO!
BUT THE CHOCO-LATE...
I TOOK PHOTOS OF THE CHOCOLATES WE MADE TODAY. WHY DON'T WE COMPARE HEARTS?

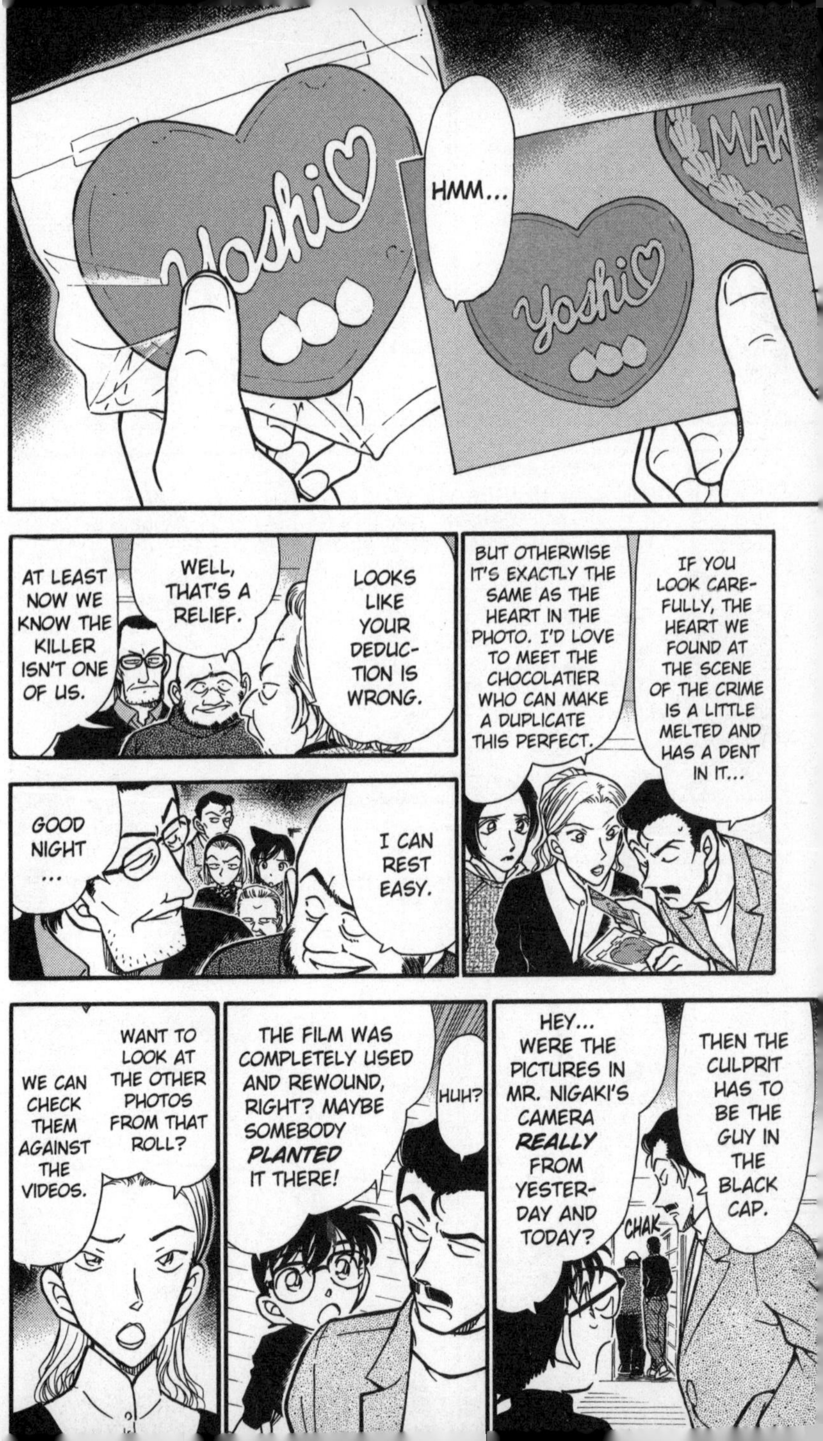
HMM...
Yoshi♡
Yoshi♡
IF YOU LOOK CAREFULLY, THE HEART WE FOUND AT THE SCENE OF THE CRIME IS A LITTLE MELTED AND HAS A DENT IN IT...
BUT OTHERWISE IT'S EXACTLY THE SAME AS THE HEART IN THE PHOTO. I'D LOVE TO MEET THE CHOCOLATIER WHO CAN MAKE A DUPLICATE THIS PERFECT.
LOOKS LIKE YOUR DEDUCTION IS WRONG.
WELL, THAT'S A RELIEF.
AT LEAST NOW WE KNOW THE KILLER ISN'T ONE OF US.
I CAN REST EASY.
GOOD NIGHT ...
THEN THE CULPRIT HAS TO BE THE GUY IN THE BLACK CAP.
CHAK
HEY... WERE THE PICTURES IN MR. NIGAKI'S CAMERA **REALLY** FROM YESTERDAY AND TODAY?
HUH?
THE FILM WAS COMPLETELY USED AND REWOUND, RIGHT? MAYBE SOMEBODY ***PLANTED*** IT THERE!
WANT TO LOOK AT THE OTHER PHOTOS FROM THAT ROLL?
WE CAN CHECK THEM AGAINST THE VIDEOS.

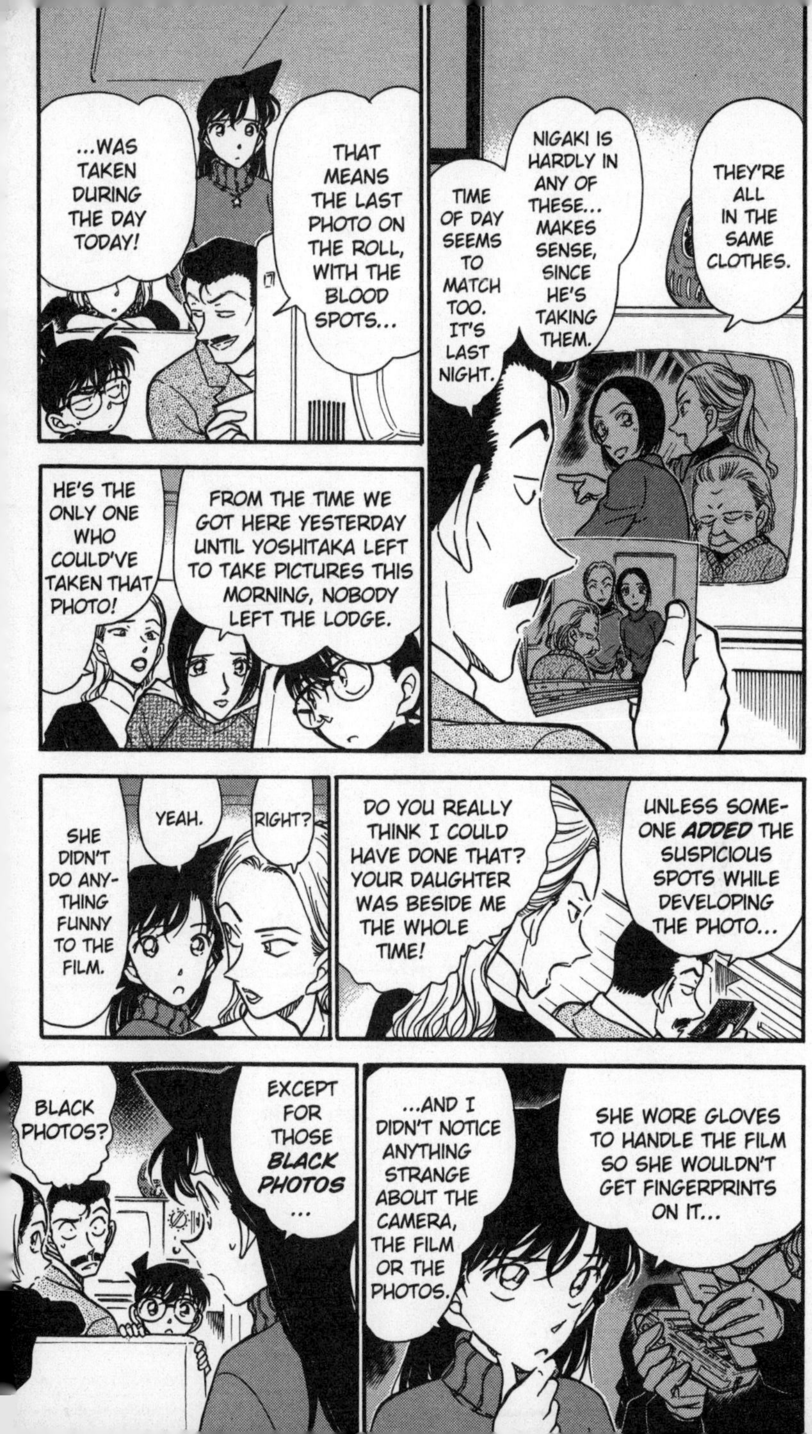
THEY'RE ALL IN THE SAME CLOTHES.
NIGAKI IS HARDLY IN ANY OF THESE... MAKES SENSE, SINCE HE'S TAKING THEM.
TIME OF DAY SEEMS TO MATCH TOO. IT'S LAST NIGHT.
THAT MEANS THE LAST PHOTO ON THE ROLL, WITH THE BLOOD SPOTS...
...WAS TAKEN DURING THE DAY TODAY!
FROM THE TIME WE GOT HERE YESTERDAY UNTIL YOSHITAKA LEFT TO TAKE PICTURES THIS MORNING, NOBODY LEFT THE LODGE.
HE'S THE ONLY ONE WHO COULD'VE TAKEN THAT PHOTO!
UNLESS SOME-ONE ***ADDED*** THE SUSPICIOUS SPOTS WHILE DEVELOPING THE PHOTO...
DO YOU REALLY THINK I COULD HAVE DONE THAT? YOUR DAUGHTER WAS BESIDE ME THE WHOLE TIME!
RIGHT?
YEAH.
SHE DIDN'T DO ANY-THING FUNNY TO THE FILM.
SHE WORE GLOVES TO HANDLE THE FILM SO SHE WOULDN'T GET FINGERPRINTS ON IT...
...AND I DIDN'T NOTICE ANYTHING STRANGE ABOUT THE CAMERA, THE FILM OR THE PHOTOS.
EXCEPT FOR THOSE ***BLACK PHOTOS***...
BLACK PHOTOS?

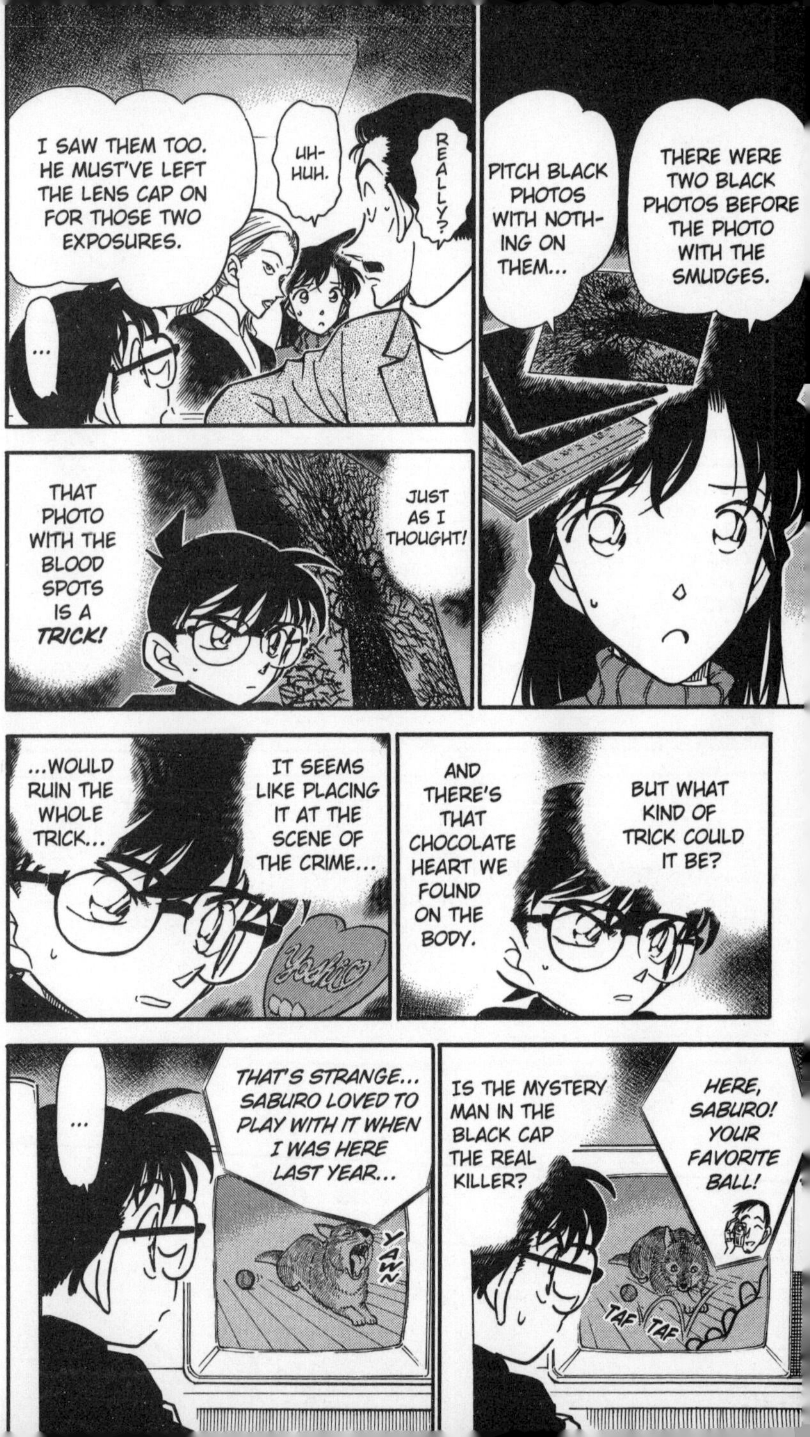
THERE WERE TWO BLACK PHOTOS BEFORE THE PHOTO WITH THE SMUDGES.
PITCH BLACK PHOTOS WITH NOTHING ON THEM...
REALLY?
UH-HUH.
I SAW THEM TOO. HE MUST'VE LEFT THE LENS CAP ON FOR THOSE TWO EXPOSURES.
...
JUST AS I THOUGHT!
THAT PHOTO WITH THE BLOOD SPOTS IS A *TRICK!*
BUT WHAT KIND OF TRICK COULD IT BE?
AND THERE'S THAT CHOCOLATE HEART WE FOUND ON THE BODY.
IT SEEMS LIKE PLACING IT AT THE SCENE OF THE CRIME...
...WOULD RUIN THE WHOLE TRICK...
HERE, SABURO! YOUR FAVORITE BALL!
IS THE MYSTERY MAN IN THE BLACK CAP THE REAL KILLER?
TAF TAF
THAT'S STRANGE... SABURO LOVED TO PLAY WITH IT WHEN I WAS HERE LAST YEAR...
YAWN
...

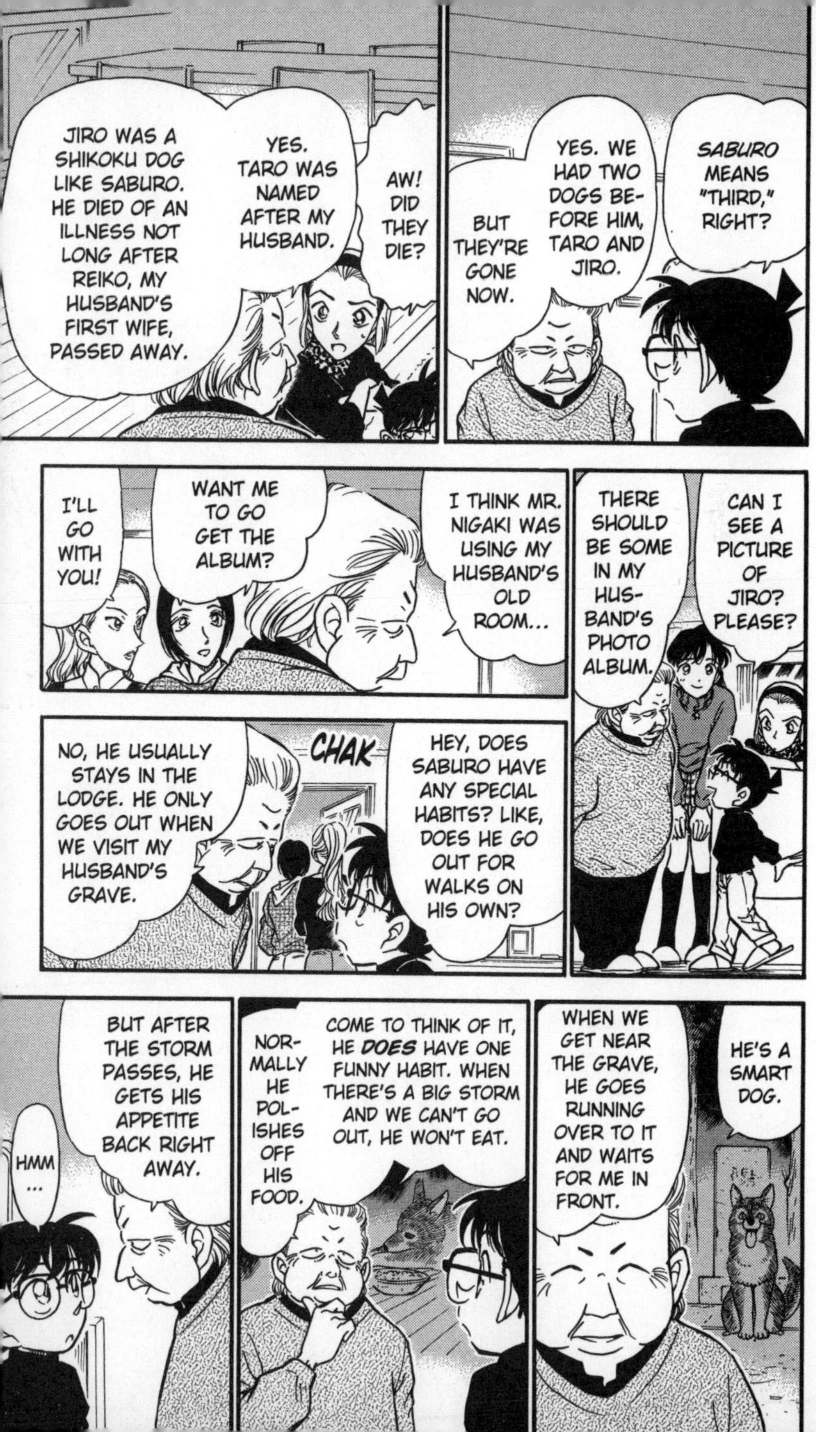
SABURO MEANS "THIRD," RIGHT?
YES. WE HAD TWO DOGS BEFORE HIM, TARO AND JIRO.
BUT THEY'RE GONE NOW.
AW! DID THEY DIE?
YES. TARO WAS NAMED AFTER MY HUSBAND.
JIRO WAS A SHIKOKU DOG LIKE SABURO. HE DIED OF AN ILLNESS NOT LONG AFTER REIKO, MY HUSBAND'S FIRST WIFE, PASSED AWAY.
CAN I SEE A PICTURE OF JIRO? PLEASE?
THERE SHOULD BE SOME IN MY HUSBAND'S PHOTO ALBUM.
I THINK MR. NIGAKI WAS USING MY HUSBAND'S OLD ROOM...
WANT ME TO GO GET THE ALBUM?
I'LL GO WITH YOU!
HEY, DOES SABURO HAVE ANY SPECIAL HABITS? LIKE, DOES HE GO OUT FOR WALKS ON HIS OWN?
CHAK
NO, HE USUALLY STAYS IN THE LODGE. HE ONLY GOES OUT WHEN WE VISIT MY HUSBAND'S GRAVE.
HE'S A SMART DOG.
WHEN WE GET NEAR THE GRAVE, HE GOES RUNNING OVER TO IT AND WAITS FOR ME IN FRONT.
COME TO THINK OF IT, HE *DOES* HAVE ONE FUNNY HABIT. WHEN THERE'S A BIG STORM AND WE CAN'T GO OUT, HE WON'T EAT.
NORMALLY HE POLISHES OFF HIS FOOD.
BUT AFTER THE STORM PASSES, HE GETS HIS APPETITE BACK RIGHT AWAY.
HMM...

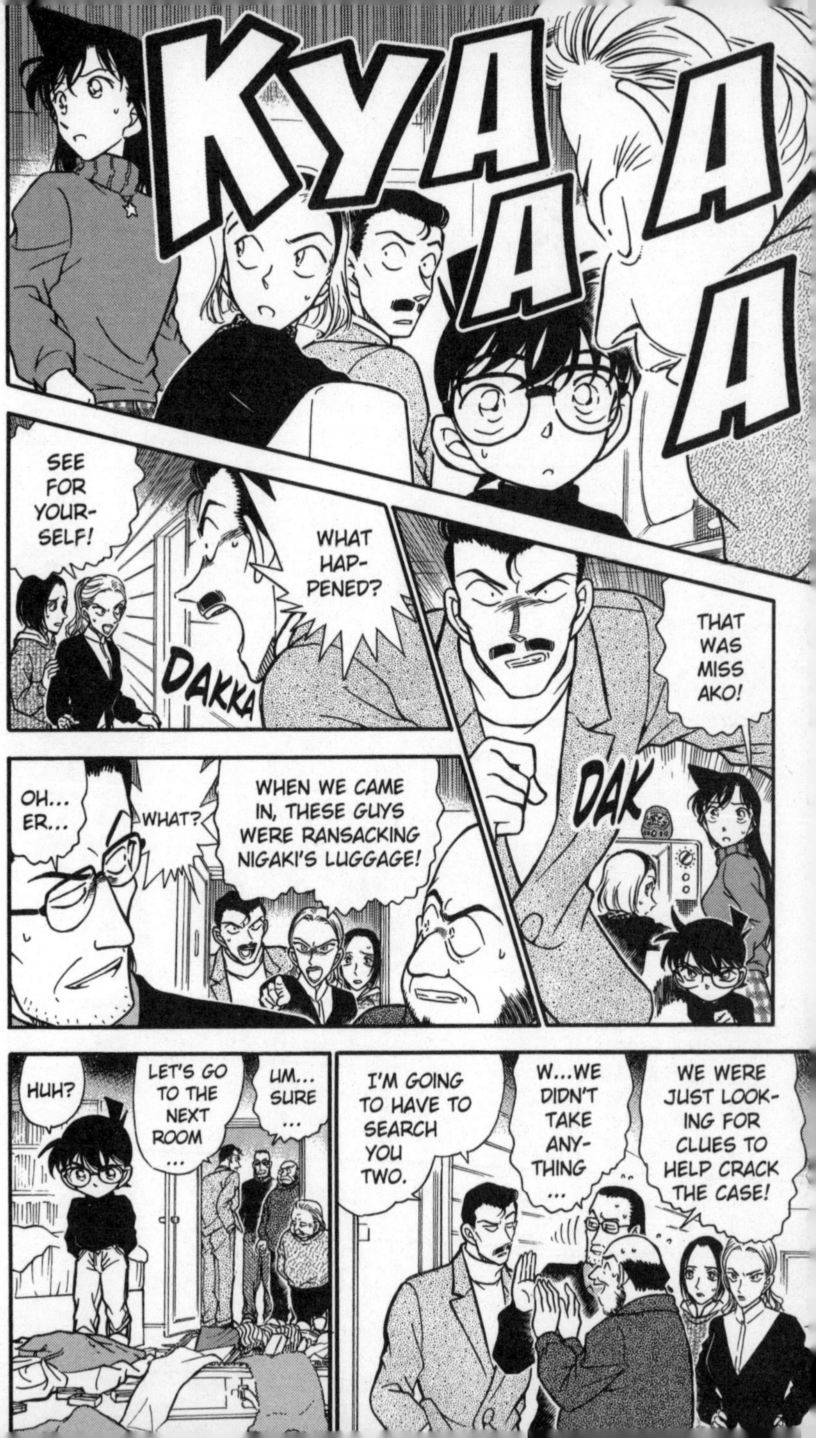
KYAAAAA
THAT WAS MISS AKO!
DAK
WHAT HAPPENED?
DAKKA
SEE FOR YOURSELF!
WHEN WE CAME IN, THESE GUYS WERE RANSACKING NIGAKI'S LUGGAGE!
WHAT?
OH... ER...
WE WERE JUST LOOKING FOR CLUES TO HELP CRACK THE CASE!
W...WE DIDN'T TAKE ANYTHING...
I'M GOING TO HAVE TO SEARCH YOU TWO.
UM... SURE...
LET'S GO TO THE NEXT ROOM...
HUH?

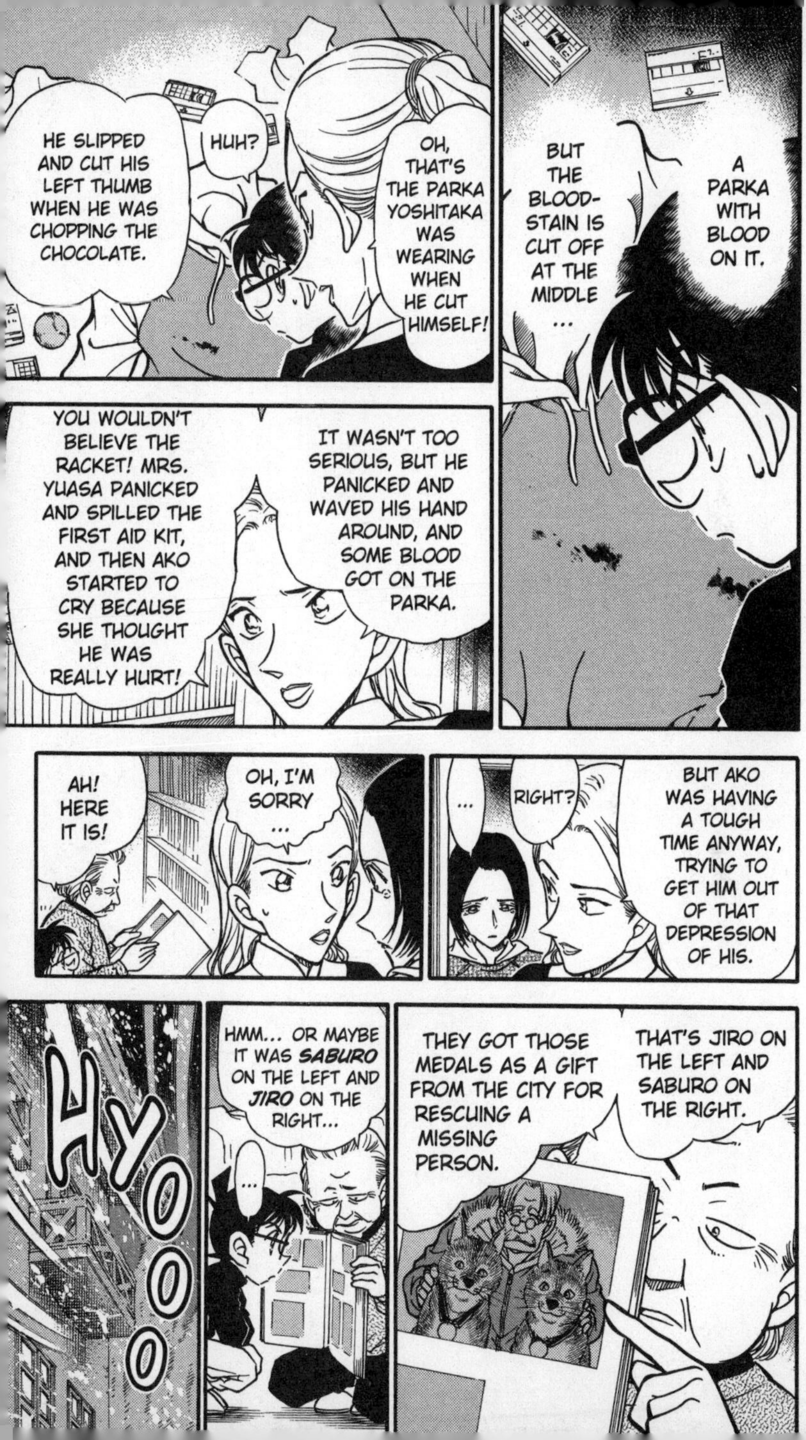
A PARKA WITH BLOOD ON IT.
BUT THE BLOOD-STAIN IS CUT OFF AT THE MIDDLE ...
OH, THAT'S THE PARKA YOSHITAKA WAS WEARING WHEN HE CUT HIMSELF!
HUH?
HE SLIPPED AND CUT HIS LEFT THUMB WHEN HE WAS CHOPPING THE CHOCOLATE.
IT WASN'T TOO SERIOUS, BUT HE PANICKED AND WAVED HIS HAND AROUND, AND SOME BLOOD GOT ON THE PARKA.
YOU WOULDN'T BELIEVE THE RACKET! MRS. YUASA PANICKED AND SPILLED THE FIRST AID KIT, AND THEN AKO STARTED TO CRY BECAUSE SHE THOUGHT HE WAS REALLY HURT!
BUT AKO WAS HAVING A TOUGH TIME ANYWAY, TRYING TO GET HIM OUT OF THAT DEPRESSION OF HIS.
RIGHT?
...
OH, I'M SORRY ...
AH! HERE IT IS!
THAT'S JIRO ON THE LEFT AND SABURO ON THE RIGHT.
THEY GOT THOSE MEDALS AS A GIFT FROM THE CITY FOR RESCUING A MISSING PERSON.
HMM... OR MAYBE IT WAS *SABURO* ON THE LEFT AND *JIRO* ON THE RIGHT...
...
HYOOO

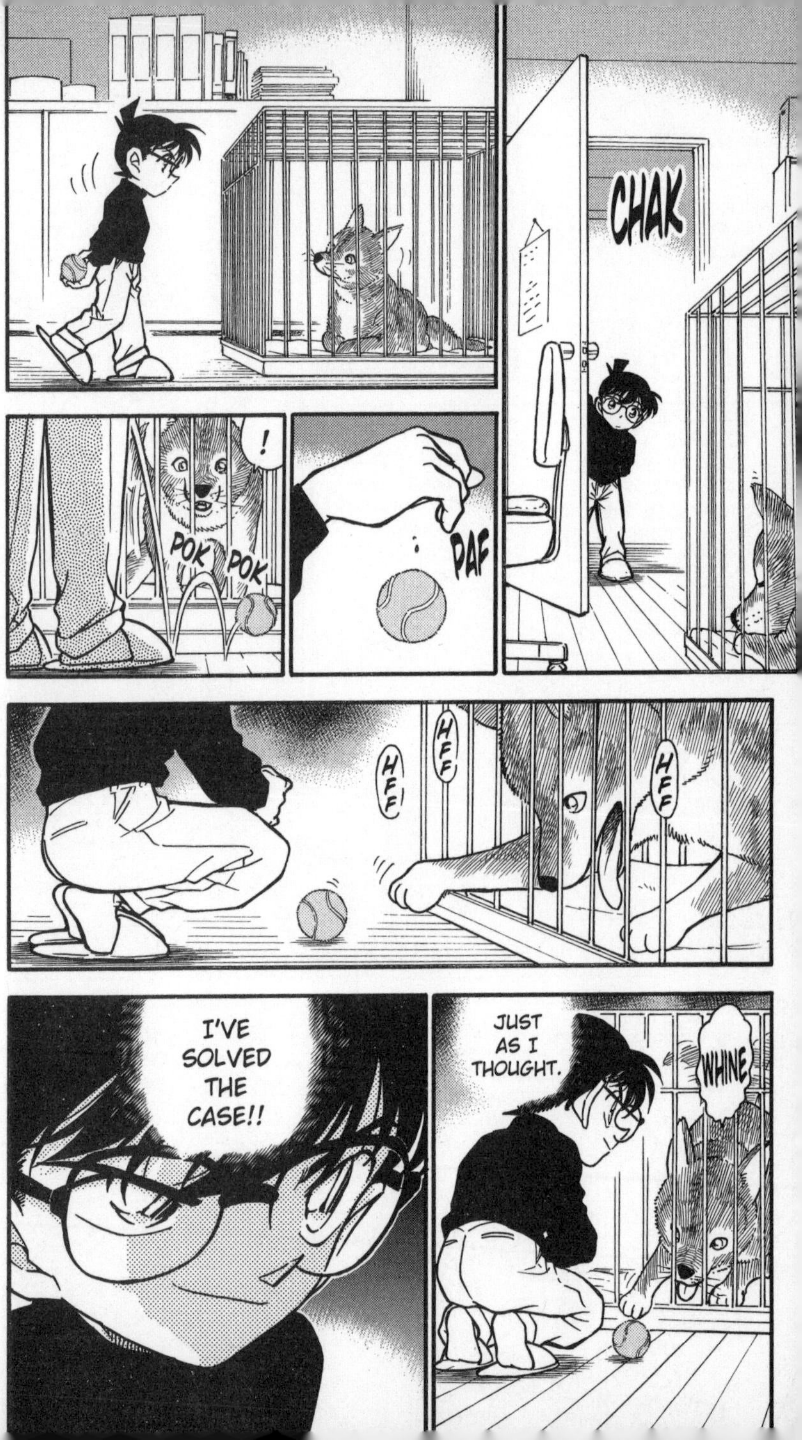
CHAK
PAF
!
POK POK
HFF
HFF
HFF
JUST AS I THOUGHT.
WHINE
I'VE SOLVED THE CASE!!

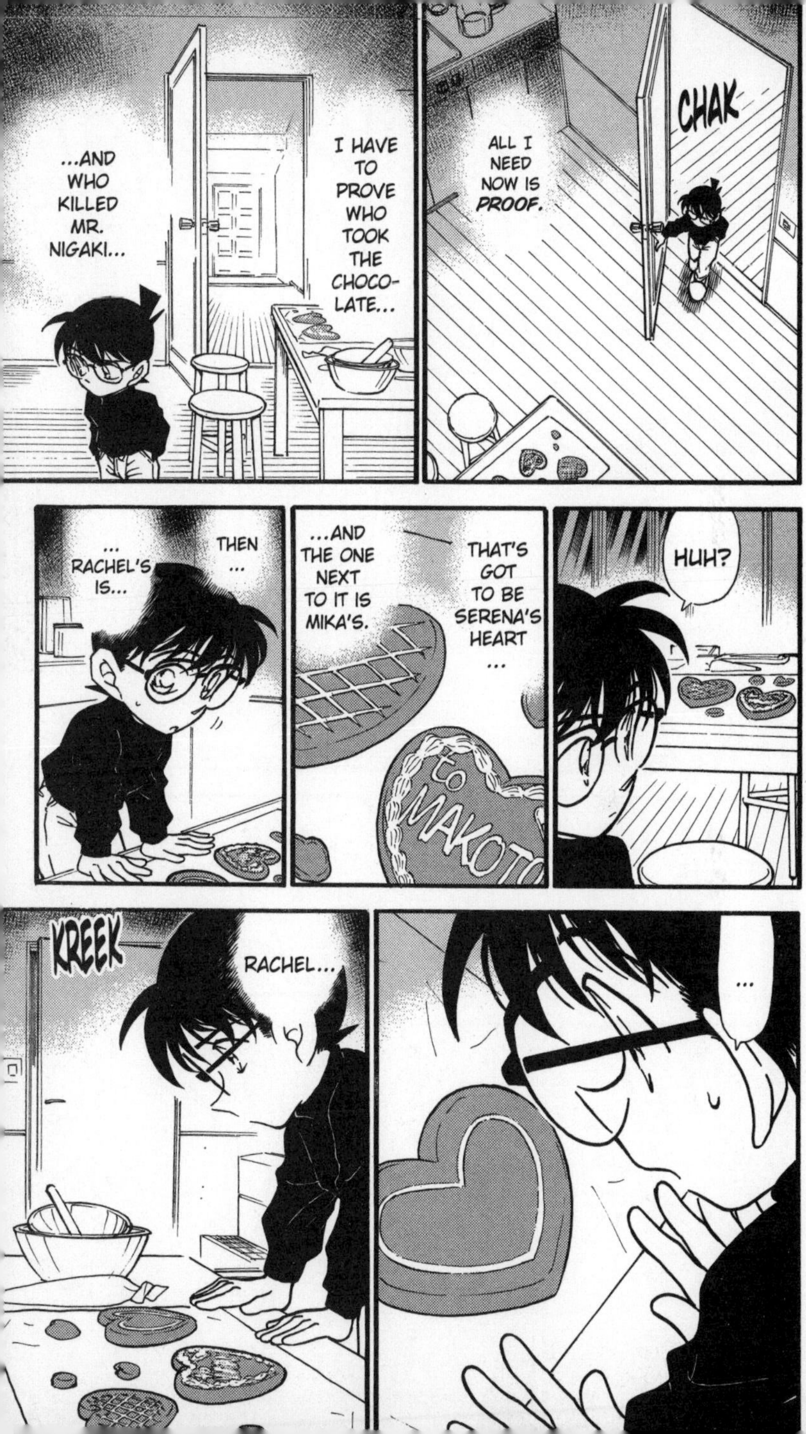
CHAK
ALL I NEED NOW IS *PROOF*.
I HAVE TO PROVE WHO TOOK THE CHOCOLATE...
...AND WHO KILLED MR. NIGAKI...
HUH?
THAT'S GOT TO BE SERENA'S HEART...
...AND THE ONE NEXT TO IT IS MIKA'S.
to MAKOTO
THEN...
...RACHEL'S IS...
...
KREEK
RACHEL...

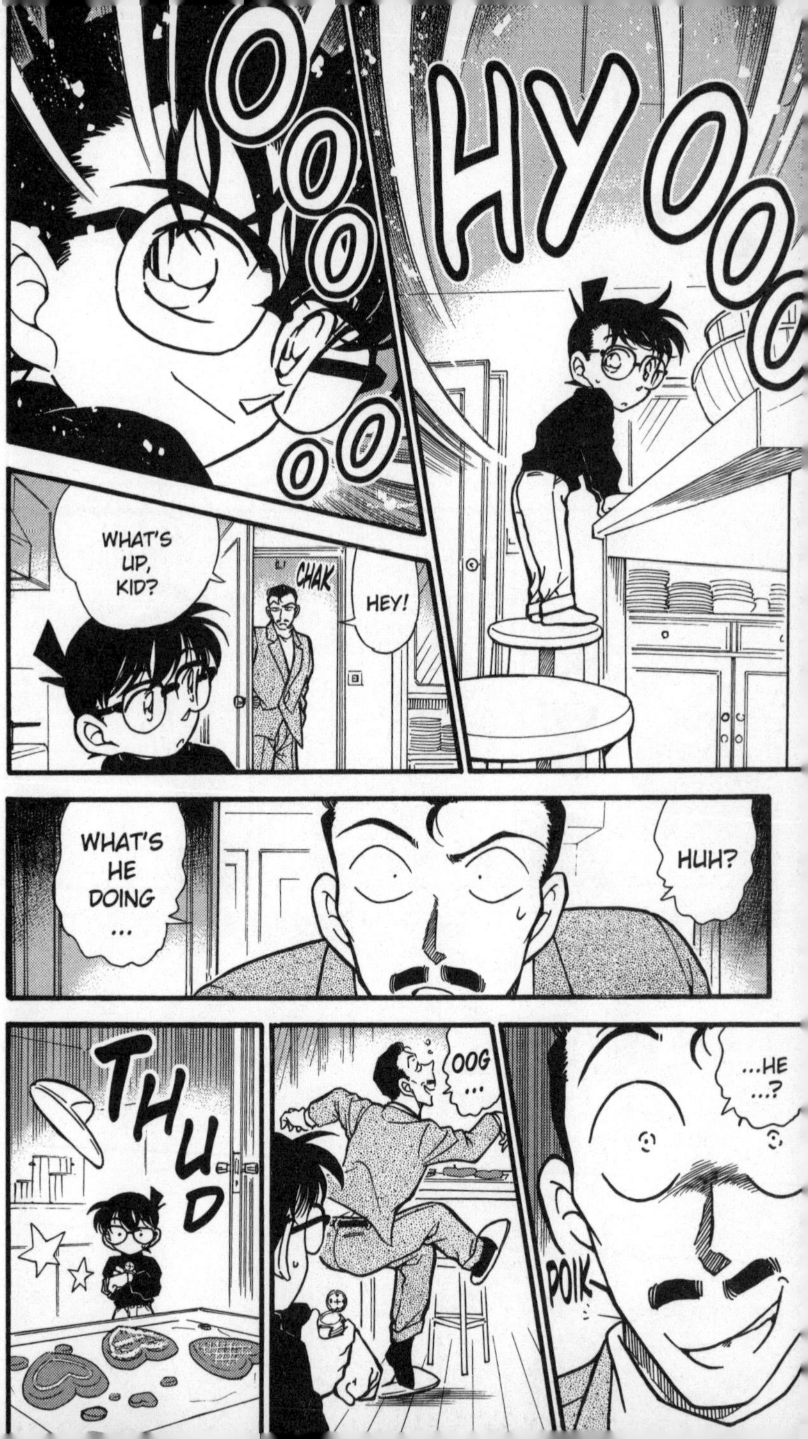
HYOOOO
OOOOOO
CHAK
HEY!
WHAT'S UP, KID?
HUH?
WHAT'S HE DOING ...
...HE ...?
POIK
OOG ...
THUD

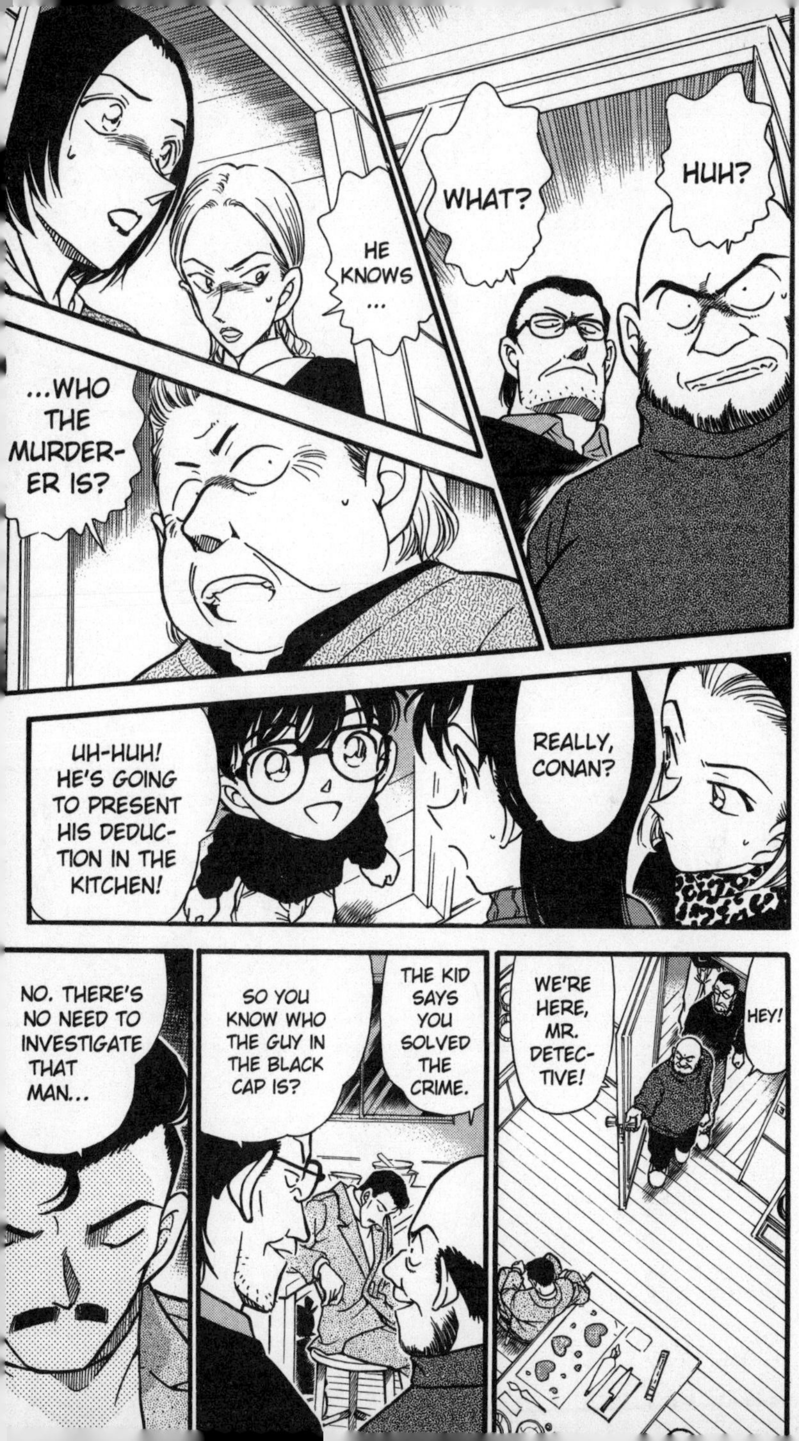
HUH?
WHAT?
HE KNOWS ...
...WHO THE MURDER-ER IS?
REALLY, CONAN?
UH-HUH! HE'S GOING TO PRESENT HIS DEDUC-TION IN THE KITCHEN!
HEY!
WE'RE HERE, MR. DETEC-TIVE!
THE KID SAYS YOU SOLVED THE CRIME.
SO YOU KNOW WHO THE GUY IN THE BLACK CAP IS?
NO. THERE'S NO NEED TO INVESTIGATE THAT MAN...

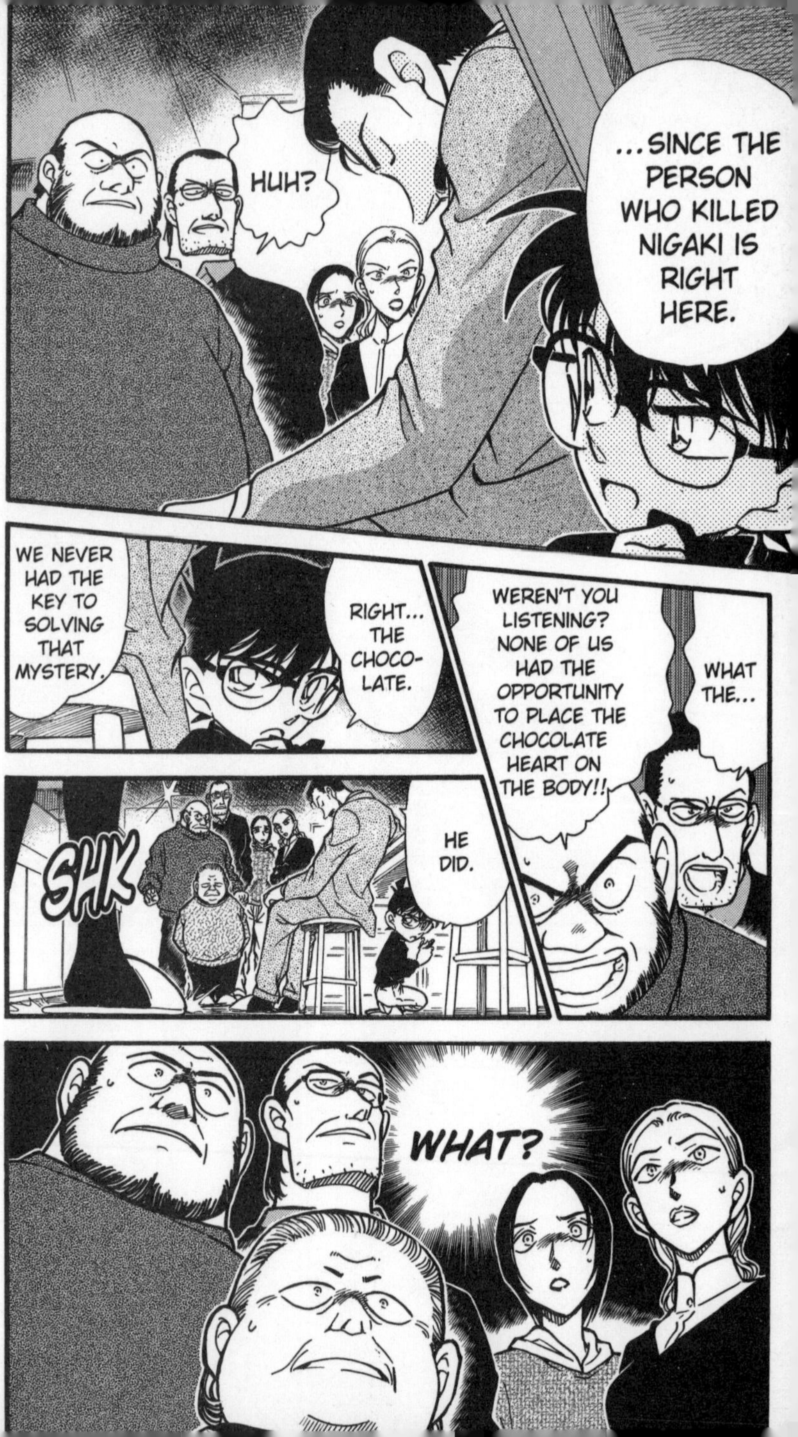
...SINCE THE PERSON WHO KILLED NIGAKI IS RIGHT HERE.
HUH?
WHAT THE...
WEREN'T YOU LISTENING? NONE OF US HAD THE OPPORTUNITY TO PLACE THE CHOCOLATE HEART ON THE BODY!!
WE NEVER HAD THE KEY TO SOLVING THAT MYSTERY.
RIGHT... THE CHOCO-LATE.
HE DID.
SHK
WHAT?

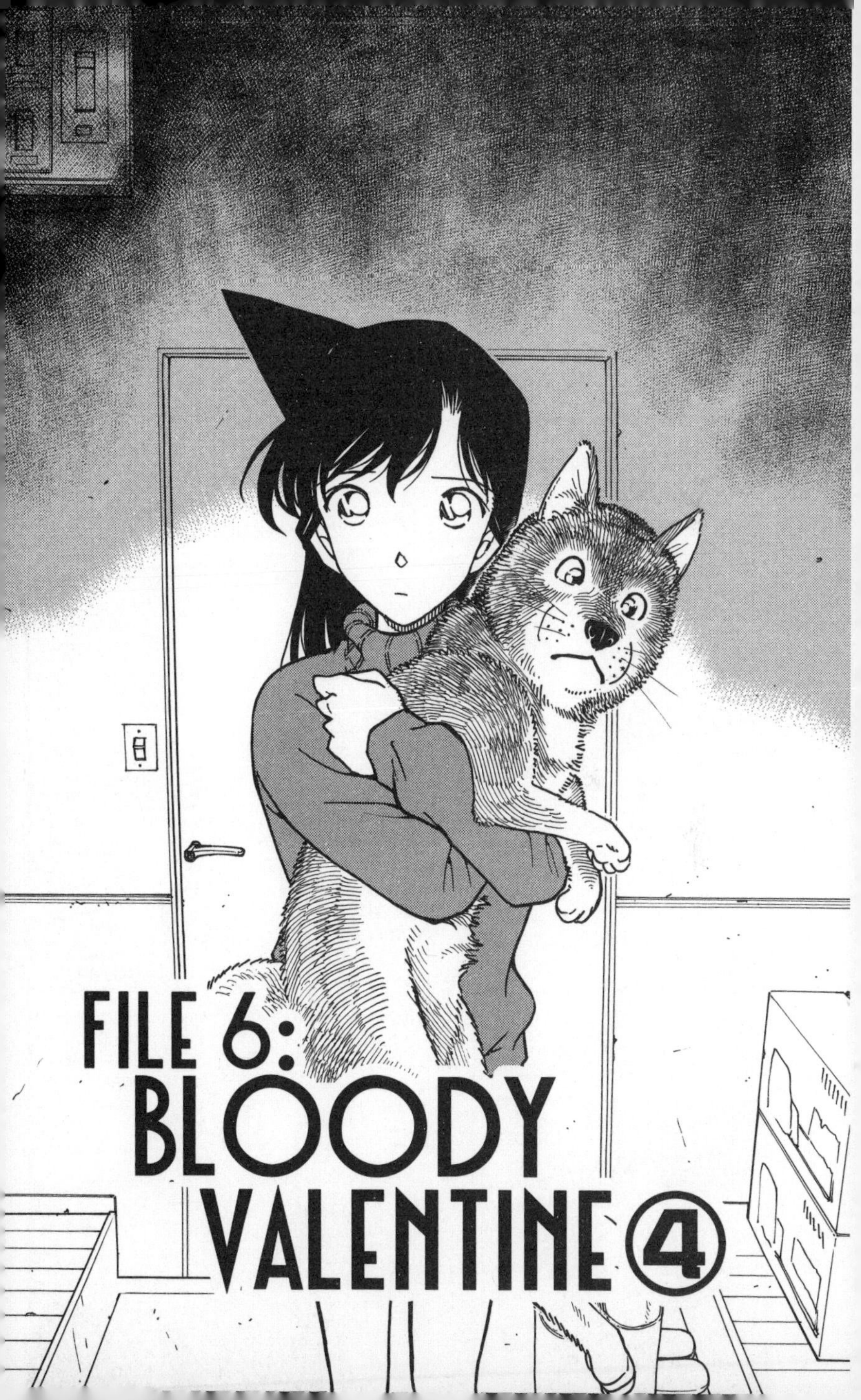
FILE 6:
BLOODY
VALENTINE ④

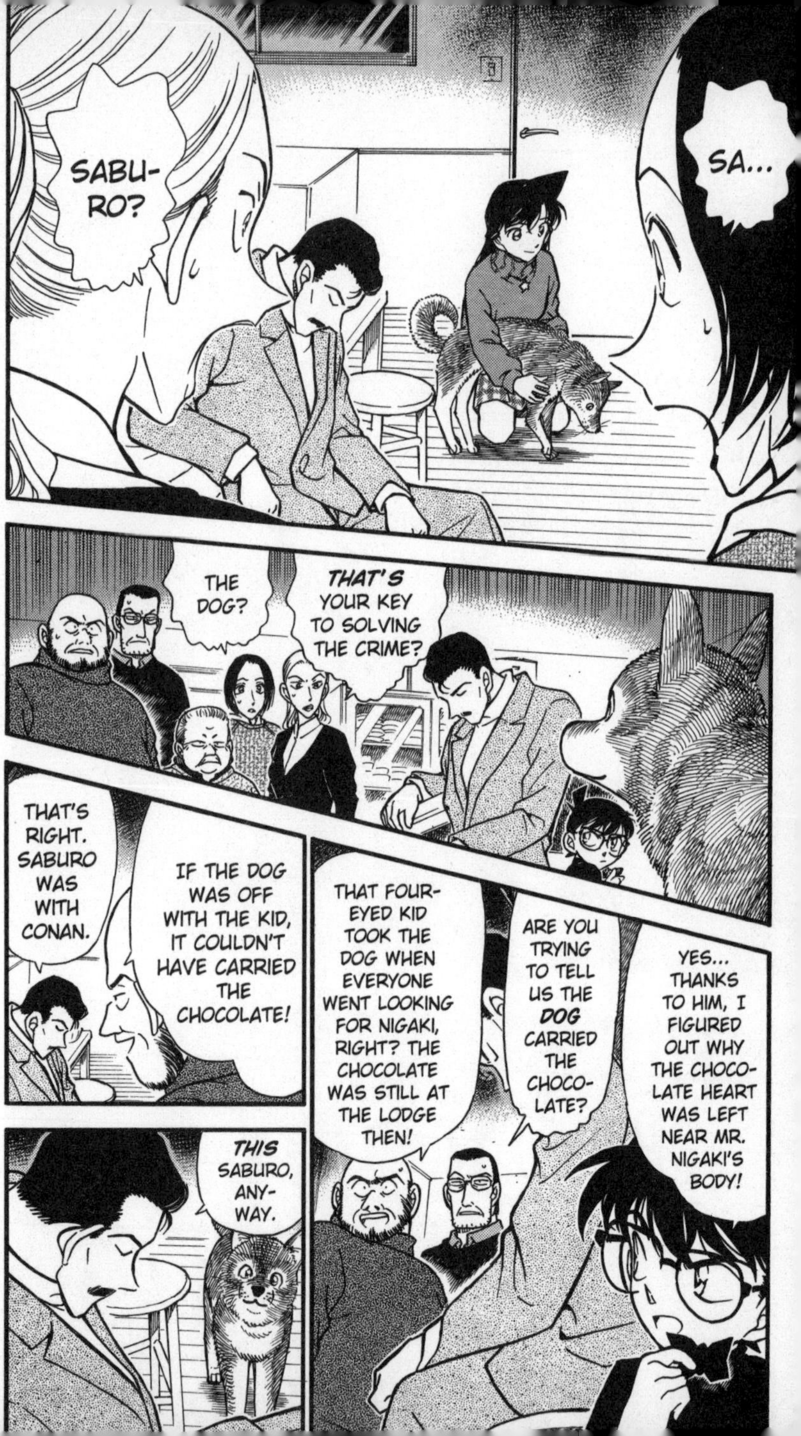
SA...
SABU-RO?
THAT'S YOUR KEY TO SOLVING THE CRIME?
THE DOG?
ARE YOU TRYING TO TELL US THE *DOG* CARRIED THE CHOCO-LATE?
YES... THANKS TO HIM, I FIGURED OUT WHY THE CHOCO-LATE HEART WAS LEFT NEAR MR. NIGAKI'S BODY!
THAT FOUR-EYED KID TOOK THE DOG WHEN EVERYONE WENT LOOKING FOR NIGAKI, RIGHT? THE CHOCOLATE WAS STILL AT THE LODGE THEN!
IF THE DOG WAS OFF WITH THE KID, IT COULDN'T HAVE CARRIED THE CHOCOLATE!
THAT'S RIGHT. SABURO WAS WITH CONAN.
THIS SABURO, ANY-WAY.

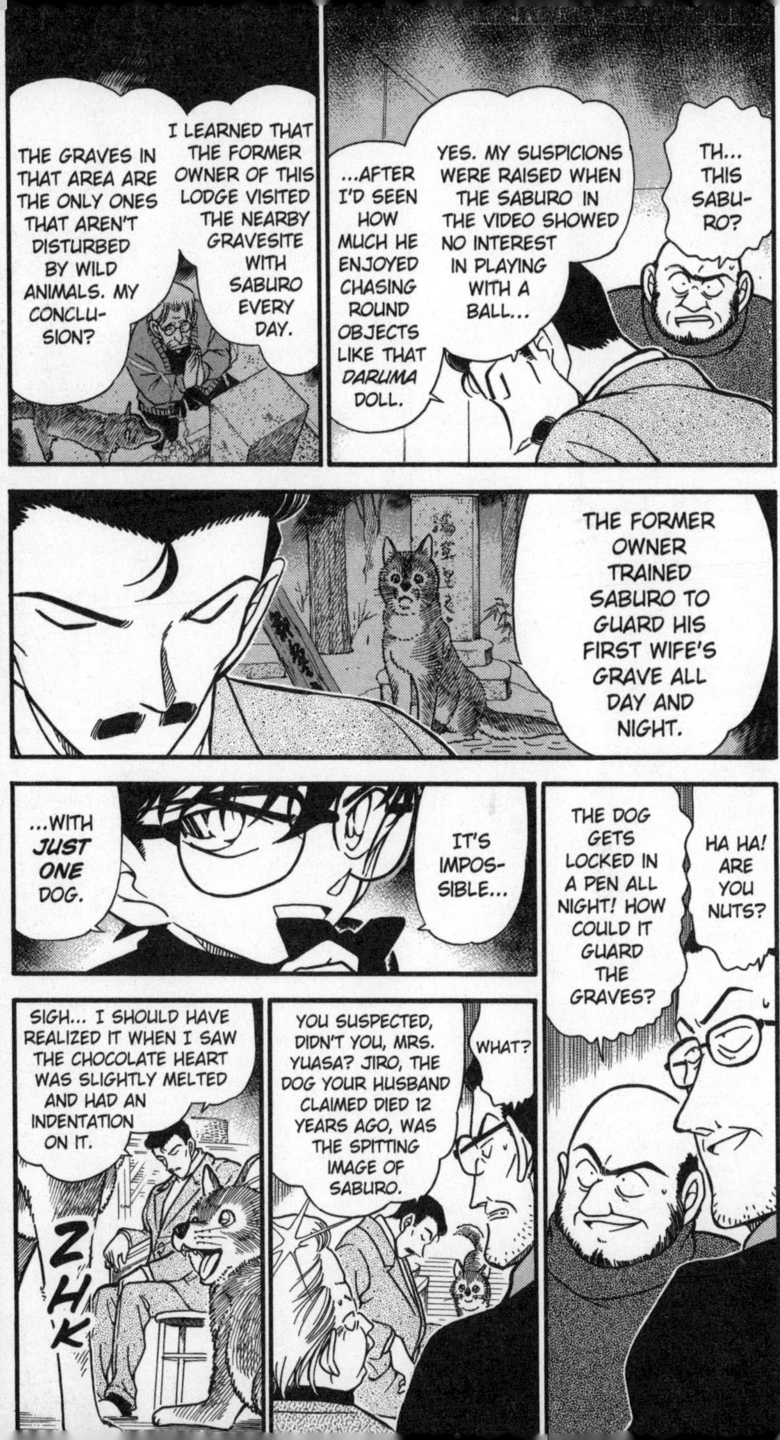
TH... THIS SABU-RO?
YES. MY SUSPICIONS WERE RAISED WHEN THE SABURO IN THE VIDEO SHOWED NO INTEREST IN PLAYING WITH A BALL...
...AFTER I'D SEEN HOW MUCH HE ENJOYED CHASING ROUND OBJECTS LIKE THAT *DARUMA* DOLL.
I LEARNED THAT THE FORMER OWNER OF THIS LODGE VISITED THE NEARBY GRAVESITE WITH SABURO EVERY DAY.
THE GRAVES IN THAT AREA ARE THE ONLY ONES THAT AREN'T DISTURBED BY WILD ANIMALS. MY CONCLU-SION?
THE FORMER OWNER TRAINED SABURO TO GUARD HIS FIRST WIFE'S GRAVE ALL DAY AND NIGHT.
HA HA! ARE YOU NUTS?
THE DOG GETS LOCKED IN A PEN ALL NIGHT! HOW COULD IT GUARD THE GRAVES?
IT'S IMPOS-SIBLE...
...WITH ***JUST ONE*** DOG.
WHAT?
YOU SUSPECTED, DIDN'T YOU, MRS. YUASA? JIRO, THE DOG YOUR HUSBAND CLAIMED DIED 12 YEARS AGO, WAS THE SPITTING IMAGE OF SABURO.
SIGH... I SHOULD HAVE REALIZED IT WHEN I SAW THE CHOCOLATE HEART WAS SLIGHTLY MELTED AND HAD AN INDENTATION ON IT.
ZHK

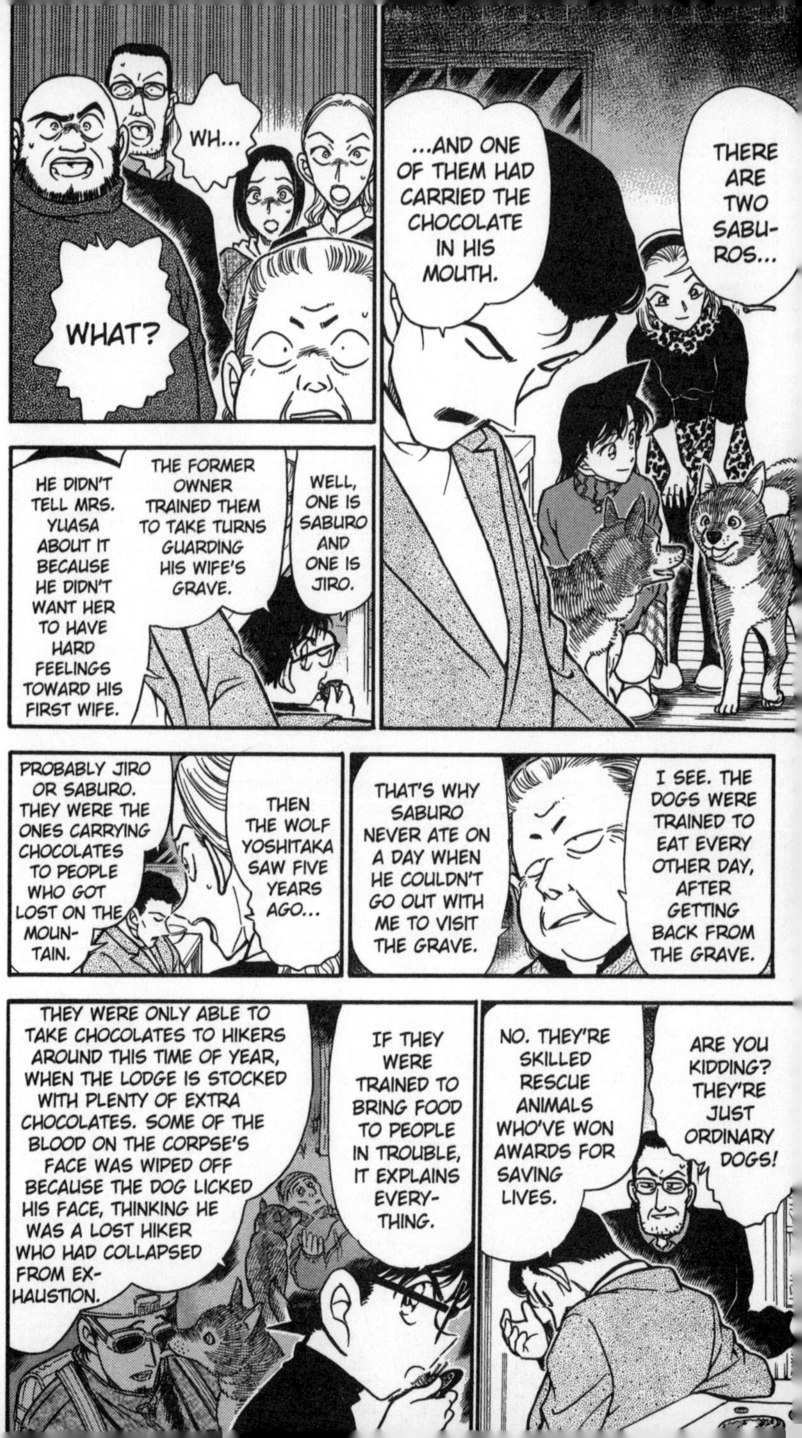
THERE ARE TWO SABU-ROS...
...AND ONE OF THEM HAD CARRIED THE CHOCOLATE IN HIS MOUTH.
WH...
WHAT?
WELL, ONE IS SABURO AND ONE IS JIRO.
THE FORMER OWNER TRAINED THEM TO TAKE TURNS GUARDING HIS WIFE'S GRAVE.
HE DIDN'T TELL MRS. YUASA ABOUT IT BECAUSE HE DIDN'T WANT HER TO HAVE HARD FEELINGS TOWARD HIS FIRST WIFE.
I SEE. THE DOGS WERE TRAINED TO EAT EVERY OTHER DAY, AFTER GETTING BACK FROM THE GRAVE.
THAT'S WHY SABURO NEVER ATE ON A DAY WHEN HE COULDN'T GO OUT WITH ME TO VISIT THE GRAVE.
THEN THE WOLF YOSHITAKA SAW FIVE YEARS AGO...
PROBABLY JIRO OR SABURO. THEY WERE THE ONES CARRYING CHOCOLATES TO PEOPLE WHO GOT LOST ON THE MOUN-TAIN.
ARE YOU KIDDING? THEY'RE JUST ORDINARY DOGS!
NO. THEY'RE SKILLED RESCUE ANIMALS WHO'VE WON AWARDS FOR SAVING LIVES.
IF THEY WERE TRAINED TO BRING FOOD TO PEOPLE IN TROUBLE, IT EXPLAINS EVERY-THING.
THEY WERE ONLY ABLE TO TAKE CHOCOLATES TO HIKERS AROUND THIS TIME OF YEAR, WHEN THE LODGE IS STOCKED WITH PLENTY OF EXTRA CHOCOLATES. SOME OF THE BLOOD ON THE CORPSE'S FACE WAS WIPED OFF BECAUSE THE DOG LICKED HIS FACE, THINKING HE WAS A LOST HIKER WHO HAD COLLAPSED FROM EX-HAUSTION.

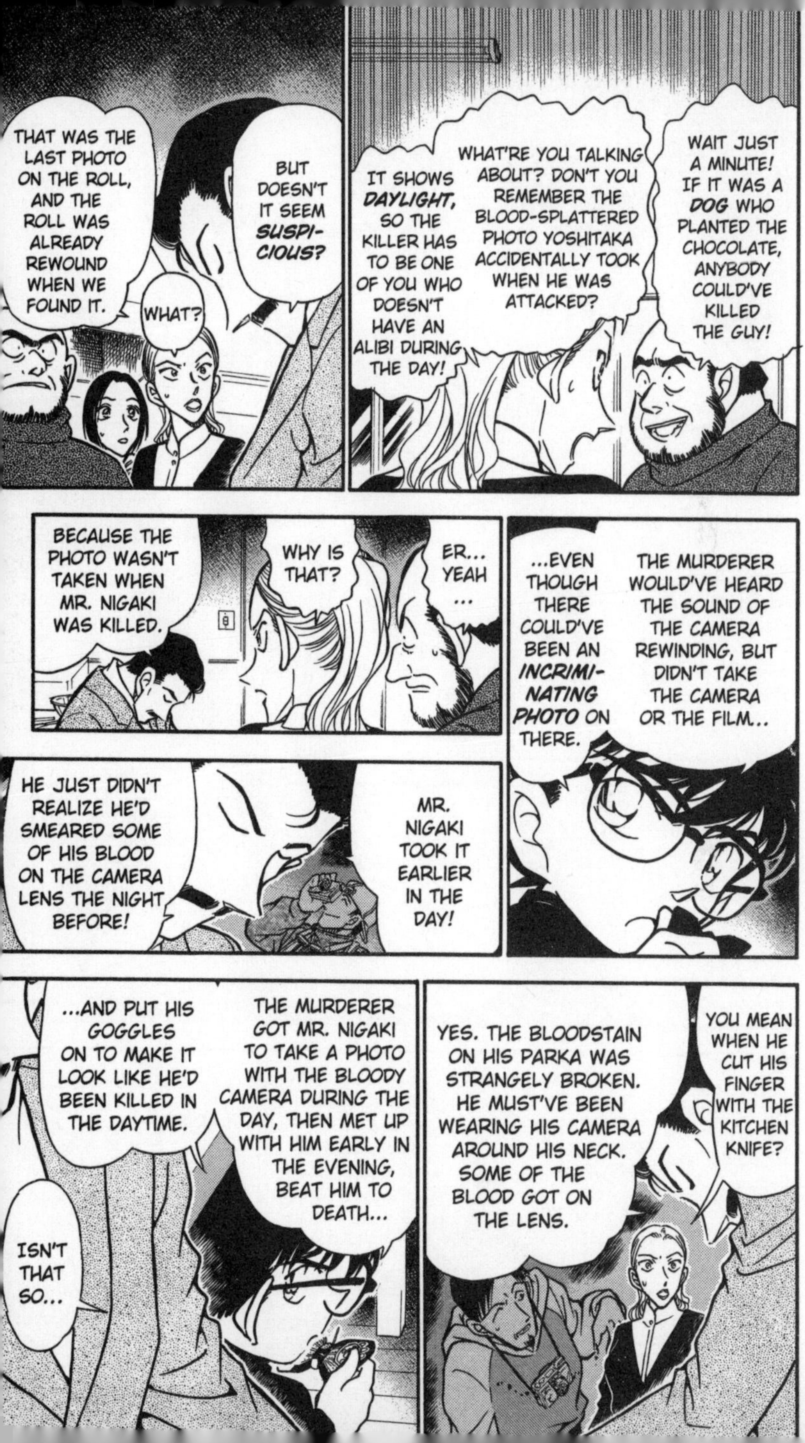
WAIT JUST A MINUTE! IF IT WAS A DOG WHO PLANTED THE CHOCOLATE, ANYBODY COULD'VE KILLED THE GUY!
WHAT'RE YOU TALKING ABOUT? DON'T YOU REMEMBER THE BLOOD-SPLATTERED PHOTO YOSHITAKA ACCIDENTALLY TOOK WHEN HE WAS ATTACKED?
IT SHOWS DAYLIGHT, SO THE KILLER HAS TO BE ONE OF YOU WHO DOESN'T HAVE AN ALIBI DURING THE DAY!
BUT DOESN'T IT SEEM SUSPICIOUS?
THAT WAS THE LAST PHOTO ON THE ROLL, AND THE ROLL WAS ALREADY REWOUND WHEN WE FOUND IT.
WHAT?
THE MURDERER WOULD'VE HEARD THE SOUND OF THE CAMERA REWINDING, BUT DIDN'T TAKE THE CAMERA OR THE FILM...
...EVEN THOUGH THERE COULD'VE BEEN AN INCRIMINATING PHOTO ON THERE.
ER... YEAH ...
WHY IS THAT?
BECAUSE THE PHOTO WASN'T TAKEN WHEN MR. NIGAKI WAS KILLED.
MR. NIGAKI TOOK IT EARLIER IN THE DAY!
HE JUST DIDN'T REALIZE HE'D SMEARED SOME OF HIS BLOOD ON THE CAMERA LENS THE NIGHT BEFORE!
YOU MEAN WHEN HE CUT HIS FINGER WITH THE KITCHEN KNIFE?
YES. THE BLOODSTAIN ON HIS PARKA WAS STRANGELY BROKEN. HE MUST'VE BEEN WEARING HIS CAMERA AROUND HIS NECK. SOME OF THE BLOOD GOT ON THE LENS.
THE MURDERER GOT MR. NIGAKI TO TAKE A PHOTO WITH THE BLOODY CAMERA DURING THE DAY, THEN MET UP WITH HIM EARLY IN THE EVENING, BEAT HIM TO DEATH...
...AND PUT HIS GOGGLES ON TO MAKE IT LOOK LIKE HE'D BEEN KILLED IN THE DAYTIME.
ISN'T THAT SO...

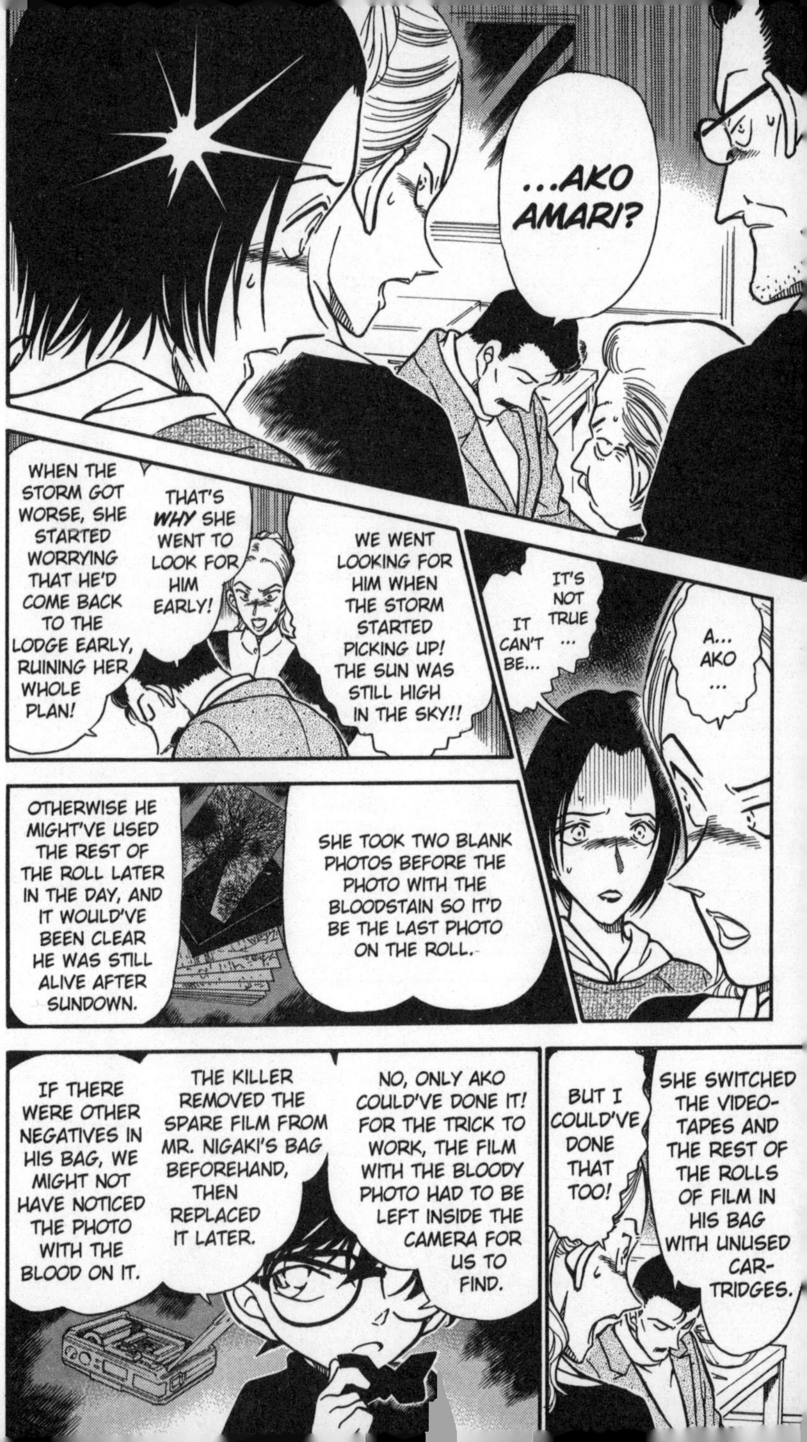
...AKO AMARI?
A... AKO ...
IT'S NOT TRUE ...
IT CAN'T BE...
WE WENT LOOKING FOR HIM WHEN THE STORM STARTED PICKING UP! THE SUN WAS STILL HIGH IN THE SKY!!
THAT'S *WHY* SHE WENT TO LOOK FOR HIM EARLY!
WHEN THE STORM GOT WORSE, SHE STARTED WORRYING THAT HE'D COME BACK TO THE LODGE EARLY, RUINING HER WHOLE PLAN!
SHE TOOK TWO BLANK PHOTOS BEFORE THE PHOTO WITH THE BLOODSTAIN SO IT'D BE THE LAST PHOTO ON THE ROLL.
OTHERWISE HE MIGHT'VE USED THE REST OF THE ROLL LATER IN THE DAY, AND IT WOULD'VE BEEN CLEAR HE WAS STILL ALIVE AFTER SUNDOWN.
SHE SWITCHED THE VIDEO-TAPES AND THE REST OF THE ROLLS OF FILM IN HIS BAG WITH UNUSED CAR-TRIDGES.
BUT I COULD'VE DONE THAT TOO!
NO, ONLY AKO COULD'VE DONE IT! FOR THE TRICK TO WORK, THE FILM WITH THE BLOODY PHOTO HAD TO BE LEFT INSIDE THE CAMERA FOR US TO FIND.
THE KILLER REMOVED THE SPARE FILM FROM MR. NIGAKI'S BAG BEFOREHAND, THEN REPLACED IT LATER.
IF THERE WERE OTHER NEGATIVES IN HIS BAG, WE MIGHT NOT HAVE NOTICED THE PHOTO WITH THE BLOOD ON IT.

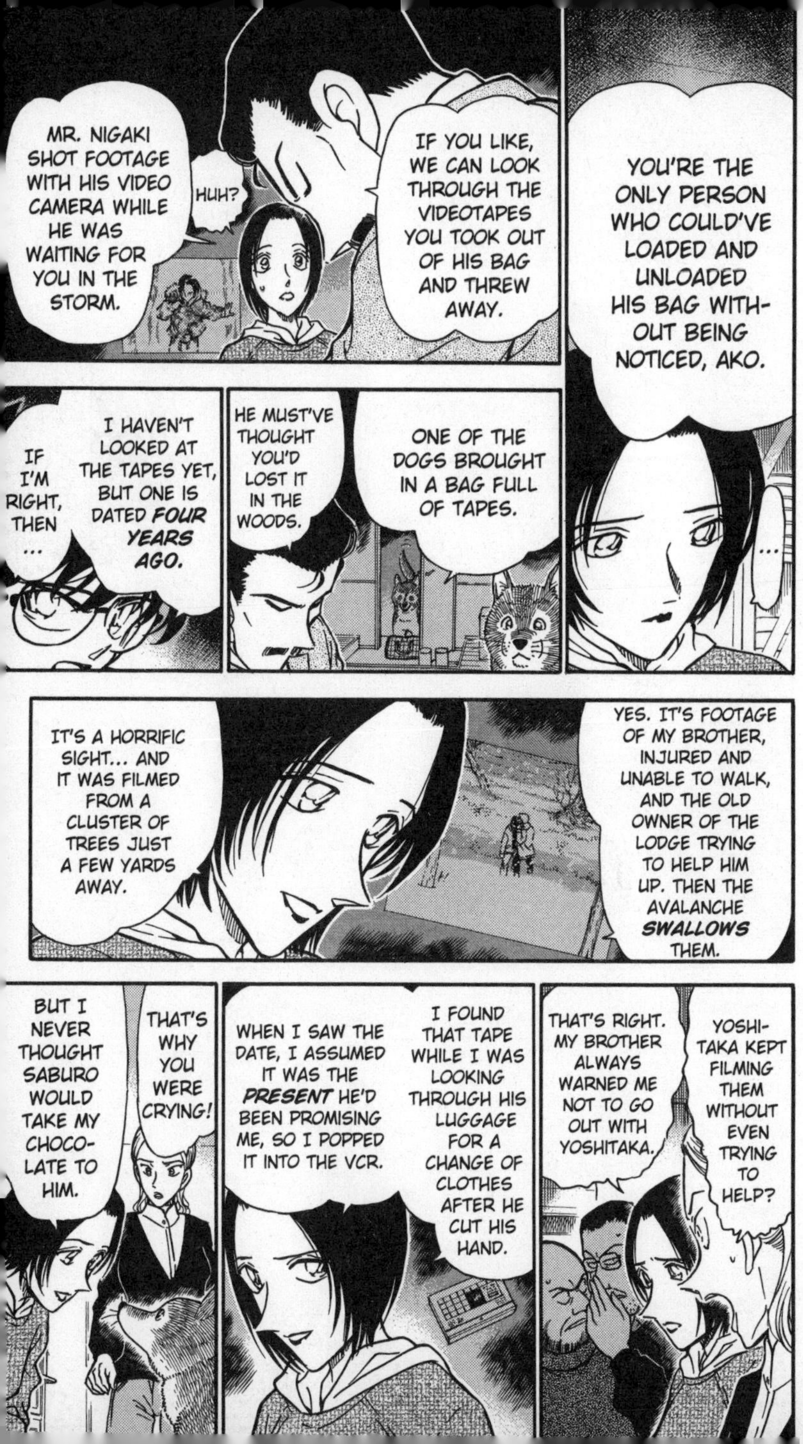
YOU'RE THE ONLY PERSON WHO COULD'VE LOADED AND UNLOADED HIS BAG WITHOUT BEING NOTICED, AKO.
IF YOU LIKE, WE CAN LOOK THROUGH THE VIDEOTAPES YOU TOOK OUT OF HIS BAG AND THREW AWAY.
HUH?
MR. NIGAKI SHOT FOOTAGE WITH HIS VIDEO CAMERA WHILE HE WAS WAITING FOR YOU IN THE STORM.
...
ONE OF THE DOGS BROUGHT IN A BAG FULL OF TAPES.
HE MUST'VE THOUGHT YOU'D LOST IT IN THE WOODS.
I HAVEN'T LOOKED AT THE TAPES YET, BUT ONE IS DATED ***FOUR YEARS AGO.***
IF I'M RIGHT, THEN ...
YES. IT'S FOOTAGE OF MY BROTHER, INJURED AND UNABLE TO WALK, AND THE OLD OWNER OF THE LODGE TRYING TO HELP HIM UP. THEN THE AVALANCHE ***SWALLOWS*** THEM.
IT'S A HORRIFIC SIGHT... AND IT WAS FILMED FROM A CLUSTER OF TREES JUST A FEW YARDS AWAY.
YOSHITAKA KEPT FILMING THEM WITHOUT EVEN TRYING TO HELP?
THAT'S RIGHT. MY BROTHER ALWAYS WARNED ME NOT TO GO OUT WITH YOSHITAKA.
I FOUND THAT TAPE WHILE I WAS LOOKING THROUGH HIS LUGGAGE FOR A CHANGE OF CLOTHES AFTER HE CUT HIS HAND.
WHEN I SAW THE DATE, I ASSUMED IT WAS THE ***PRESENT*** HE'D BEEN PROMISING ME, SO I POPPED IT INTO THE VCR.
THAT'S WHY YOU WERE CRYING!
BUT I NEVER THOUGHT SABURO WOULD TAKE MY CHOCOLATE TO HIM.

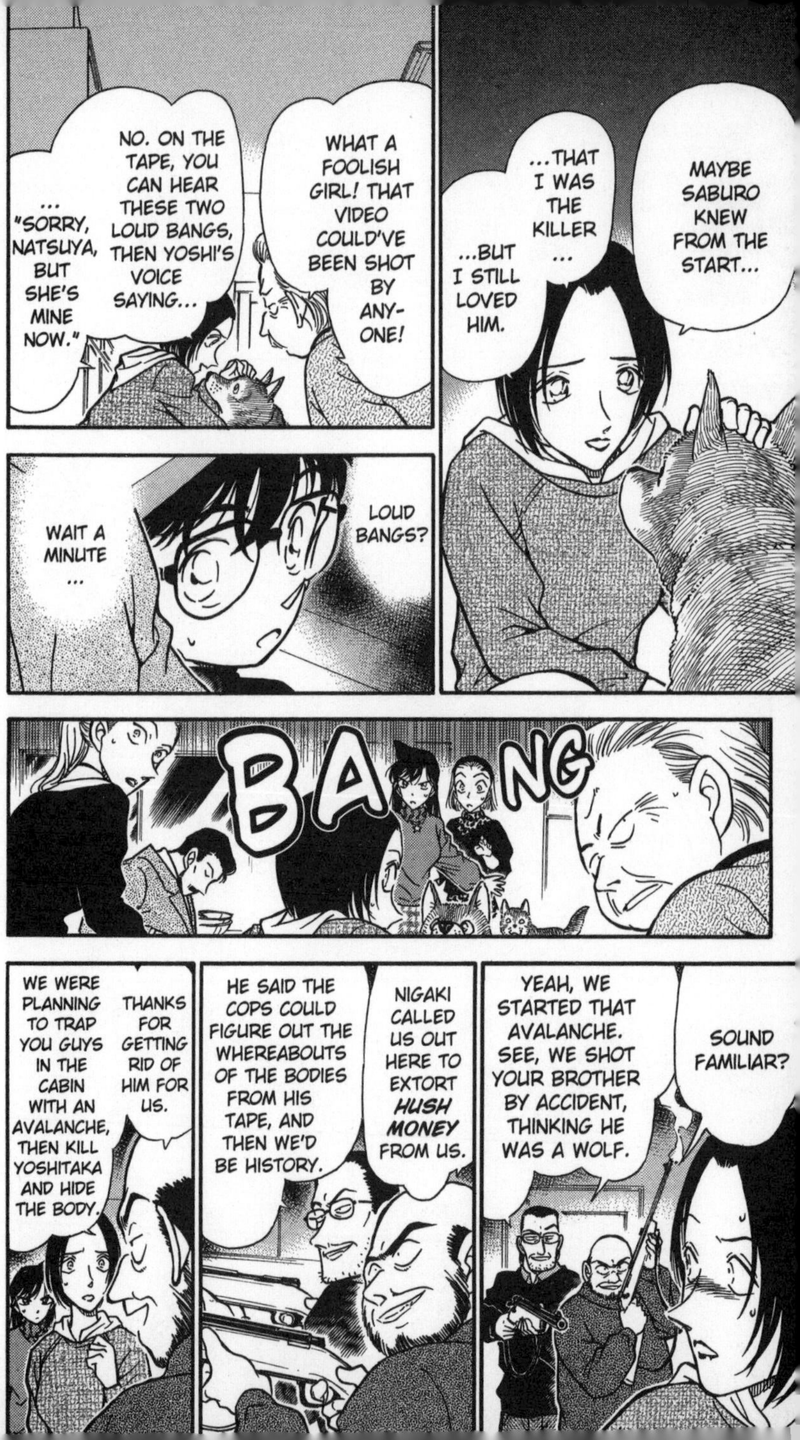
MAYBE SABURO KNEW FROM THE START...
...THAT I WAS THE KILLER...
...BUT I STILL LOVED HIM.
WHAT A FOOLISH GIRL! THAT VIDEO COULD'VE BEEN SHOT BY ANY-ONE!
NO. ON THE TAPE, YOU CAN HEAR THESE TWO LOUD BANGS, THEN YOSHI'S VOICE SAYING...
... "SORRY, NATSUYA, BUT SHE'S MINE NOW."
LOUD BANGS?
WAIT A MINUTE ...
BANG
SOUND FAMILIAR?
YEAH, WE STARTED THAT AVALANCHE. SEE, WE SHOT YOUR BROTHER BY ACCIDENT, THINKING HE WAS A WOLF.
NIGAKI CALLED US OUT HERE TO EXTORT ***HUSH MONEY*** FROM US.
HE SAID THE COPS COULD FIGURE OUT THE WHEREABOUTS OF THE BODIES FROM HIS TAPE, AND THEN WE'D BE HISTORY.
THANKS FOR GETTING RID OF HIM FOR US.
WE WERE PLANNING TO TRAP YOU GUYS IN THE CABIN WITH AN AVALANCHE, THEN KILL YOSHITAKA AND HIDE THE BODY.

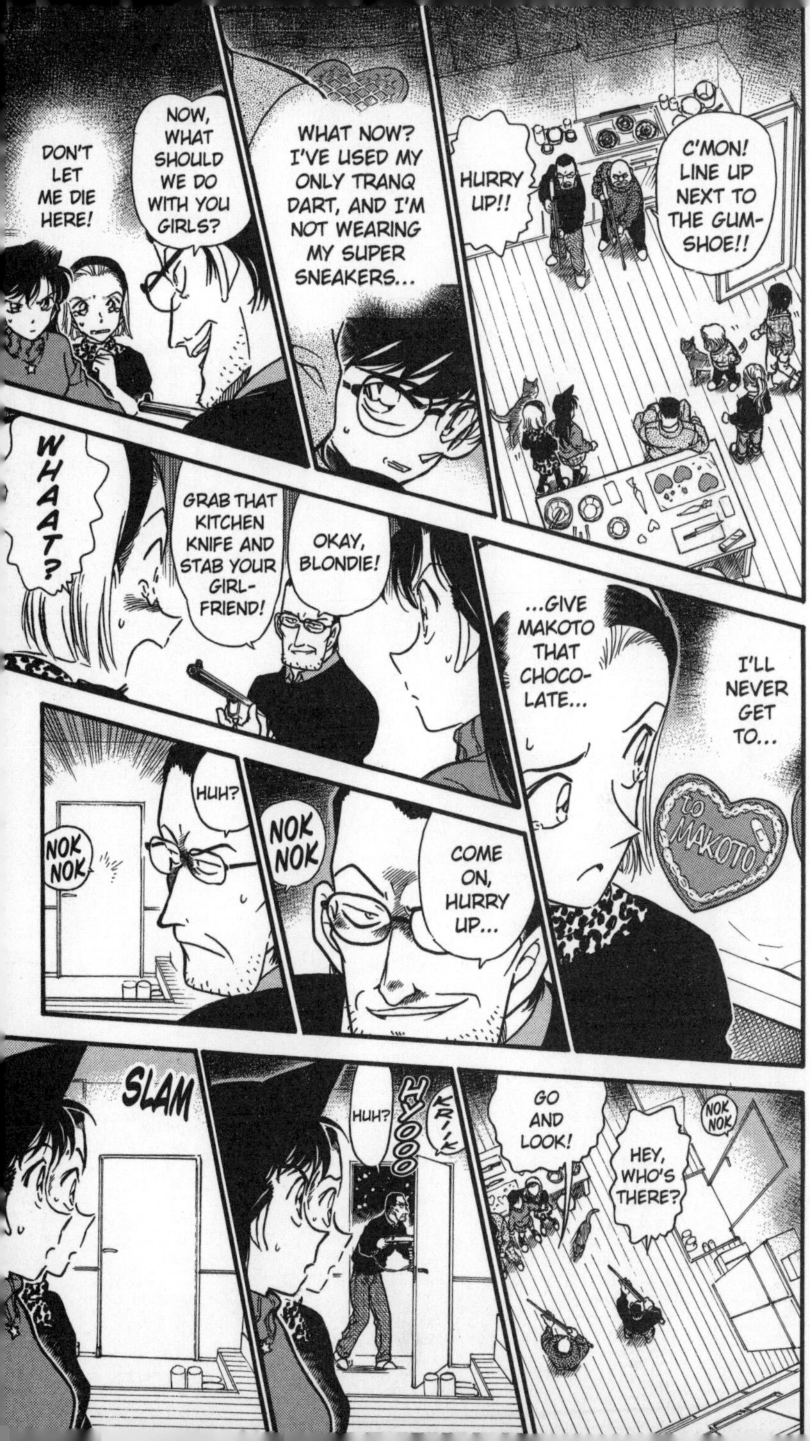
C'MON! LINE UP NEXT TO THE GUM-SHOE!!
HURRY UP!!
WHAT NOW? I'VE USED MY ONLY TRANQ DART, AND I'M NOT WEARING MY SUPER SNEAKERS...
NOW, WHAT SHOULD WE DO WITH YOU GIRLS?
DON'T LET ME DIE HERE!
OKAY, BLONDIE!
GRAB THAT KITCHEN KNIFE AND STAB YOUR GIRL-FRIEND!
WHAAT?
I'LL NEVER GET TO...
...GIVE MAKOTO THAT CHOCO-LATE...
to MAKOTO
COME ON, HURRY UP...
NOK NOK
HUH?
NOK NOK
NOK NOK
HEY, WHO'S THERE?
GO AND LOOK!
KRIK
HYOOOO
HUH?
SLAM

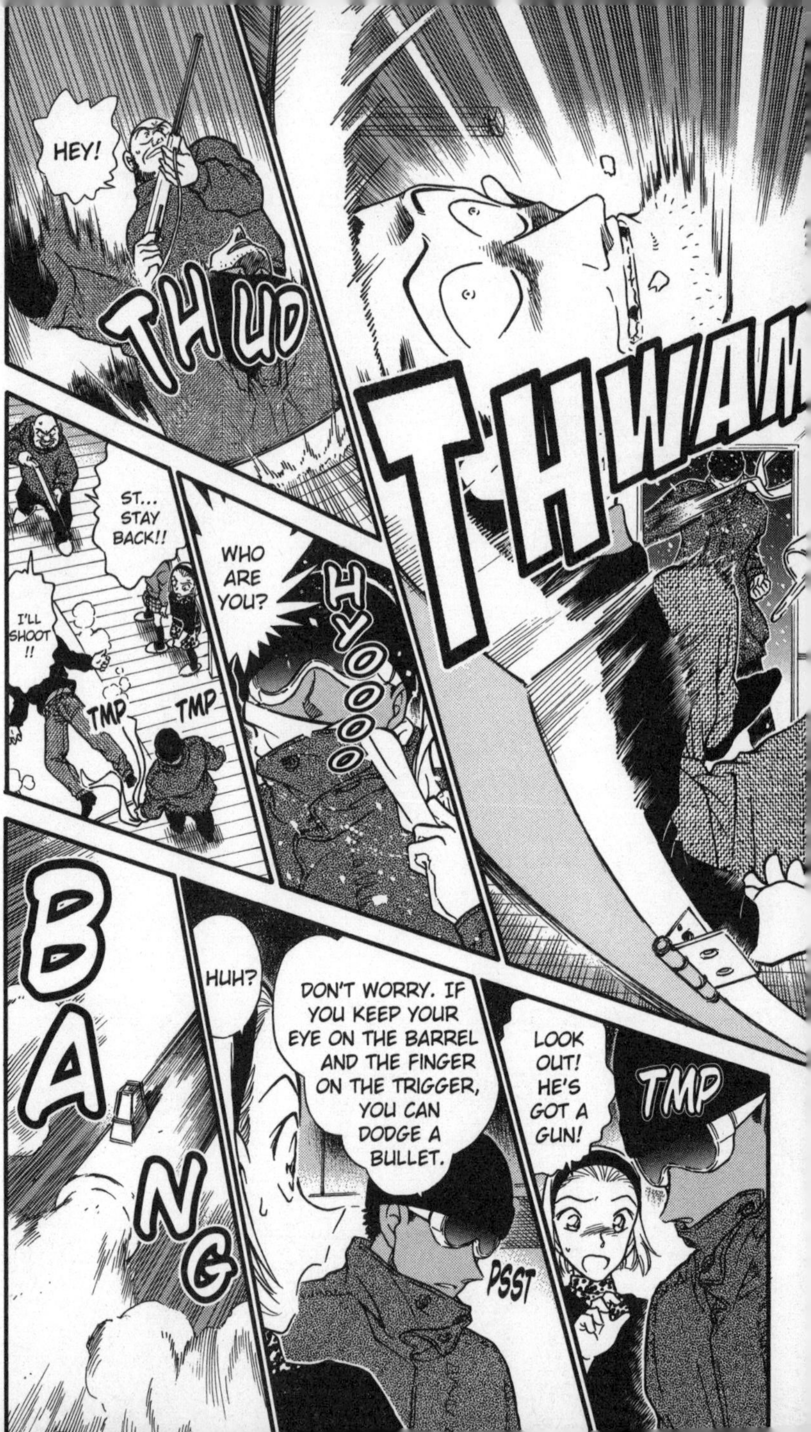
THWAM
HEY!
THUD
WHO ARE YOU?
HYOOOOO
ST... STAY BACK!!
I'LL SHOOT !!
TMP
TMP
LOOK OUT! HE'S GOT A GUN!
TMP
HUH?
DON'T WORRY. IF YOU KEEP YOUR EYE ON THE BARREL AND THE FINGER ON THE TRIGGER, YOU CAN DODGE A BULLET.
PSST
BANG

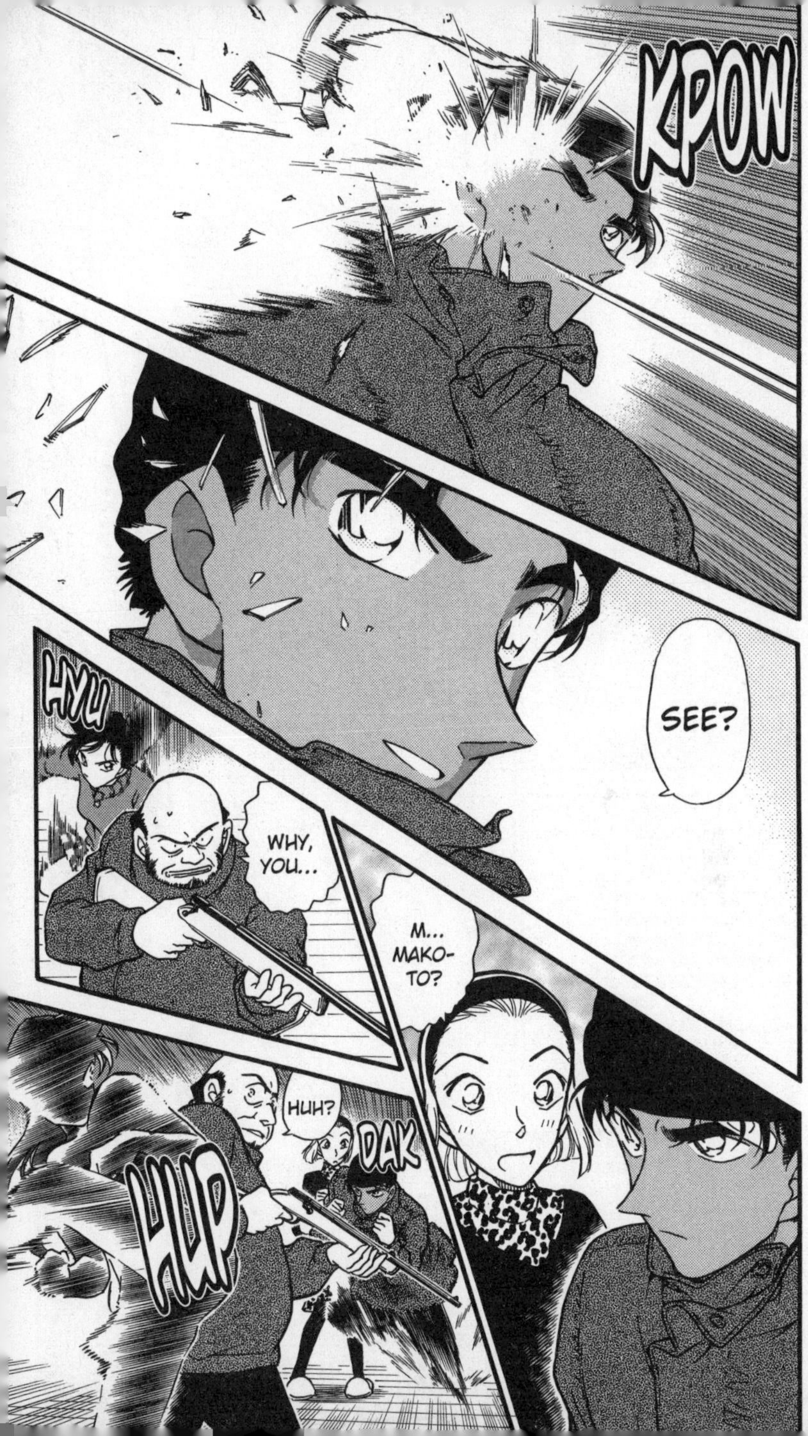
KPOW
SEE?
M... MAKO-TO?
HYU
WHY, YOU...
DAK
HUH?
HUP

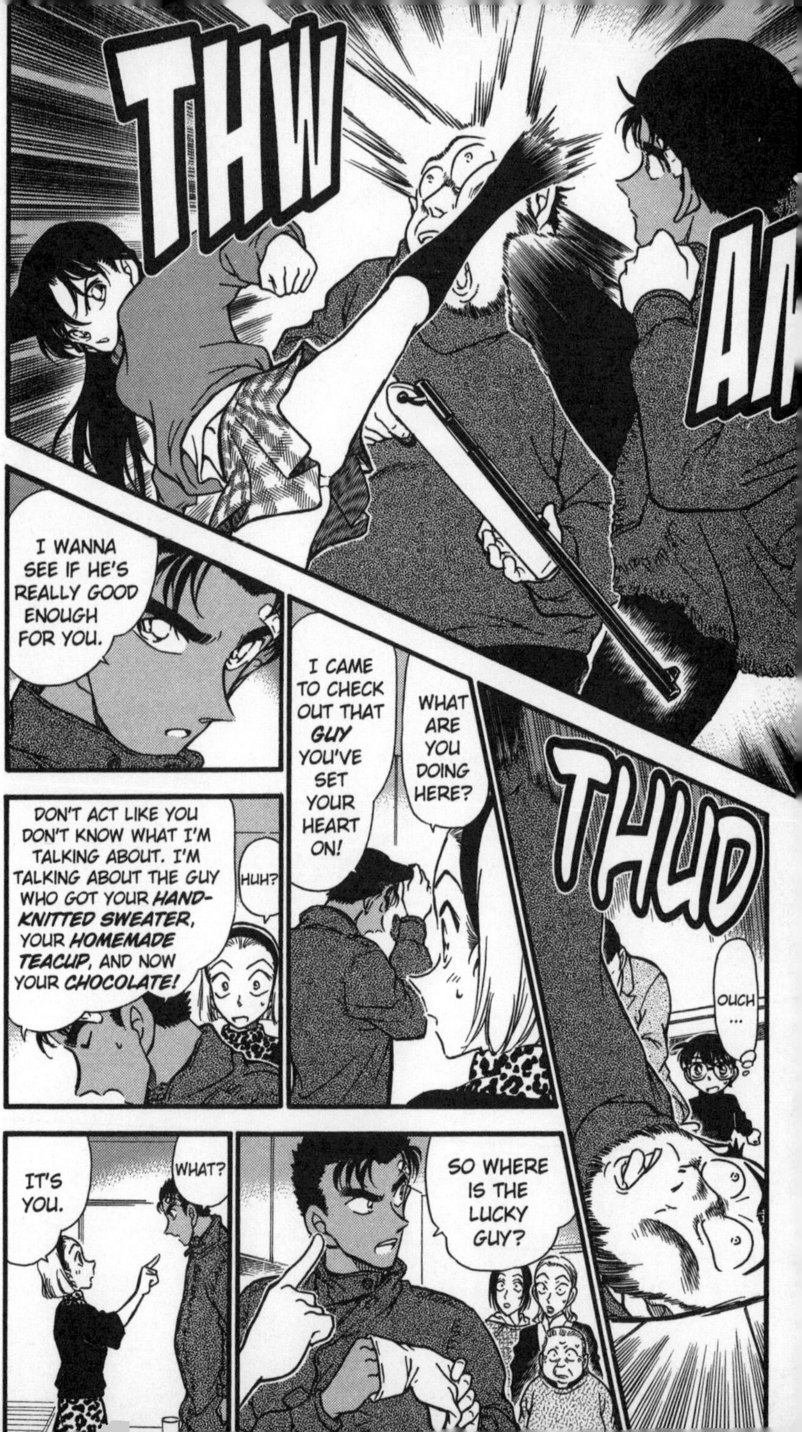

THW
A
THUD
OUCH ...
WHAT ARE YOU DOING HERE?
I CAME TO CHECK OUT THAT **GUY** YOU'VE SET YOUR HEART ON!
HUH?
I WANNA SEE IF HE'S REALLY GOOD ENOUGH FOR YOU.
DON'T ACT LIKE YOU DON'T KNOW WHAT I'M TALKING ABOUT. I'M TALKING ABOUT THE GUY WHO GOT YOUR ***HAND-KNITTED SWEATER***, YOUR ***HOMEMADE TEACUP***, AND NOW YOUR ***CHOCOLATE!***
SO WHERE IS THE LUCKY GUY?
WHAT?
IT'S YOU.

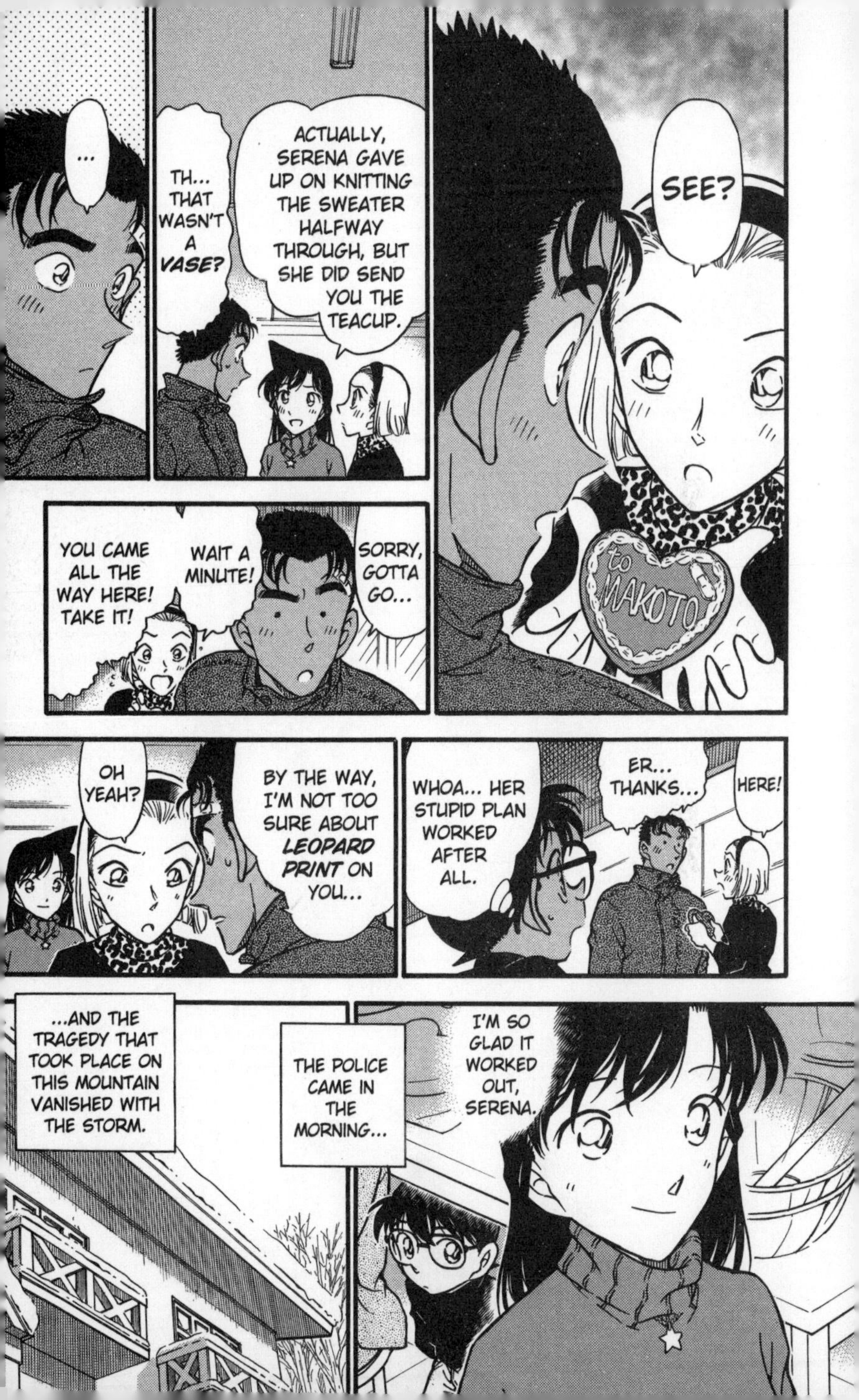

SEE?
ACTUALLY, SERENA GAVE UP ON KNITTING THE SWEATER HALFWAY THROUGH, BUT SHE DID SEND YOU THE TEACUP.
TH... THAT WASN'T A *VASE?*
...
SORRY, GOTTA GO...
WAIT A MINUTE!
YOU CAME ALL THE WAY HERE! TAKE IT!
to MAKOTO
HERE!
ER... THANKS...
WHOA... HER STUPID PLAN WORKED AFTER ALL.
BY THE WAY, I'M NOT TOO SURE ABOUT *LEOPARD PRINT* ON YOU...
OH YEAH?
I'M SO GLAD IT WORKED OUT, SERENA.
THE POLICE CAME IN THE MORNING...
...AND THE TRAGEDY THAT TOOK PLACE ON THIS MOUNTAIN VANISHED WITH THE STORM.

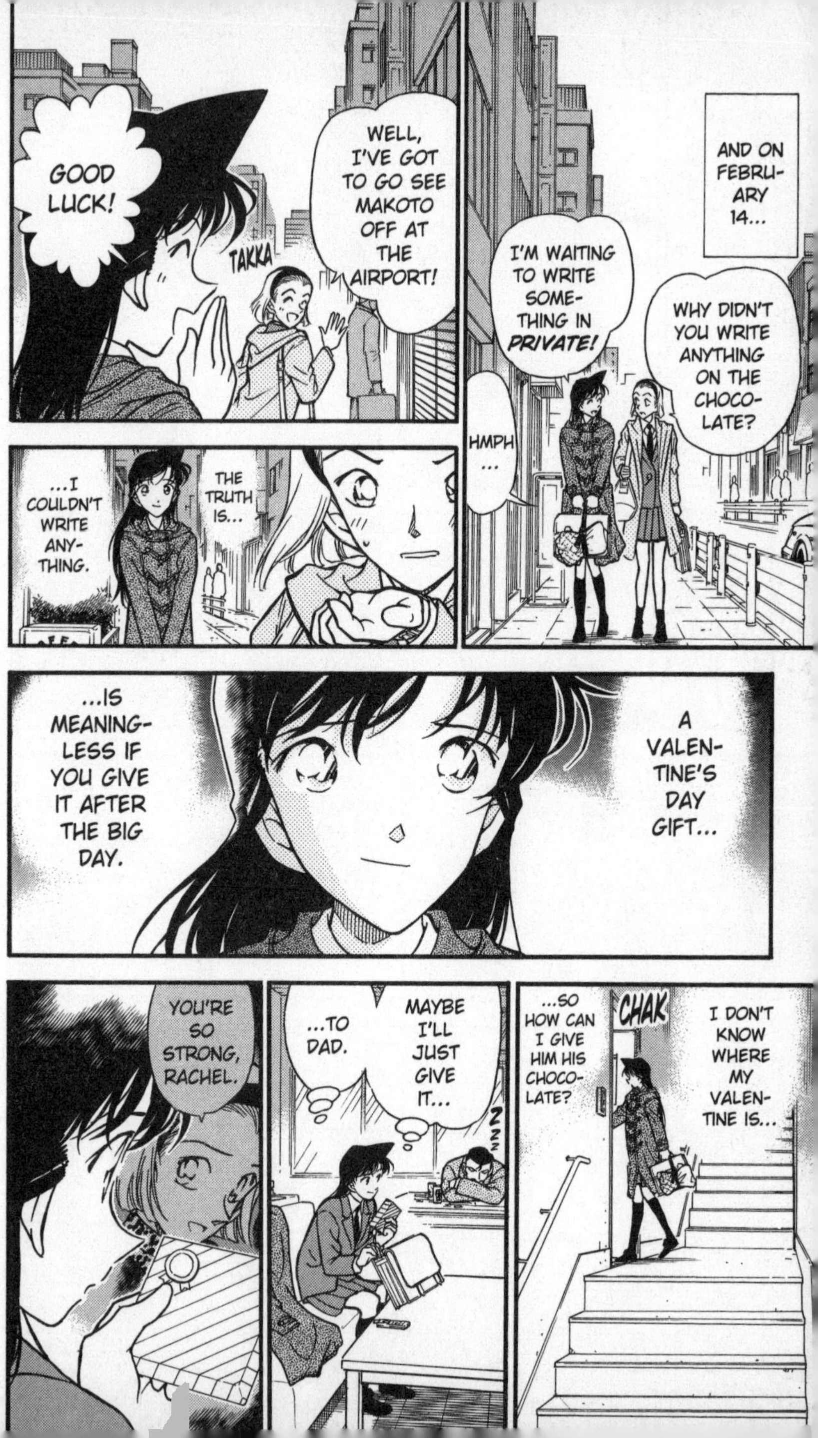
AND ON FEBRUARY 14...
WHY DIDN'T YOU WRITE ANYTHING ON THE CHOCOLATE?
I'M WAITING TO WRITE SOMETHING IN *PRIVATE!*
HMPH...
WELL, I'VE GOT TO GO SEE MAKOTO OFF AT THE AIRPORT!
TAKKA
GOOD LUCK!
THE TRUTH IS...
...I COULDN'T WRITE ANYTHING.
A VALENTINE'S DAY GIFT...
...IS MEANINGLESS IF YOU GIVE IT AFTER THE BIG DAY.
I DON'T KNOW WHERE MY VALENTINE IS...
CHAK
...SO HOW CAN I GIVE HIM HIS CHOCOLATE?
MAYBE I'LL JUST GIVE IT...
...TO DAD.
ZZZ
YOU'RE SO STRONG, RACHEL.

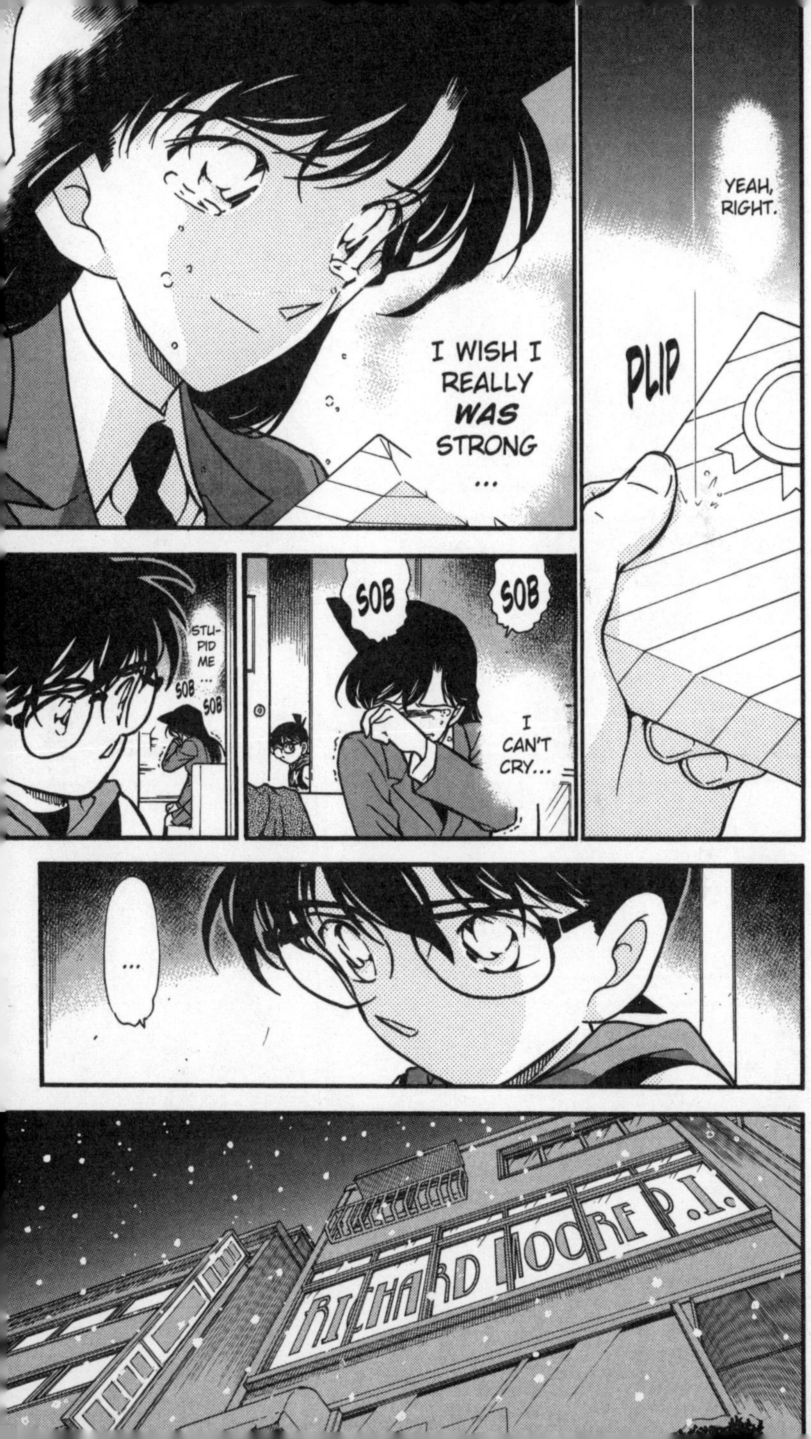
YEAH, RIGHT.
PLIP
I WISH I REALLY WAS STRONG ...
SOB
SOB
I CAN'T CRY...
STU-PID ME ...
SOB
SOB
...
RICHARD MOORE P.I.

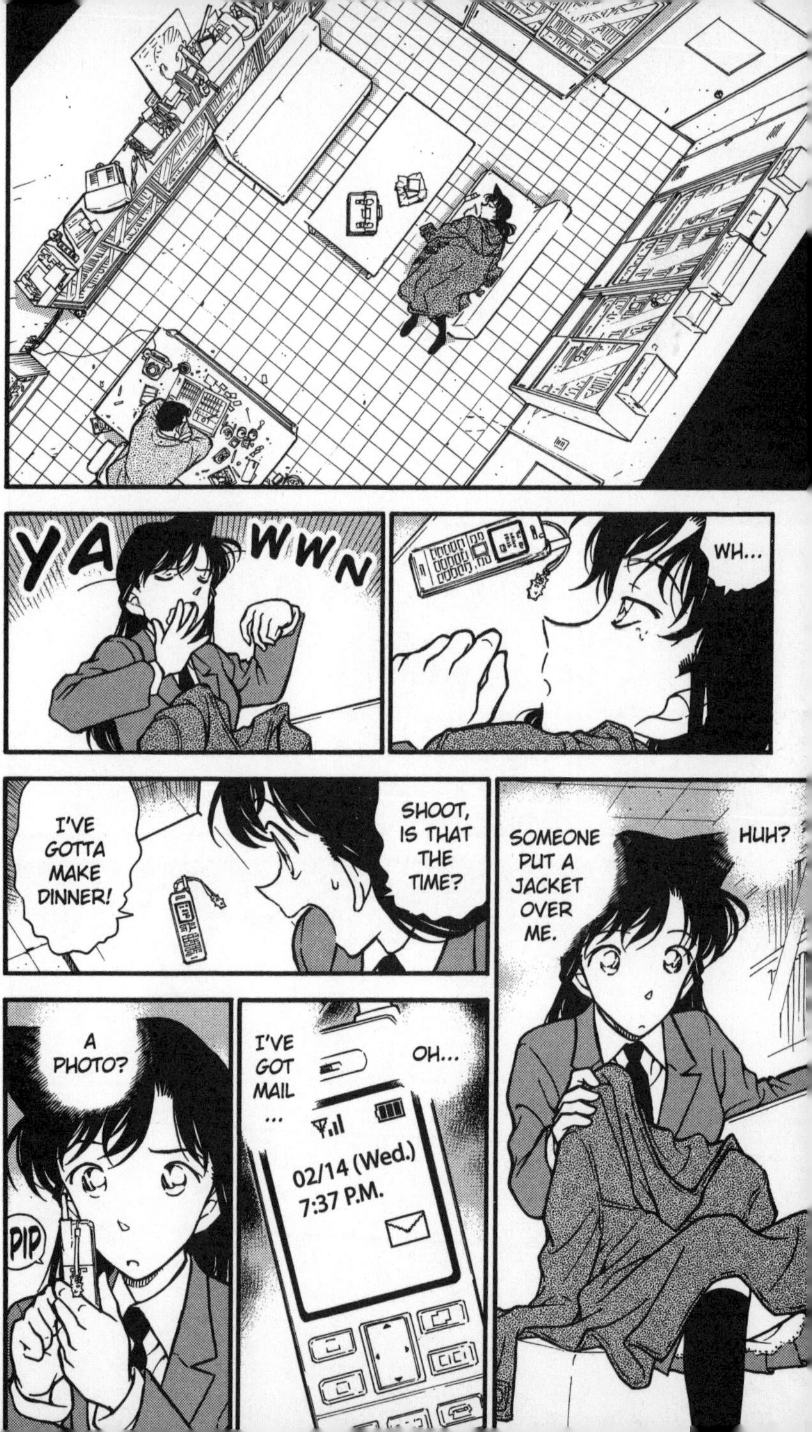
WH...
YAWWN
HUH?
SOMEONE PUT A JACKET OVER ME.
SHOOT, IS THAT THE TIME?
I'VE GOTTA MAKE DINNER!
OH...
I'VE GOT MAIL ...
02/14 (Wed.)
7:37 P.M.
A PHOTO?
PIP

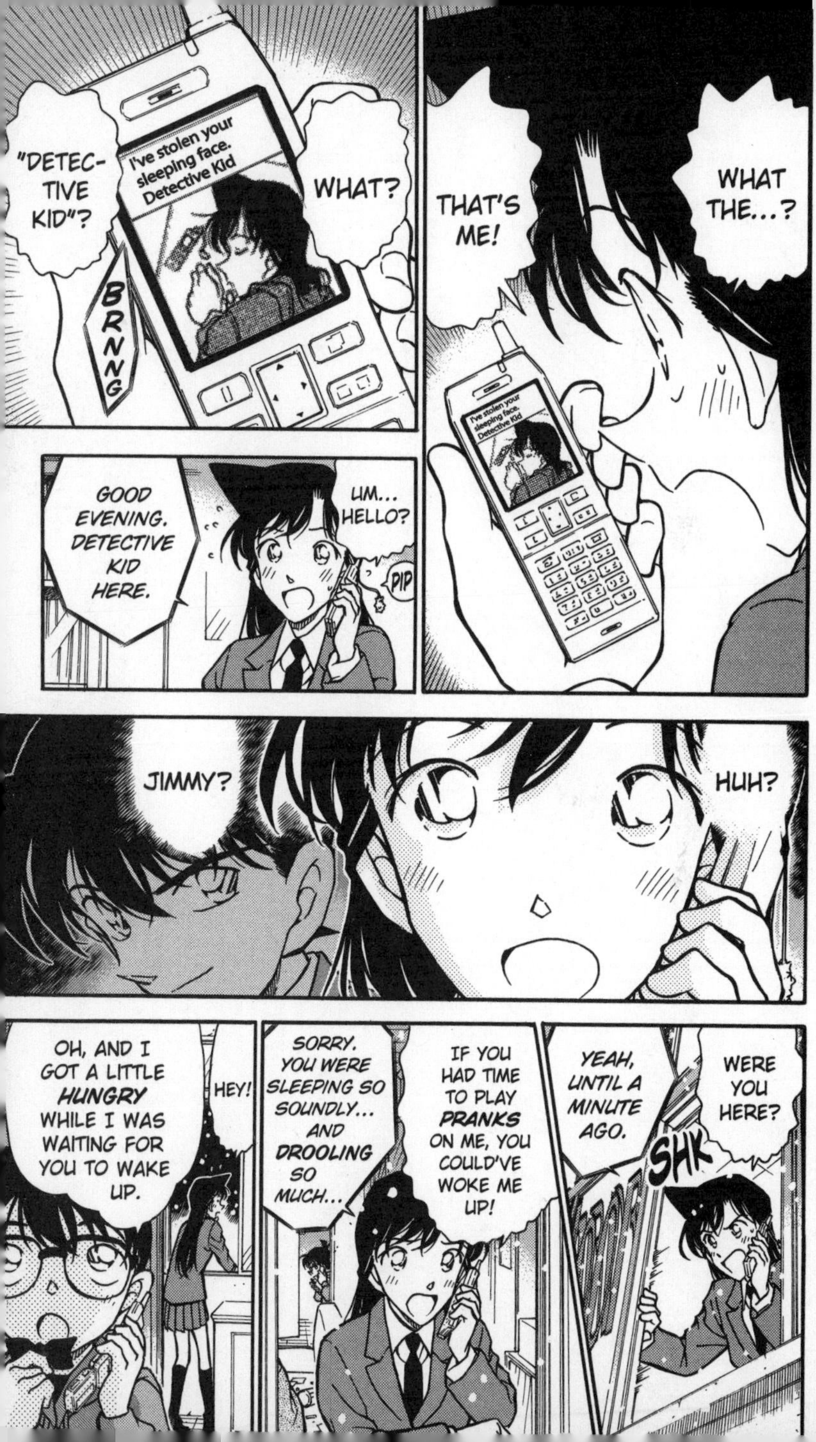
WHAT THE...?
THAT'S ME!
I've stolen your sleeping face. Detective Kid
WHAT?
I've stolen your sleeping face. Detective Kid
"DETEC-TIVE KID"?
BRNNG
UM... HELLO?
PIP
GOOD EVENING. DETECTIVE KID HERE.
HUH?
JIMMY?
WERE YOU HERE?
YEAH, UNTIL A MINUTE AGO.
SHK
IF YOU HAD TIME TO PLAY PRANKS ON ME, YOU COULD'VE WOKE ME UP!
SORRY. YOU WERE SLEEPING SO SOUNDLY... AND DROOLING SO MUCH...
HEY!
OH, AND I GOT A LITTLE HUNGRY WHILE I WAS WAITING FOR YOU TO WAKE UP.

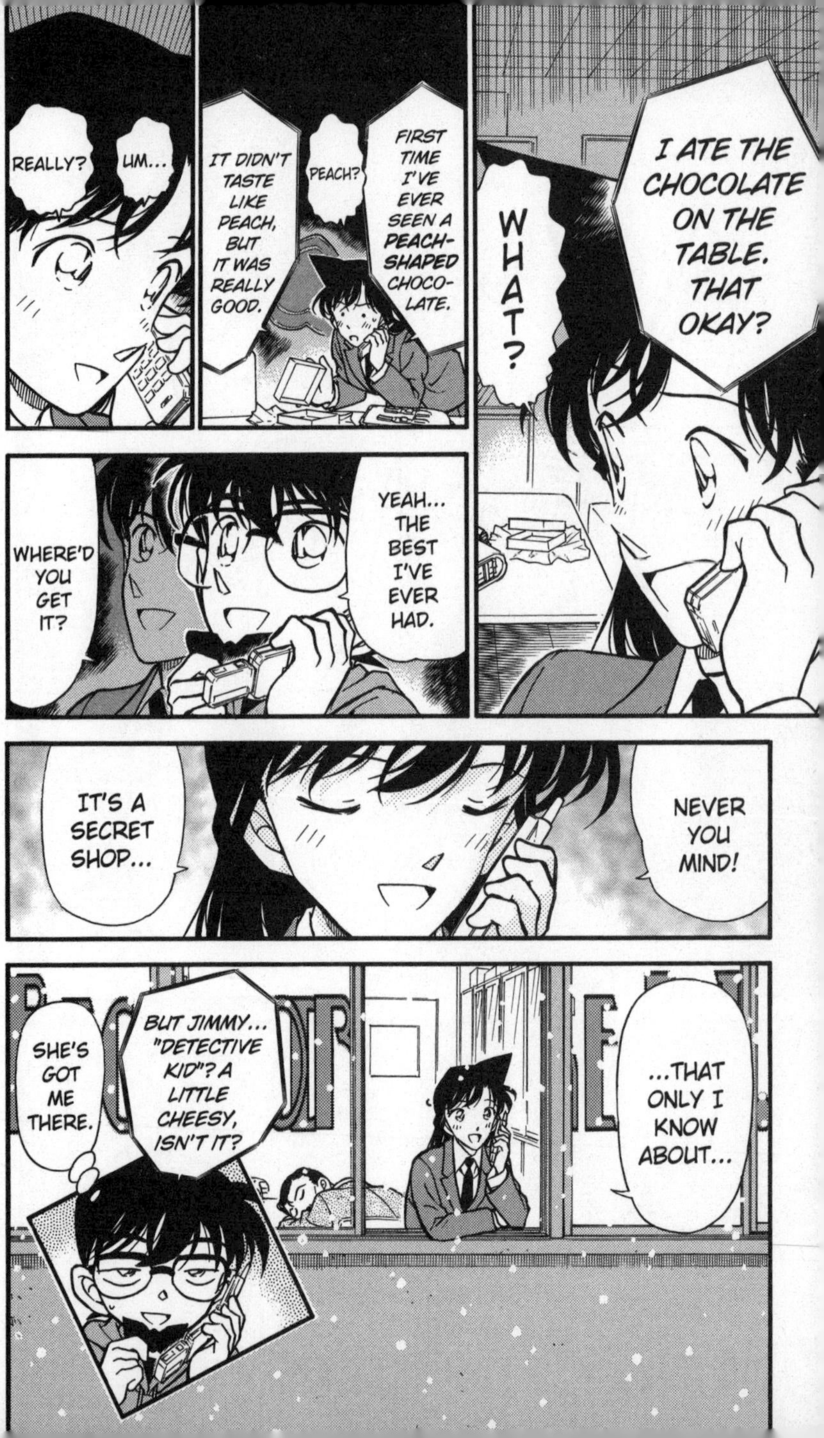

I ATE THE CHOCOLATE ON THE TABLE. THAT OKAY?
WHAT?
FIRST TIME I'VE EVER SEEN A PEACH-SHAPED CHOCOLATE.
PEACH?
IT DIDN'T TASTE LIKE PEACH, BUT IT WAS REALLY GOOD.
UM...
REALLY?
YEAH... THE BEST I'VE EVER HAD.
WHERE'D YOU GET IT?
NEVER YOU MIND!
IT'S A SECRET SHOP...
...THAT ONLY I KNOW ABOUT...
BUT JIMMY... "DETECTIVE KID"? A LITTLE CHEESY, ISN'T IT?
SHE'S GOT ME THERE.

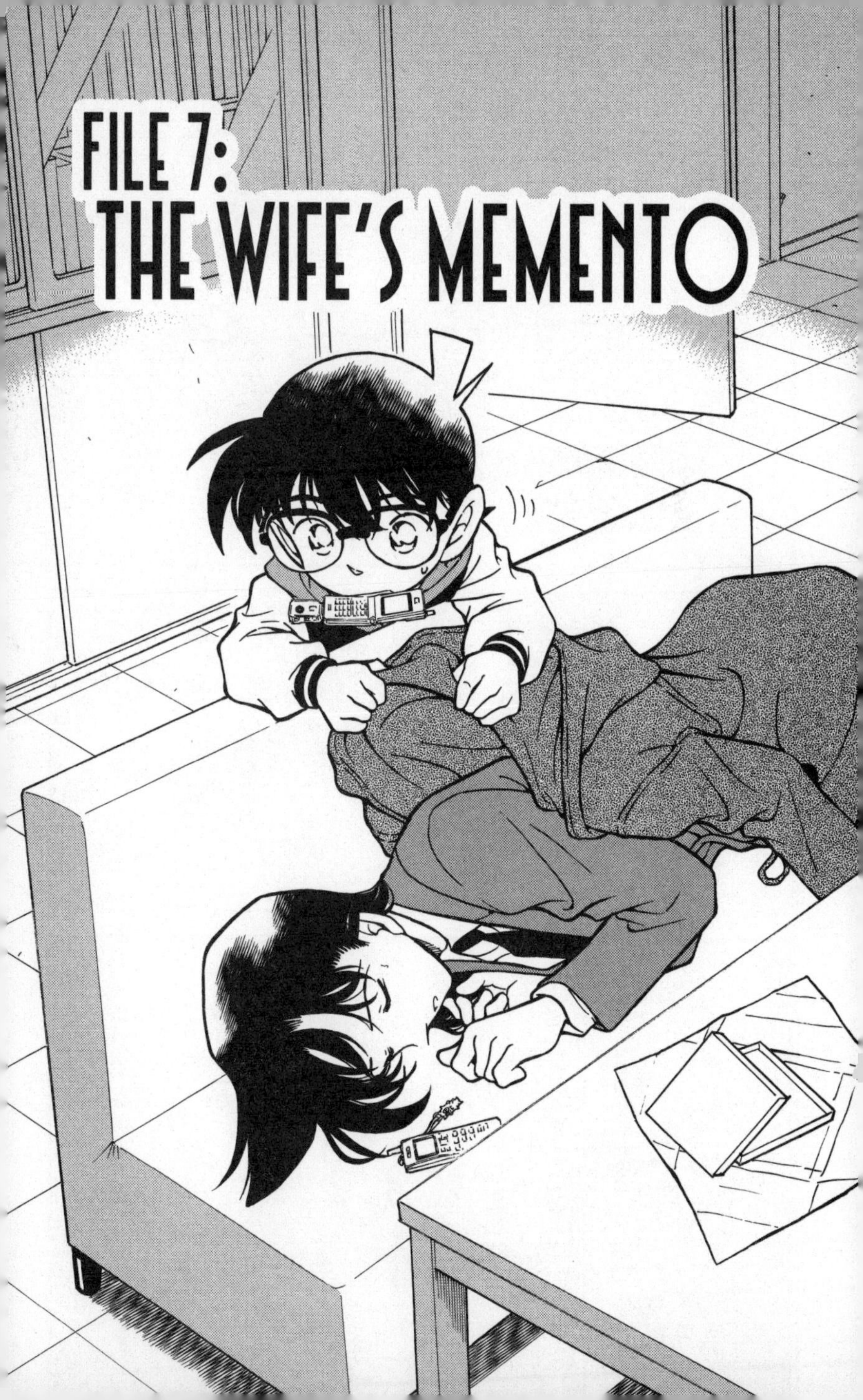
FILE 7:
THE WIFE'S MEMENTO

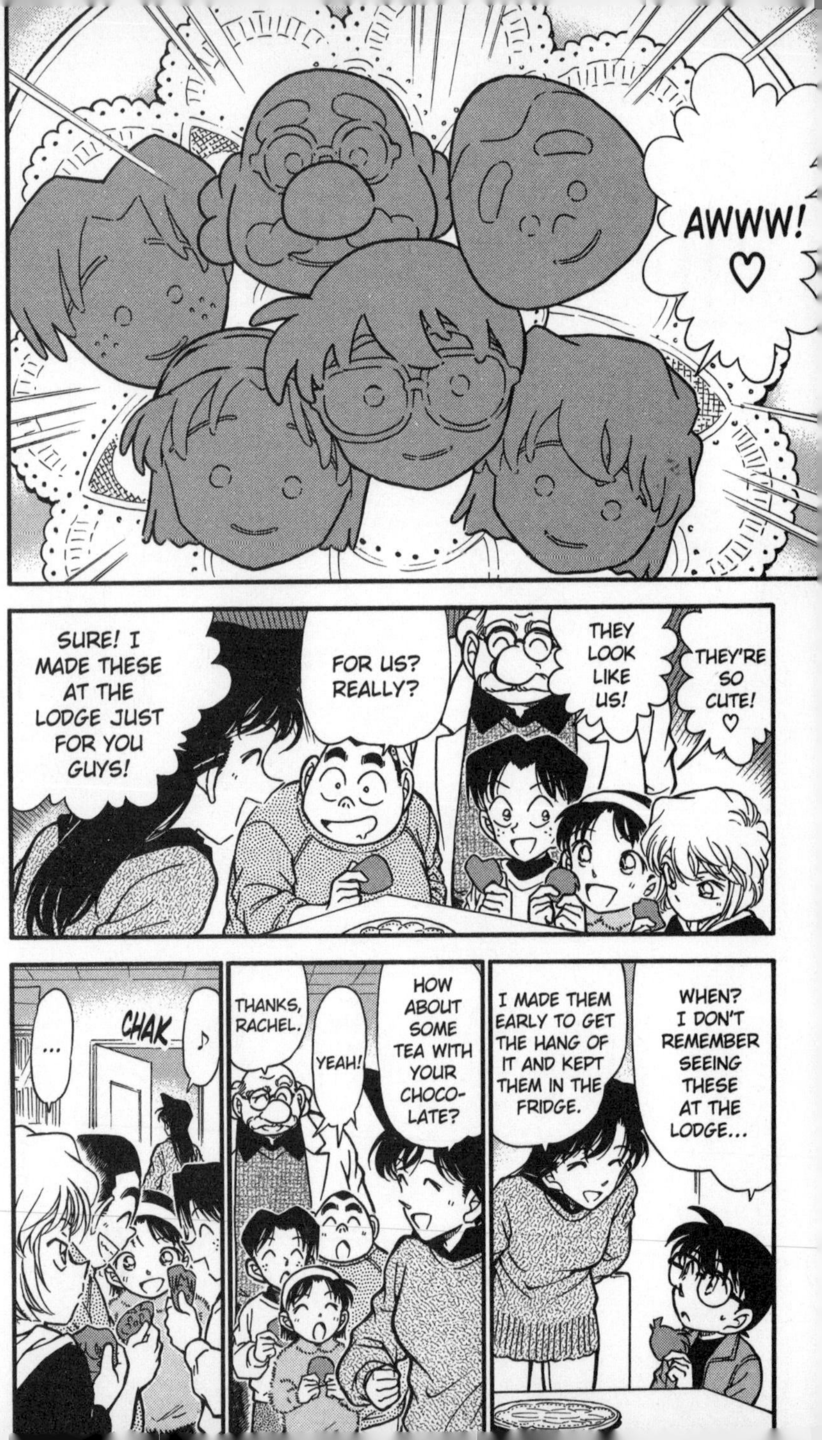
AWWW! ♥
THEY'RE SO CUTE! ♥
THEY LOOK LIKE US!
FOR US? REALLY?
SURE! I MADE THESE AT THE LODGE JUST FOR YOU GUYS!
WHEN? I DON'T REMEMBER SEEING THESE AT THE LODGE...
I MADE THEM EARLY TO GET THE HANG OF IT AND KEPT THEM IN THE FRIDGE.
HOW ABOUT SOME TEA WITH YOUR CHOCOLATE?
YEAH!
THANKS, RACHEL.
♪
CHAK
...

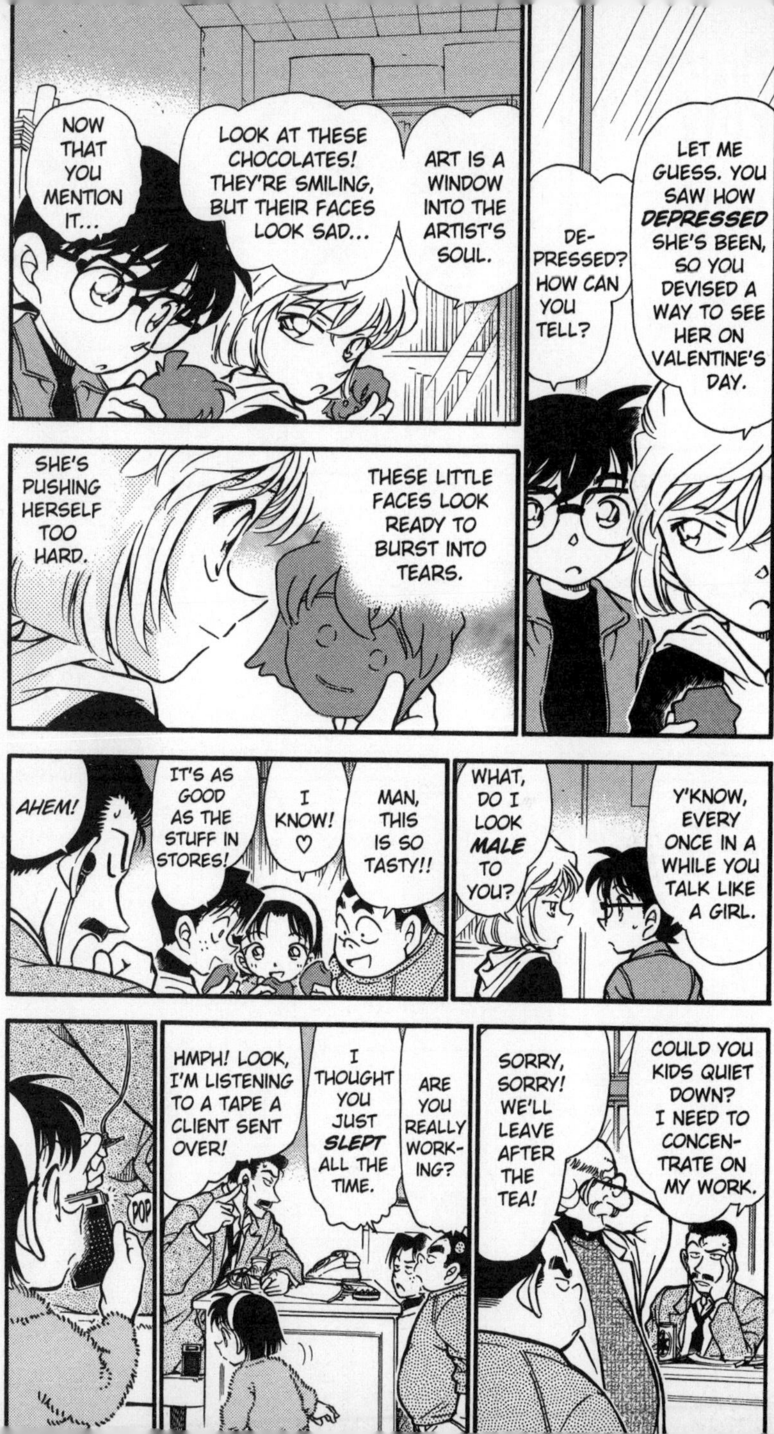
LET ME GUESS. YOU SAW HOW **DEPRESSED** SHE'S BEEN, SO YOU DEVISED A WAY TO SEE HER ON VALENTINE'S DAY.
DE-PRESSED? HOW CAN YOU TELL?
ART IS A WINDOW INTO THE ARTIST'S SOUL.
LOOK AT THESE CHOCOLATES! THEY'RE SMILING, BUT THEIR FACES LOOK SAD...
NOW THAT YOU MENTION IT...
THESE LITTLE FACES LOOK READY TO BURST INTO TEARS.
SHE'S PUSHING HERSELF TOO HARD.
Y'KNOW, EVERY ONCE IN A WHILE YOU TALK LIKE A GIRL.
WHAT, DO I LOOK **MALE** TO YOU?
MAN, THIS IS SO TASTY!!
I KNOW! ♡
IT'S AS GOOD AS THE STUFF IN STORES!
AHEM!
COULD YOU KIDS QUIET DOWN? I NEED TO CONCENTRATE ON MY WORK.
SORRY, SORRY! WE'LL LEAVE AFTER THE TEA!
ARE YOU REALLY WORKING?
I THOUGHT YOU JUST **SLEPT** ALL THE TIME.
HMPH! LOOK, I'M LISTENING TO A TAPE A CLIENT SENT OVER!
POP

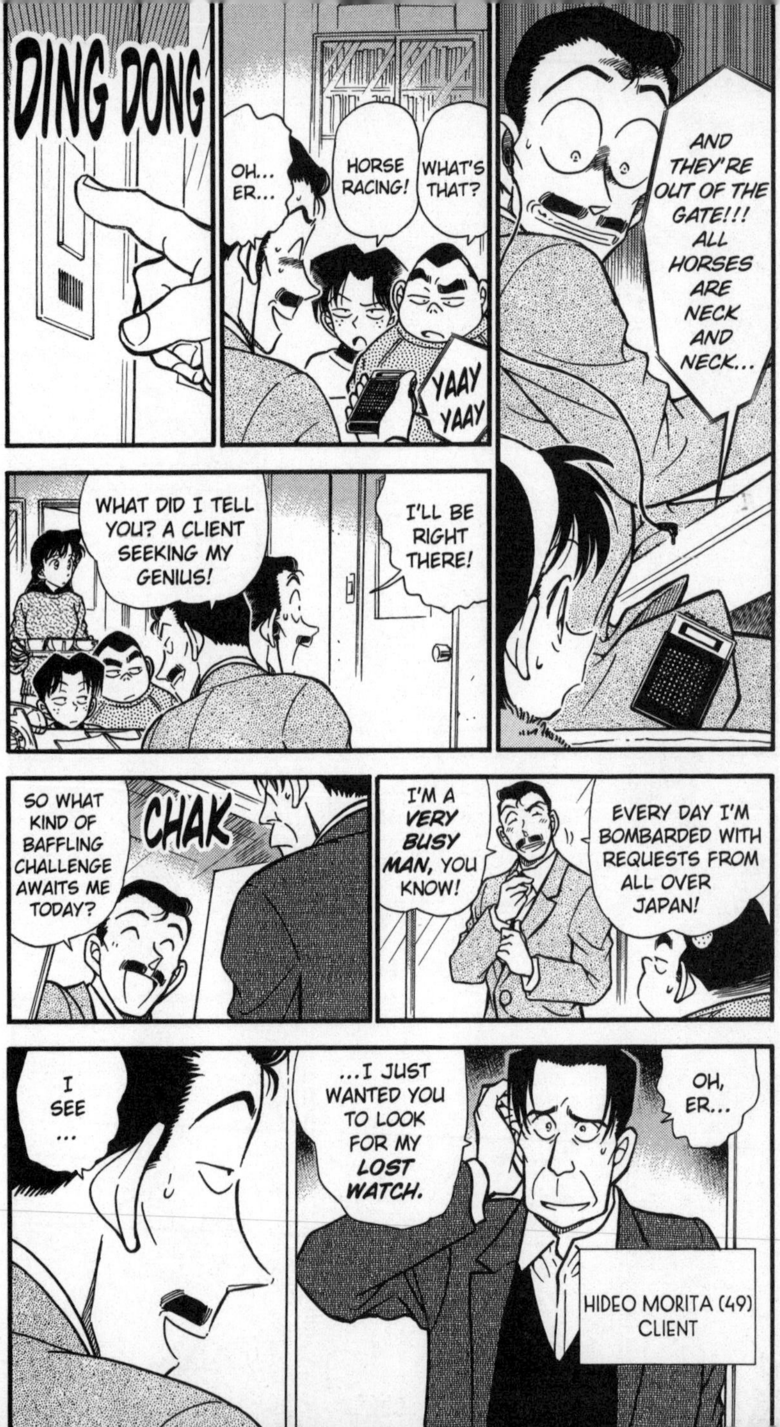
AND THEY'RE OUT OF THE GATE!!! ALL HORSES ARE NECK AND NECK...
WHAT'S THAT?
HORSE RACING!
YAAY YAAY
OH... ER...
DING DONG
I'LL BE RIGHT THERE!
WHAT DID I TELL YOU? A CLIENT SEEKING MY GENIUS!
EVERY DAY I'M BOMBARDED WITH REQUESTS FROM ALL OVER JAPAN!
I'M A VERY BUSY MAN, YOU KNOW!
CHAK
SO WHAT KIND OF BAFFLING CHALLENGE AWAITS ME TODAY?
OH, ER...
...I JUST WANTED YOU TO LOOK FOR MY LOST WATCH.
HIDEO MORITA (49) CLIENT
I SEE...

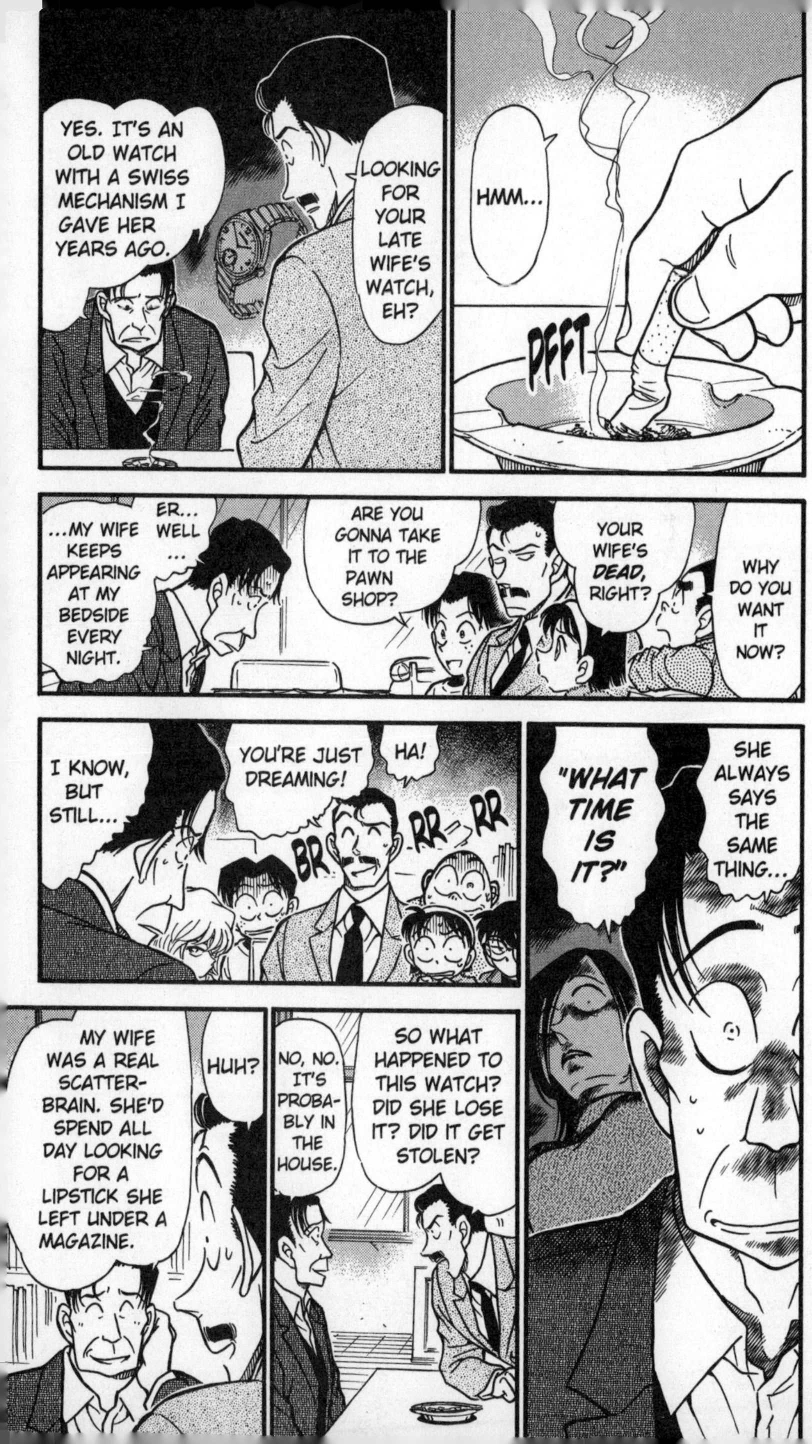
HMM...
PFFT
LOOKING FOR YOUR LATE WIFE'S WATCH, EH?
YES. IT'S AN OLD WATCH WITH A SWISS MECHANISM I GAVE HER YEARS AGO.
WHY DO YOU WANT IT NOW?
YOUR WIFE'S *DEAD*, RIGHT?
ARE YOU GONNA TAKE IT TO THE PAWN SHOP?
ER... WELL...
...MY WIFE KEEPS APPEARING AT MY BEDSIDE EVERY NIGHT.
SHE ALWAYS SAYS THE SAME THING...
"WHAT TIME IS IT?"
HA!
YOU'RE JUST DREAMING!
BR
RR
RR
I KNOW, BUT STILL...
SO WHAT HAPPENED TO THIS WATCH? DID SHE LOSE IT? DID IT GET STOLEN?
NO, NO. IT'S PROBABLY IN THE HOUSE.
HUH?
MY WIFE WAS A REAL SCATTER-BRAIN. SHE'D SPEND ALL DAY LOOKING FOR A LIPSTICK SHE LEFT UNDER A MAGAZINE.

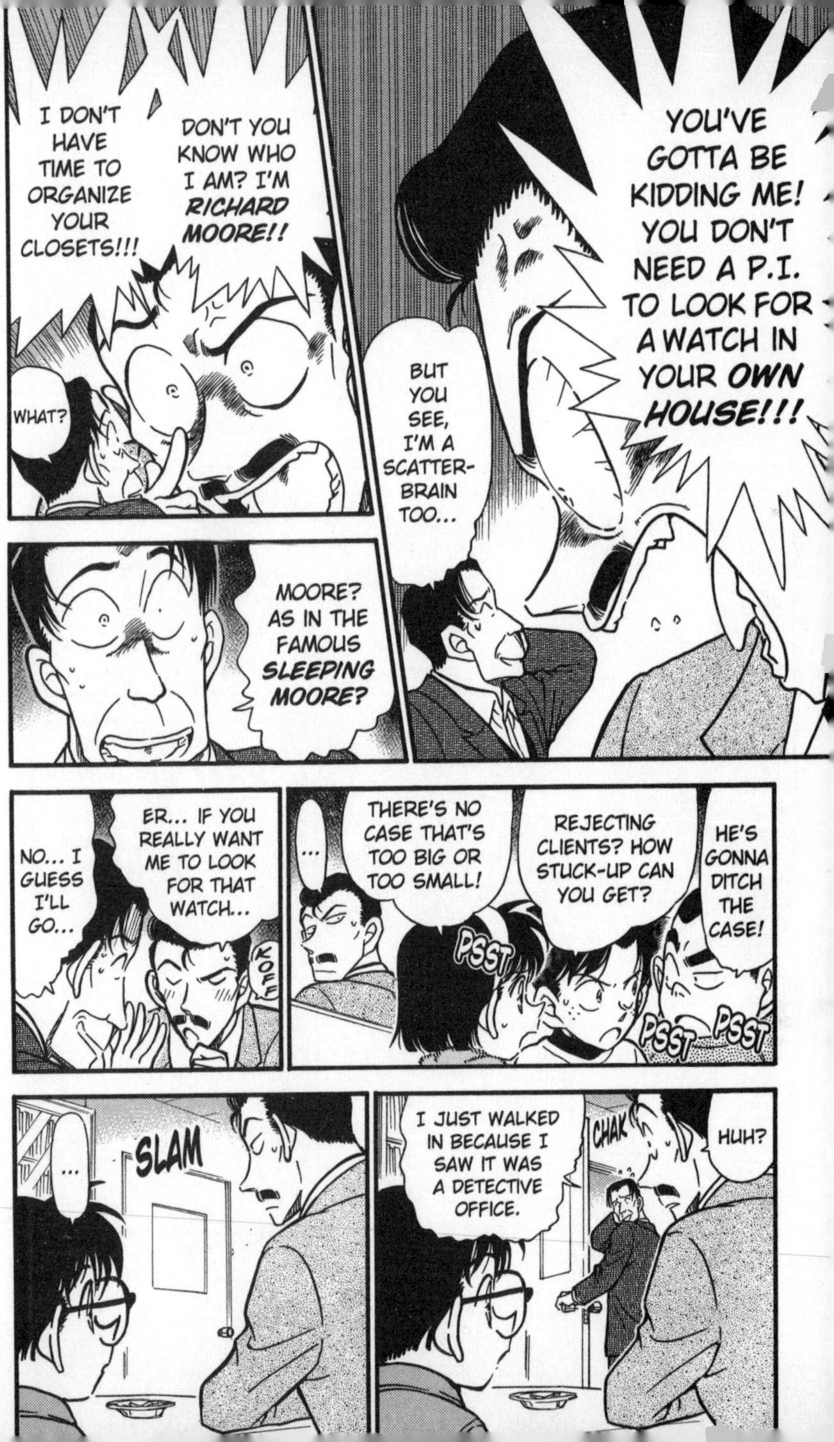

YOU'VE GOTTA BE KIDDING ME! YOU DON'T NEED A P.I. TO LOOK FOR A WATCH IN YOUR OWN HOUSE!!!
BUT YOU SEE, I'M A SCATTER-BRAIN TOO...
DON'T YOU KNOW WHO I AM? I'M RICHARD MOORE!!
I DON'T HAVE TIME TO ORGANIZE YOUR CLOSETS!!!
WHAT?
MOORE? AS IN THE FAMOUS SLEEPING MOORE?
HE'S GONNA DITCH THE CASE!
REJECTING CLIENTS? HOW STUCK-UP CAN YOU GET?
THERE'S NO CASE THAT'S TOO BIG OR TOO SMALL!
...
PSST
PSST
PSST
ER... IF YOU REALLY WANT ME TO LOOK FOR THAT WATCH...
KOFF
NO... I GUESS I'LL GO...
HUH?
CHAK
I JUST WALKED IN BECAUSE I SAW IT WAS A DETECTIVE OFFICE.
SLAM
...

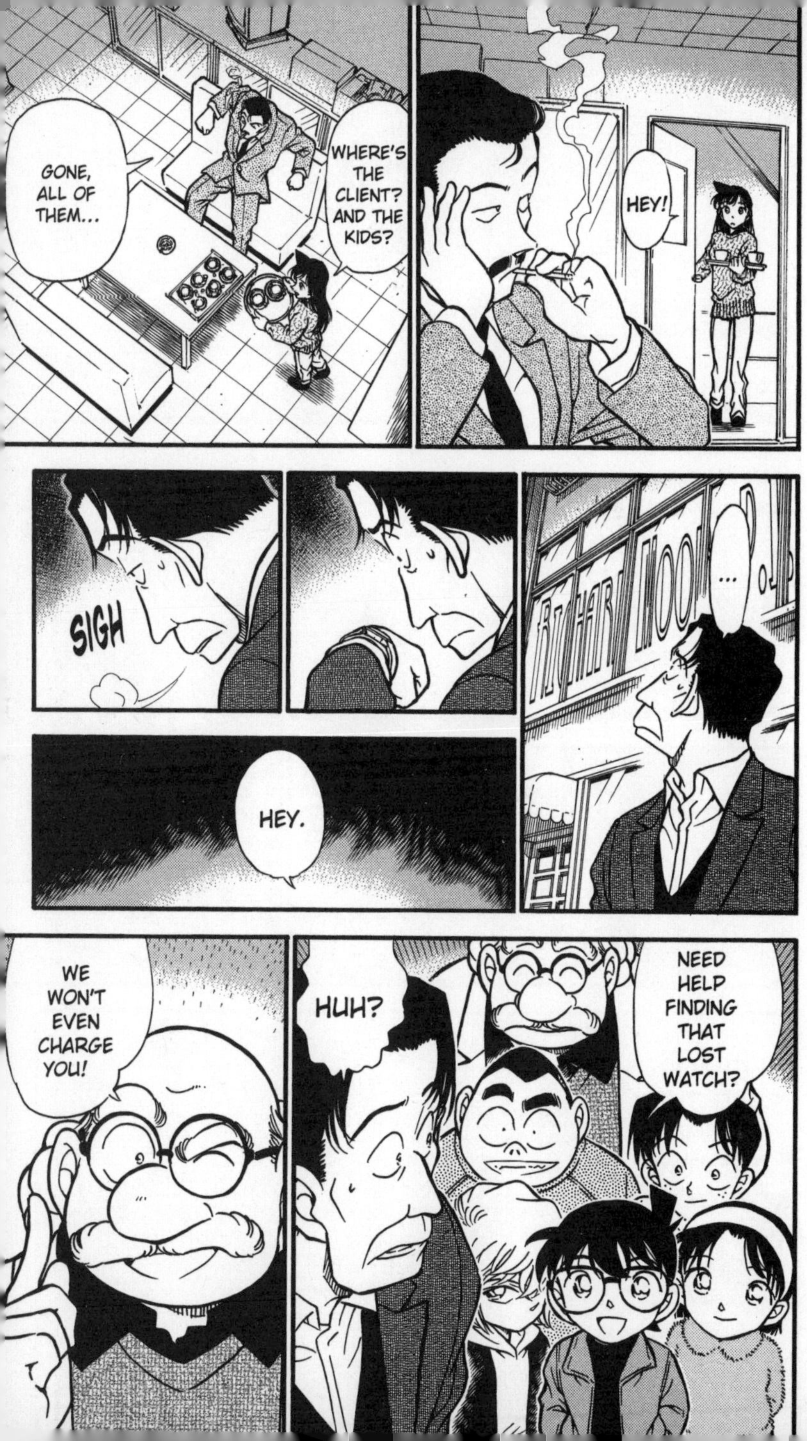
HEY!
WHERE'S THE CLIENT? AND THE KIDS?
GONE, ALL OF THEM...
...
SIGH
HEY.
NEED HELP FINDING THAT LOST WATCH?
HUH?
WE WON'T EVEN CHARGE YOU!

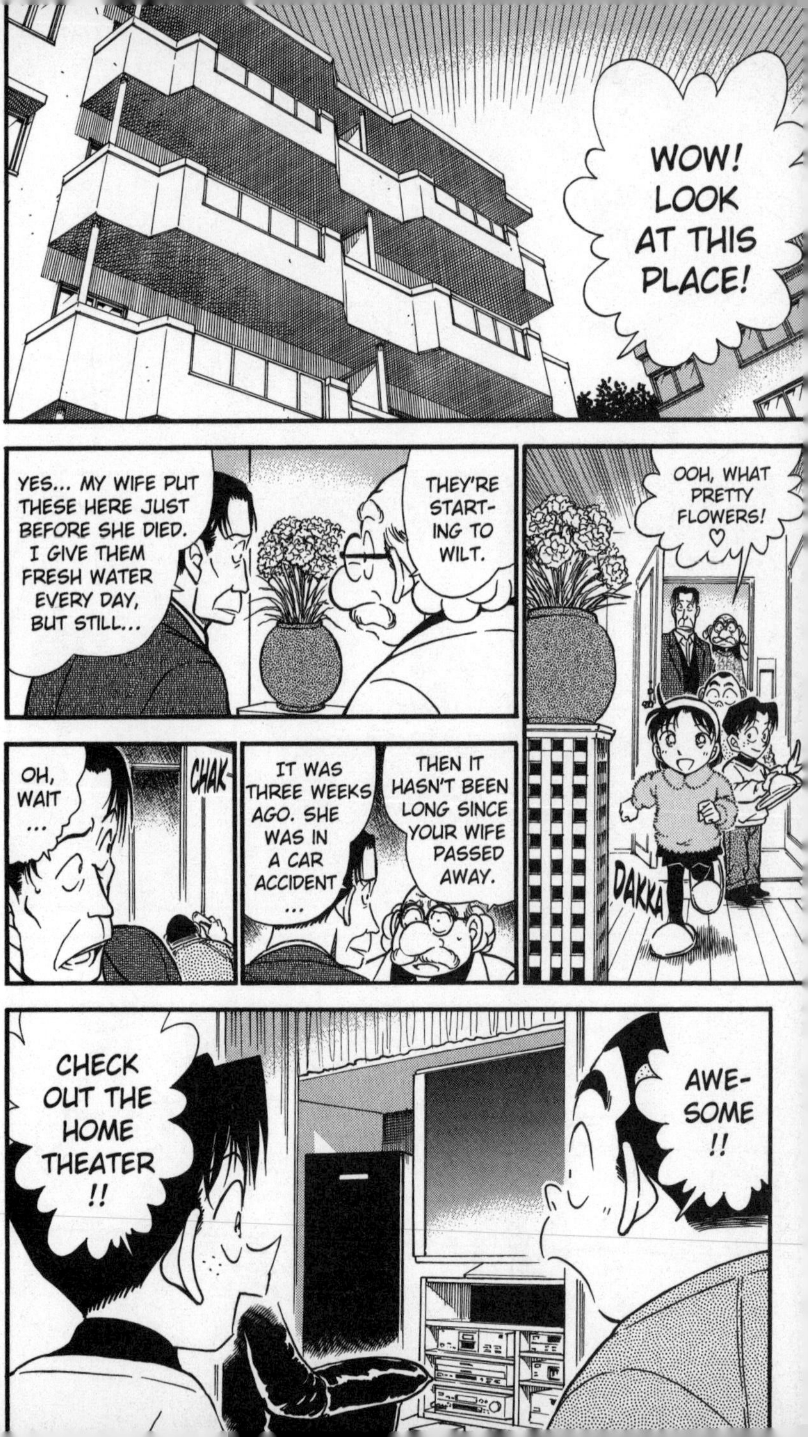
WOW! LOOK AT THIS PLACE!
OOH, WHAT PRETTY FLOWERS! ♡
DAKKA
THEY'RE START- ING TO WILT.
YES... MY WIFE PUT THESE HERE JUST BEFORE SHE DIED. I GIVE THEM FRESH WATER EVERY DAY, BUT STILL...
THEN IT HASN'T BEEN LONG SINCE YOUR WIFE PASSED AWAY.
IT WAS THREE WEEKS AGO. SHE WAS IN A CAR ACCIDENT ...
CHAK
OH, WAIT ...
AWE- SOME !!
CHECK OUT THE HOME THEATER !!

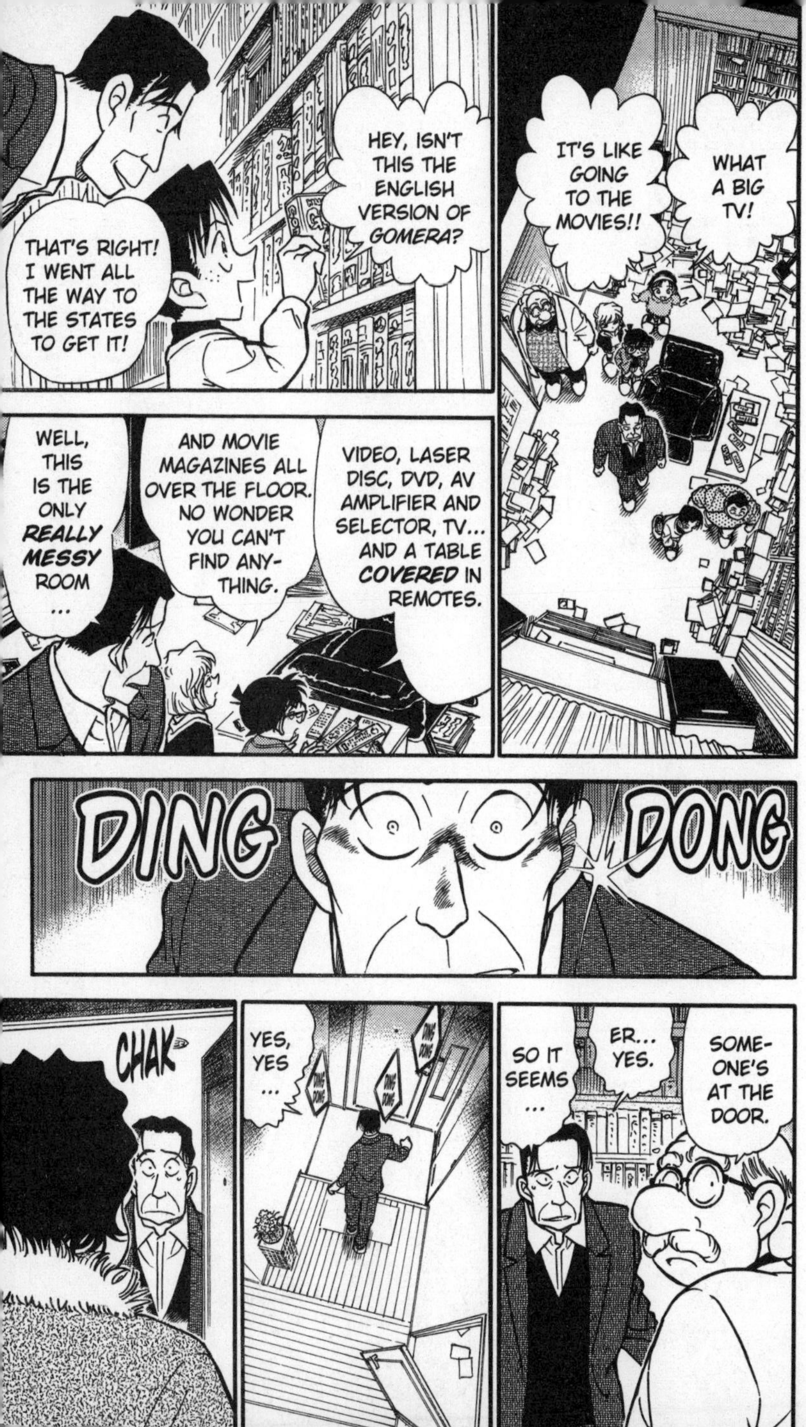
WHAT A BIG TV!
IT'S LIKE GOING TO THE MOVIES!!
HEY, ISN'T THIS THE ENGLISH VERSION OF *GOMERA*?
THAT'S RIGHT! I WENT ALL THE WAY TO THE STATES TO GET IT!
VIDEO, LASER DISC, DVD, AV AMPLIFIER AND SELECTOR, TV... AND A TABLE *COVERED* IN REMOTES.
AND MOVIE MAGAZINES ALL OVER THE FLOOR. NO WONDER YOU CAN'T FIND ANY-THING.
WELL, THIS IS THE ONLY *REALLY MESSY* ROOM ...
DING DONG
SOME-ONE'S AT THE DOOR.
ER... YES.
SO IT SEEMS ...
DING DONG
DING DONG
DING DONG
YES, YES ...
CHAK

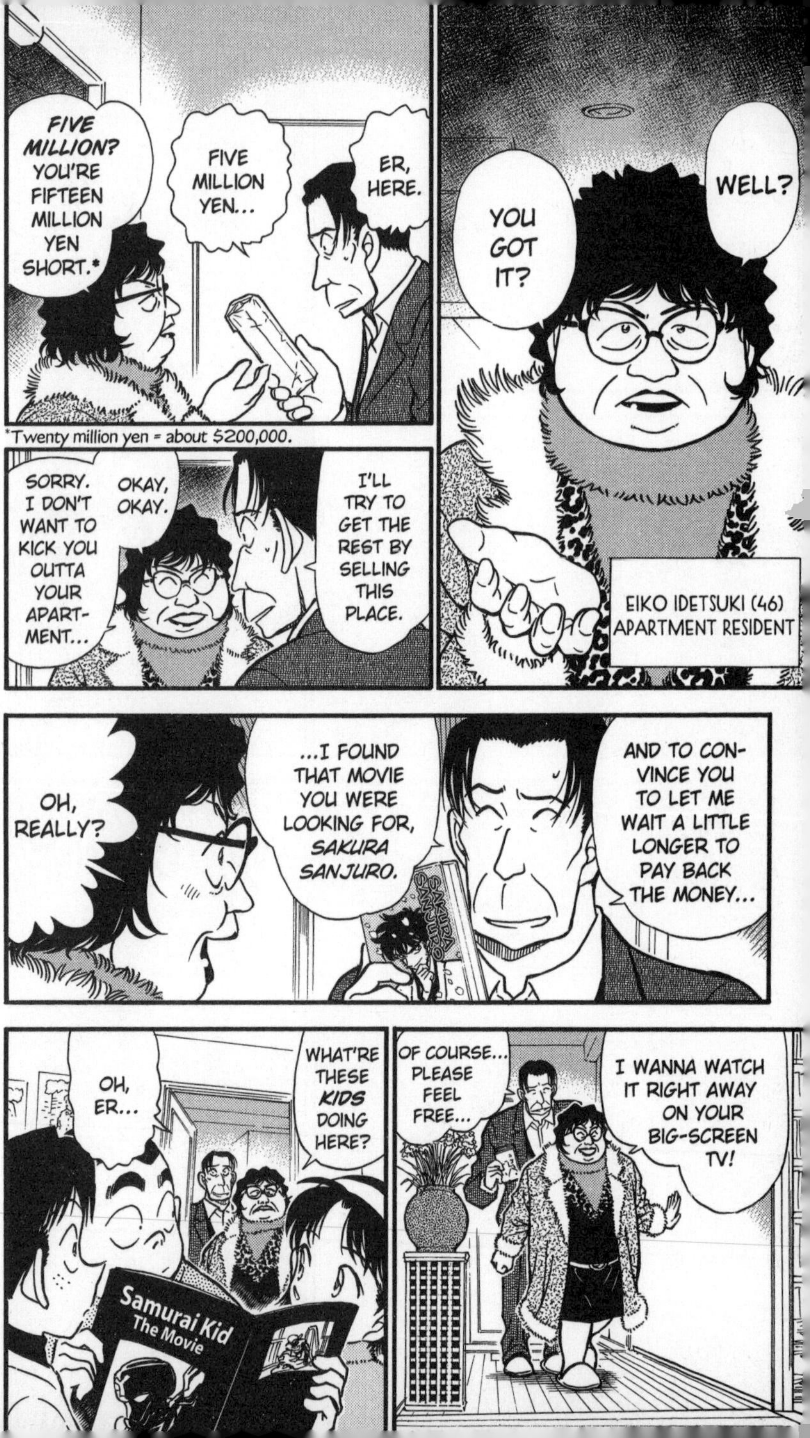
WELL?
YOU GOT IT?
EIKO IDETSUKI (46) APARTMENT RESIDENT
ER, HERE.
FIVE MILLION YEN...
FIVE MILLION? YOU'RE FIFTEEN MILLION YEN SHORT.*
I'LL TRY TO GET THE REST BY SELLING THIS PLACE.
OKAY, OKAY.
SORRY. I DON'T WANT TO KICK YOU OUTTA YOUR APARTMENT...
AND TO CONVINCE YOU TO LET ME WAIT A LITTLE LONGER TO PAY BACK THE MONEY...
...I FOUND THAT MOVIE YOU WERE LOOKING FOR, *SAKURA SANJURO.*
SAKURA SANJURO
OH, REALLY?
I WANNA WATCH IT RIGHT AWAY ON YOUR BIG-SCREEN TV!
OF COURSE... PLEASE FEEL FREE...
WHAT'RE THESE *KIDS* DOING HERE?
OH, ER...
Samurai Kid The Movie
*Twenty million yen = about $200,000.

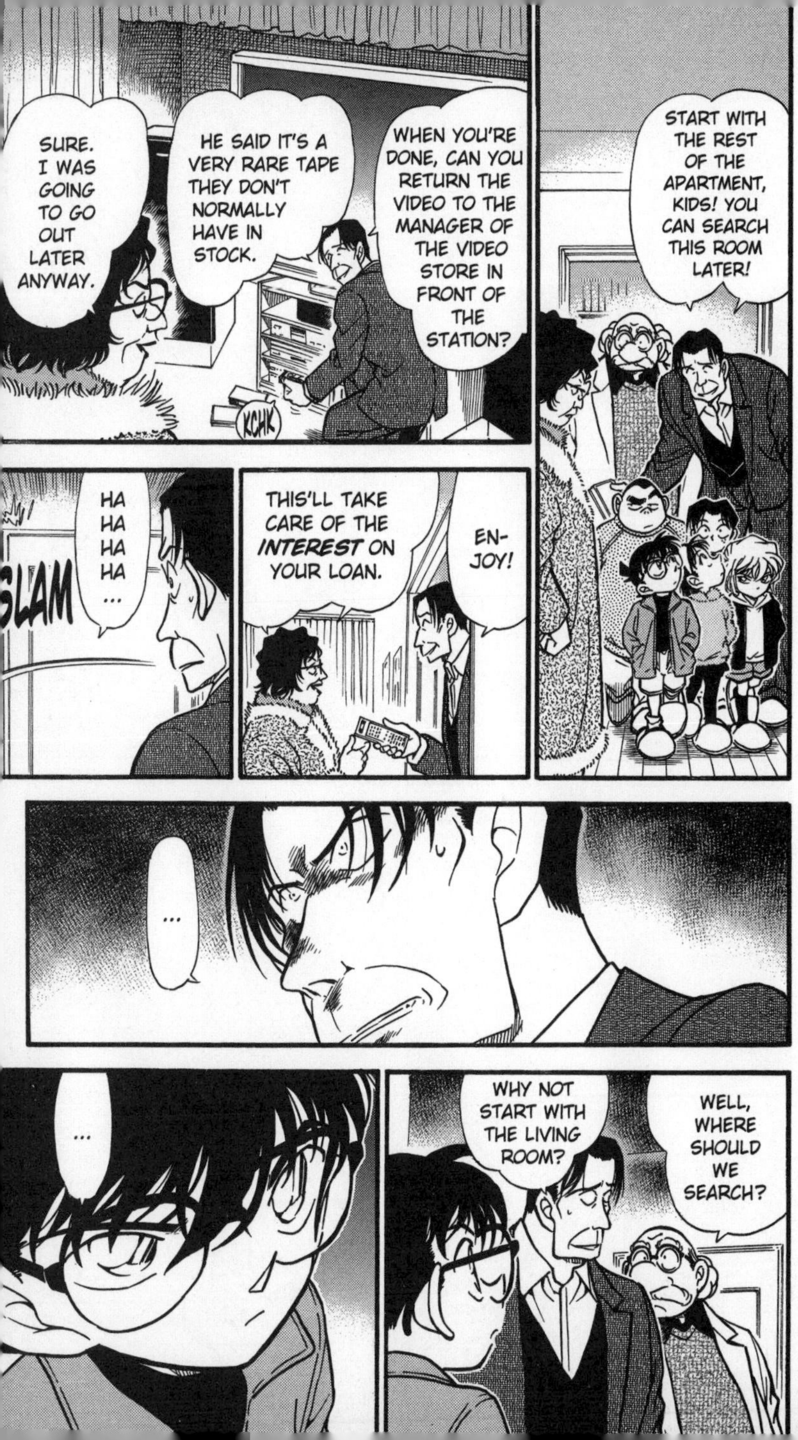
START WITH THE REST OF THE APARTMENT, KIDS! YOU CAN SEARCH THIS ROOM LATER!
WHEN YOU'RE DONE, CAN YOU RETURN THE VIDEO TO THE MANAGER OF THE VIDEO STORE IN FRONT OF THE STATION?
HE SAID IT'S A VERY RARE TAPE THEY DON'T NORMALLY HAVE IN STOCK.
SURE. I WAS GOING TO GO OUT LATER ANYWAY.
KCHK
EN-JOY!
THIS'LL TAKE CARE OF THE *INTEREST* ON YOUR LOAN.
HA HA HA HA ...
SLAM
...
WELL, WHERE SHOULD WE SEARCH?
WHY NOT START WITH THE LIVING ROOM?
...

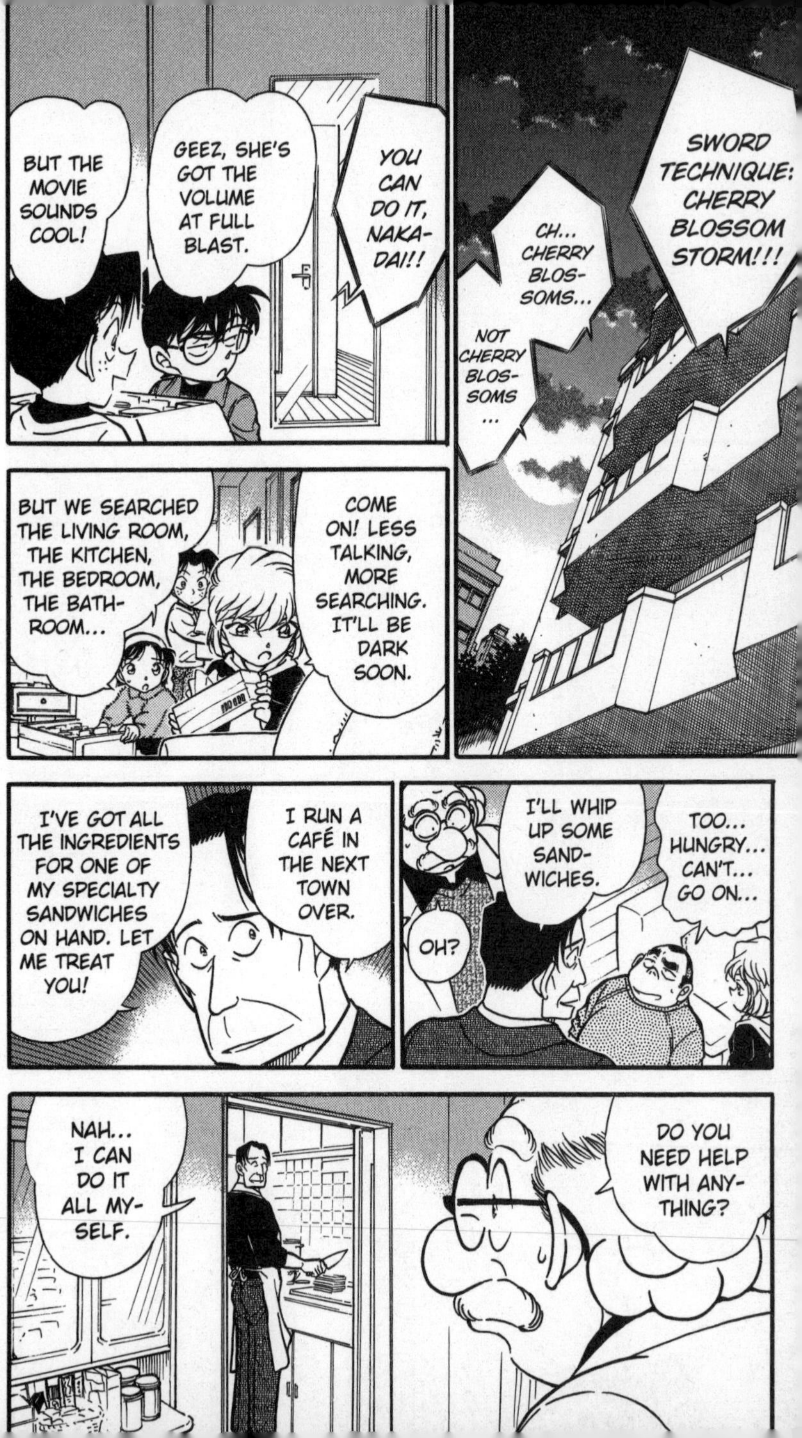
SWORD TECHNIQUE: CHERRY BLOSSOM STORM!!!
CH... CHERRY BLOSSOMS...
NOT CHERRY BLOSSOMS ...
YOU CAN DO IT, NAKADAI!!
GEEZ, SHE'S GOT THE VOLUME AT FULL BLAST.
BUT THE MOVIE SOUNDS COOL!
COME ON! LESS TALKING, MORE SEARCHING. IT'LL BE DARK SOON.
BUT WE SEARCHED THE LIVING ROOM, THE KITCHEN, THE BEDROOM, THE BATHROOM...
TOO... HUNGRY... CAN'T... GO ON...
I'LL WHIP UP SOME SANDWICHES.
OH?
I RUN A CAFÉ IN THE NEXT TOWN OVER.
I'VE GOT ALL THE INGREDIENTS FOR ONE OF MY SPECIALTY SANDWICHES ON HAND. LET ME TREAT YOU!
DO YOU NEED HELP WITH ANYTHING?
NAH... I CAN DO IT ALL MYSELF.

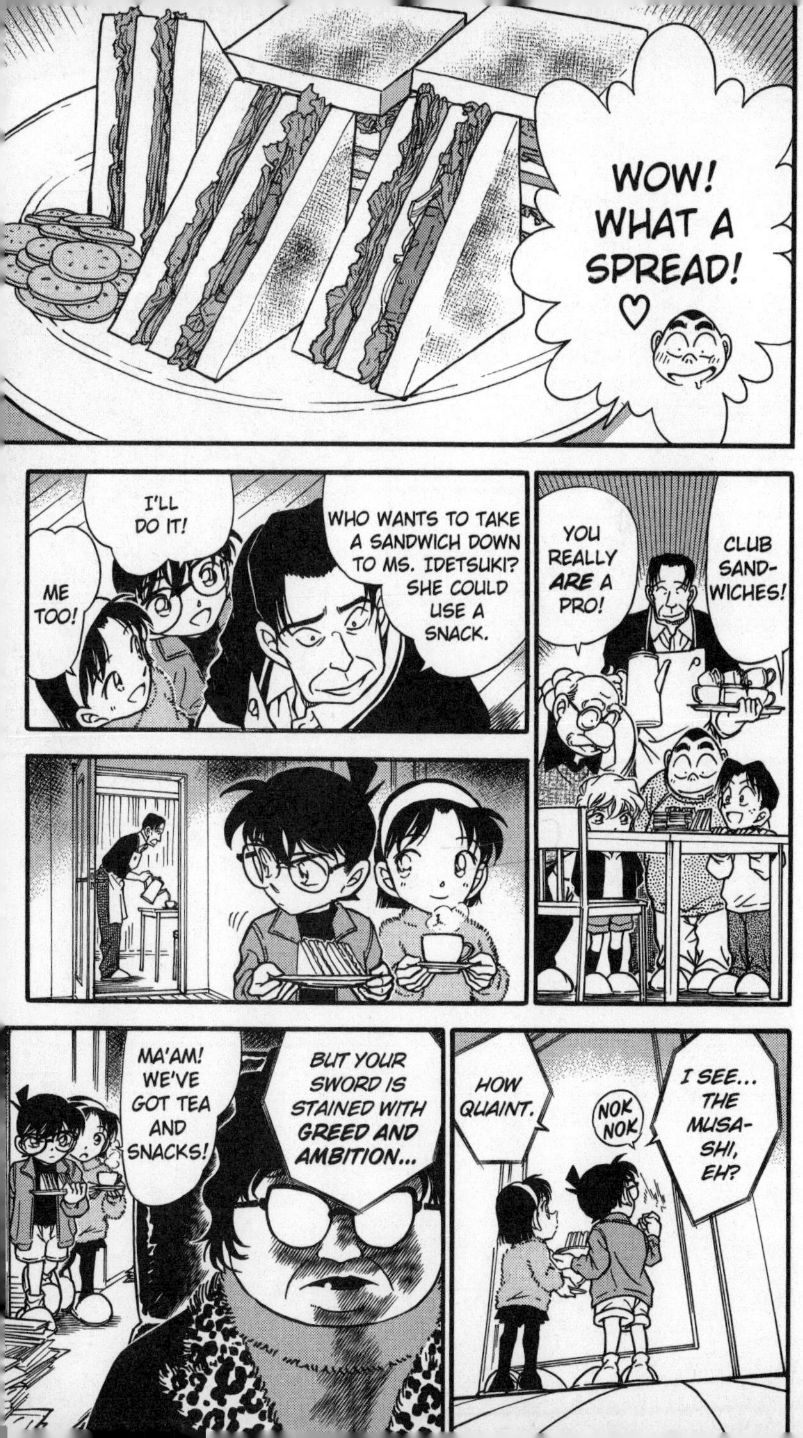
WOW! WHAT A SPREAD! ♡
CLUB SANDWICHES!
YOU REALLY *ARE* A PRO!
WHO WANTS TO TAKE A SANDWICH DOWN TO MS. IDETSUKI? SHE COULD USE A SNACK.
I'LL DO IT!
ME TOO!
I SEE... THE MUSASHI, EH?
NOK NOK
HOW QUAINT.
BUT YOUR SWORD IS STAINED WITH **GREED AND AMBITION...**
MA'AM! WE'VE GOT TEA AND SNACKS!

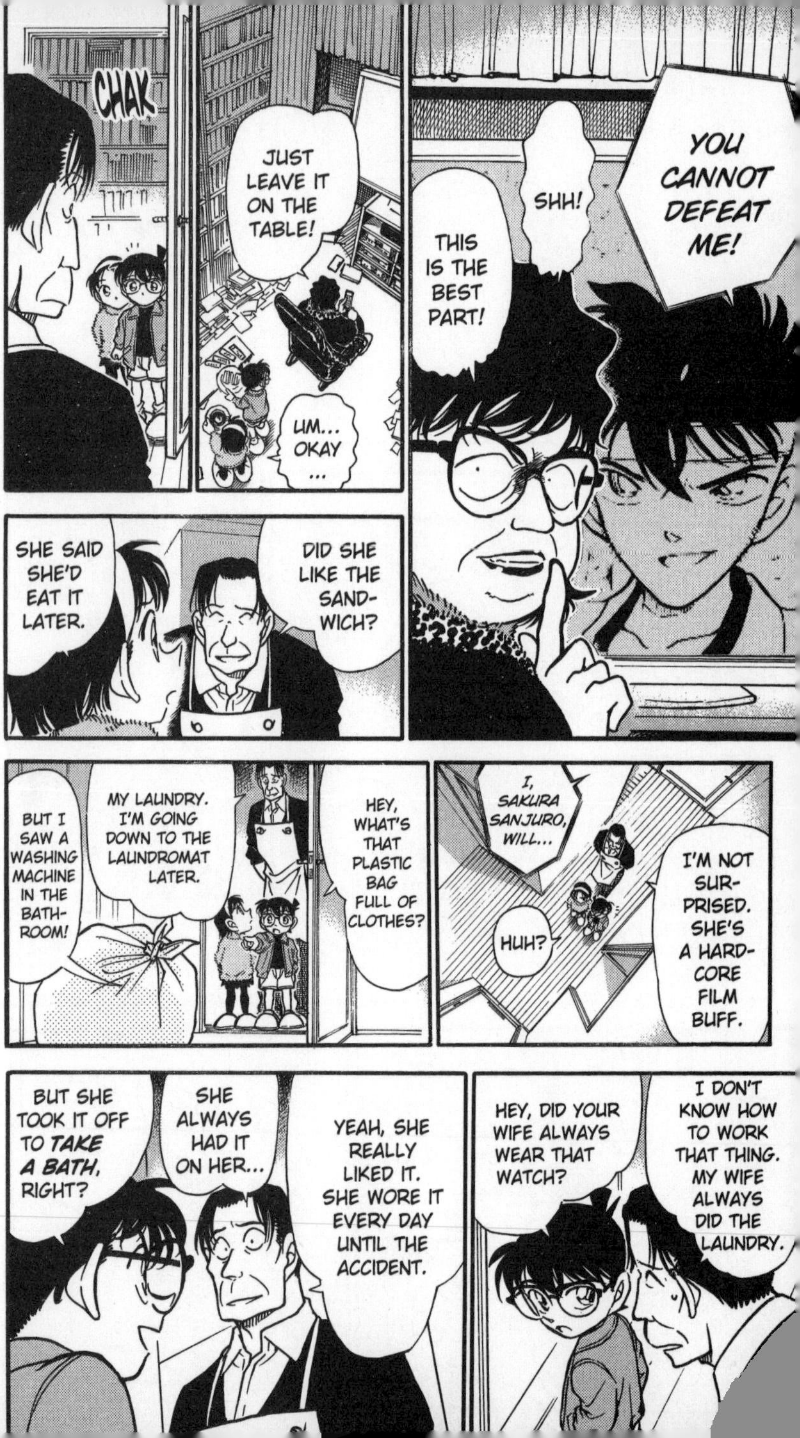
YOU CANNOT DEFEAT ME!
SHH!
THIS IS THE BEST PART!
JUST LEAVE IT ON THE TABLE!
UM... OKAY ...
CHAK
DID SHE LIKE THE SANDWICH?
SHE SAID SHE'D EAT IT LATER.
I, SAKURA SANJURO, WILL...
I'M NOT SURPRISED. SHE'S A HARDCORE FILM BUFF.
HUH?
HEY, WHAT'S THAT PLASTIC BAG FULL OF CLOTHES?
MY LAUNDRY. I'M GOING DOWN TO THE LAUNDROMAT LATER.
BUT I SAW A WASHING MACHINE IN THE BATHROOM!
I DON'T KNOW HOW TO WORK THAT THING. MY WIFE ALWAYS DID THE LAUNDRY.
HEY, DID YOUR WIFE ALWAYS WEAR THAT WATCH?
YEAH, SHE REALLY LIKED IT. SHE WORE IT EVERY DAY UNTIL THE ACCIDENT.
SHE ALWAYS HAD IT ON HER...
BUT SHE TOOK IT OFF TO *TAKE A BATH*, RIGHT?

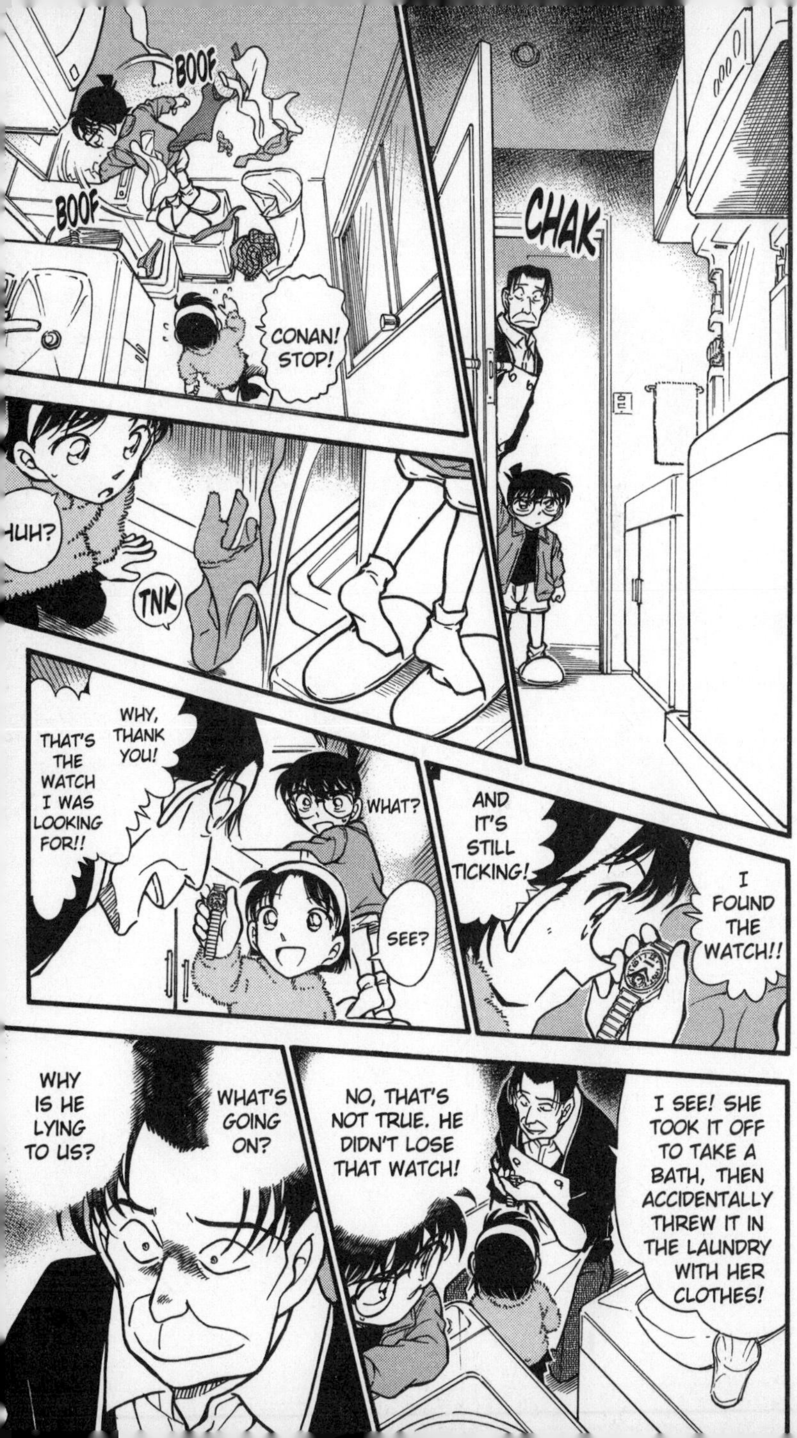
CHAK
BOOF
BOOF
CONAN! STOP!
HUH?
TNK
I FOUND THE WATCH!!
AND IT'S STILL TICKING!
SEE?
WHAT?
WHY, THANK YOU!
THAT'S THE WATCH I WAS LOOKING FOR!!
I SEE! SHE TOOK IT OFF TO TAKE A BATH, THEN ACCIDENTALLY THREW IT IN THE LAUNDRY WITH HER CLOTHES!
NO, THAT'S NOT TRUE. HE DIDN'T LOSE THAT WATCH!
WHAT'S GOING ON?
WHY IS HE LYING TO US?

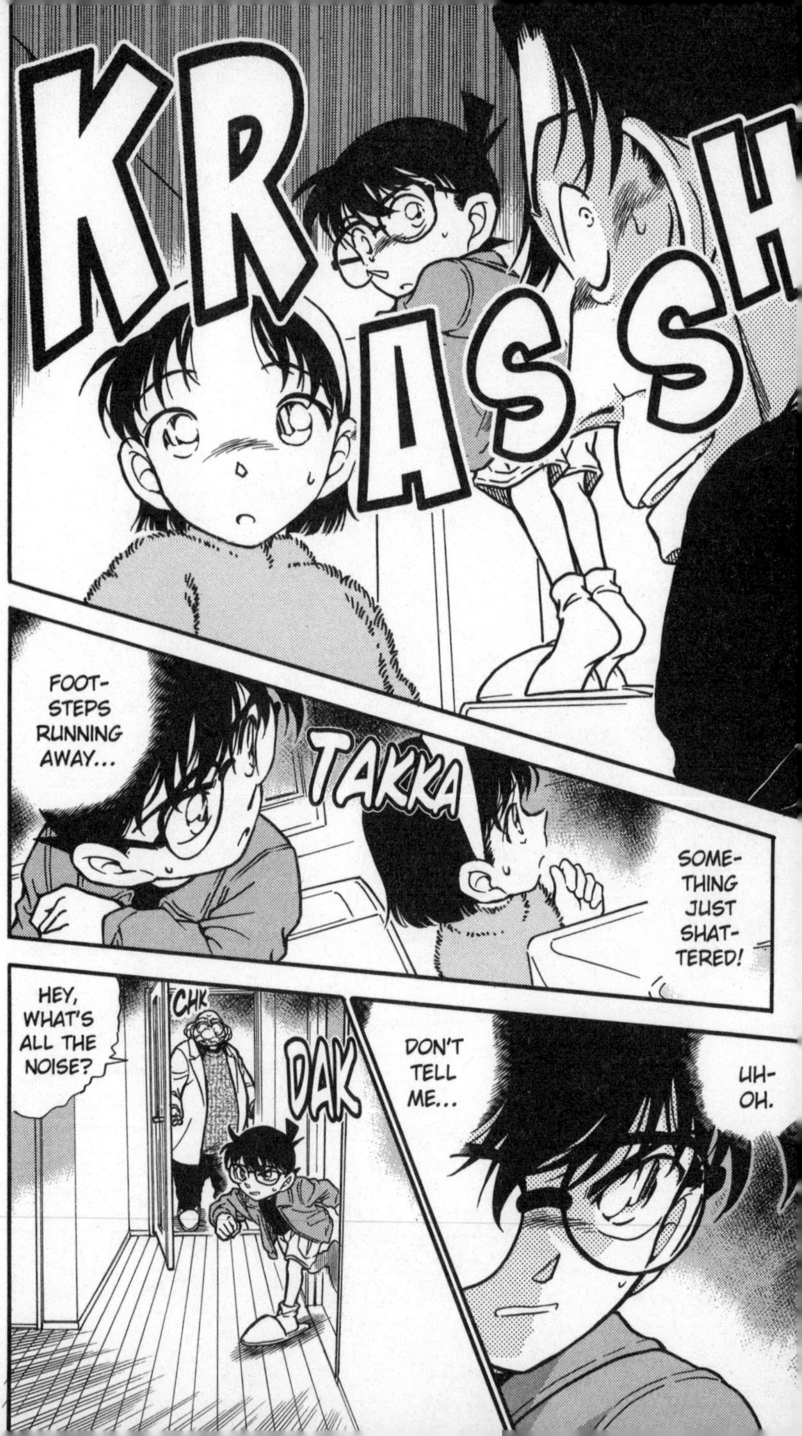
KRASSH
SOMETHING JUST SHATTERED!
TAKKA
FOOTSTEPS RUNNING AWAY...
UH-OH.
DON'T TELL ME...
CHK
HEY, WHAT'S ALL THE NOISE?
DAK

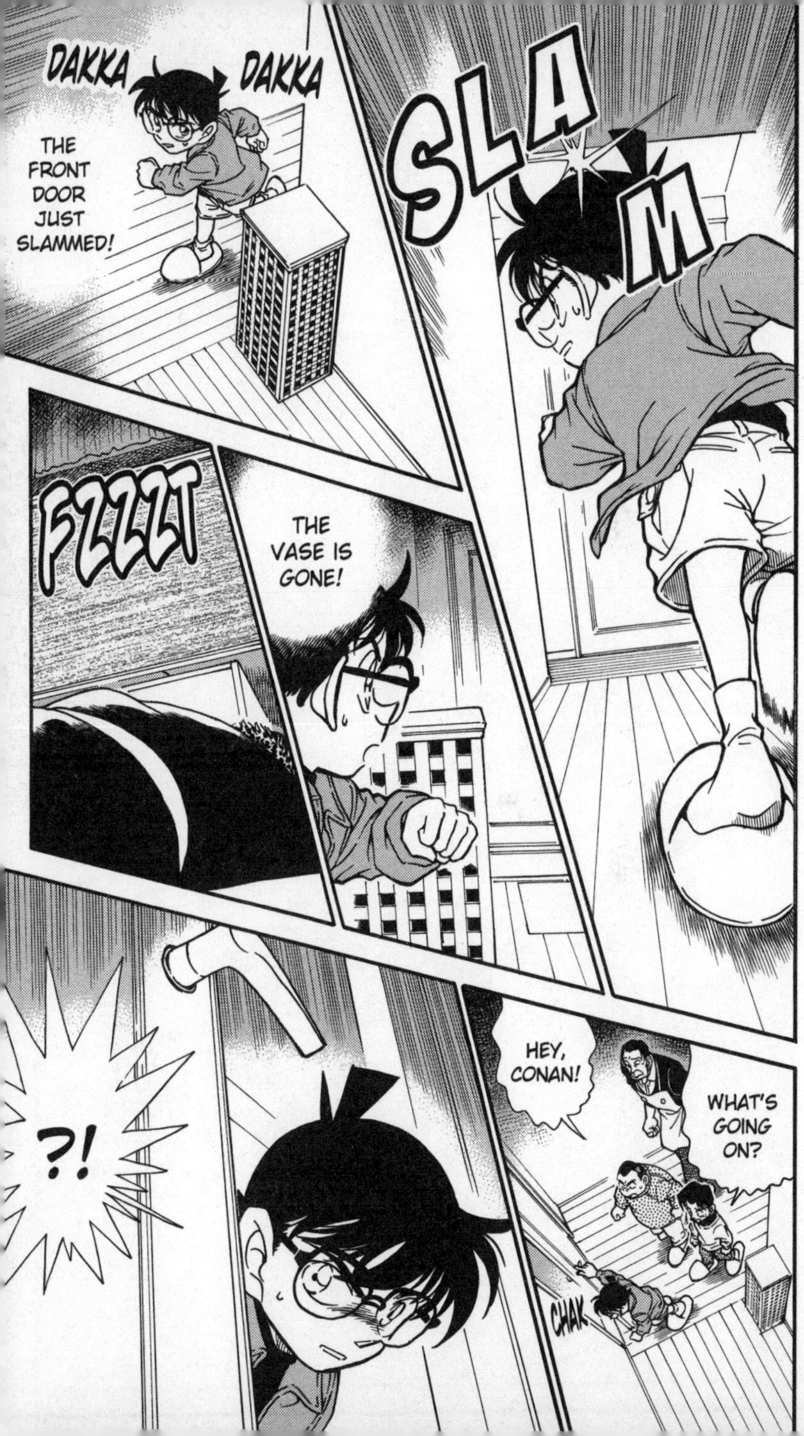
SLAM
DAKKA DAKKA
THE FRONT DOOR JUST SLAMMED!
THE VASE IS GONE!
FZZZT
HEY, CONAN!
WHAT'S GOING ON?
CHAK
?!

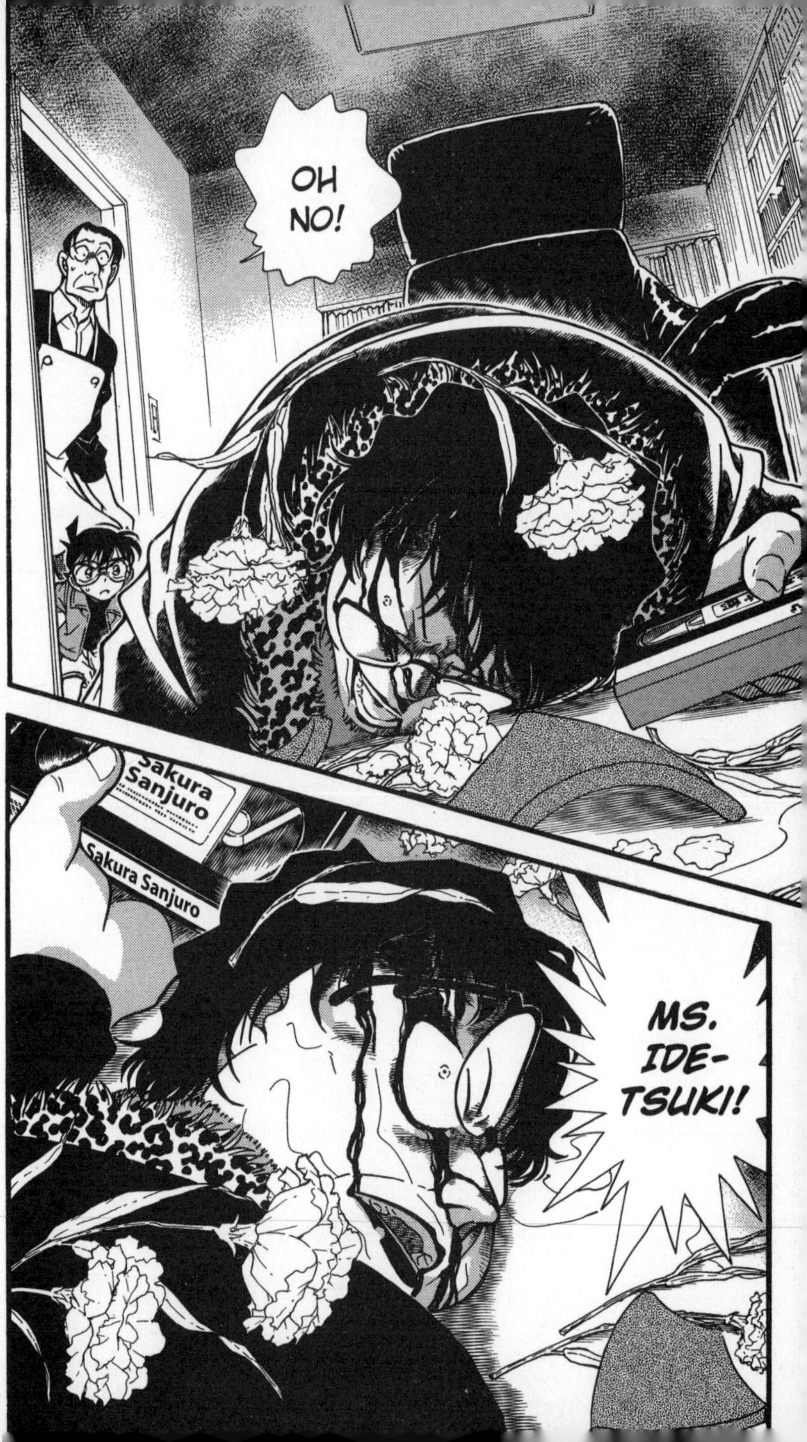
OH NO!
Sakura Sanjuro
Sakura Sanjuro
MS. IDE-TSUKI!

FILE 8: A PURE SCENT

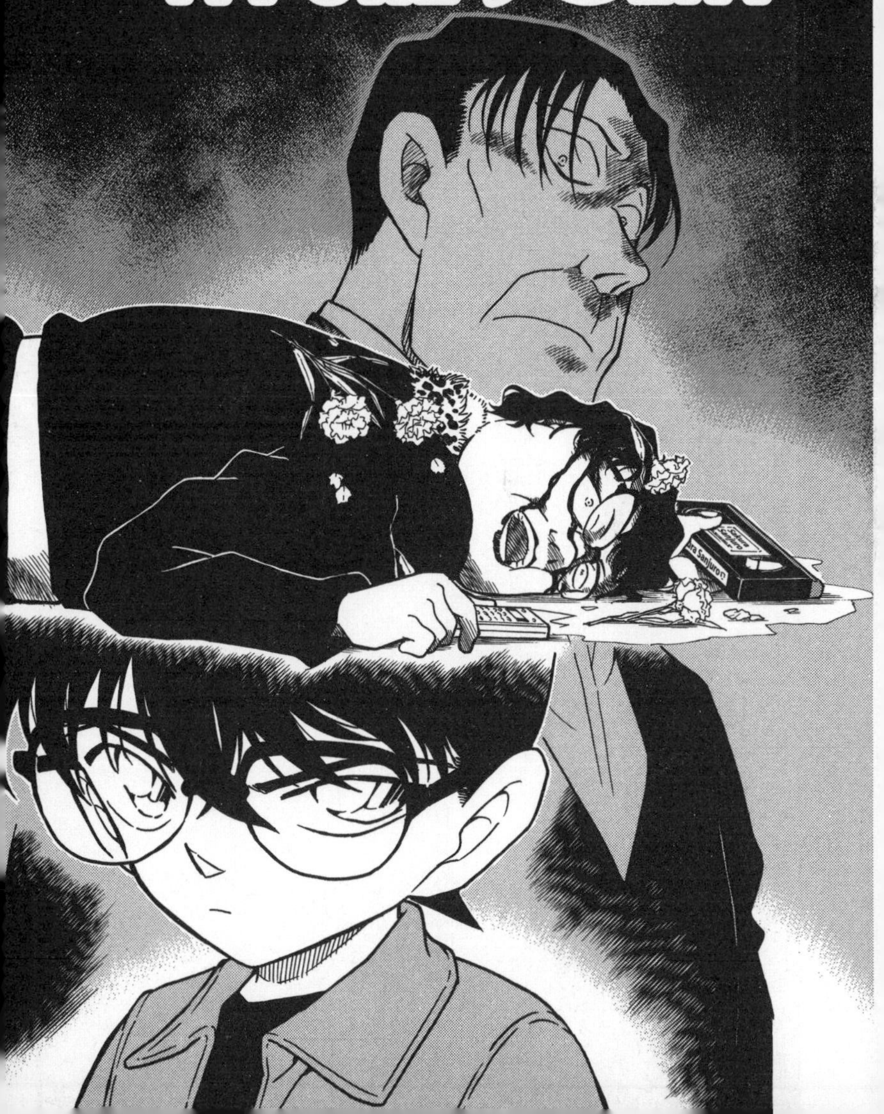

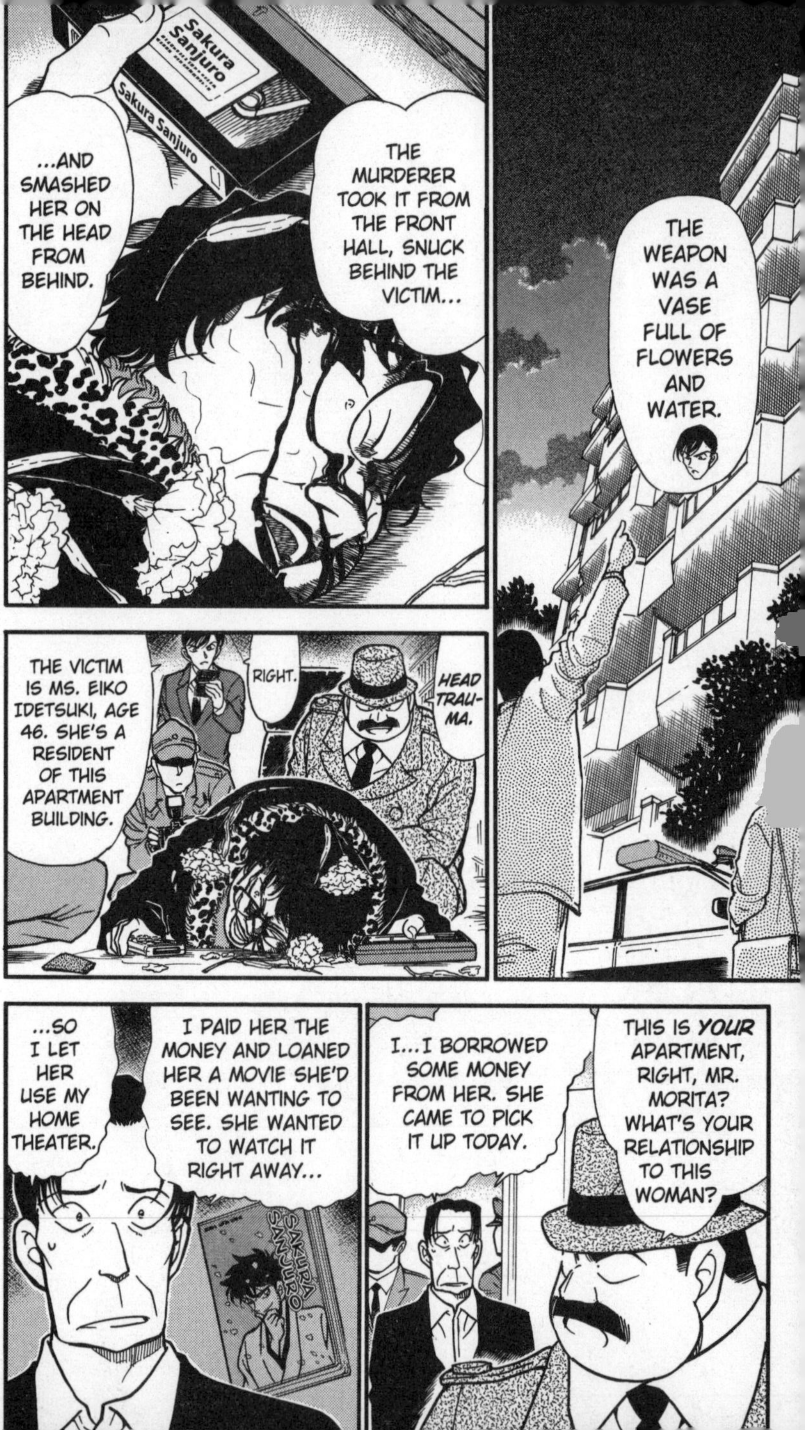
THE WEAPON WAS A VASE FULL OF FLOWERS AND WATER.
Sakura Sanjuro
THE MURDERER TOOK IT FROM THE FRONT HALL, SNUCK BEHIND THE VICTIM...
...AND SMASHED HER ON THE HEAD FROM BEHIND.
HEAD TRAUMA.
RIGHT.
THE VICTIM IS MS. EIKO IDETSUKI, AGE 46. SHE'S A RESIDENT OF THIS APARTMENT BUILDING.
THIS IS *YOUR* APARTMENT, RIGHT, MR. MORITA? WHAT'S YOUR RELATIONSHIP TO THIS WOMAN?
I...I BORROWED SOME MONEY FROM HER. SHE CAME TO PICK IT UP TODAY.
I PAID HER THE MONEY AND LOANED HER A MOVIE SHE'D BEEN WANTING TO SEE. SHE WANTED TO WATCH IT RIGHT AWAY...
...SO I LET HER USE MY HOME THEATER.
SAKURA SANJURO

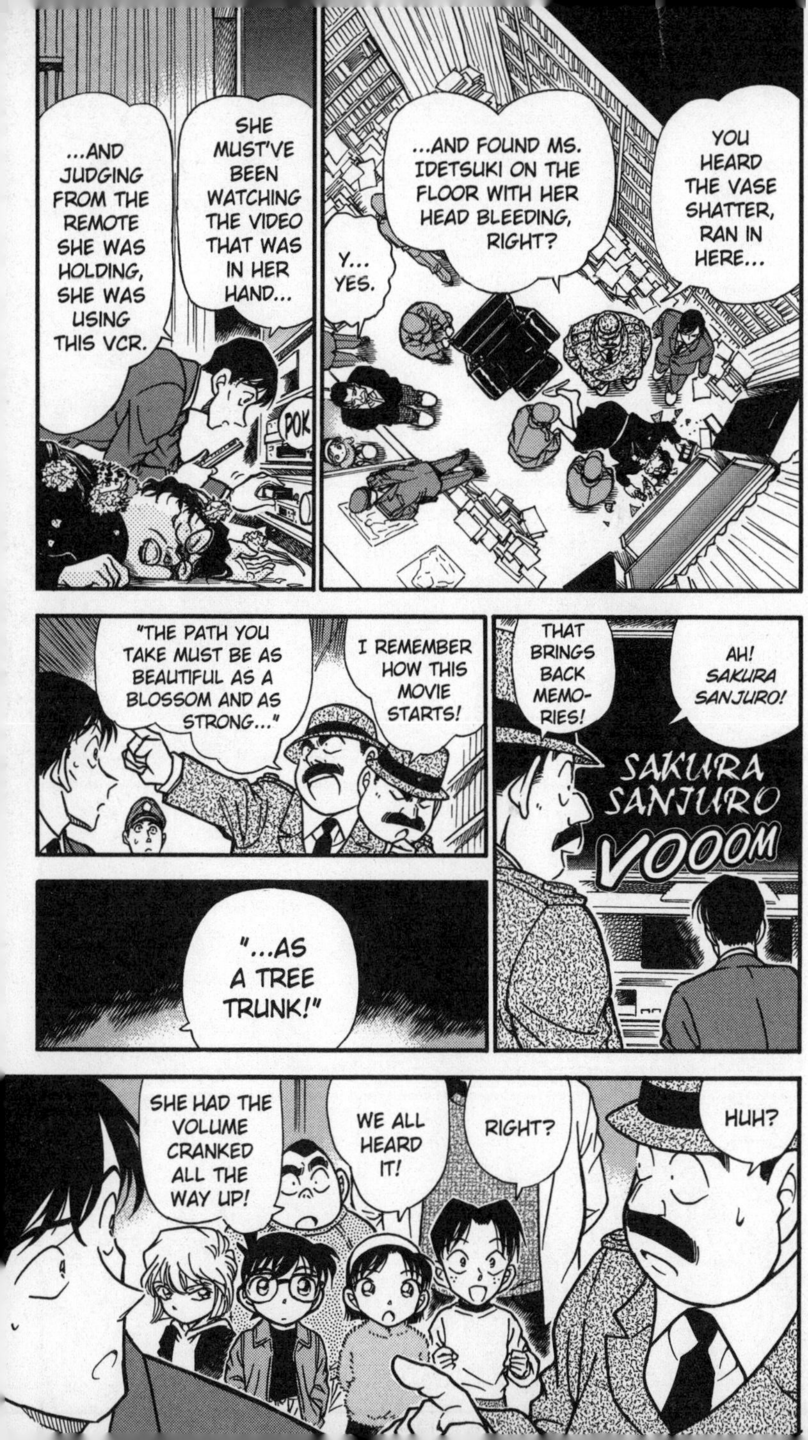
YOU HEARD THE VASE SHATTER, RAN IN HERE...
...AND FOUND MS. IDETSUKI ON THE FLOOR WITH HER HEAD BLEEDING, RIGHT?
Y... YES.
SHE MUST'VE BEEN WATCHING THE VIDEO THAT WAS IN HER HAND...
...AND JUDGING FROM THE REMOTE SHE WAS HOLDING, SHE WAS USING THIS VCR.
POK
AH! SAKURA SANJURO!
THAT BRINGS BACK MEMO-RIES!
SAKURA SANJURO
VOOOM
I REMEMBER HOW THIS MOVIE STARTS!
"THE PATH YOU TAKE MUST BE AS BEAUTIFUL AS A BLOSSOM AND AS STRONG..."
"...AS A TREE TRUNK!"
HUH?
RIGHT?
WE ALL HEARD IT!
SHE HAD THE VOLUME CRANKED ALL THE WAY UP!

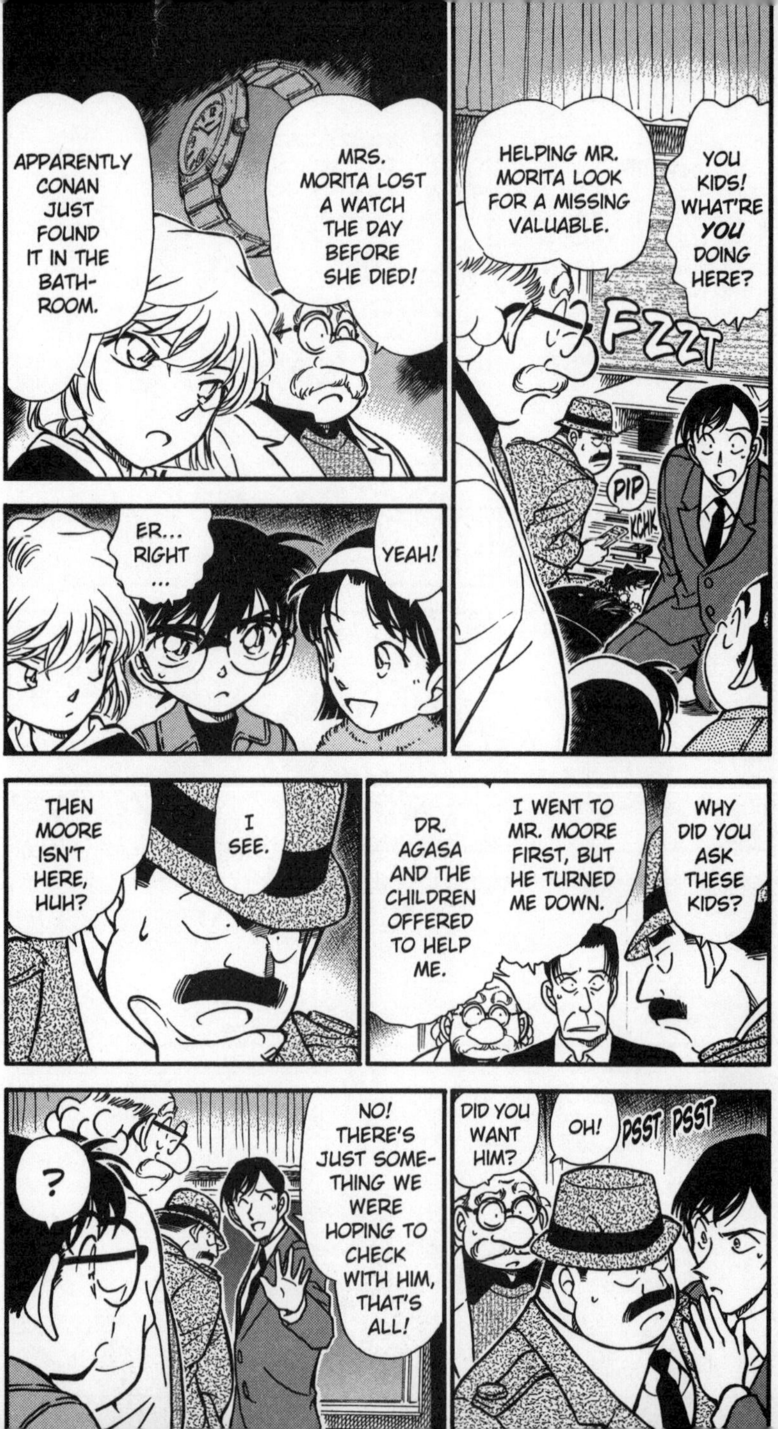
YOU KIDS! WHAT'RE YOU DOING HERE?
HELPING MR. MORITA LOOK FOR A MISSING VALUABLE.
FZZT
PIP
KCHK
MRS. MORITA LOST A WATCH THE DAY BEFORE SHE DIED!
APPARENTLY CONAN JUST FOUND IT IN THE BATH-ROOM.
YEAH!
ER... RIGHT ...
WHY DID YOU ASK THESE KIDS?
I WENT TO MR. MOORE FIRST, BUT HE TURNED ME DOWN.
DR. AGASA AND THE CHILDREN OFFERED TO HELP ME.
I SEE.
THEN MOORE ISN'T HERE, HUH?
PSST PSST
OH!
DID YOU WANT HIM?
NO! THERE'S JUST SOMETHING WE WERE HOPING TO CHECK WITH HIM, THAT'S ALL!
?

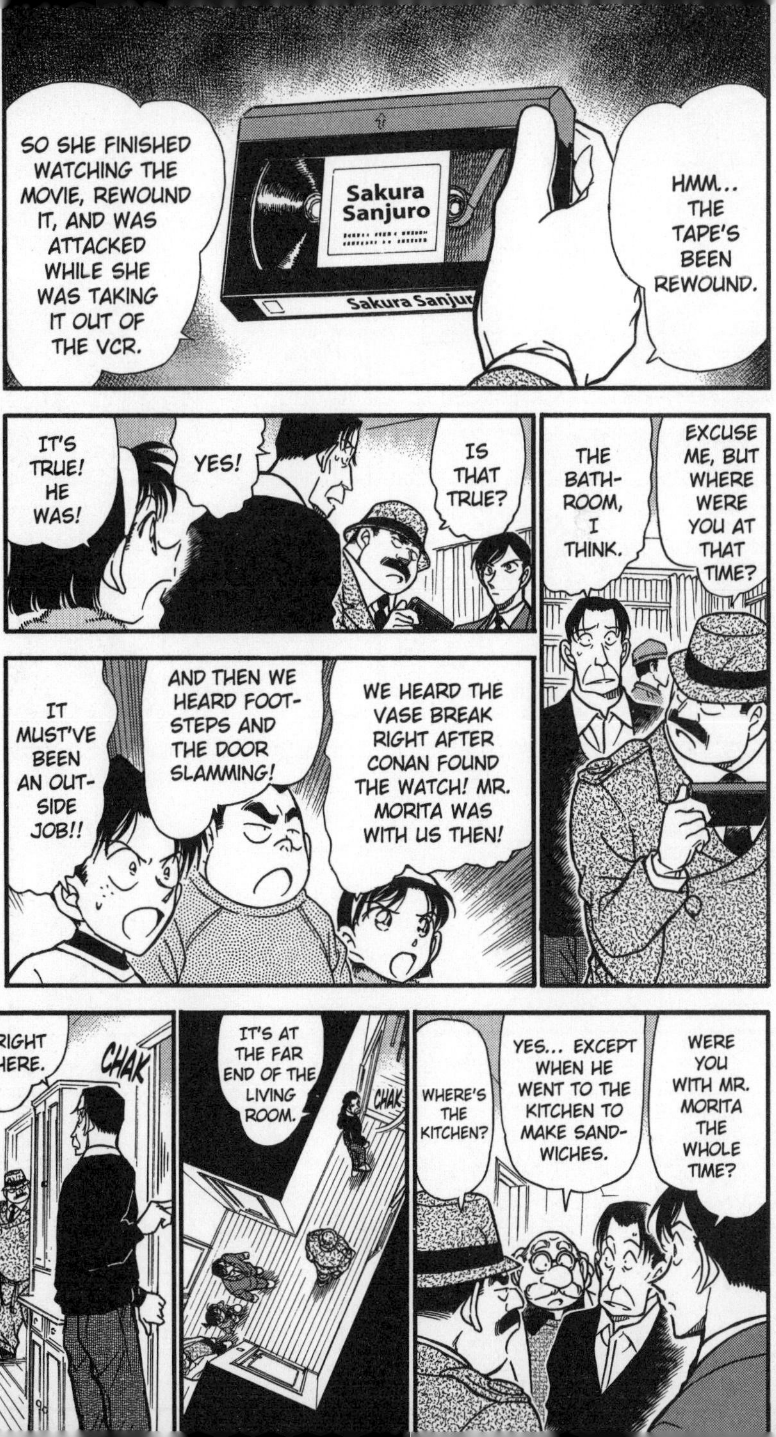
HMM... THE TAPE'S BEEN REWOUND.
Sakura Sanjuro
Sakura Sanjuro
SO SHE FINISHED WATCHING THE MOVIE, REWOUND IT, AND WAS ATTACKED WHILE SHE WAS TAKING IT OUT OF THE VCR.
EXCUSE ME, BUT WHERE WERE YOU AT THAT TIME?
THE BATH-ROOM, I THINK.
IS THAT TRUE?
YES!
IT'S TRUE! HE WAS!
WE HEARD THE VASE BREAK RIGHT AFTER CONAN FOUND THE WATCH! MR. MORITA WAS WITH US THEN!
AND THEN WE HEARD FOOT-STEPS AND THE DOOR SLAMMING!
IT MUST'VE BEEN AN OUT-SIDE JOB!!
WERE YOU WITH MR. MORITA THE WHOLE TIME?
YES... EXCEPT WHEN HE WENT TO THE KITCHEN TO MAKE SAND-WICHES.
WHERE'S THE KITCHEN?
IT'S AT THE FAR END OF THE LIVING ROOM.
CHAK
RIGHT HERE.
CHAK

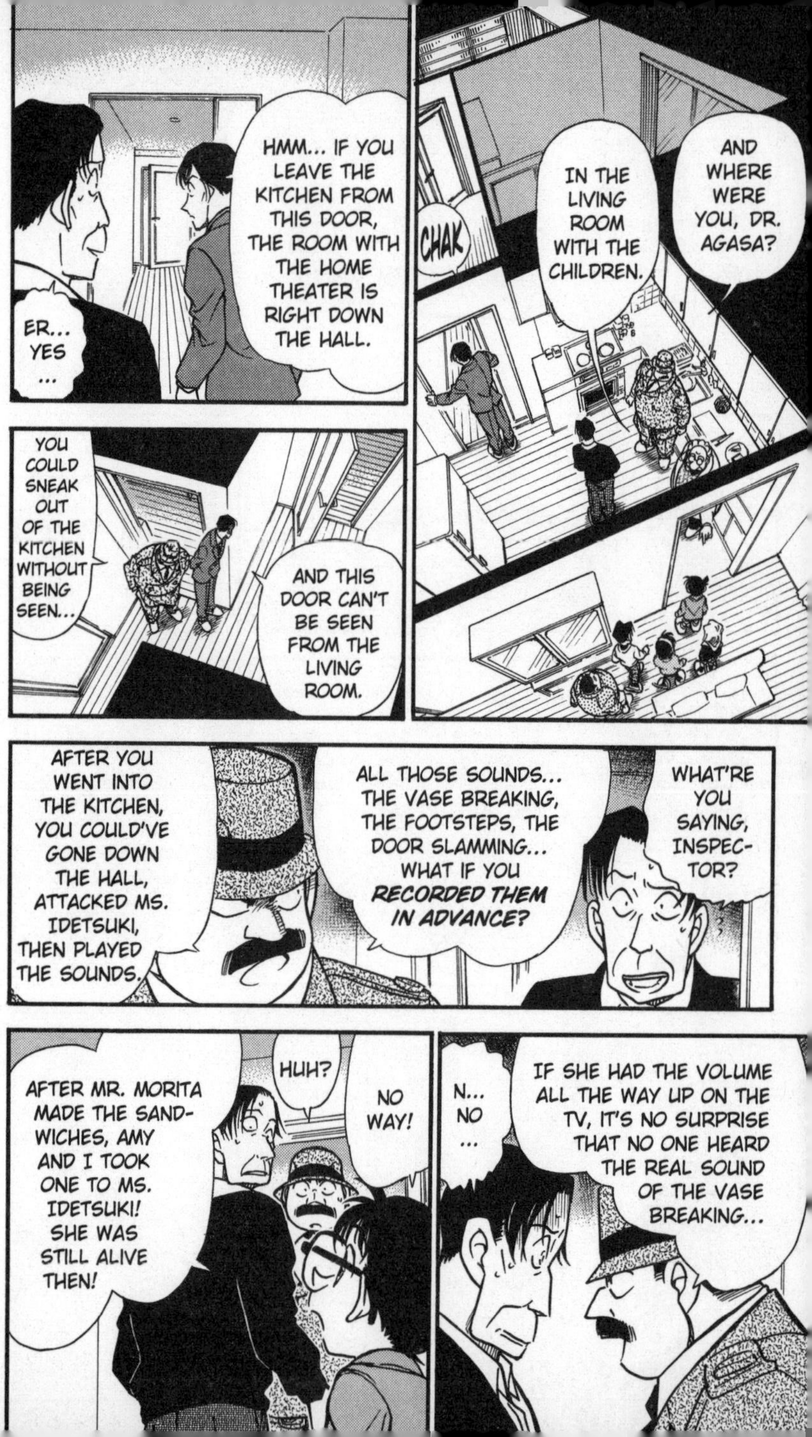
AND WHERE WERE YOU, DR. AGASA?
IN THE LIVING ROOM WITH THE CHILDREN.
CHAK
HMM... IF YOU LEAVE THE KITCHEN FROM THIS DOOR, THE ROOM WITH THE HOME THEATER IS RIGHT DOWN THE HALL.
ER... YES ...
YOU COULD SNEAK OUT OF THE KITCHEN WITHOUT BEING SEEN...
AND THIS DOOR CAN'T BE SEEN FROM THE LIVING ROOM.
WHAT'RE YOU SAYING, INSPECTOR?
ALL THOSE SOUNDS... THE VASE BREAKING, THE FOOTSTEPS, THE DOOR SLAMMING... WHAT IF YOU RECORDED THEM IN ADVANCE?
AFTER YOU WENT INTO THE KITCHEN, YOU COULD'VE GONE DOWN THE HALL, ATTACKED MS. IDETSUKI, THEN PLAYED THE SOUNDS.
IF SHE HAD THE VOLUME ALL THE WAY UP ON THE TV, IT'S NO SURPRISE THAT NO ONE HEARD THE REAL SOUND OF THE VASE BREAKING...
N... NO ...
HUH?
NO WAY!
AFTER MR. MORITA MADE THE SANDWICHES, AMY AND I TOOK ONE TO MS. IDETSUKI! SHE WAS STILL ALIVE THEN!

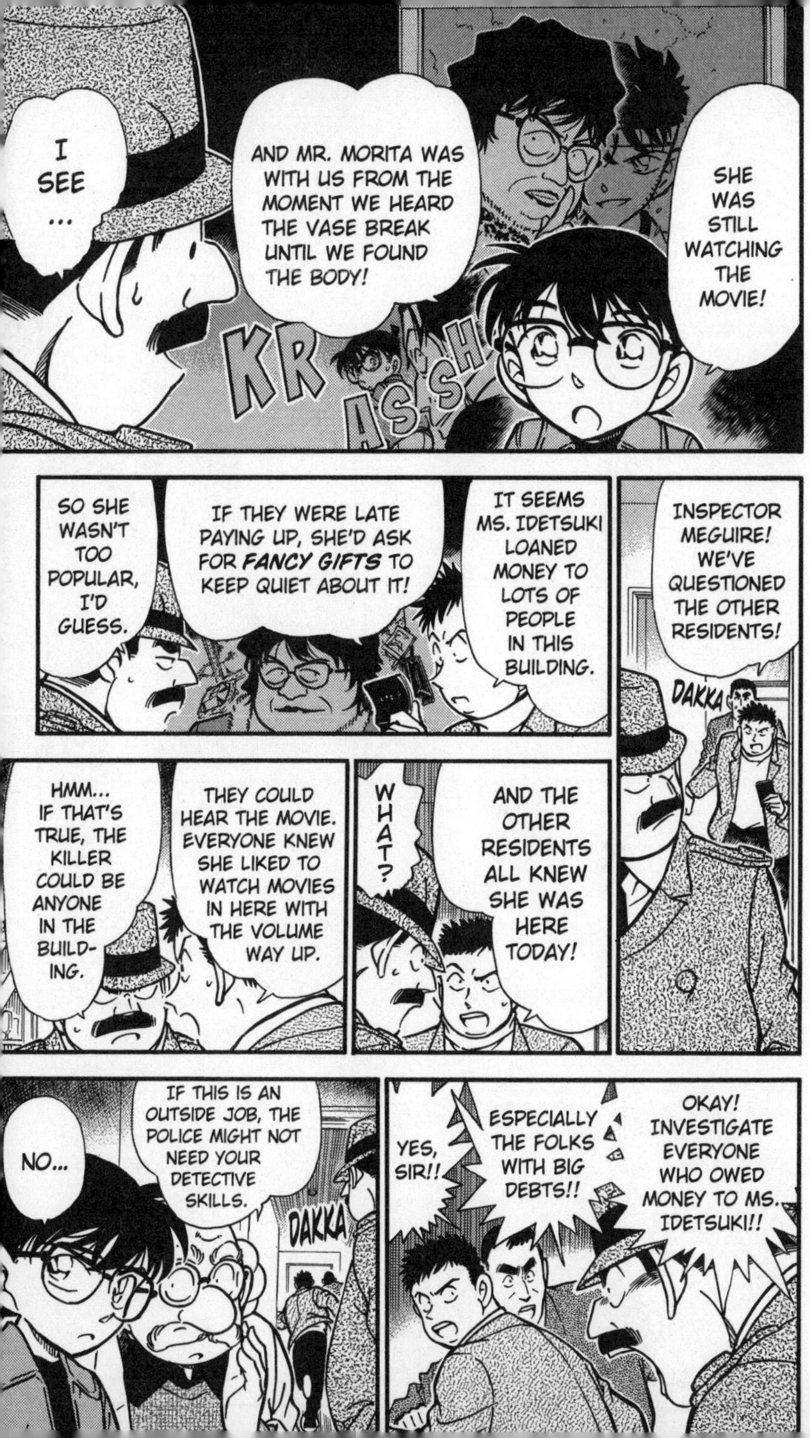
SHE WAS STILL WATCHING THE MOVIE!
AND MR. MORITA WAS WITH US FROM THE MOMENT WE HEARD THE VASE BREAK UNTIL WE FOUND THE BODY!
I SEE ...
KRASH
INSPECTOR MEGUIRE! WE'VE QUESTIONED THE OTHER RESIDENTS!
DAKKA
IT SEEMS MS. IDETSUKI LOANED MONEY TO LOTS OF PEOPLE IN THIS BUILDING.
IF THEY WERE LATE PAYING UP, SHE'D ASK FOR FANCY GIFTS TO KEEP QUIET ABOUT IT!
SO SHE WASN'T TOO POPULAR, I'D GUESS.
AND THE OTHER RESIDENTS ALL KNEW SHE WAS HERE TODAY!
WHAT?
THEY COULD HEAR THE MOVIE. EVERYONE KNEW SHE LIKED TO WATCH MOVIES IN HERE WITH THE VOLUME WAY UP.
HMM... IF THAT'S TRUE, THE KILLER COULD BE ANYONE IN THE BUILDING.
OKAY! INVESTIGATE EVERYONE WHO OWED MONEY TO MS. IDETSUKI!!
ESPECIALLY THE FOLKS WITH BIG DEBTS!!
YES, SIR!!
DAKKA
IF THIS IS AN OUTSIDE JOB, THE POLICE MIGHT NOT NEED YOUR DETECTIVE SKILLS.
NO...

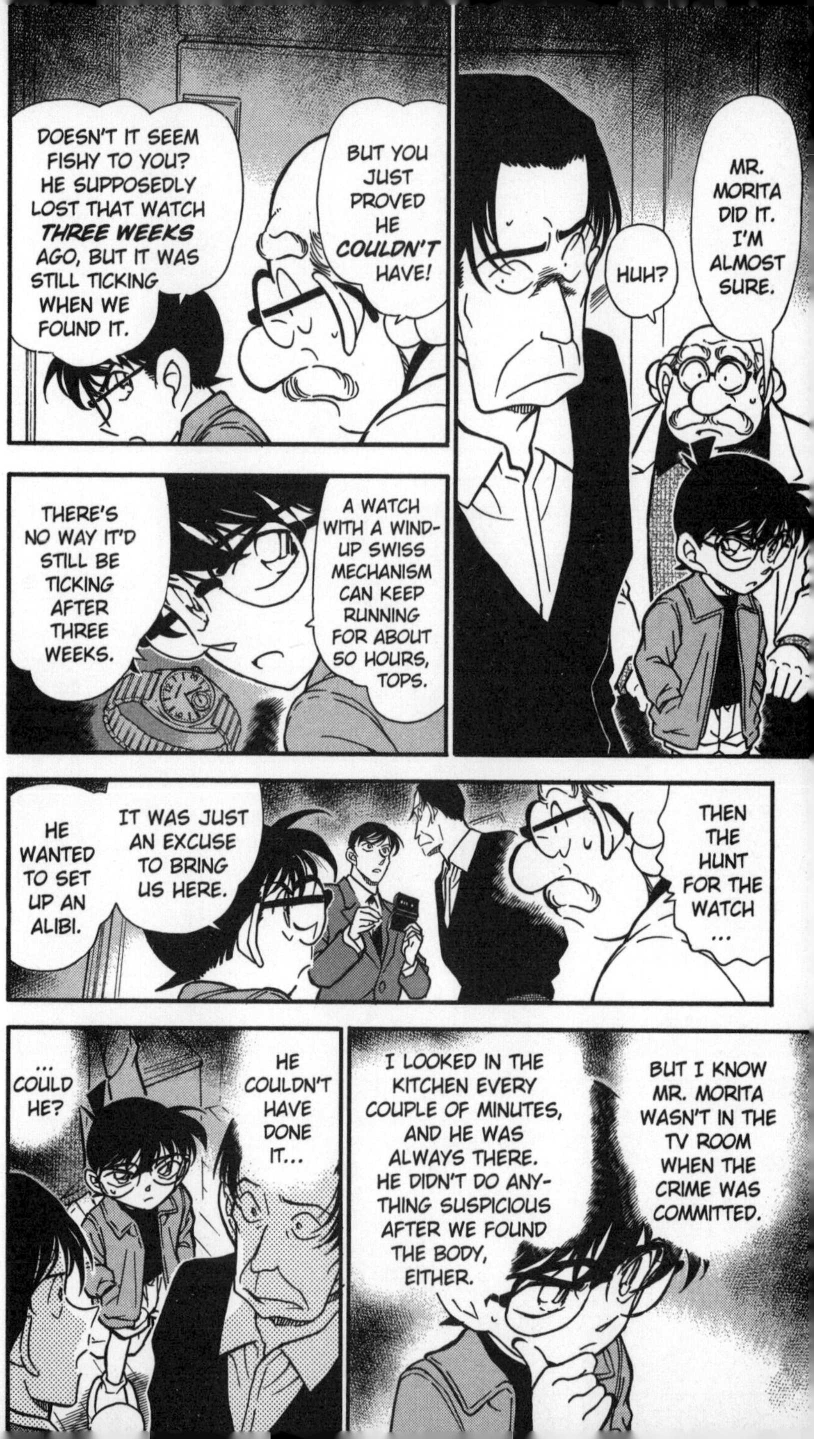

MR. MORITA DID IT. I'M ALMOST SURE.
HUH?
BUT YOU JUST PROVED HE ***COULDN'T*** HAVE!
DOESN'T IT SEEM FISHY TO YOU? HE SUPPOSEDLY LOST THAT WATCH ***THREE WEEKS*** AGO, BUT IT WAS STILL TICKING WHEN WE FOUND IT.
A WATCH WITH A WIND-UP SWISS MECHANISM CAN KEEP RUNNING FOR ABOUT 50 HOURS, TOPS.
THERE'S NO WAY IT'D STILL BE TICKING AFTER THREE WEEKS.
THEN THE HUNT FOR THE WATCH...
IT WAS JUST AN EXCUSE TO BRING US HERE.
HE WANTED TO SET UP AN ALIBI.
BUT I KNOW MR. MORITA WASN'T IN THE TV ROOM WHEN THE CRIME WAS COMMITTED.
I LOOKED IN THE KITCHEN EVERY COUPLE OF MINUTES, AND HE WAS ALWAYS THERE. HE DIDN'T DO ANY-THING SUSPICIOUS AFTER WE FOUND THE BODY, EITHER.
HE COULDN'T HAVE DONE IT...
...COULD HE?

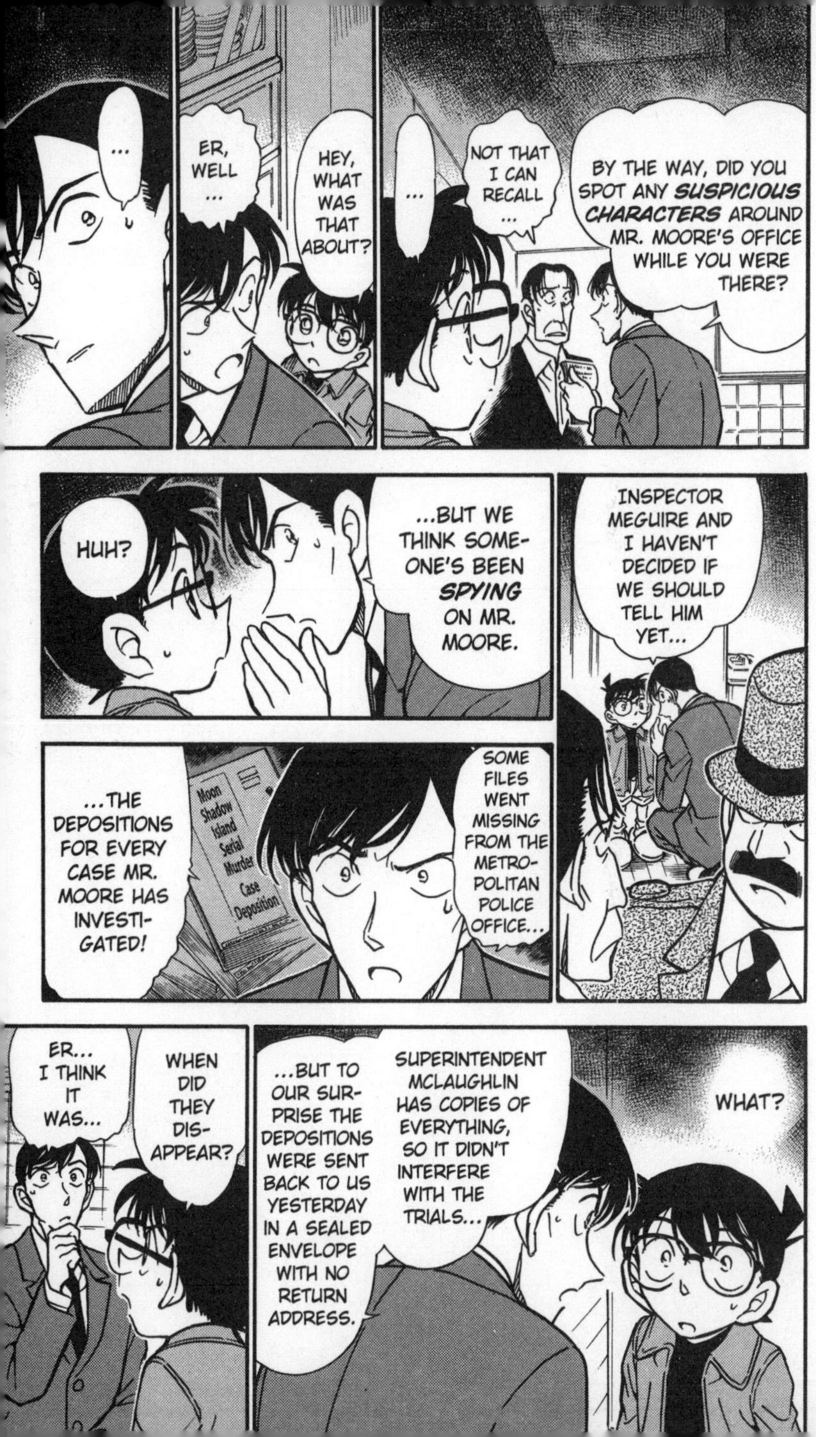
BY THE WAY, DID YOU SPOT ANY SUSPICIOUS CHARACTERS AROUND MR. MOORE'S OFFICE WHILE YOU WERE THERE?
NOT THAT I CAN RECALL ...
...
HEY, WHAT WAS THAT ABOUT?
ER, WELL ...
...
INSPECTOR MEGUIRE AND I HAVEN'T DECIDED IF WE SHOULD TELL HIM YET...
...BUT WE THINK SOME-ONE'S BEEN SPYING ON MR. MOORE.
HUH?
SOME FILES WENT MISSING FROM THE METRO-POLITAN POLICE OFFICE...
Moon Shadow Island Serial Murder Case Deposition
...THE DEPOSITIONS FOR EVERY CASE MR. MOORE HAS INVESTI-GATED!
WHAT?
SUPERINTENDENT MCLAUGHLIN HAS COPIES OF EVERYTHING, SO IT DIDN'T INTERFERE WITH THE TRIALS...
...BUT TO OUR SUR-PRISE THE DEPOSITIONS WERE SENT BACK TO US YESTERDAY IN A SEALED ENVELOPE WITH NO RETURN ADDRESS.
WHEN DID THEY DIS-APPEAR?
ER... I THINK IT WAS...

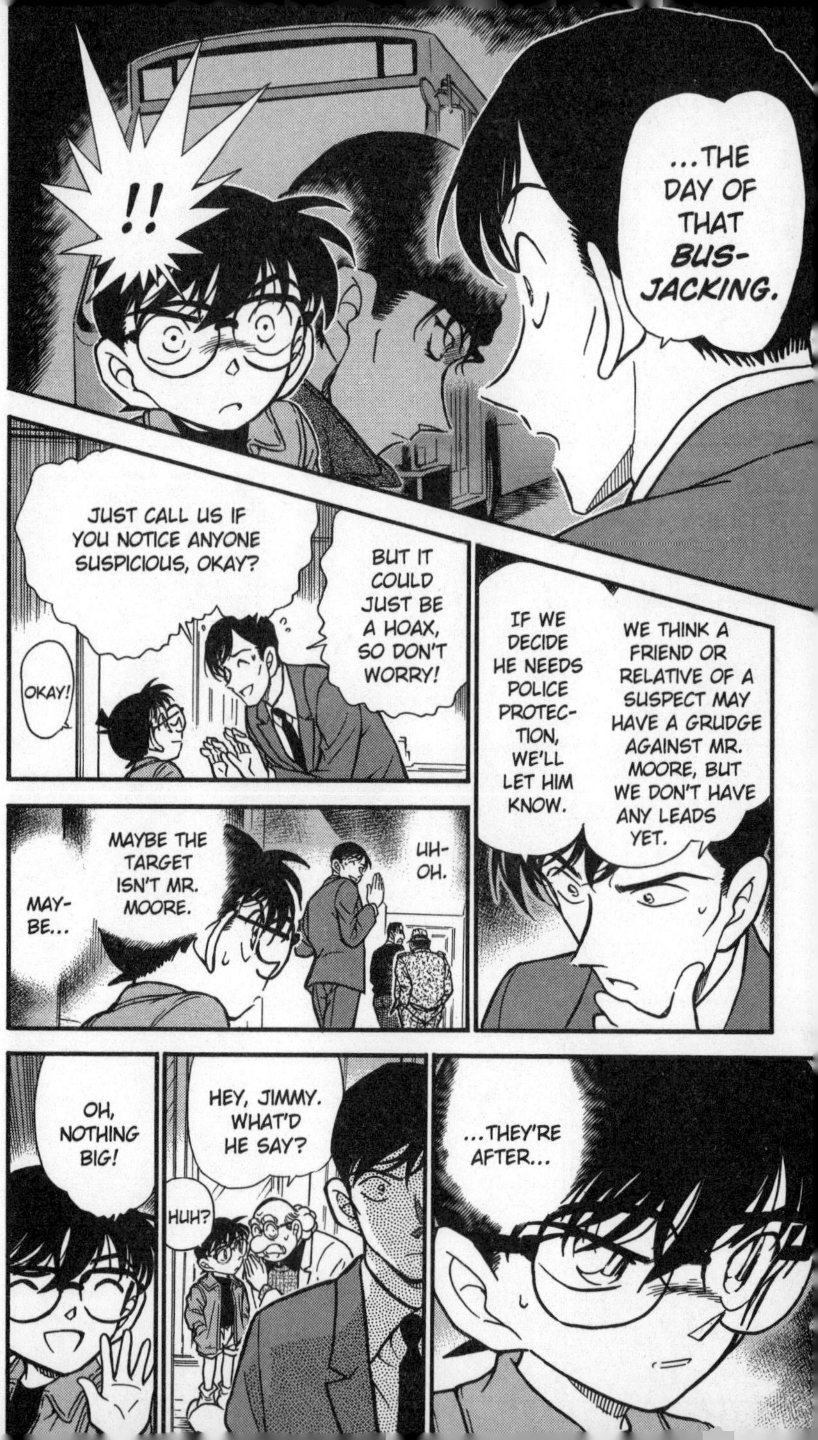
...THE DAY OF THAT BUS-JACKING.
!!
WE THINK A FRIEND OR RELATIVE OF A SUSPECT MAY HAVE A GRUDGE AGAINST MR. MOORE, BUT WE DON'T HAVE ANY LEADS YET.
IF WE DECIDE HE NEEDS POLICE PROTECTION, WE'LL LET HIM KNOW.
JUST CALL US IF YOU NOTICE ANYONE SUSPICIOUS, OKAY?
BUT IT COULD JUST BE A HOAX, SO DON'T WORRY!
OKAY!
UH-OH.
MAYBE THE TARGET ISN'T MR. MOORE.
MAY-BE...
...THEY'RE AFTER...
HEY, JIMMY. WHAT'D HE SAY?
HUH?
OH, NOTHING BIG!

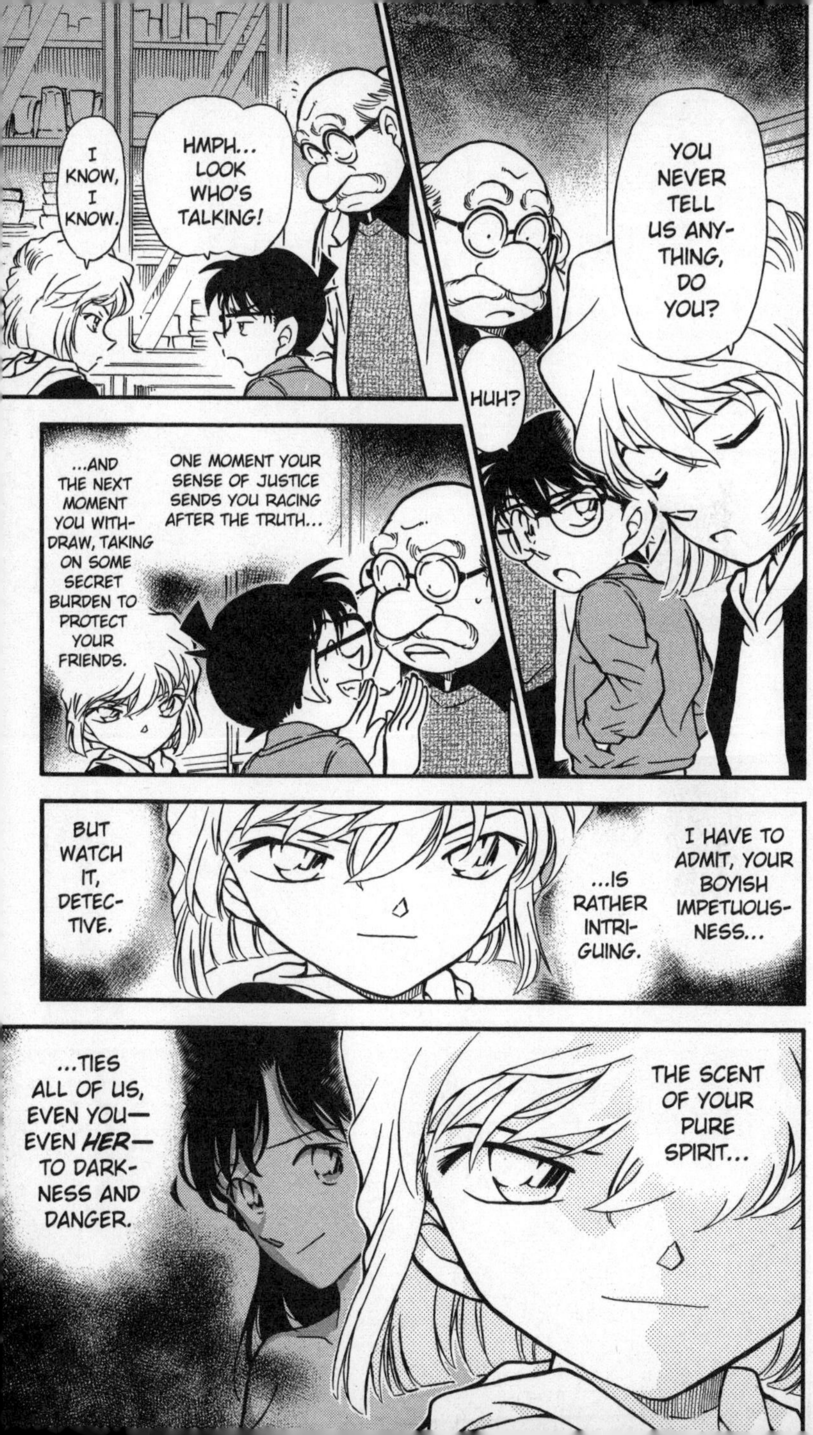
YOU NEVER TELL US ANYTHING, DO YOU?
HUH?
HMPH... LOOK WHO'S TALKING!
I KNOW, I KNOW.
ONE MOMENT YOUR SENSE OF JUSTICE SENDS YOU RACING AFTER THE TRUTH...
...AND THE NEXT MOMENT YOU WITHDRAW, TAKING ON SOME SECRET BURDEN TO PROTECT YOUR FRIENDS.
I HAVE TO ADMIT, YOUR BOYISH IMPETUOUSNESS...
...IS RATHER INTRIGUING.
BUT WATCH IT, DETECTIVE.
THE SCENT OF YOUR PURE SPIRIT...
...TIES ALL OF US, EVEN YOU—EVEN *HER*—TO DARKNESS AND DANGER.

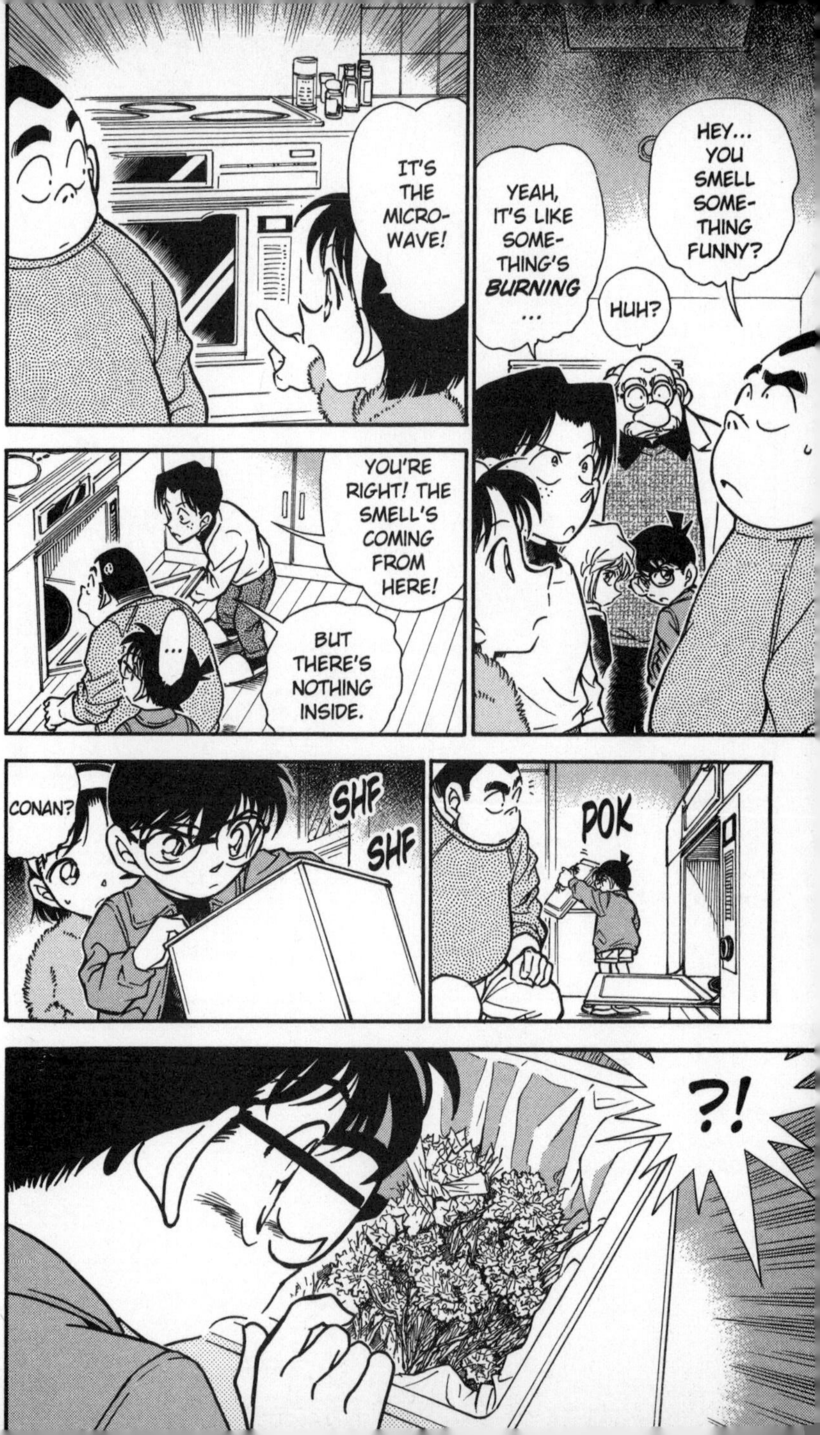
HEY... YOU SMELL SOME-THING FUNNY?
HUH?
YEAH, IT'S LIKE SOME-THING'S BURNING...
IT'S THE MICRO-WAVE!
YOU'RE RIGHT! THE SMELL'S COMING FROM HERE!
BUT THERE'S NOTHING INSIDE.
...
POK
SHF
SHF
CONAN?
?!

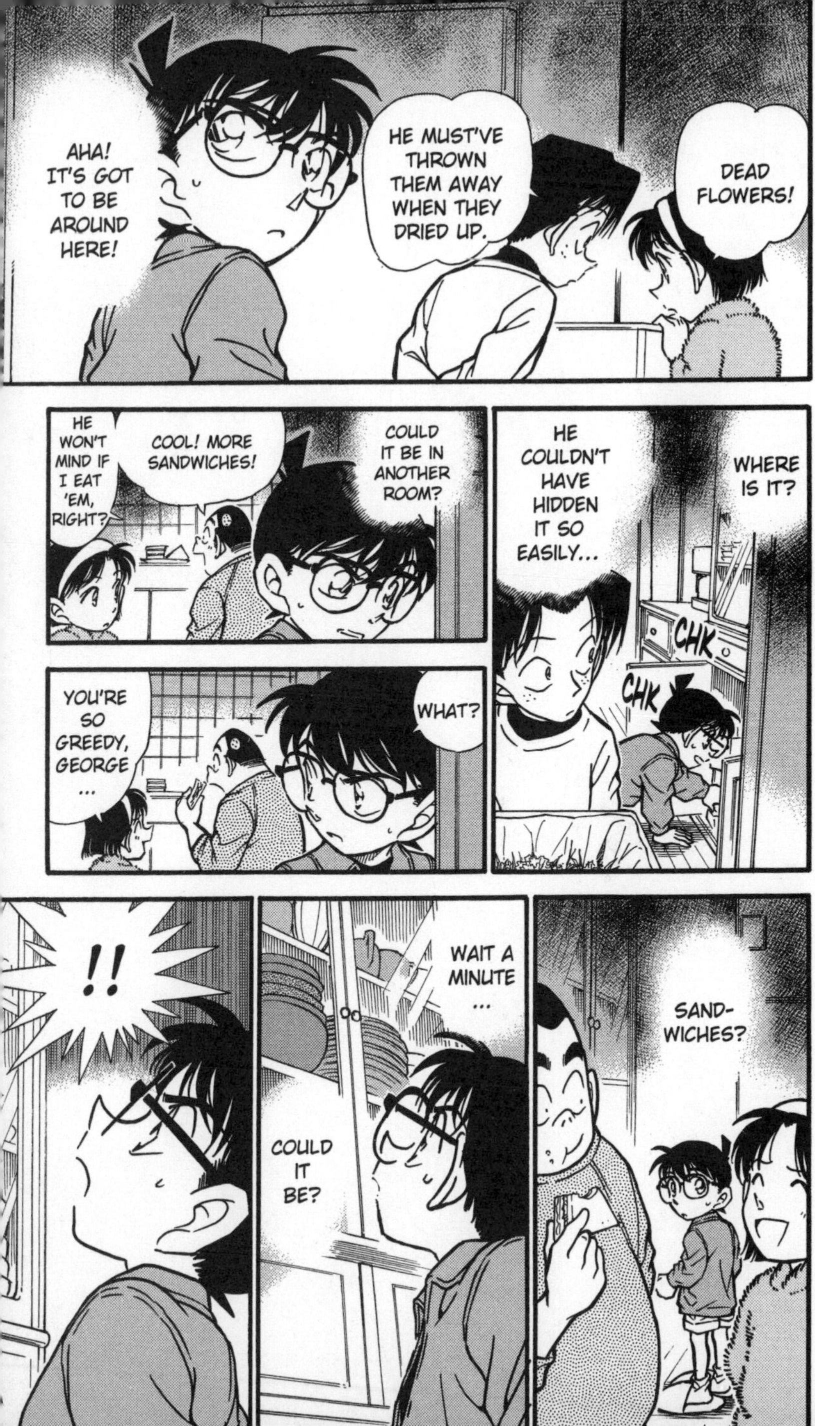
DEAD FLOWERS!
HE MUST'VE THROWN THEM AWAY WHEN THEY DRIED UP.
AHA! IT'S GOT TO BE AROUND HERE!
WHERE IS IT?
HE COULDN'T HAVE HIDDEN IT SO EASILY...
CHK
CHK
COULD IT BE IN ANOTHER ROOM?
COOL! MORE SANDWICHES!
HE WON'T MIND IF I EAT 'EM, RIGHT?
WHAT?
YOU'RE SO GREEDY, GEORGE ...
SAND-WICHES?
WAIT A MINUTE ...
COULD IT BE?
!!

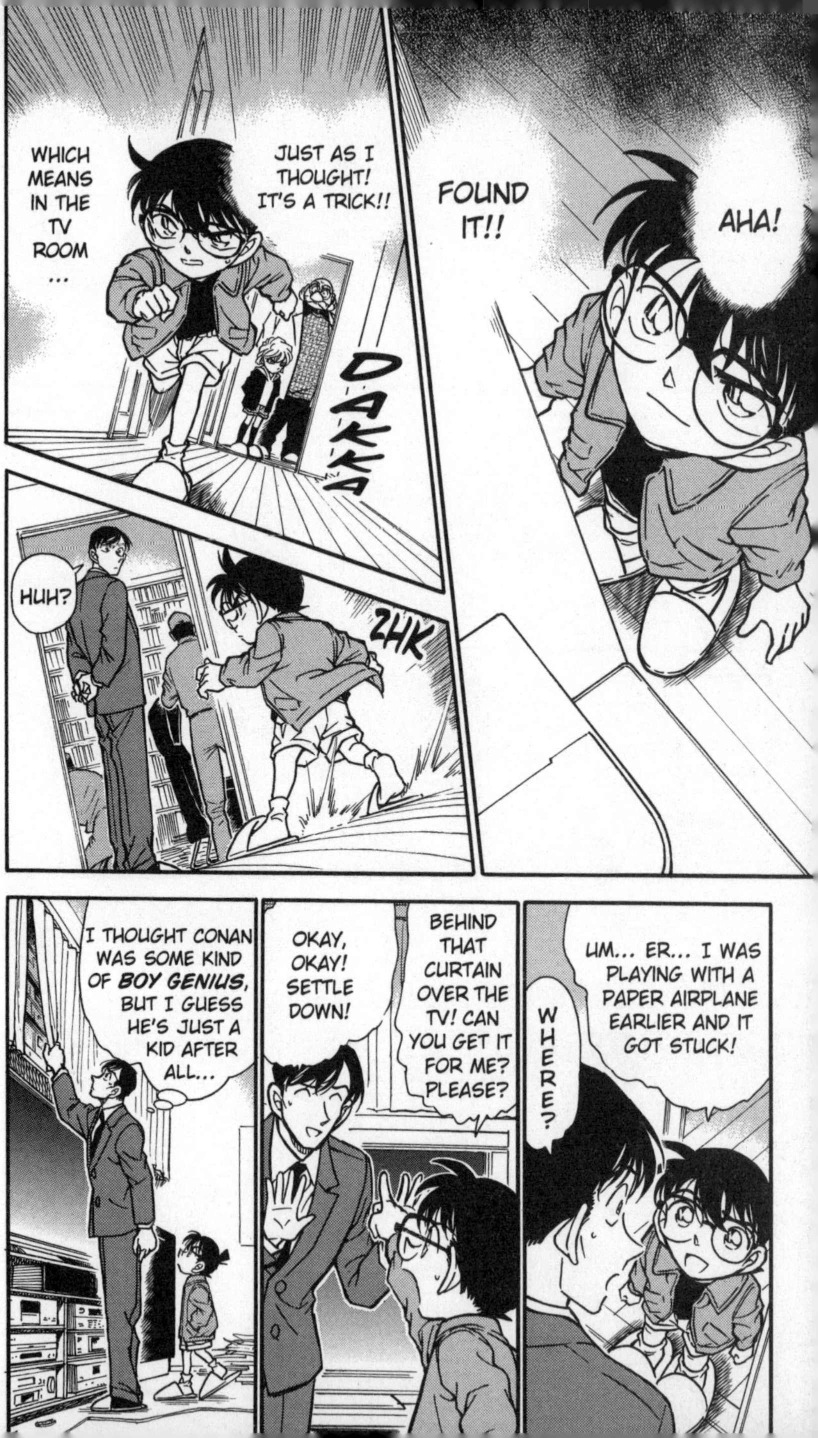
JUST AS I THOUGHT! IT'S A TRICK!!
WHICH MEANS IN THE TV ROOM ...
DAKKA
ZHK
HUH?
AHA!
FOUND IT!!
UM... ER... I WAS PLAYING WITH A PAPER AIRPLANE EARLIER AND IT GOT STUCK!
WHERE?
BEHIND THAT CURTAIN OVER THE TV! CAN YOU GET IT FOR ME? PLEASE?
OKAY, OKAY! SETTLE DOWN!
I THOUGHT CONAN WAS SOME KIND OF ***BOY GENIUS***, BUT I GUESS HE'S JUST A KID AFTER ALL...

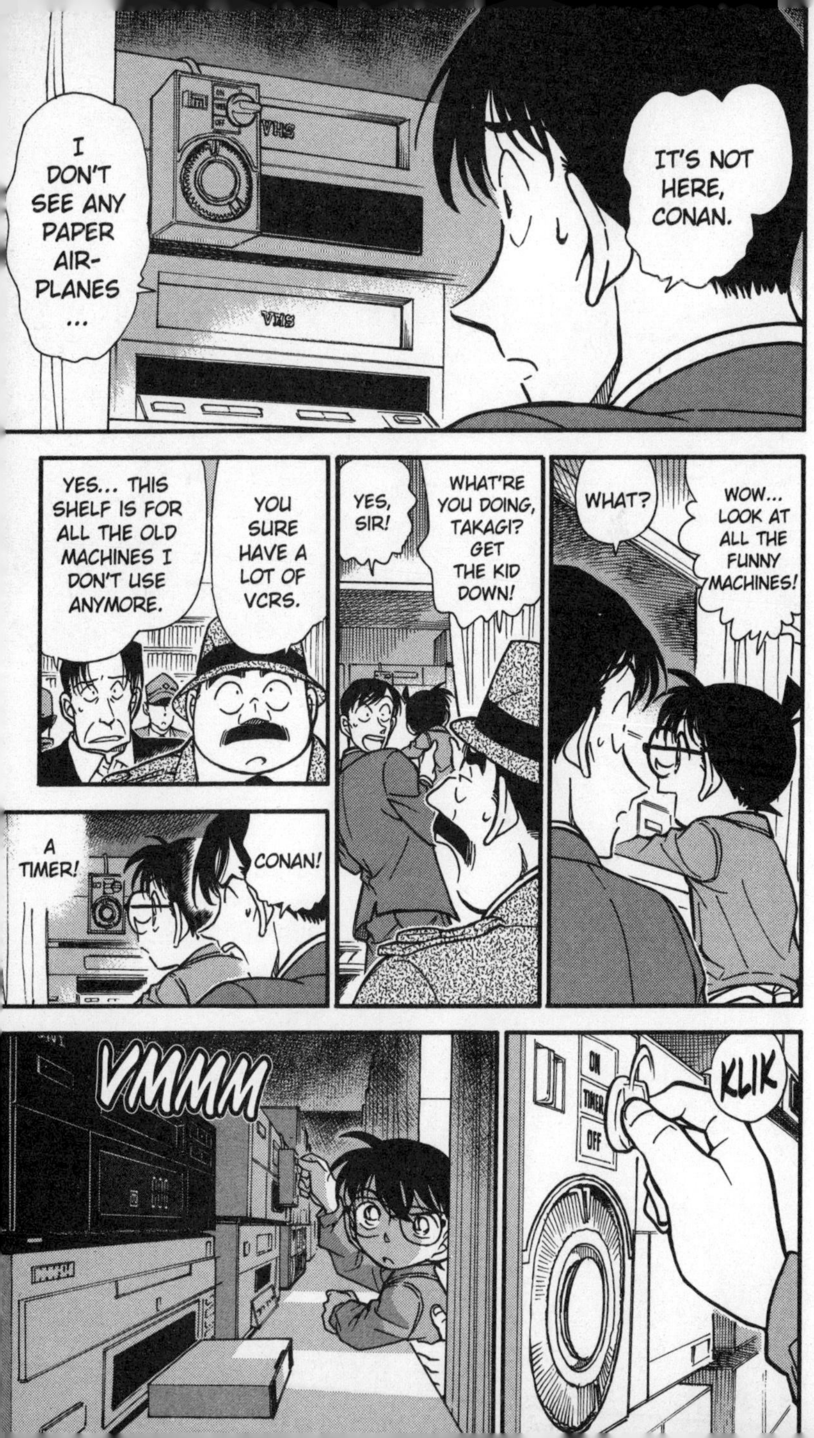
IT'S NOT HERE, CONAN.
I DON'T SEE ANY PAPER AIR-PLANES ...
WOW... LOOK AT ALL THE FUNNY MACHINES!
WHAT?
WHAT'RE YOU DOING, TAKAGI? GET THE KID DOWN!
YES, SIR!
YOU SURE HAVE A LOT OF VCRS.
YES... THIS SHELF IS FOR ALL THE OLD MACHINES I DON'T USE ANYMORE.
CONAN!
A TIMER!
KLIK
VMMM

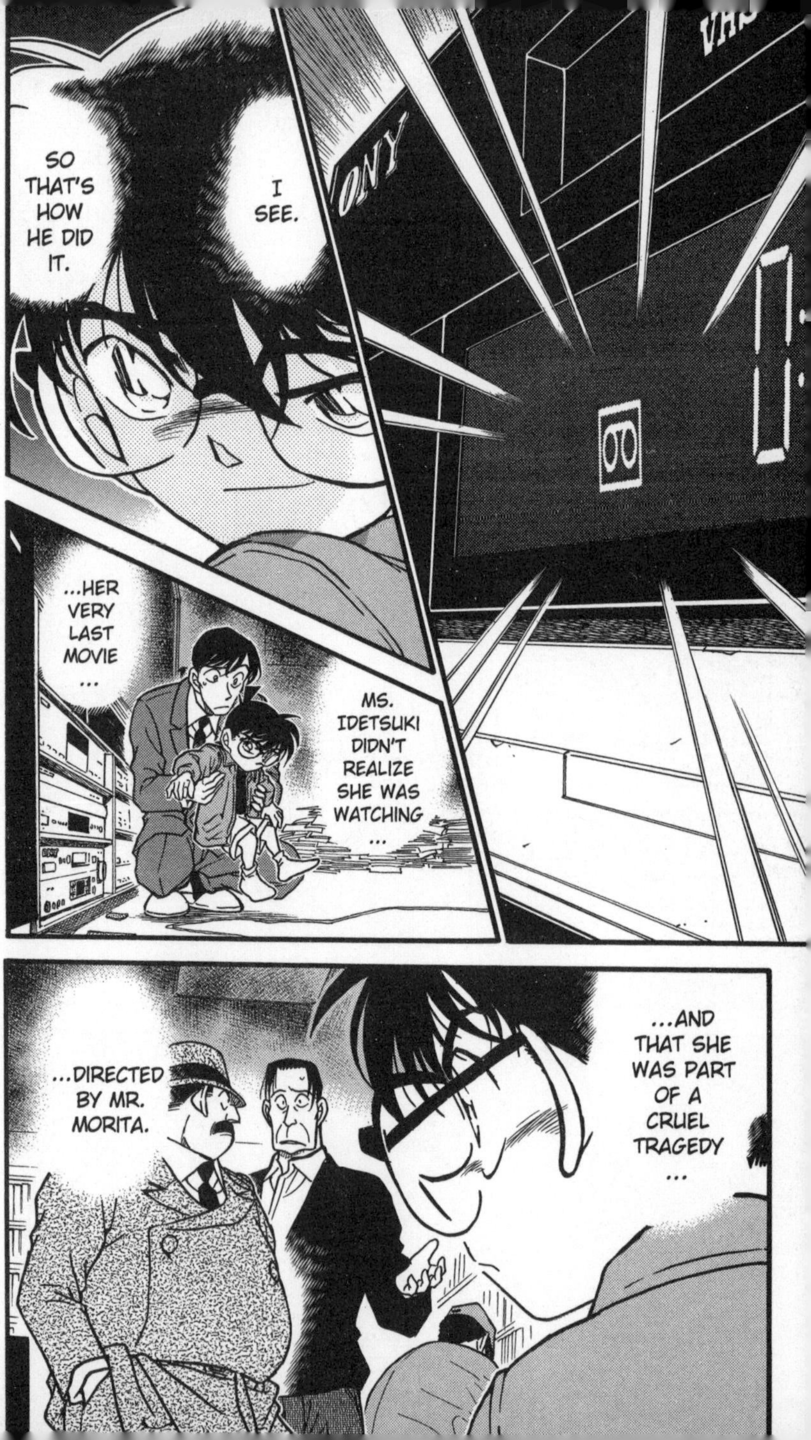
I SEE.
SO THAT'S HOW HE DID IT.
MS. IDETSUKI DIDN'T REALIZE SHE WAS WATCHING...
...HER VERY LAST MOVIE...
...AND THAT SHE WAS PART OF A CRUEL TRAGEDY...
...DIRECTED BY MR. MORITA.

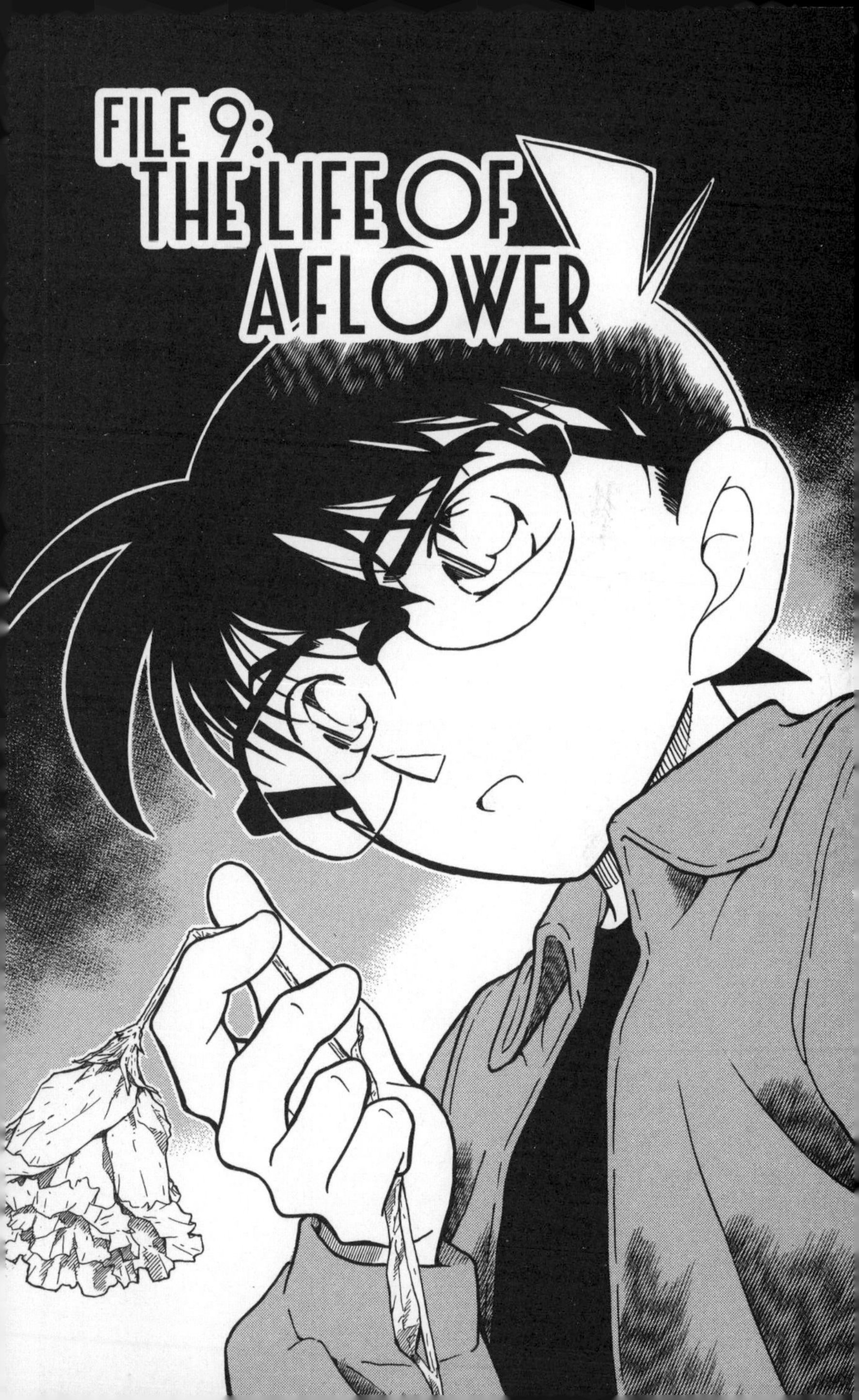
FILE 9:
THE LIFE OF
A FLOWER

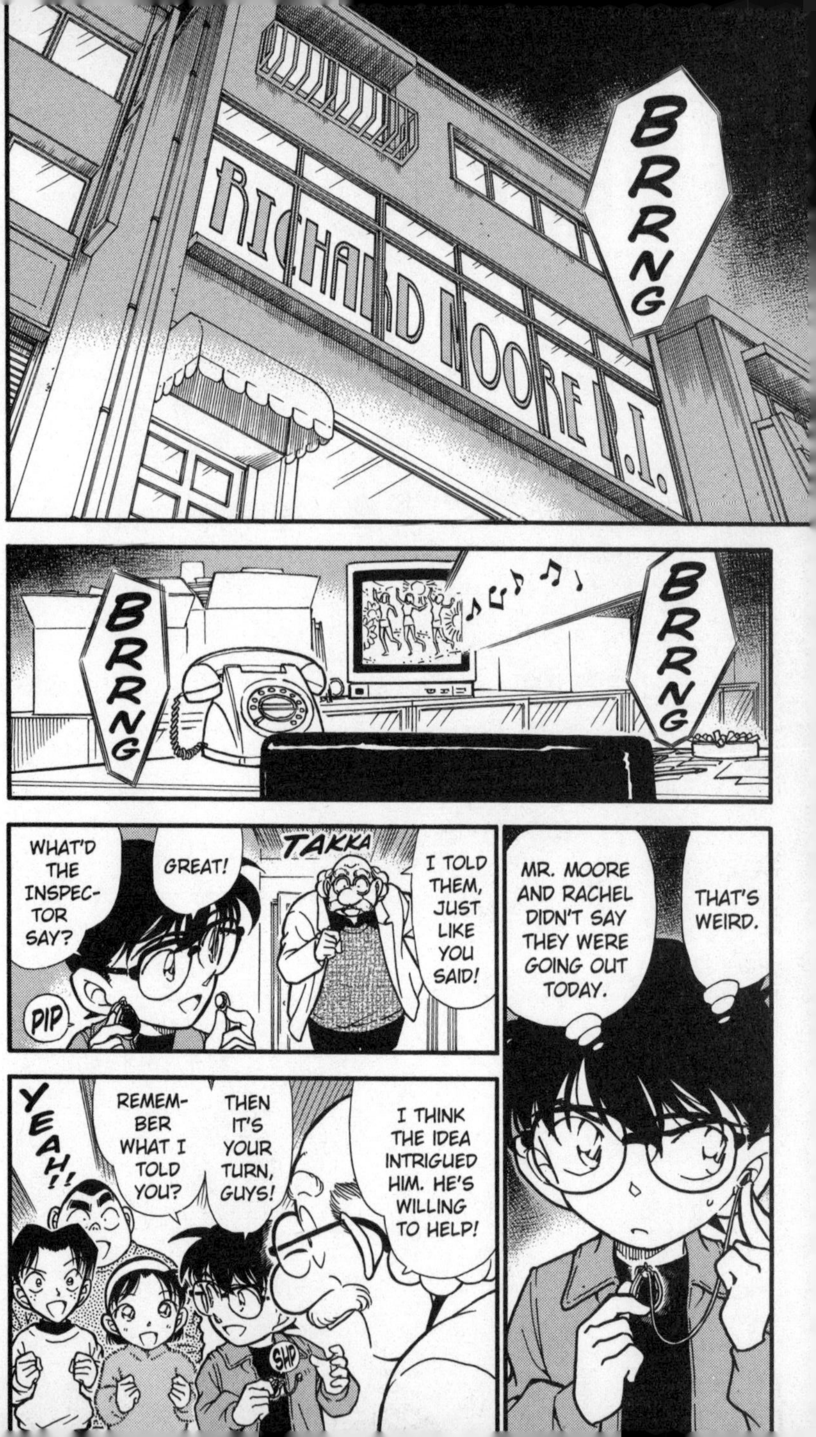
RICHARD MOORE P.I.
BRRNG
BRRNG
BRRNG
THAT'S WEIRD.
MR. MOORE AND RACHEL DIDN'T SAY THEY WERE GOING OUT TODAY.
I TOLD THEM, JUST LIKE YOU SAID!
TAKKA
GREAT!
WHAT'D THE INSPECTOR SAY?
PIP
I THINK THE IDEA INTRIGUED HIM. HE'S WILLING TO HELP!
THEN IT'S YOUR TURN, GUYS!
REMEMBER WHAT I TOLD YOU?
SHP
YEAH!!

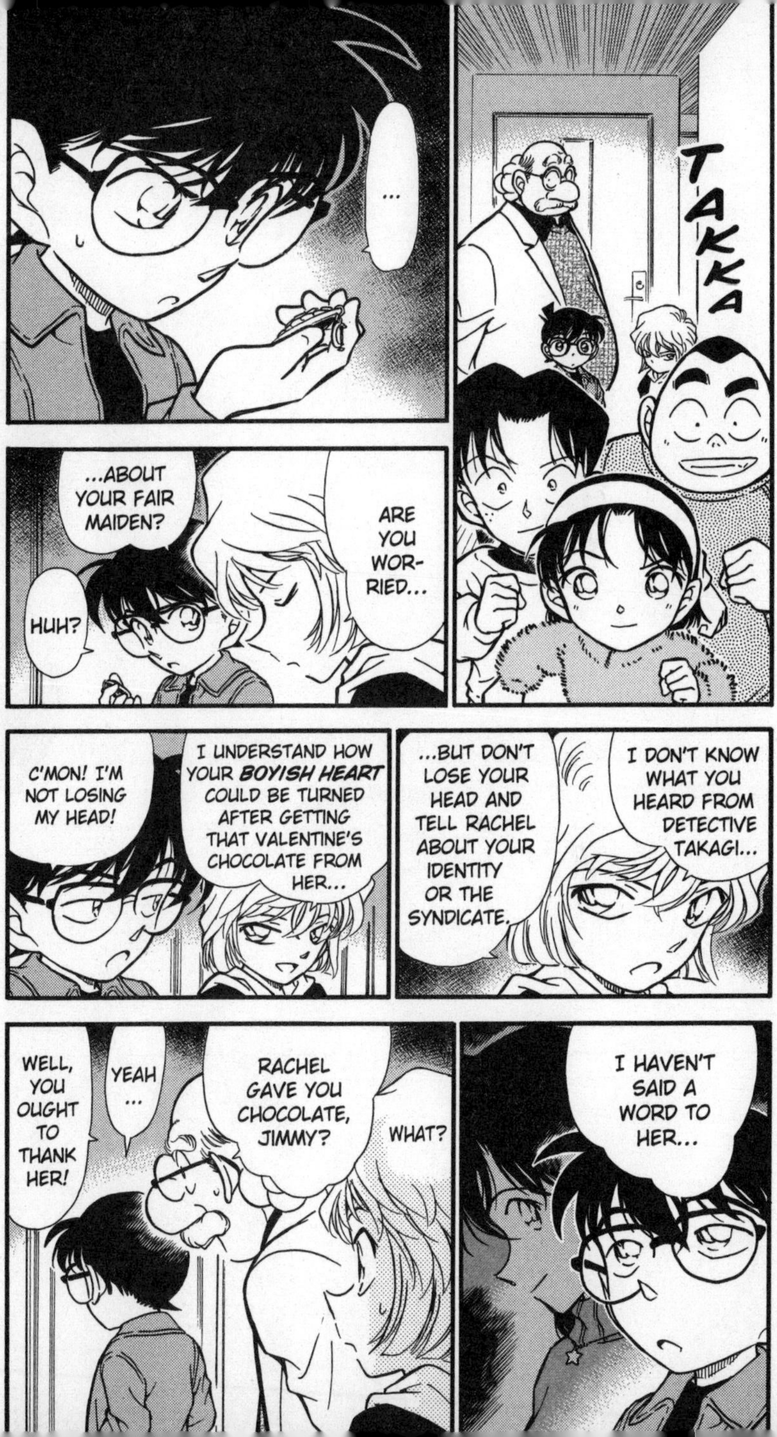
TAKKA
...
ARE YOU WORRIED...
...ABOUT YOUR FAIR MAIDEN?
HUH?
I DON'T KNOW WHAT YOU HEARD FROM DETECTIVE TAKAGI...
...BUT DON'T LOSE YOUR HEAD AND TELL RACHEL ABOUT YOUR IDENTITY OR THE SYNDICATE.
I UNDERSTAND HOW YOUR **BOYISH HEART** COULD BE TURNED AFTER GETTING THAT VALENTINE'S CHOCOLATE FROM HER...
C'MON! I'M NOT LOSING MY HEAD!
I HAVEN'T SAID A WORD TO HER...
WHAT?
RACHEL GAVE YOU CHOCOLATE, JIMMY?
YEAH...
WELL, YOU OUGHT TO THANK HER!

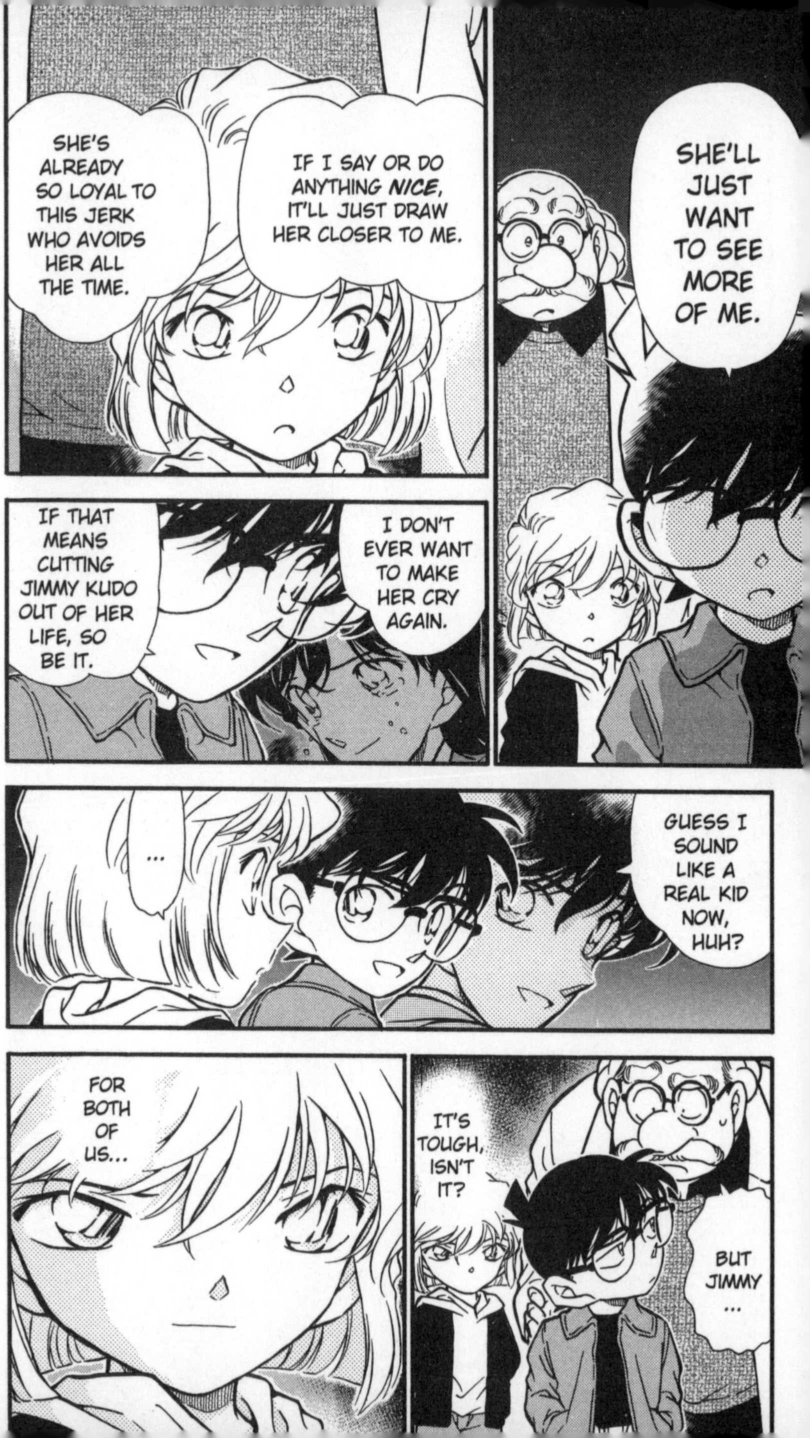
SHE'LL JUST WANT TO SEE MORE OF ME.
IF I SAY OR DO ANYTHING NICE, IT'LL JUST DRAW HER CLOSER TO ME.
SHE'S ALREADY SO LOYAL TO THIS JERK WHO AVOIDS HER ALL THE TIME.
I DON'T EVER WANT TO MAKE HER CRY AGAIN.
IF THAT MEANS CUTTING JIMMY KUDO OUT OF HER LIFE, SO BE IT.
GUESS I SOUND LIKE A REAL KID NOW, HUH?
...
BUT JIMMY ...
IT'S TOUGH, ISN'T IT?
FOR BOTH OF US...

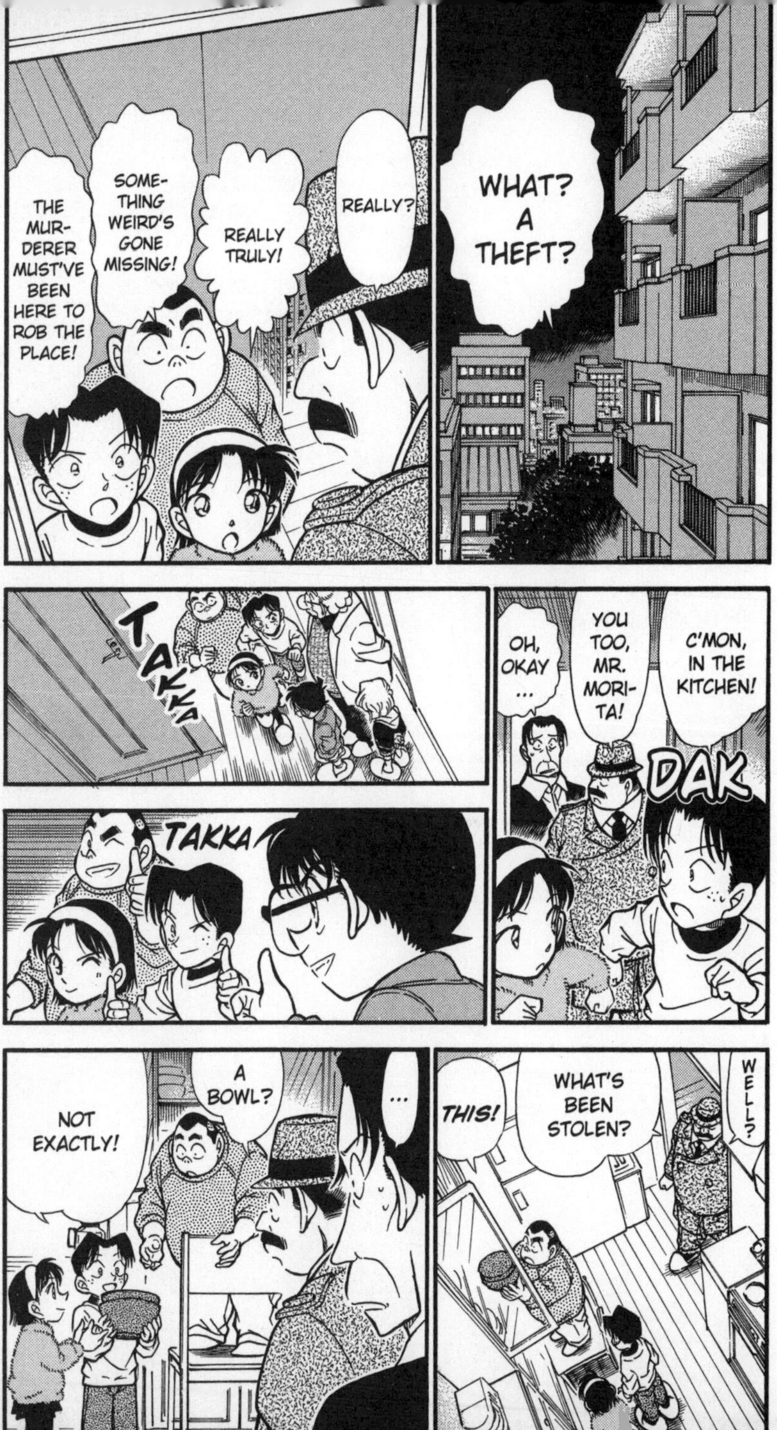
WHAT? A THEFT?
REALLY?
REALLY TRULY!
SOME-THING WEIRD'S GONE MISSING!
THE MUR-DERER MUST'VE BEEN HERE TO ROB THE PLACE!
C'MON, IN THE KITCHEN!
YOU TOO, MR. MORI-TA!
OH, OKAY ...
DAK
TAKKA
TAKKA
WELL?
WHAT'S BEEN STOLEN?
THIS!
...
A BOWL?
NOT EXACTLY!

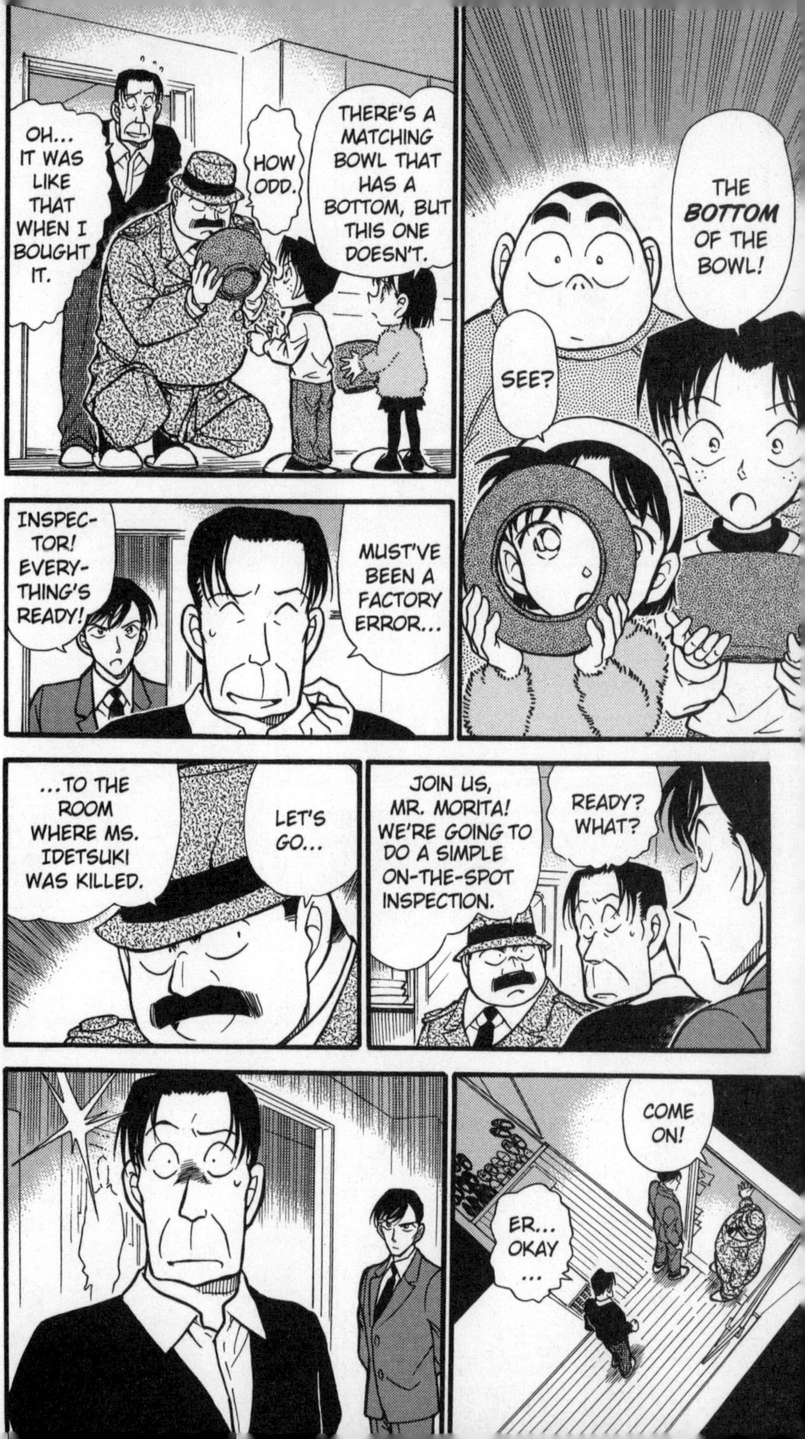
THE *BOTTOM* OF THE BOWL!
SEE?
THERE'S A MATCHING BOWL THAT HAS A BOTTOM, BUT THIS ONE DOESN'T.
HOW ODD.
OH... IT WAS LIKE THAT WHEN I BOUGHT IT.
MUST'VE BEEN A FACTORY ERROR...
INSPECTOR! EVERYTHING'S READY!
READY? WHAT?
JOIN US, MR. MORITA! WE'RE GOING TO DO A SIMPLE ON-THE-SPOT INSPECTION.
LET'S GO...
...TO THE ROOM WHERE MS. IDETSUKI WAS KILLED.
COME ON!
ER... OKAY ...

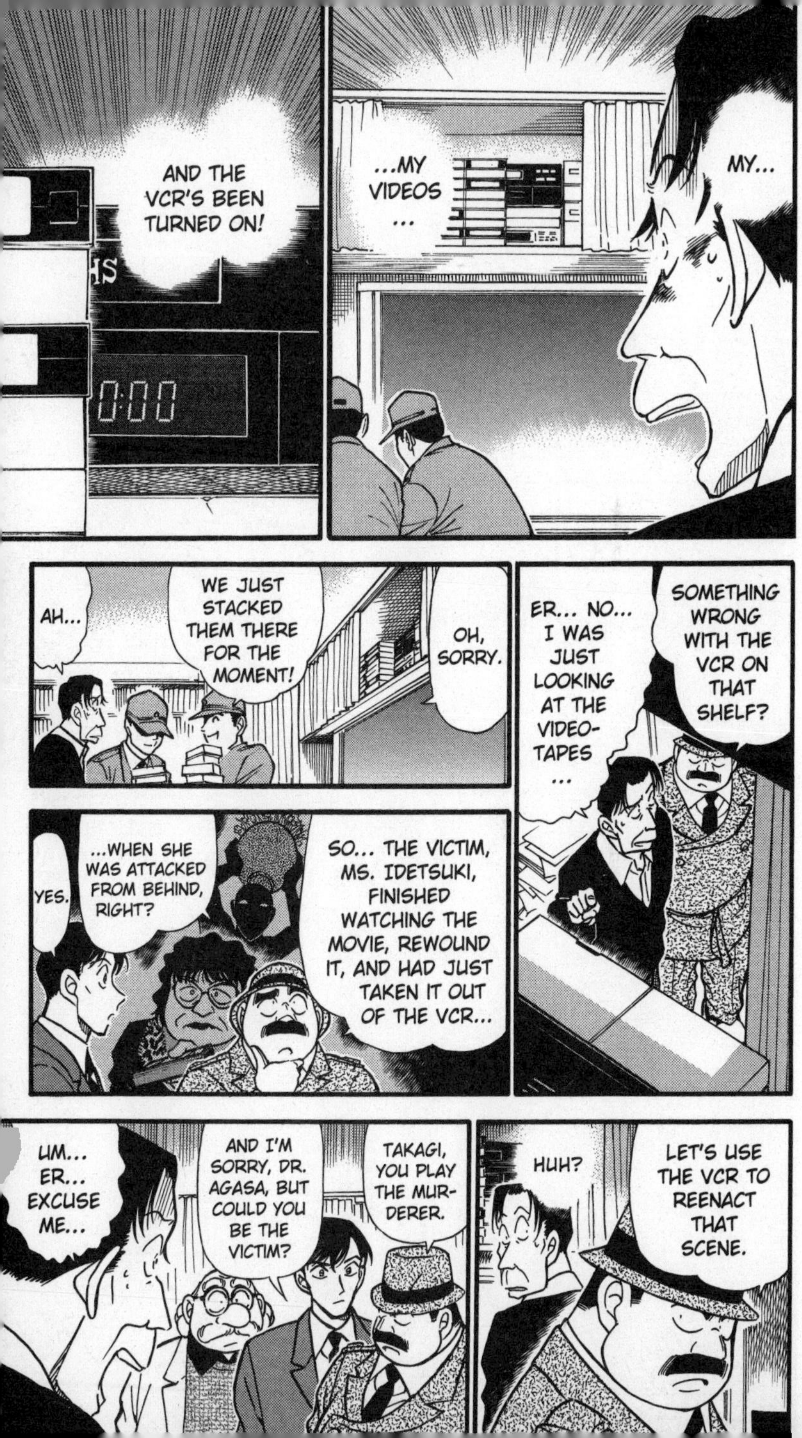
MY...
...MY VIDEOS ...
AND THE VCR'S BEEN TURNED ON!
SOMETHING WRONG WITH THE VCR ON THAT SHELF?
ER... NO... I WAS JUST LOOKING AT THE VIDEO-TAPES ...
OH, SORRY.
WE JUST STACKED THEM THERE FOR THE MOMENT!
AH...
SO... THE VICTIM, MS. IDETSUKI, FINISHED WATCHING THE MOVIE, REWOUND IT, AND HAD JUST TAKEN IT OUT OF THE VCR...
...WHEN SHE WAS ATTACKED FROM BEHIND, RIGHT?
YES.
LET'S USE THE VCR TO REENACT THAT SCENE.
HUH?
TAKAGI, YOU PLAY THE MUR-DERER.
AND I'M SORRY, DR. AGASA, BUT COULD YOU BE THE VICTIM?
UM... ER... EXCUSE ME...

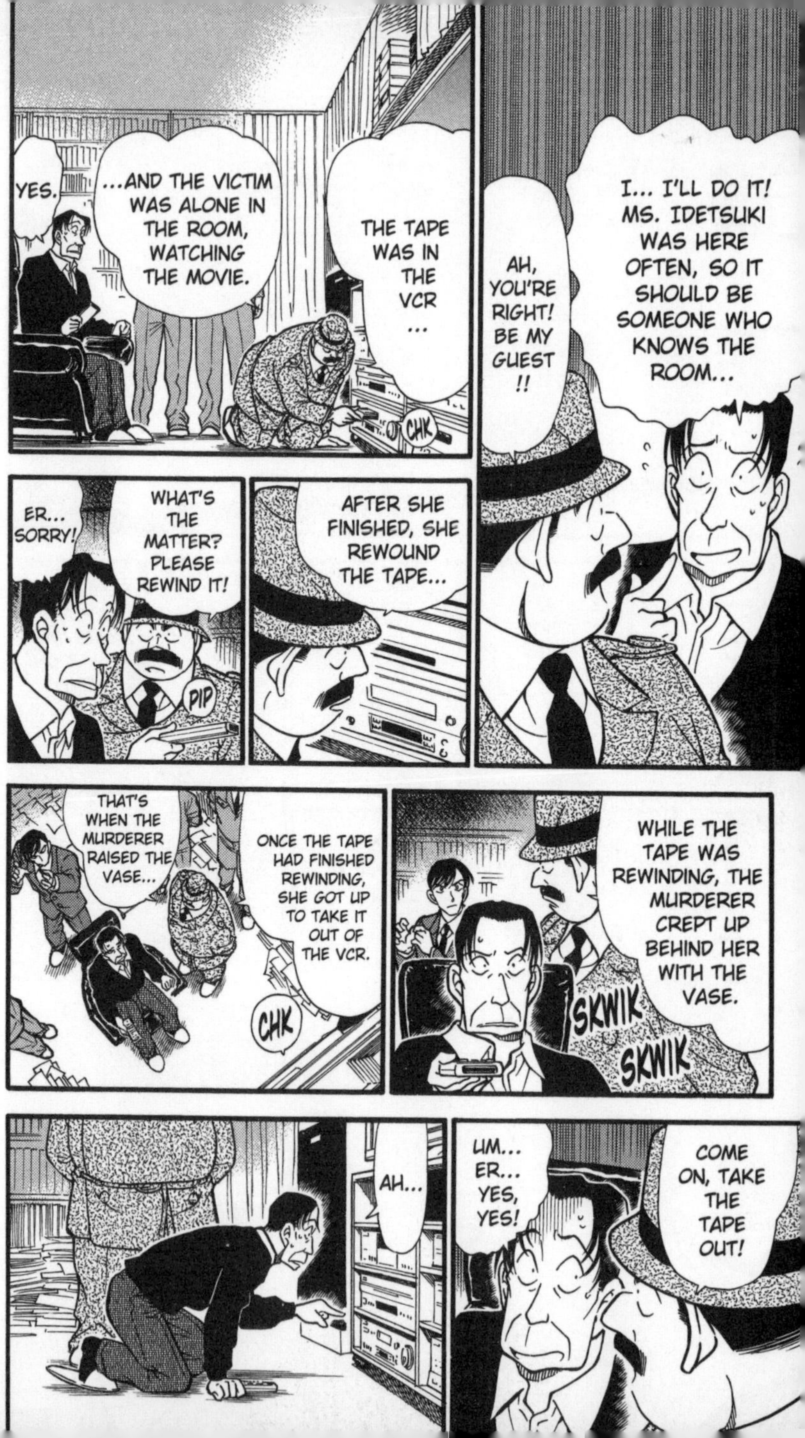
I... I'LL DO IT! MS. IDETSUKI WAS HERE OFTEN, SO IT SHOULD BE SOMEONE WHO KNOWS THE ROOM...
AH, YOU'RE RIGHT! BE MY GUEST!!
THE TAPE WAS IN THE VCR...
CHK
...AND THE VICTIM WAS ALONE IN THE ROOM, WATCHING THE MOVIE.
YES.
AFTER SHE FINISHED, SHE REWOUND THE TAPE...
WHAT'S THE MATTER? PLEASE REWIND IT!
ER... SORRY!
PIP
WHILE THE TAPE WAS REWINDING, THE MURDERER CREPT UP BEHIND HER WITH THE VASE.
SKWIK
SKWIK
ONCE THE TAPE HAD FINISHED REWINDING, SHE GOT UP TO TAKE IT OUT OF THE VCR.
CHK
THAT'S WHEN THE MURDERER RAISED THE VASE...
COME ON, TAKE THE TAPE OUT!
UM... ER... YES, YES!
AH...

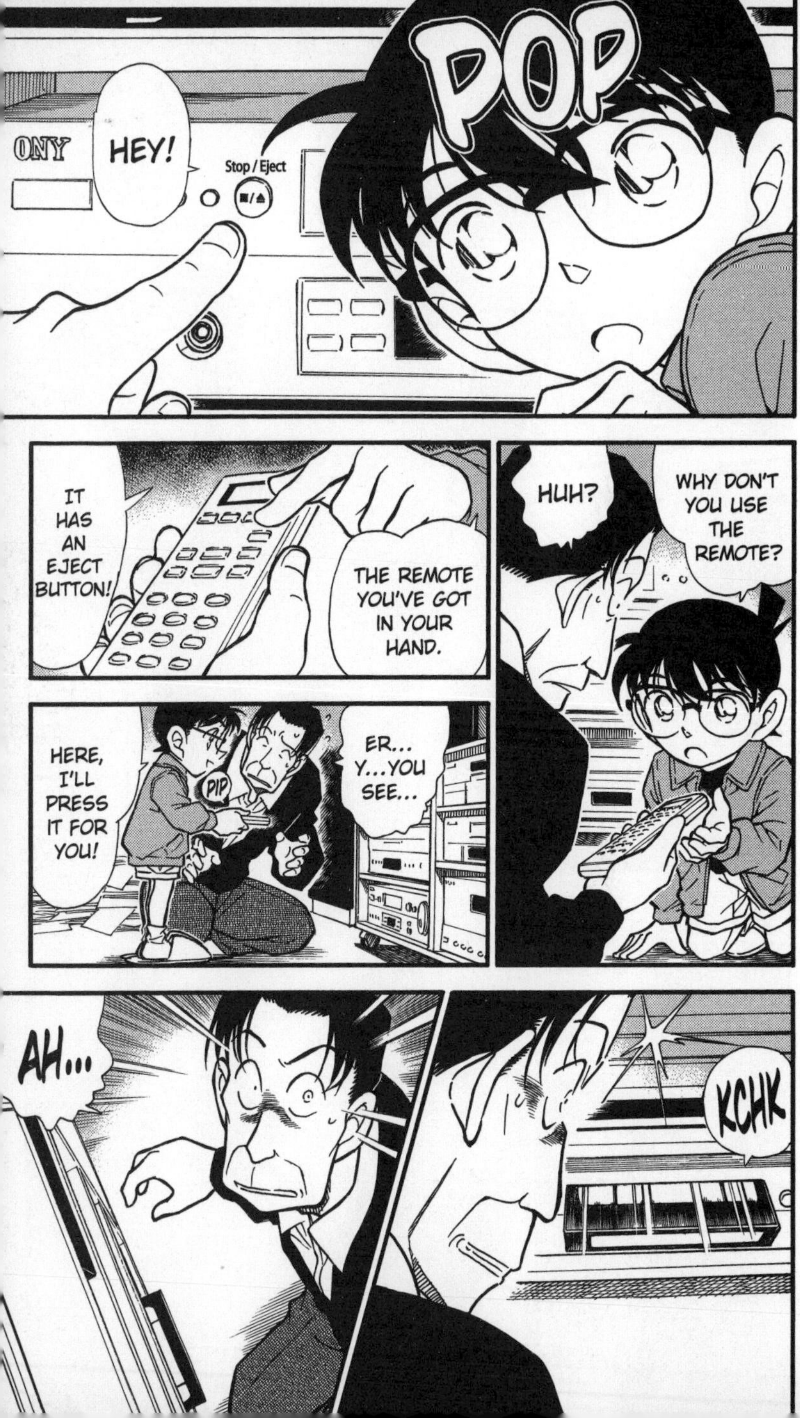
POP
Stop / Eject
ONY
HEY!
WHY DON'T YOU USE THE REMOTE?
HUH?
THE REMOTE YOU'VE GOT IN YOUR HAND.
IT HAS AN EJECT BUTTON!
ER... Y...YOU SEE...
PIP
HERE, I'LL PRESS IT FOR YOU!
KCHK
AH...

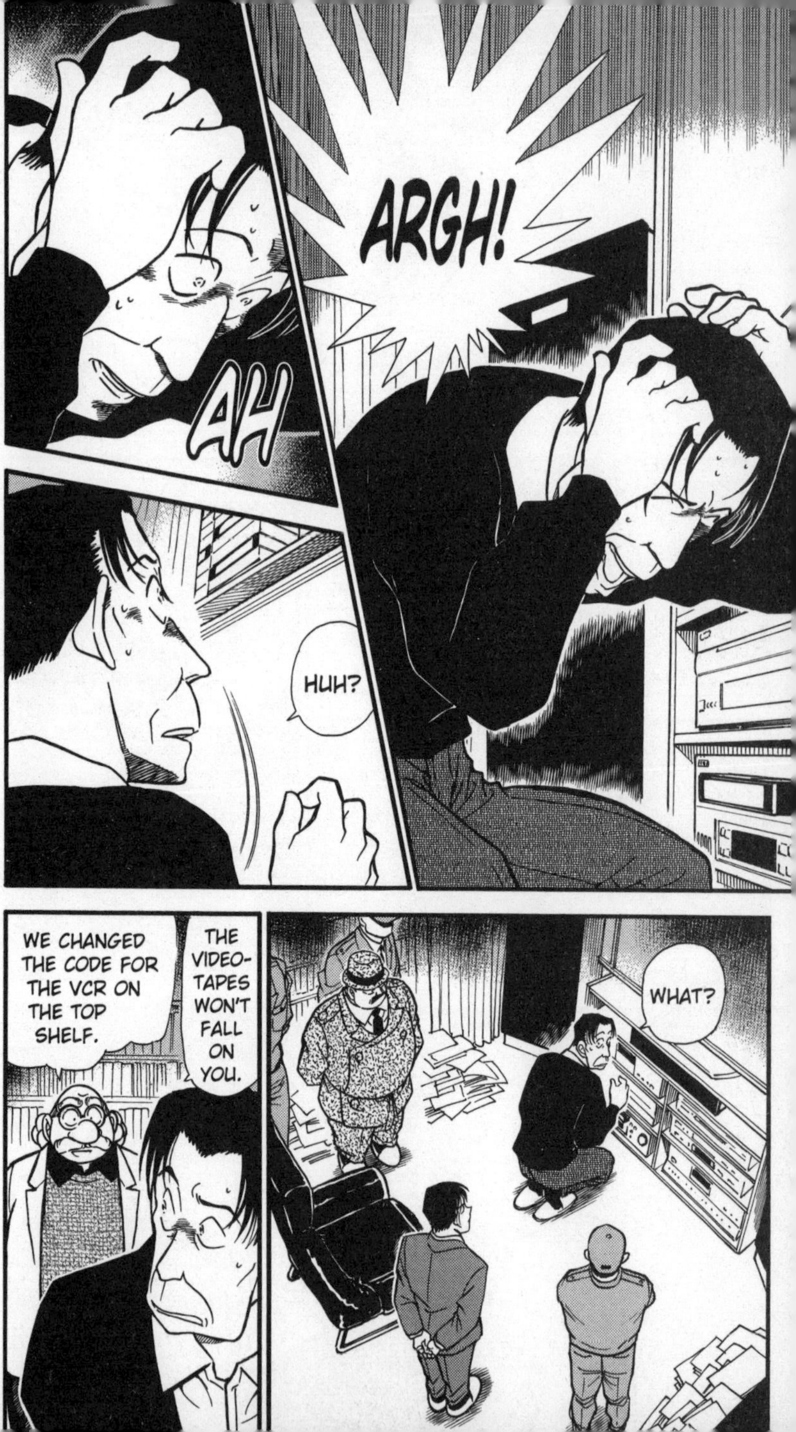
ARGH!
AH
HUH?
WHAT?
THE VIDEO-TAPES WON'T FALL ON YOU.
WE CHANGED THE CODE FOR THE VCR ON THE TOP SHELF.

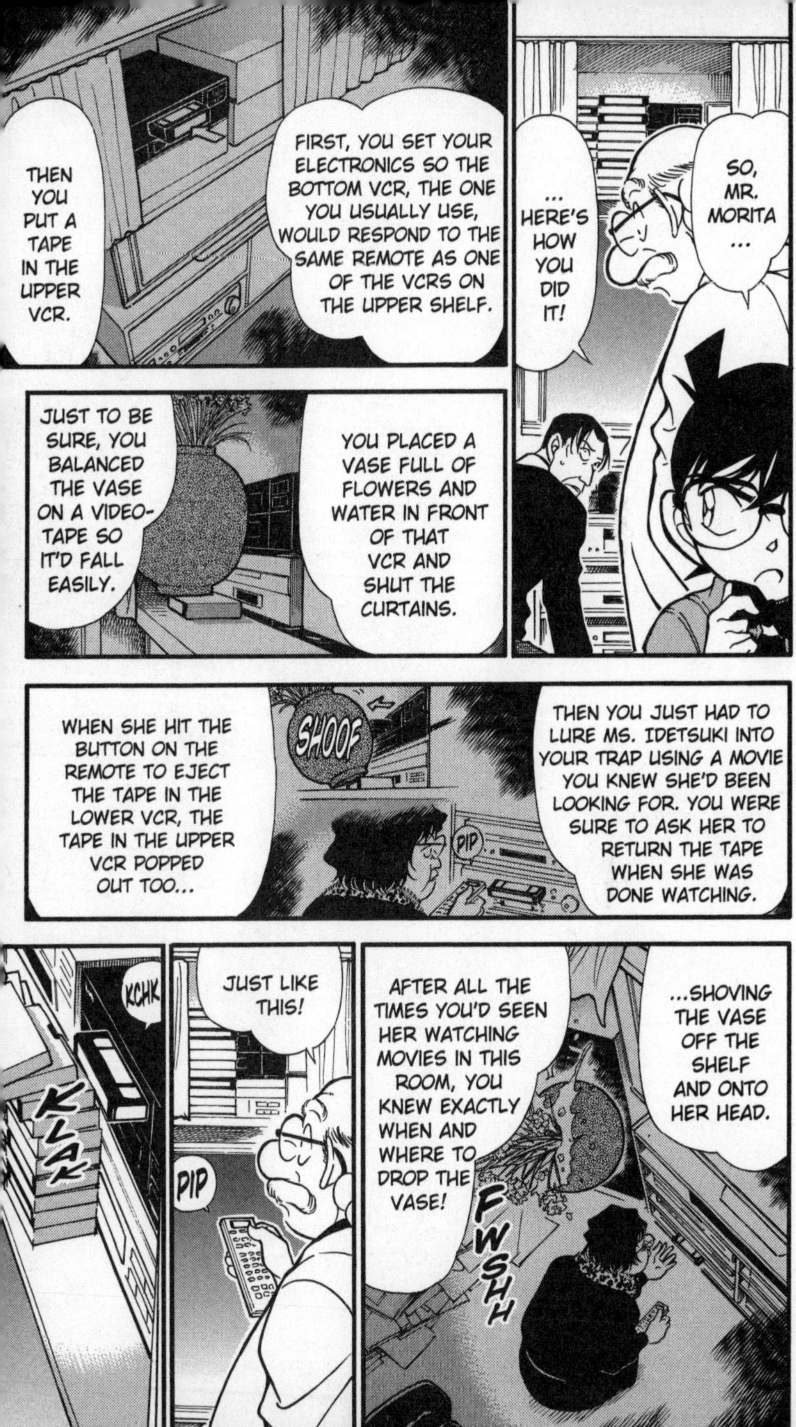
SO, MR. MORITA...
...HERE'S HOW YOU DID IT!
FIRST, YOU SET YOUR ELECTRONICS SO THE BOTTOM VCR, THE ONE YOU USUALLY USE, WOULD RESPOND TO THE SAME REMOTE AS ONE OF THE VCRS ON THE UPPER SHELF.
THEN YOU PUT A TAPE IN THE UPPER VCR.
YOU PLACED A VASE FULL OF FLOWERS AND WATER IN FRONT OF THAT VCR AND SHUT THE CURTAINS.
JUST TO BE SURE, YOU BALANCED THE VASE ON A VIDEO-TAPE SO IT'D FALL EASILY.
THEN YOU JUST HAD TO LURE MS. IDETSUKI INTO YOUR TRAP USING A MOVIE YOU KNEW SHE'D BEEN LOOKING FOR. YOU WERE SURE TO ASK HER TO RETURN THE TAPE WHEN SHE WAS DONE WATCHING.
SHOOF
PIP
WHEN SHE HIT THE BUTTON ON THE REMOTE TO EJECT THE TAPE IN THE LOWER VCR, THE TAPE IN THE UPPER VCR POPPED OUT TOO...
...SHOVING THE VASE OFF THE SHELF AND ONTO HER HEAD.
AFTER ALL THE TIMES YOU'D SEEN HER WATCHING MOVIES IN THIS ROOM, YOU KNEW EXACTLY WHEN AND WHERE TO DROP THE VASE!
FWSHH
JUST LIKE THIS!
PIP
KCHK
KLAK

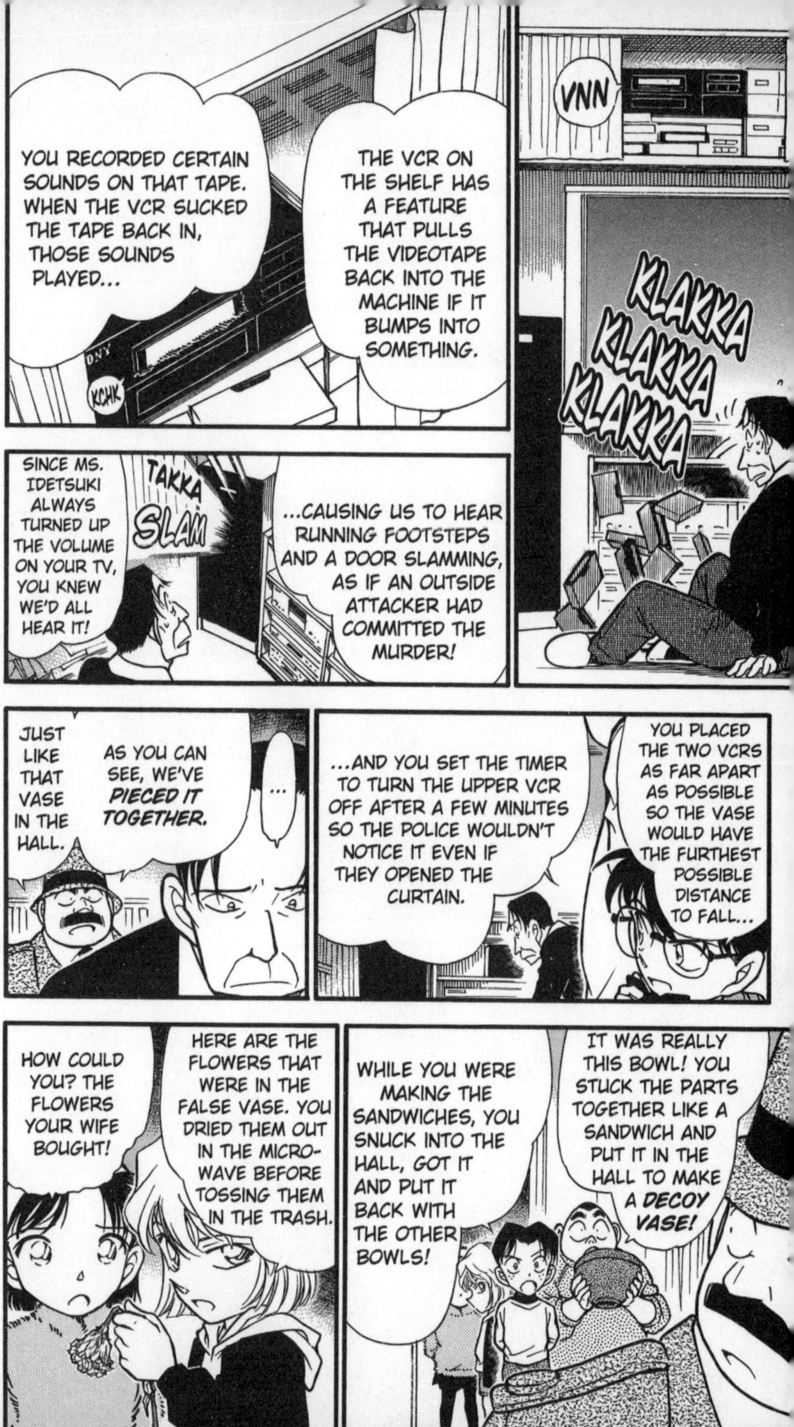
VNN
KLAKKA KLAKKA KLAKKA
THE VCR ON THE SHELF HAS A FEATURE THAT PULLS THE VIDEOTAPE BACK INTO THE MACHINE IF IT BUMPS INTO SOMETHING.
YOU RECORDED CERTAIN SOUNDS ON THAT TAPE. WHEN THE VCR SUCKED THE TAPE BACK IN, THOSE SOUNDS PLAYED...
KCHK
...CAUSING US TO HEAR RUNNING FOOTSTEPS AND A DOOR SLAMMING, AS IF AN OUTSIDE ATTACKER HAD COMMITTED THE MURDER!
TAKKA
SLAM
SINCE MS. IDETSUKI ALWAYS TURNED UP THE VOLUME ON YOUR TV, YOU KNEW WE'D ALL HEAR IT!
YOU PLACED THE TWO VCRS AS FAR APART AS POSSIBLE SO THE VASE WOULD HAVE THE FURTHEST POSSIBLE DISTANCE TO FALL...
...AND YOU SET THE TIMER TO TURN THE UPPER VCR OFF AFTER A FEW MINUTES SO THE POLICE WOULDN'T NOTICE IT EVEN IF THEY OPENED THE CURTAIN.
...
AS YOU CAN SEE, WE'VE PIECED IT TOGETHER.
JUST LIKE THAT VASE IN THE HALL.
IT WAS REALLY THIS BOWL! YOU STUCK THE PARTS TOGETHER LIKE A SANDWICH AND PUT IT IN THE HALL TO MAKE A DECOY VASE!
WHILE YOU WERE MAKING THE SANDWICHES, YOU SNUCK INTO THE HALL, GOT IT AND PUT IT BACK WITH THE OTHER BOWLS!
HERE ARE THE FLOWERS THAT WERE IN THE FALSE VASE. YOU DRIED THEM OUT IN THE MICRO-WAVE BEFORE TOSSING THEM IN THE TRASH.
HOW COULD YOU? THE FLOWERS YOUR WIFE BOUGHT!

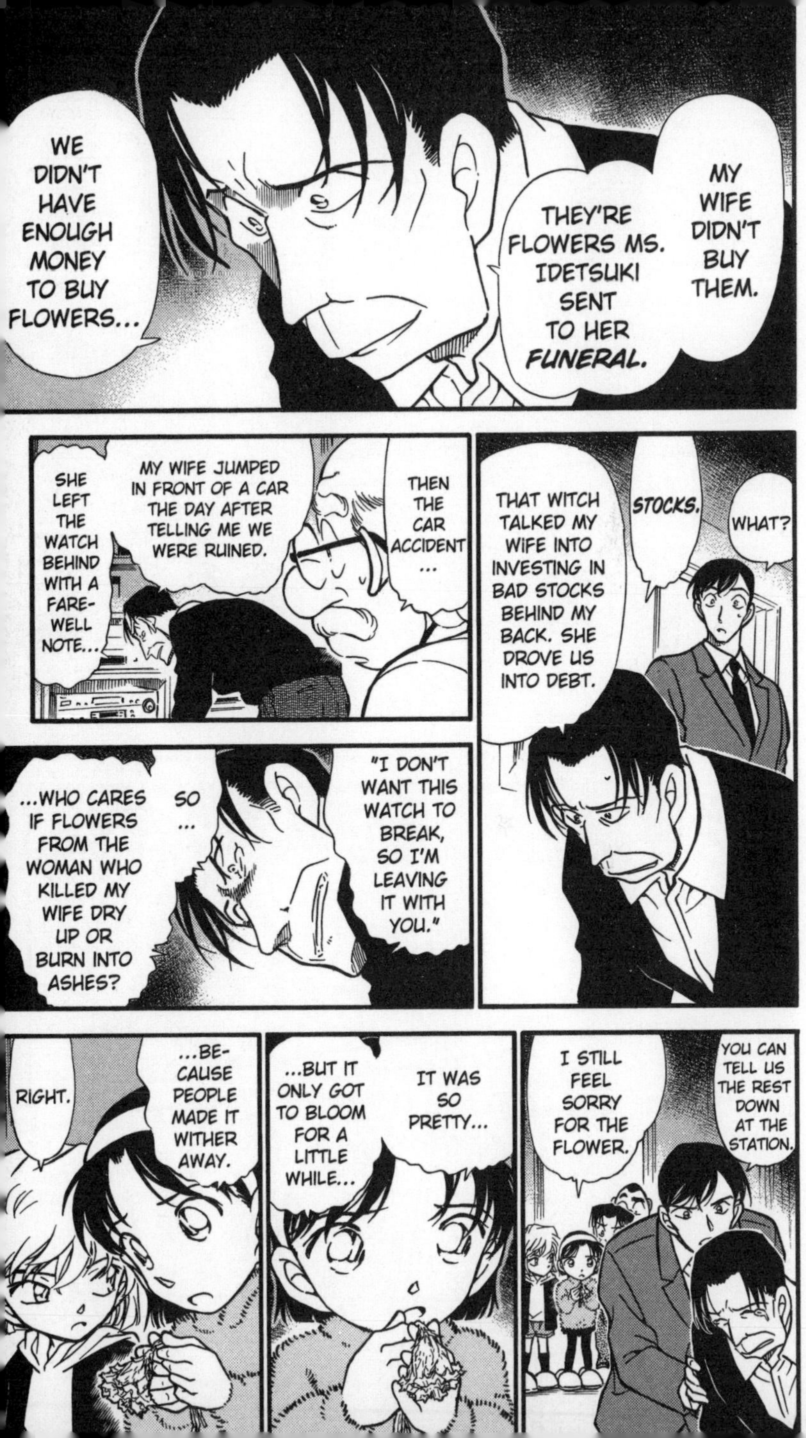
MY WIFE DIDN'T BUY THEM.
THEY'RE FLOWERS MS. IDETSUKI SENT TO HER *FUNERAL.*
WE DIDN'T HAVE ENOUGH MONEY TO BUY FLOWERS...
WHAT?
STOCKS.
THAT WITCH TALKED MY WIFE INTO INVESTING IN BAD STOCKS BEHIND MY BACK. SHE DROVE US INTO DEBT.
THEN THE CAR ACCIDENT...
MY WIFE JUMPED IN FRONT OF A CAR THE DAY AFTER TELLING ME WE WERE RUINED.
SHE LEFT THE WATCH BEHIND WITH A FARE-WELL NOTE...
"I DON'T WANT THIS WATCH TO BREAK, SO I'M LEAVING IT WITH YOU."
SO...
...WHO CARES IF FLOWERS FROM THE WOMAN WHO KILLED MY WIFE DRY UP OR BURN INTO ASHES?
YOU CAN TELL US THE REST DOWN AT THE STATION.
I STILL FEEL SORRY FOR THE FLOWER.
IT WAS SO PRETTY...
...BUT IT ONLY GOT TO BLOOM FOR A LITTLE WHILE...
...BE-CAUSE PEOPLE MADE IT WITHER AWAY.
RIGHT.

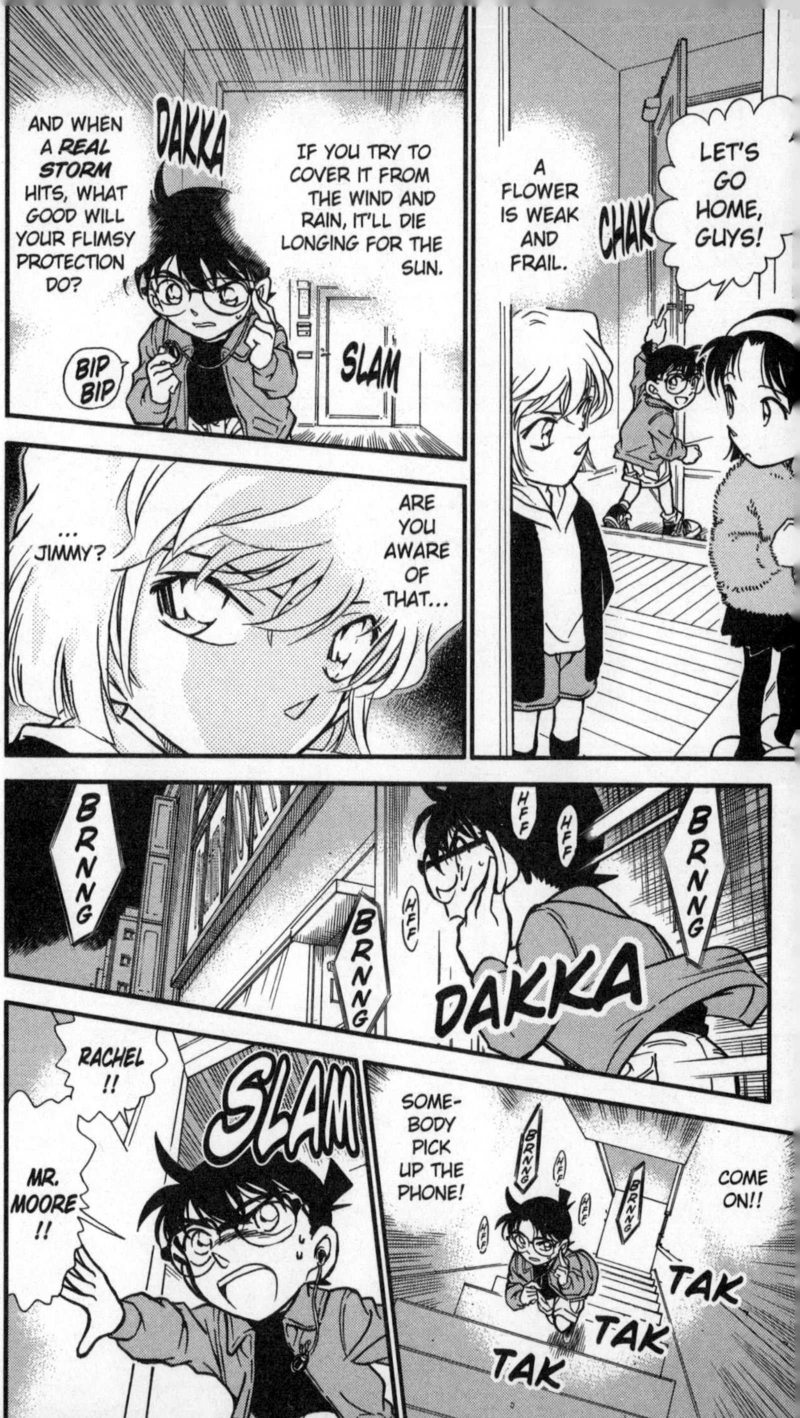

LET'S GO HOME, GUYS!
CHAK
A FLOWER IS WEAK AND FRAIL.
IF YOU TRY TO COVER IT FROM THE WIND AND RAIN, IT'LL DIE LONGING FOR THE SUN.
DAKKA
AND WHEN A *REAL STORM* HITS, WHAT GOOD WILL YOUR FLIMSY PROTECTION DO?
SLAM
BIP BIP
ARE YOU AWARE OF THAT...
... JIMMY?
BRNNG
HFF
HFF
HFF
BRNNG
BRNNG
DAKKA
COME ON!!
SOMEBODY PICK UP THE PHONE!
BRNNG
BRNNG
TAK
TAK
TAK
SLAM
RACHEL !!
MR. MOORE !!

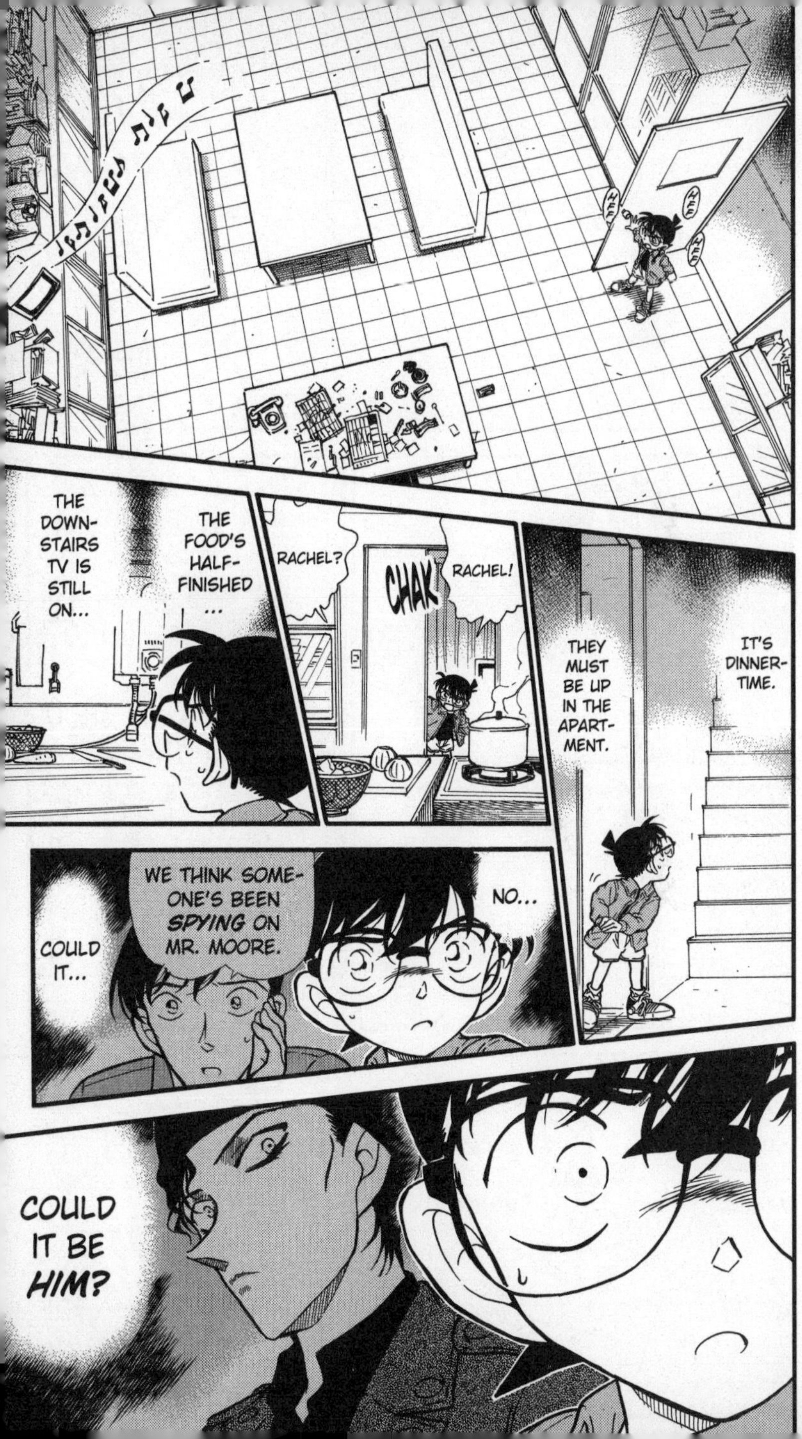
HEF
HEF
HEF
IT'S DINNER-TIME.
THEY MUST BE UP IN THE APARTMENT.
RACHEL!
CHAK
RACHEL?
THE FOOD'S HALF-FINISHED...
THE DOWN-STAIRS TV IS STILL ON...
NO...
WE THINK SOME-ONE'S BEEN *SPYING* ON MR. MOORE.
COULD IT...
COULD IT BE *HIM?*

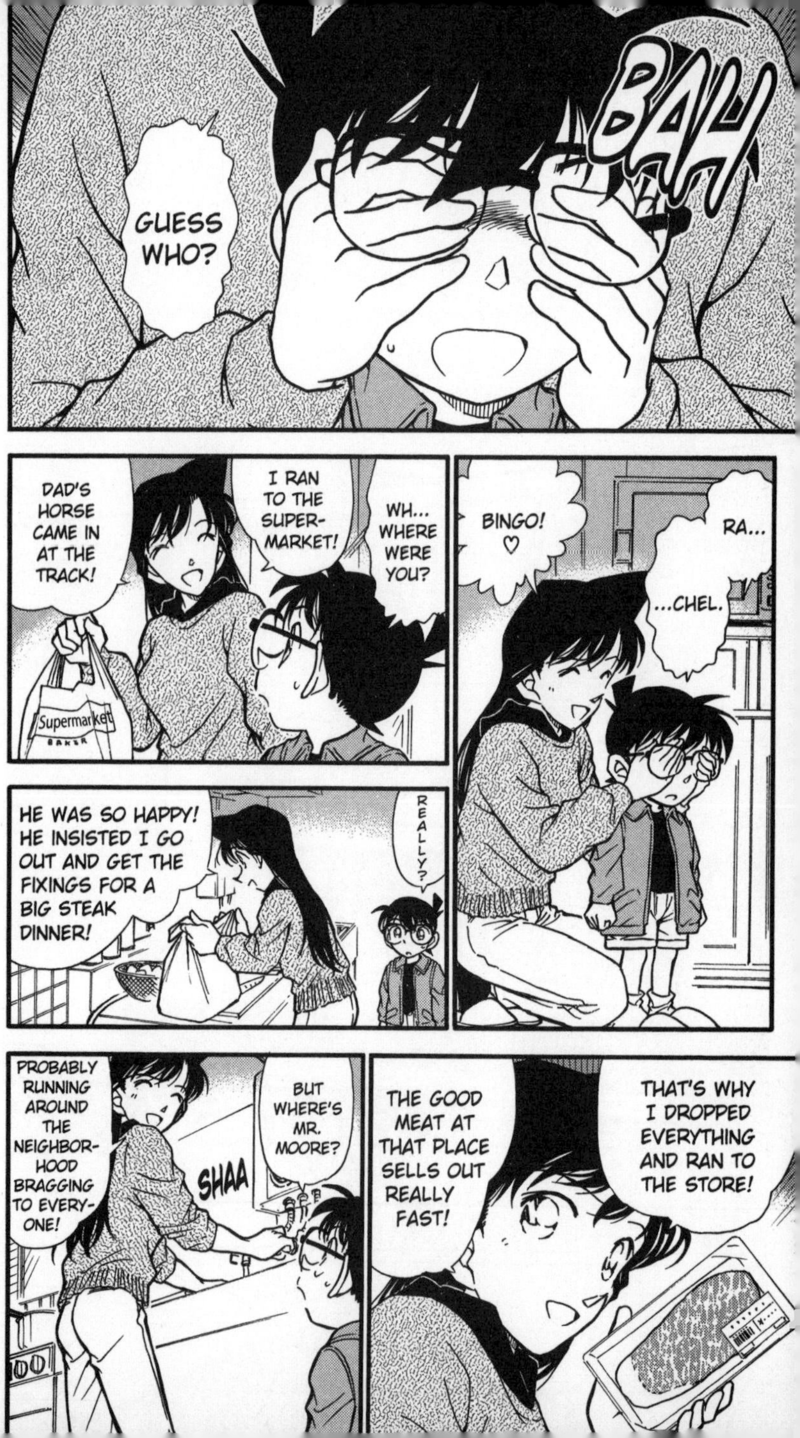
BAH
GUESS WHO?
RA...
...CHEL.
BINGO! ♡
WH... WHERE WERE YOU?
I RAN TO THE SUPER-MARKET!
DAD'S HORSE CAME IN AT THE TRACK!
Supermarket
REALLY?
HE WAS SO HAPPY! HE INSISTED I GO OUT AND GET THE FIXINGS FOR A BIG STEAK DINNER!
THAT'S WHY I DROPPED EVERYTHING AND RAN TO THE STORE!
THE GOOD MEAT AT THAT PLACE SELLS OUT REALLY FAST!
BUT WHERE'S MR. MOORE?
SHAA
PROBABLY RUNNING AROUND THE NEIGHBOR-HOOD BRAGGING TO EVERY-ONE!

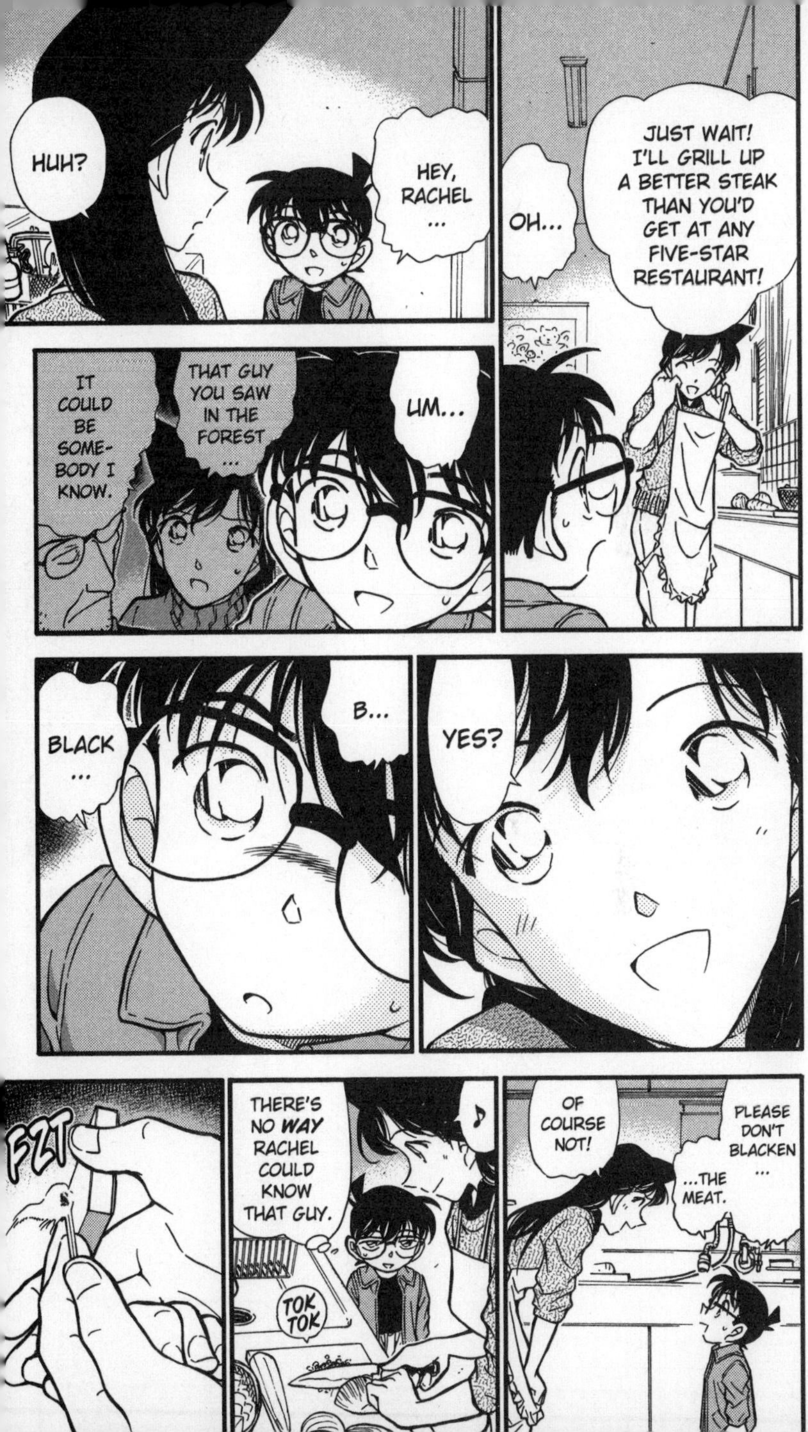
JUST WAIT! I'LL GRILL UP A BETTER STEAK THAN YOU'D GET AT ANY FIVE-STAR RESTAURANT!
OH...
HEY, RACHEL ...
HUH?
UM...
THAT GUY YOU SAW IN THE FOREST ...
IT COULD BE SOME-BODY I KNOW.
YES?
B...
BLACK ...
PLEASE DON'T BLACKEN ...
...THE MEAT.
OF COURSE NOT!
♪
THERE'S NO WAY RACHEL COULD KNOW THAT GUY.
TOK TOK
FZT

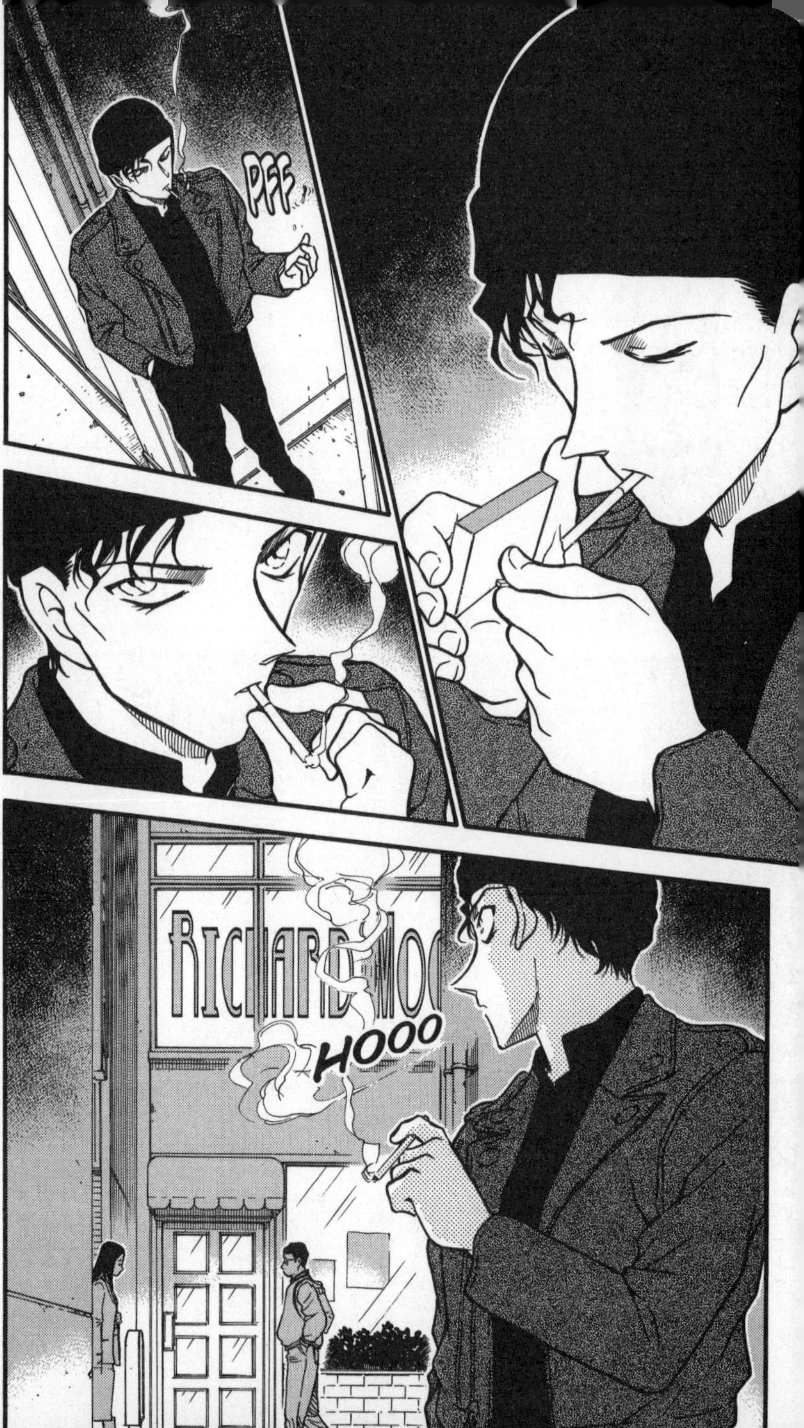
PFF
RICHARD MOO
HOOO

FILE 10: X MARKS THE SPOT

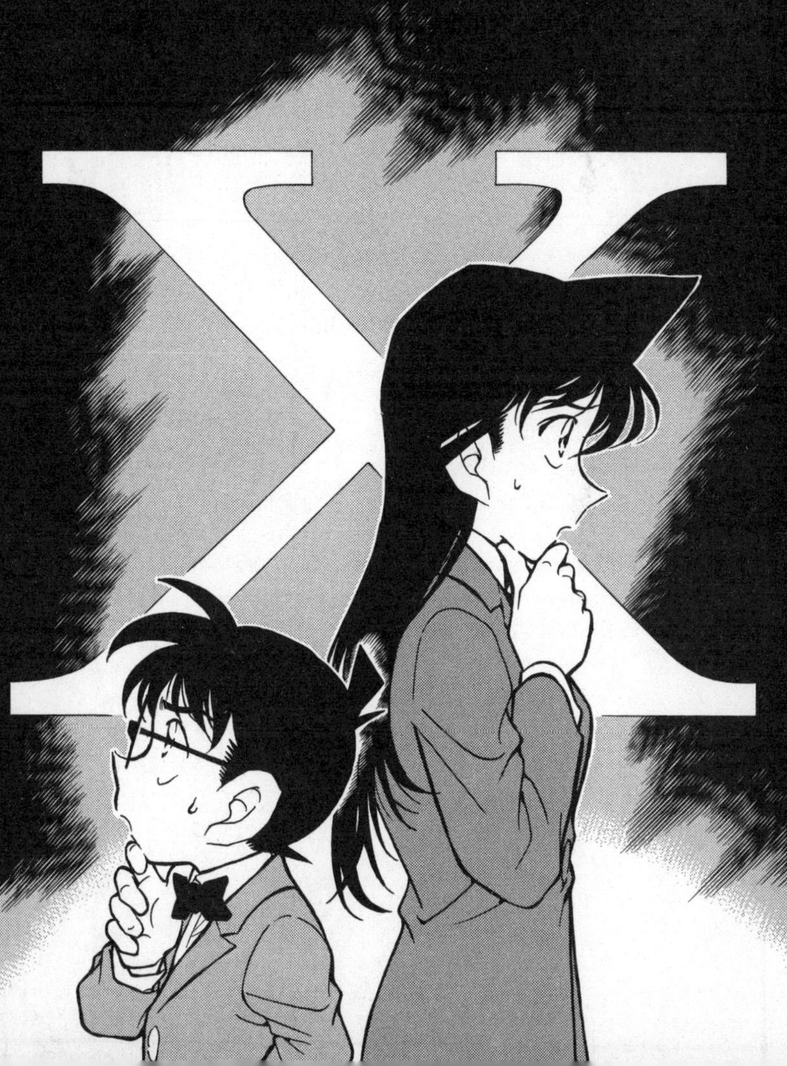

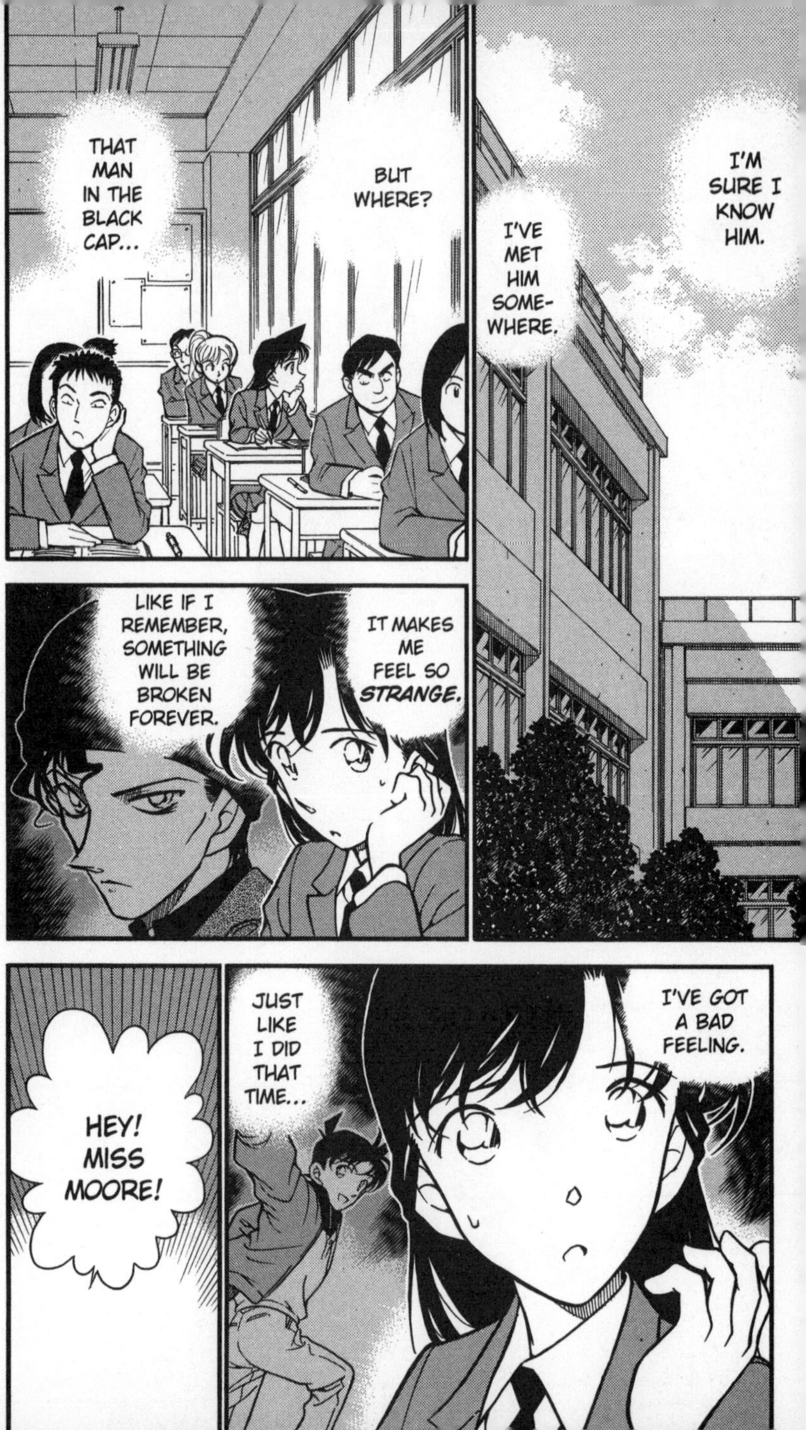
I'M SURE I KNOW HIM.
I'VE MET HIM SOMEWHERE.
BUT WHERE?
THAT MAN IN THE BLACK CAP...
IT MAKES ME FEEL SO *STRANGE.*
LIKE IF I REMEMBER, SOMETHING WILL BE BROKEN FOREVER.
I'VE GOT A BAD FEELING.
JUST LIKE I DID THAT TIME...
HEY! MISS MOORE!

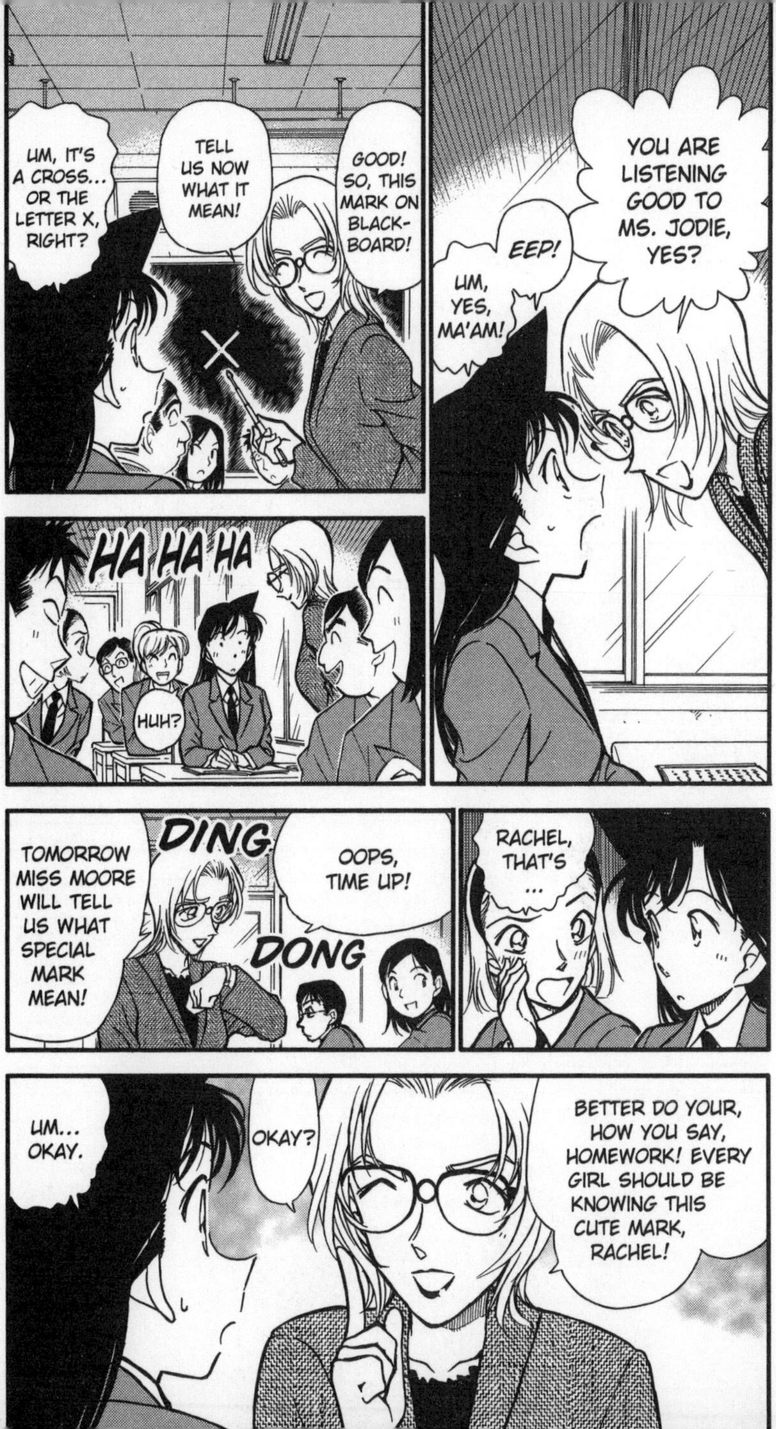
YOU ARE LISTENING GOOD TO MS. JODIE, YES?
EEP!
UM, YES, MA'AM!
GOOD! SO, THIS MARK ON BLACKBOARD!
TELL US NOW WHAT IT MEAN!
UM, IT'S A CROSS... OR THE LETTER X, RIGHT?
HA HA HA
HUH?
RACHEL, THAT'S ...
DING
OOPS, TIME UP!
DONG
TOMORROW MISS MOORE WILL TELL US WHAT SPECIAL MARK MEAN!
BETTER DO YOUR, HOW YOU SAY, HOMEWORK! EVERY GIRL SHOULD BE KNOWING THIS CUTE MARK, RACHEL!
OKAY?
UM... OKAY.

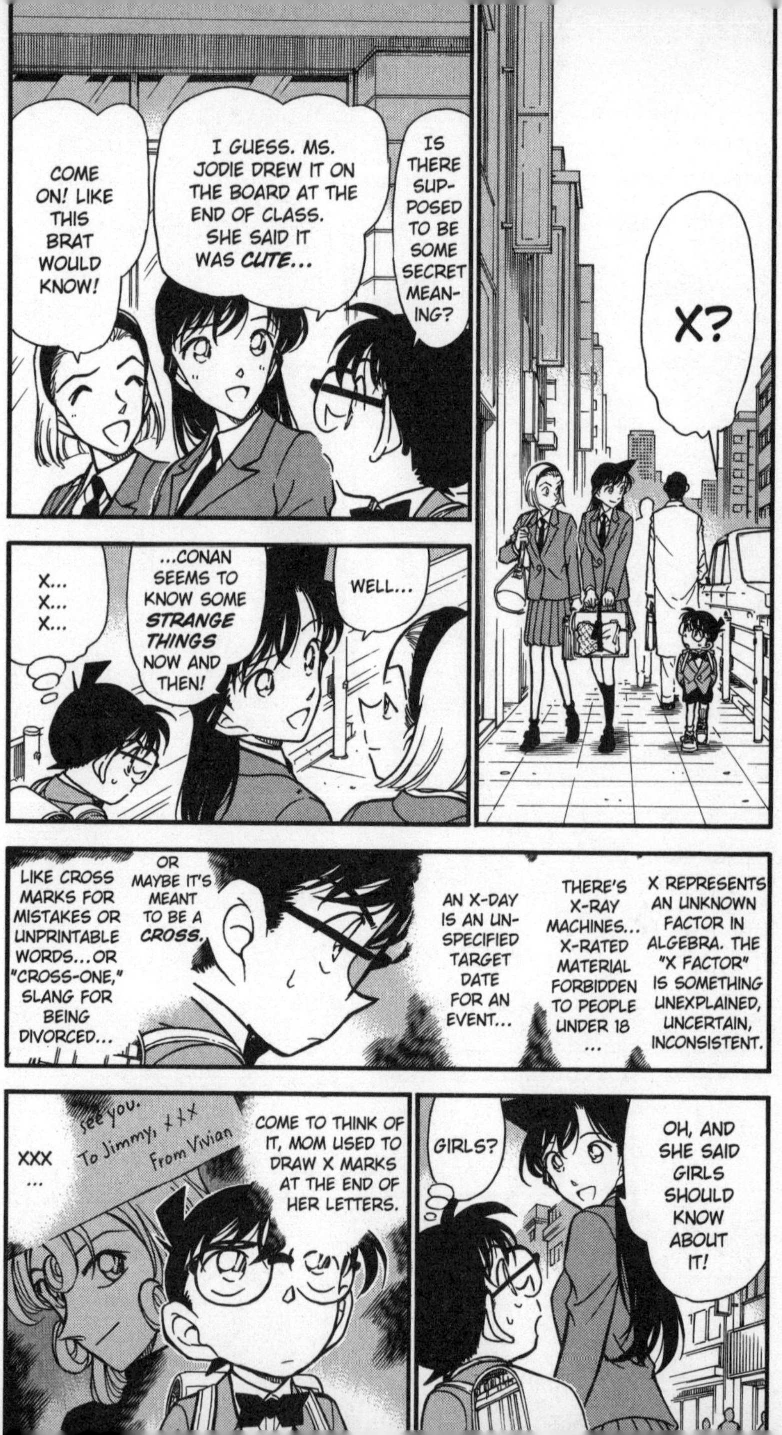
X?
IS THERE SUPPOSED TO BE SOME SECRET MEANING?
I GUESS. MS. JODIE DREW IT ON THE BOARD AT THE END OF CLASS. SHE SAID IT WAS *CUTE*...
COME ON! LIKE THIS BRAT WOULD KNOW!
WELL...
...CONAN SEEMS TO KNOW SOME *STRANGE THINGS* NOW AND THEN!
X... X... X...
X REPRESENTS AN UNKNOWN FACTOR IN ALGEBRA. THE "X FACTOR" IS SOMETHING UNEXPLAINED, UNCERTAIN, INCONSISTENT.
THERE'S X-RAY MACHINES... X-RATED MATERIAL FORBIDDEN TO PEOPLE UNDER 18 ...
AN X-DAY IS AN UNSPECIFIED TARGET DATE FOR AN EVENT...
OR MAYBE IT'S MEANT TO BE A *CROSS*.
LIKE CROSS MARKS FOR MISTAKES OR UNPRINTABLE WORDS...OR "CROSS-ONE," SLANG FOR BEING DIVORCED...
OH, AND SHE SAID GIRLS SHOULD KNOW ABOUT IT!
GIRLS?
COME TO THINK OF IT, MOM USED TO DRAW X MARKS AT THE END OF HER LETTERS.
see you.
To Jimmy, xxx
From Vivian
XXX ...

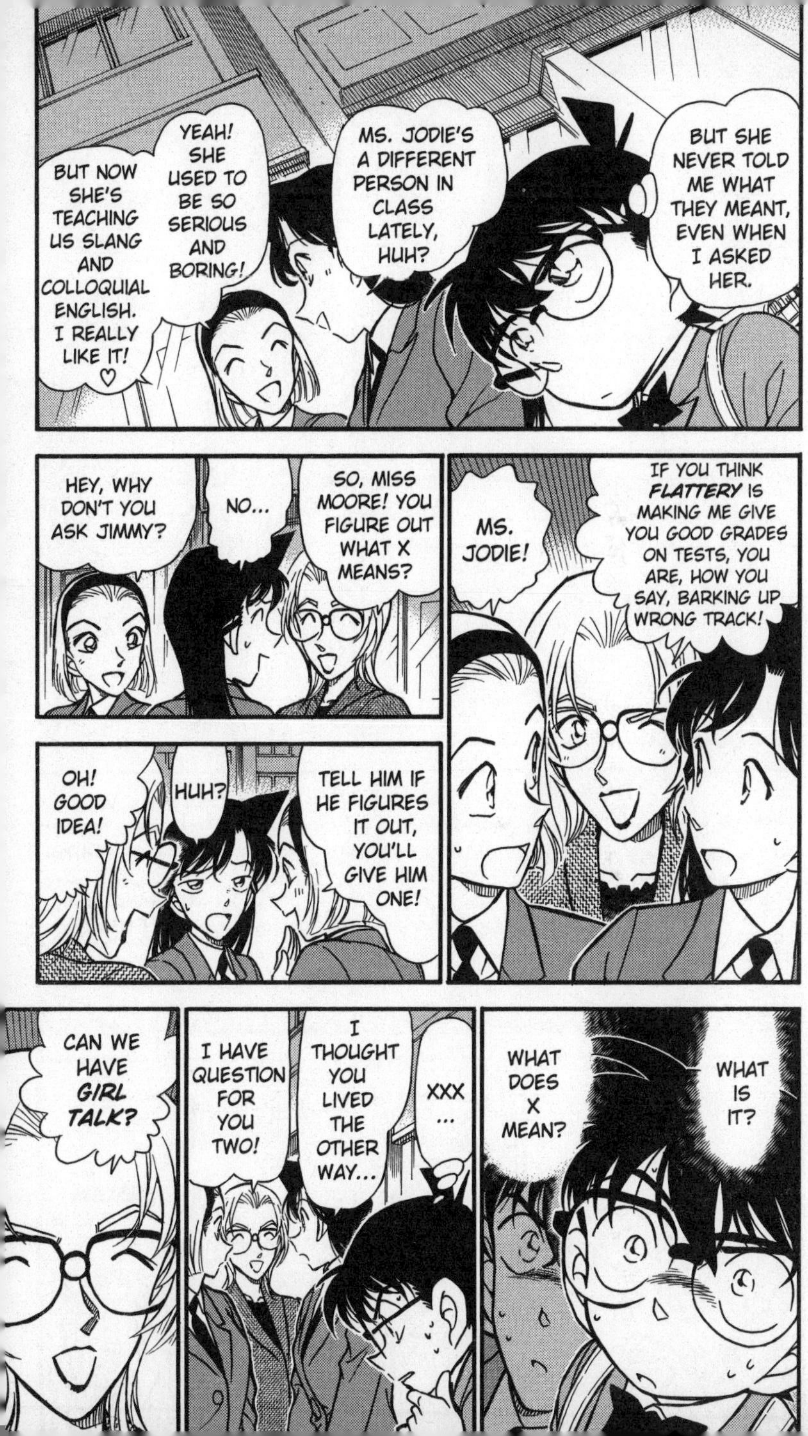
BUT SHE NEVER TOLD ME WHAT THEY MEANT, EVEN WHEN I ASKED HER.
MS. JODIE'S A DIFFERENT PERSON IN CLASS LATELY, HUH?
YEAH! SHE USED TO BE SO SERIOUS AND BORING!
BUT NOW SHE'S TEACHING US SLANG AND COLLOQUIAL ENGLISH. I REALLY LIKE IT! ♡
IF YOU THINK *FLATTERY* IS MAKING ME GIVE YOU GOOD GRADES ON TESTS, YOU ARE, HOW YOU SAY, BARKING UP WRONG TRACK!
MS. JODIE!
SO, MISS MOORE! YOU FIGURE OUT WHAT X MEANS?
NO...
HEY, WHY DON'T YOU ASK JIMMY?
TELL HIM IF HE FIGURES IT OUT, YOU'LL GIVE HIM ONE!
HUH?
OH! GOOD IDEA!
WHAT IS IT?
WHAT DOES X MEAN?
XXX ...
I THOUGHT YOU LIVED THE OTHER WAY...
I HAVE QUESTION FOR YOU TWO!
CAN WE HAVE *GIRL TALK?*

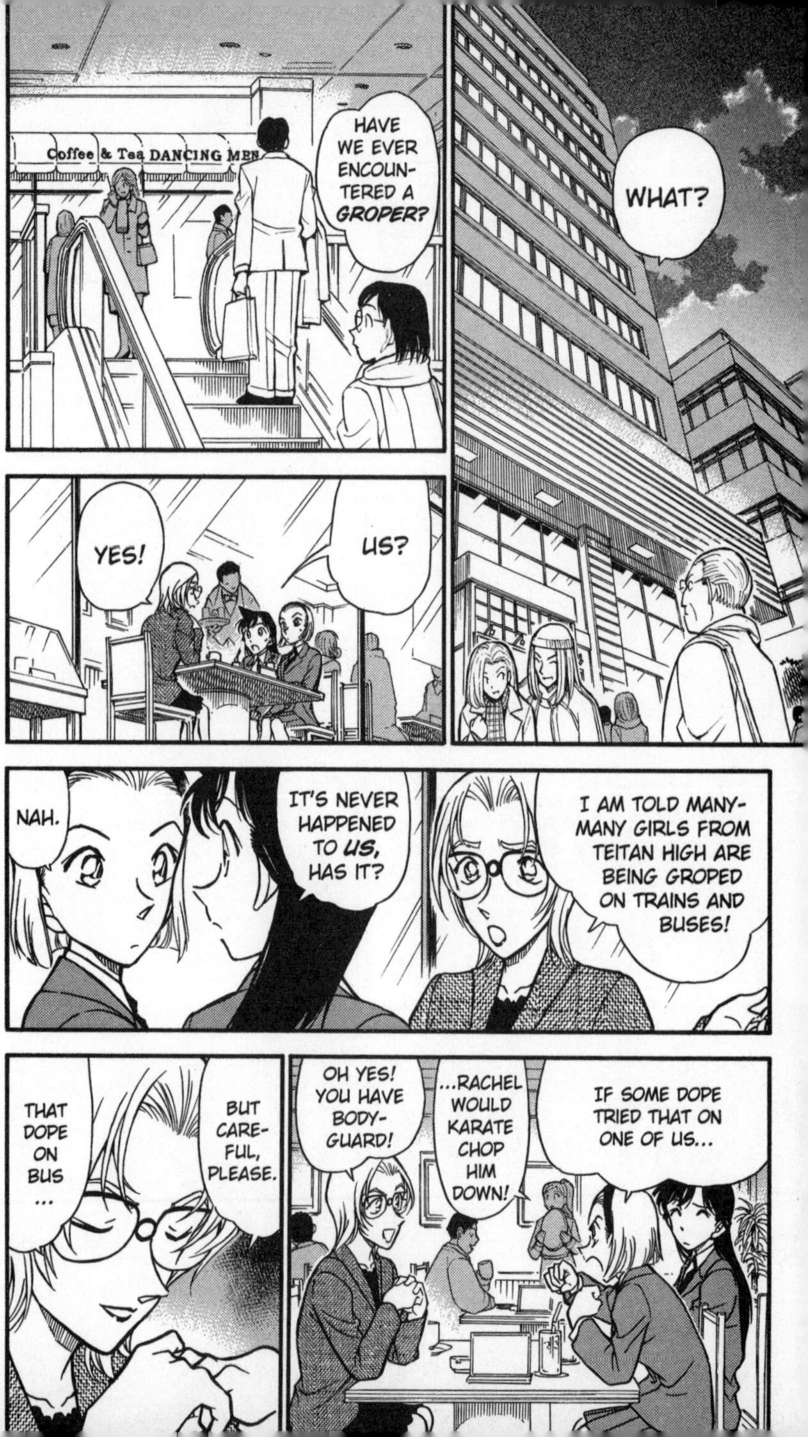
WHAT?
HAVE WE EVER ENCOUNTERED A *GROPER?*
Coffee & Tea DANCING MEN
US?
YES!
I AM TOLD MANY-MANY GIRLS FROM TEITAN HIGH ARE BEING GROPED ON TRAINS AND BUSES!
IT'S NEVER HAPPENED TO *US,* HAS IT?
NAH.
IF SOME DOPE TRIED THAT ON ONE OF US...
...RACHEL WOULD KARATE CHOP HIM DOWN!
OH YES! YOU HAVE BODY-GUARD!
BUT CARE-FUL, PLEASE.
THAT DOPE ON BUS ...

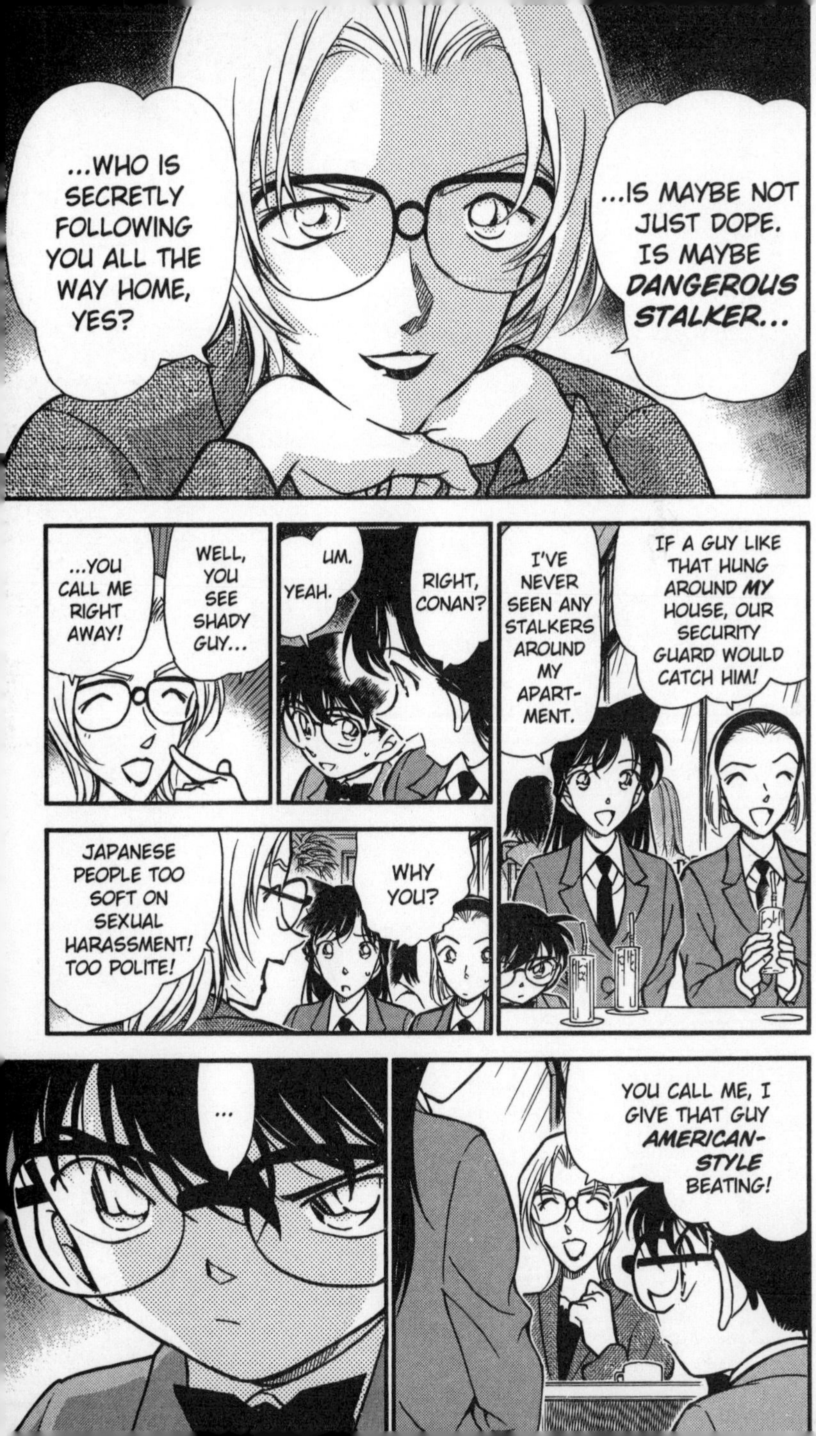
...IS MAYBE NOT JUST DOPE. IS MAYBE DANGEROUS STALKER...
...WHO IS SECRETLY FOLLOWING YOU ALL THE WAY HOME, YES?
IF A GUY LIKE THAT HUNG AROUND MY HOUSE, OUR SECURITY GUARD WOULD CATCH HIM!
I'VE NEVER SEEN ANY STALKERS AROUND MY APARTMENT.
RIGHT, CONAN?
UM. YEAH.
WELL, YOU SEE SHADY GUY...
...YOU CALL ME RIGHT AWAY!
WHY YOU?
JAPANESE PEOPLE TOO SOFT ON SEXUAL HARASSMENT! TOO POLITE!
YOU CALL ME, I GIVE THAT GUY AMERICAN-STYLE BEATING!
...

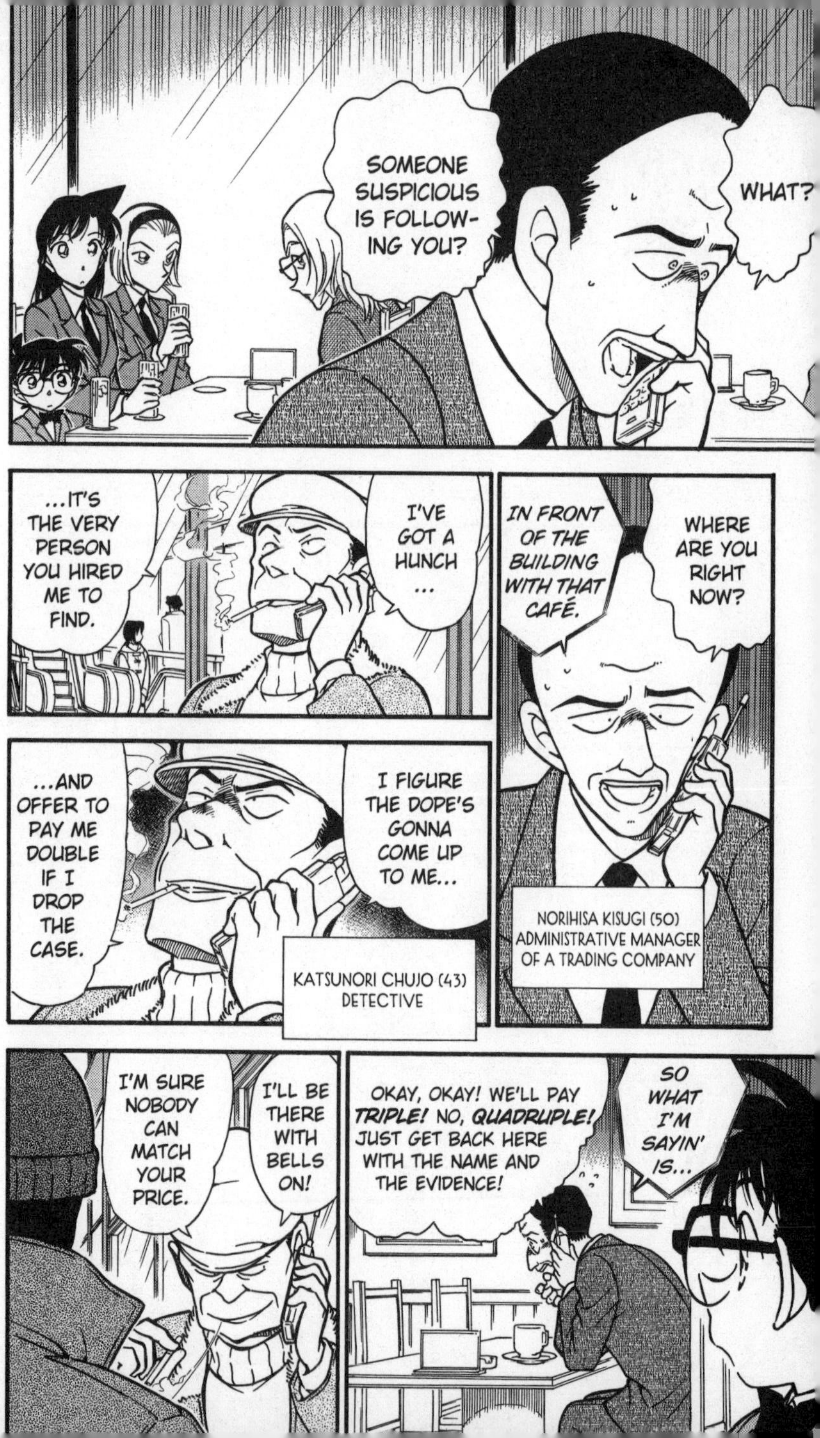
WHAT?
SOMEONE SUSPICIOUS IS FOLLOWING YOU?
WHERE ARE YOU RIGHT NOW?
IN FRONT OF THE BUILDING WITH THAT CAFÉ.
NORIHISA KISUGI (50) ADMINISTRATIVE MANAGER OF A TRADING COMPANY
I'VE GOT A HUNCH...
...IT'S THE VERY PERSON YOU HIRED ME TO FIND.
I FIGURE THE DOPE'S GONNA COME UP TO ME...
...AND OFFER TO PAY ME DOUBLE IF I DROP THE CASE.
KATSUNORI CHUJO (43) DETECTIVE
SO WHAT I'M SAYIN' IS...
OKAY, OKAY! WE'LL PAY *TRIPLE!* NO, *QUADRUPLE!* JUST GET BACK HERE WITH THE NAME AND THE EVIDENCE!
I'LL BE THERE WITH BELLS ON!
I'M SURE NOBODY CAN MATCH YOUR PRICE.

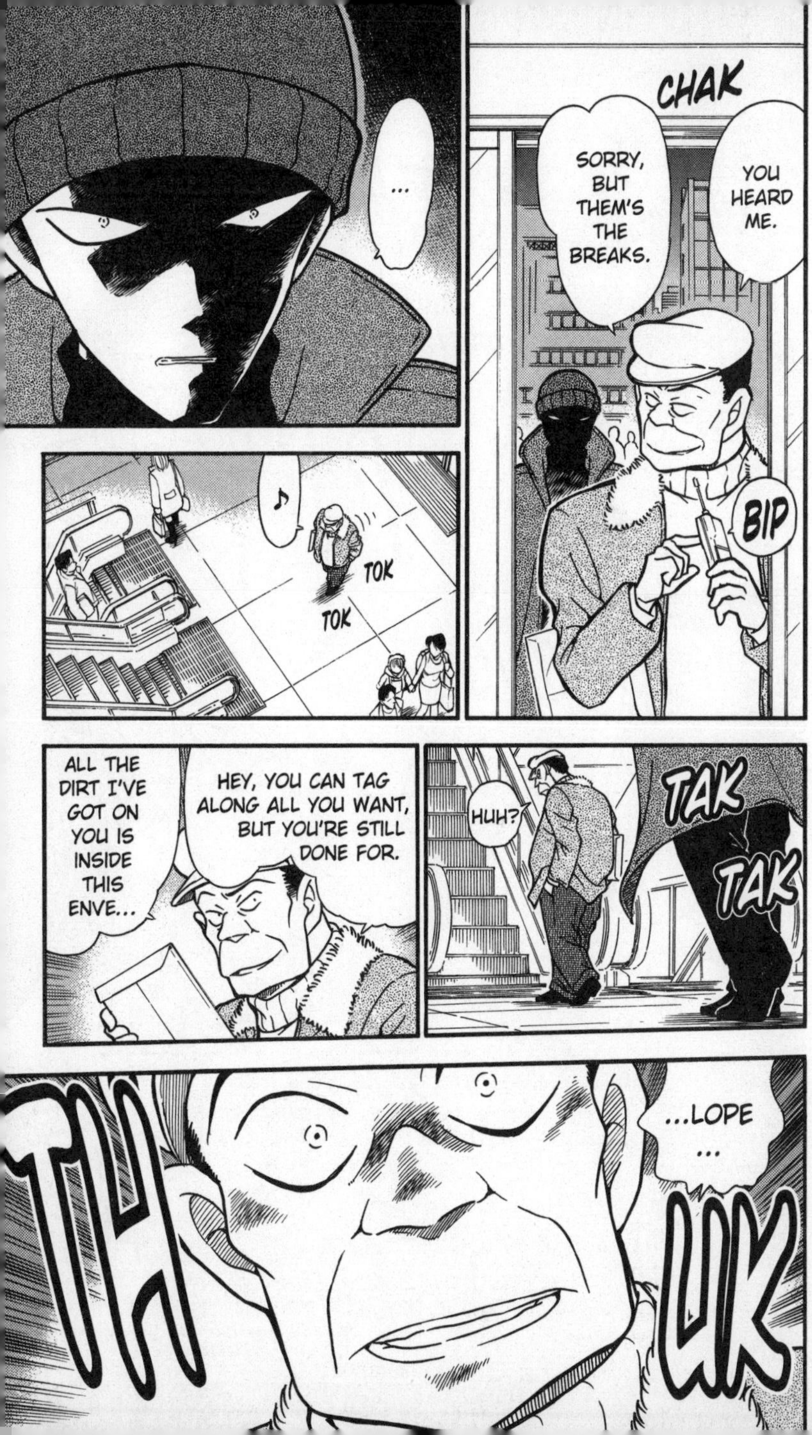
CHAK
YOU HEARD ME.
SORRY, BUT THEM'S THE BREAKS.
BIP
...
♪
TOK
TOK
TAK
TAK
HUH?
HEY, YOU CAN TAG ALONG ALL YOU WANT, BUT YOU'RE STILL DONE FOR.
ALL THE DIRT I'VE GOT ON YOU IS INSIDE THIS ENVE...
...LOPE ...
THUK

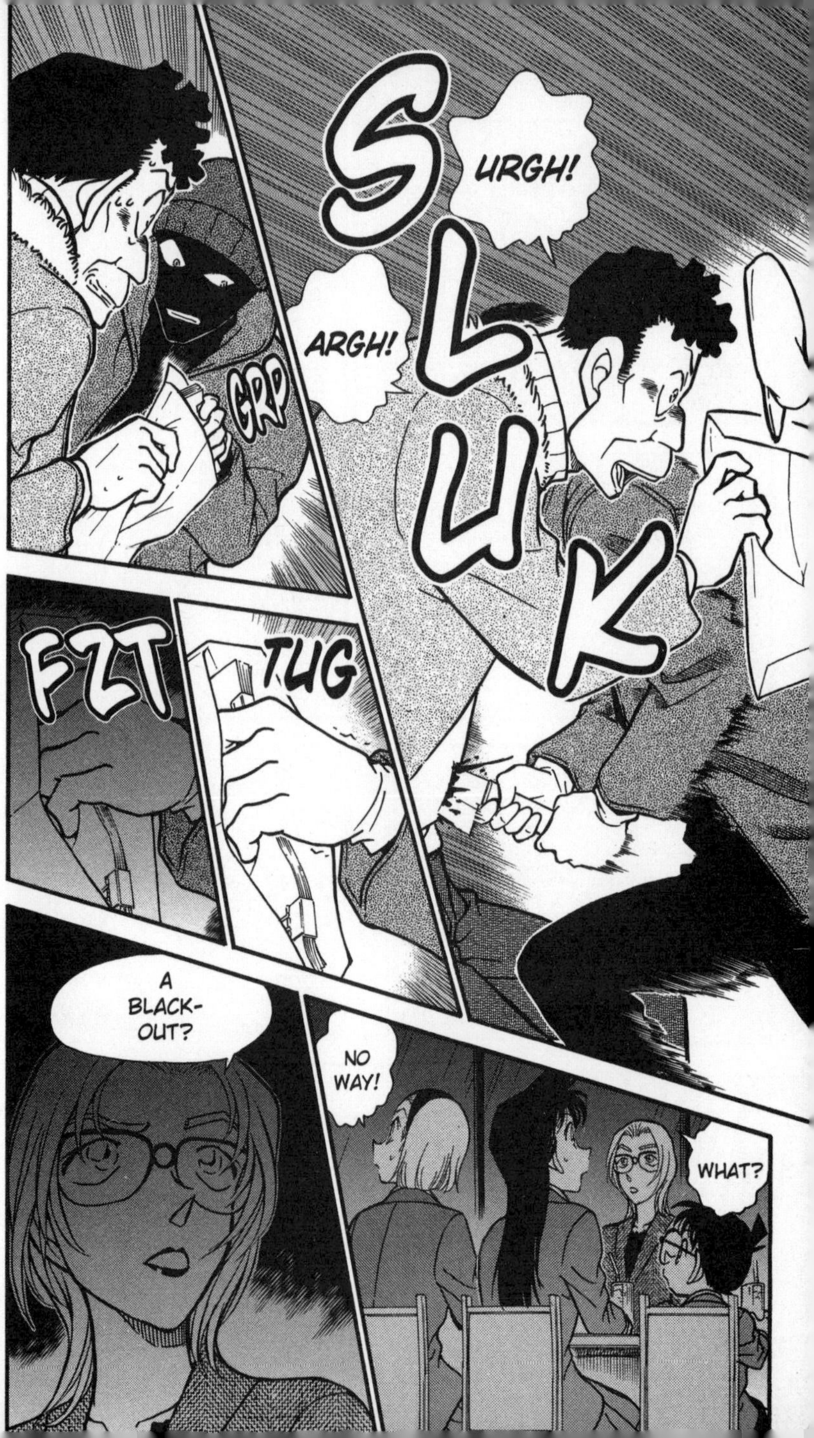
URGH!
SLUK
ARGH!
GRP
TUG
FZT
WHAT?
NO WAY!
A BLACK-OUT?

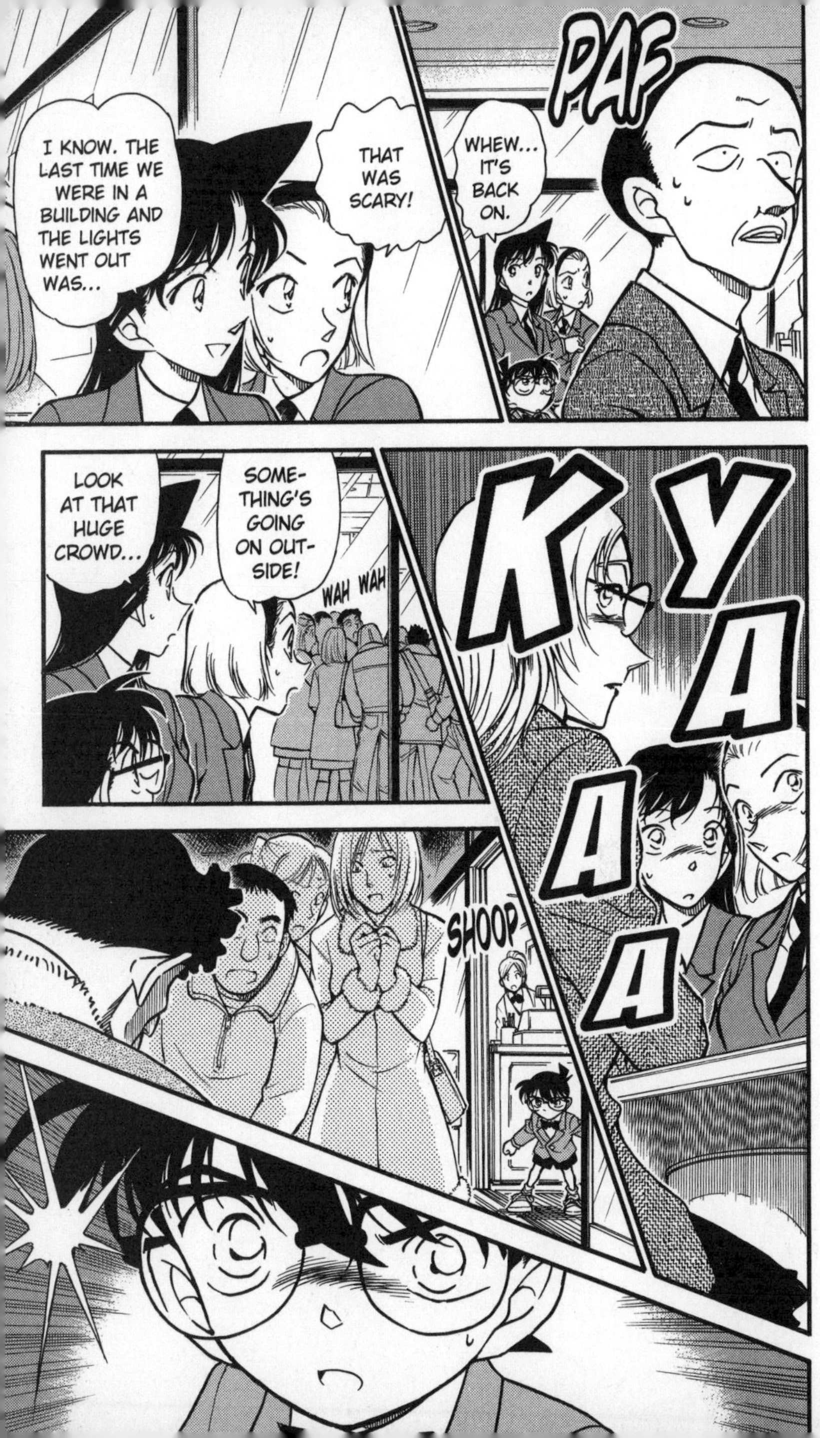
PAF
WHEW... IT'S BACK ON.
THAT WAS SCARY!
I KNOW. THE LAST TIME WE WERE IN A BUILDING AND THE LIGHTS WENT OUT WAS...
KYAAAA
SOME-THING'S GOING ON OUT-SIDE!
WAH WAH
LOOK AT THAT HUGE CROWD...
SHOOP

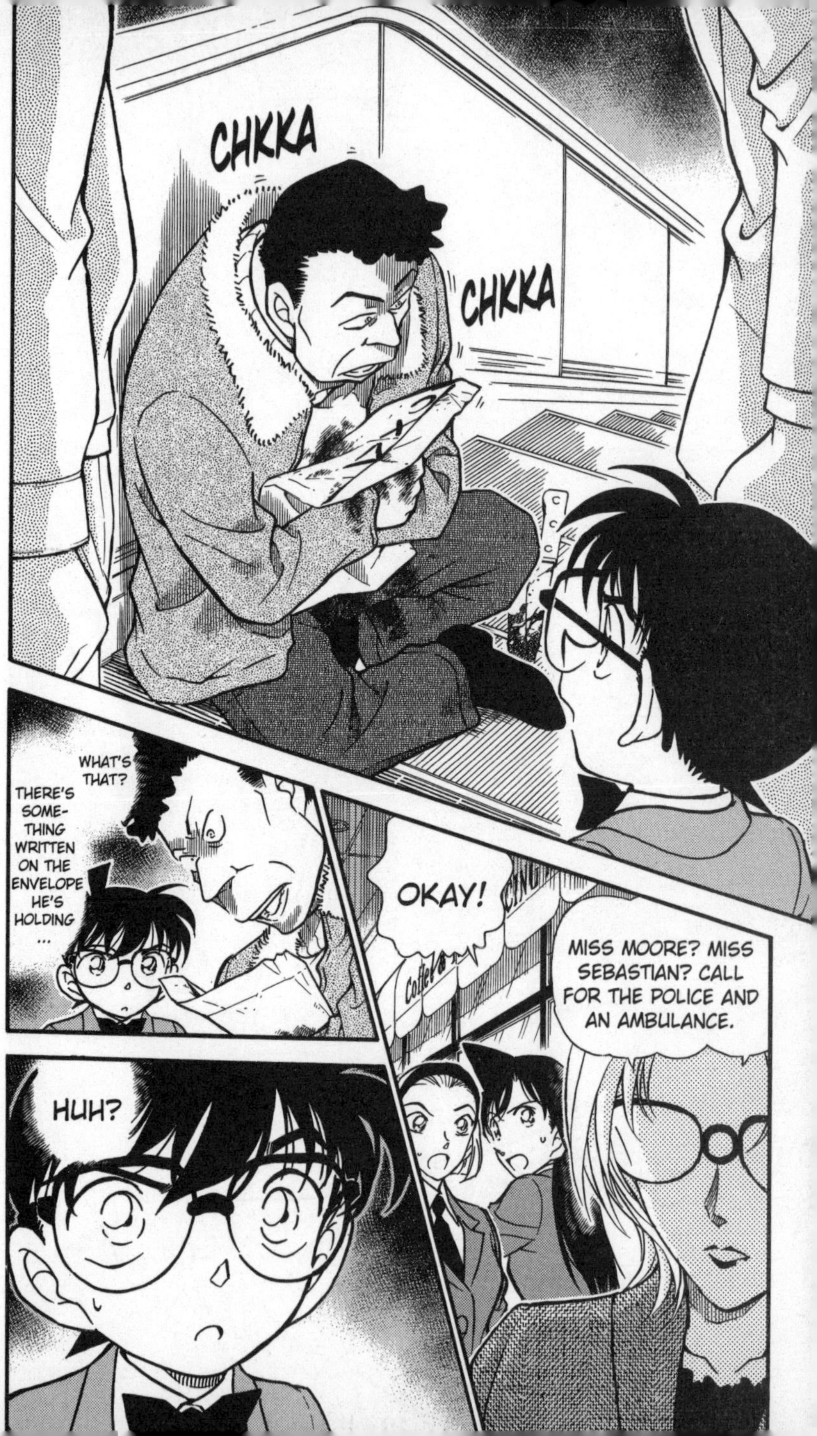
CHKKA
CHKKA
MISS MOORE? MISS SEBASTIAN? CALL FOR THE POLICE AND AN AMBULANCE.
OKAY!
WHAT'S THAT?
THERE'S SOMETHING WRITTEN ON THE ENVELOPE HE'S HOLDING...
HUH?

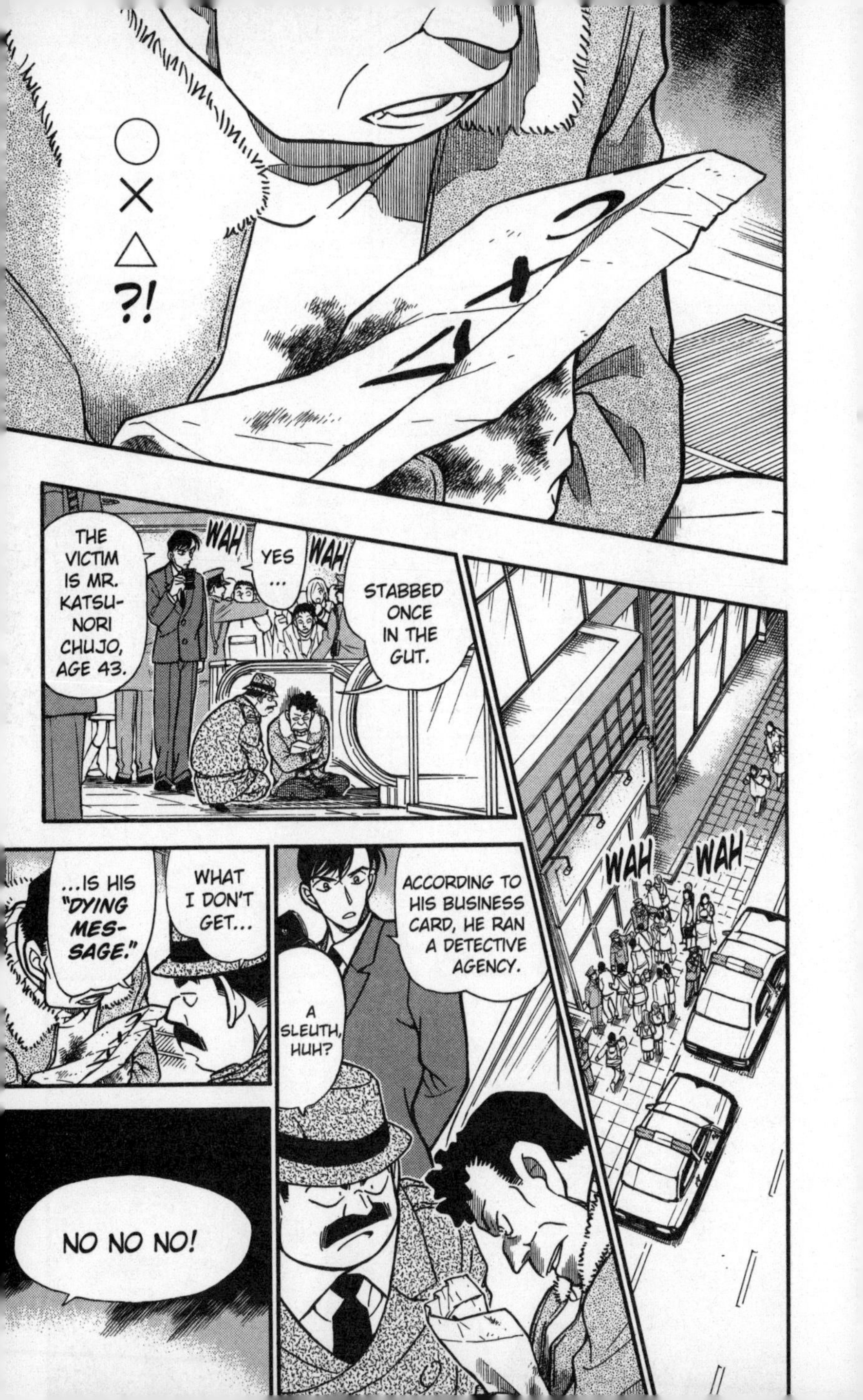

○
×
△
?!
WAH WAH
WAH WAH
THE VICTIM IS MR. KATSUNORI CHUJO, AGE 43.
YES...
STABBED ONCE IN THE GUT.
ACCORDING TO HIS BUSINESS CARD, HE RAN A DETECTIVE AGENCY.
A SLEUTH, HUH?
WHAT I DON'T GET...
...IS HIS "DYING MESSAGE."
NO NO NO!

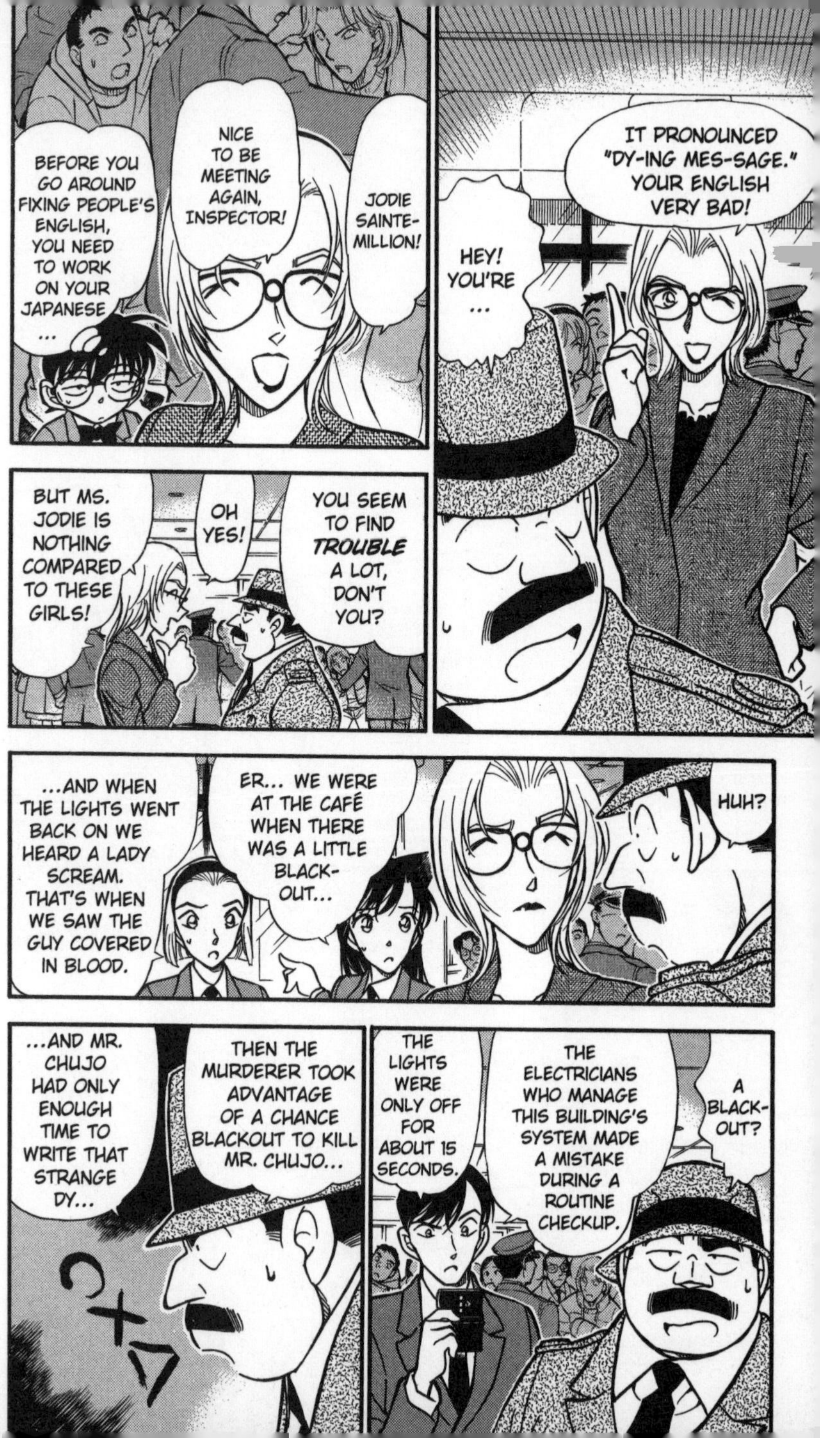
IT PRONOUNCED "DY-ING MES-SAGE." YOUR ENGLISH VERY BAD!
HEY! YOU'RE ...
JODIE SAINTE-MILLION!
NICE TO BE MEETING AGAIN, INSPECTOR!
BEFORE YOU GO AROUND FIXING PEOPLE'S ENGLISH, YOU NEED TO WORK ON YOUR JAPANESE ...
YOU SEEM TO FIND *TROUBLE* A LOT, DON'T YOU?
OH YES!
BUT MS. JODIE IS NOTHING COMPARED TO THESE GIRLS!
HUH?
ER... WE WERE AT THE CAFÉ WHEN THERE WAS A LITTLE BLACK-OUT...
...AND WHEN THE LIGHTS WENT BACK ON WE HEARD A LADY SCREAM. THAT'S WHEN WE SAW THE GUY COVERED IN BLOOD.
A BLACK-OUT?
THE ELECTRICIANS WHO MANAGE THIS BUILDING'S SYSTEM MADE A MISTAKE DURING A ROUTINE CHECKUP.
THE LIGHTS WERE ONLY OFF FOR ABOUT 15 SECONDS.
THEN THE MURDERER TOOK ADVANTAGE OF A CHANCE BLACKOUT TO KILL MR. CHUJO...
...AND MR. CHUJO HAD ONLY ENOUGH TIME TO WRITE THAT STRANGE DY...

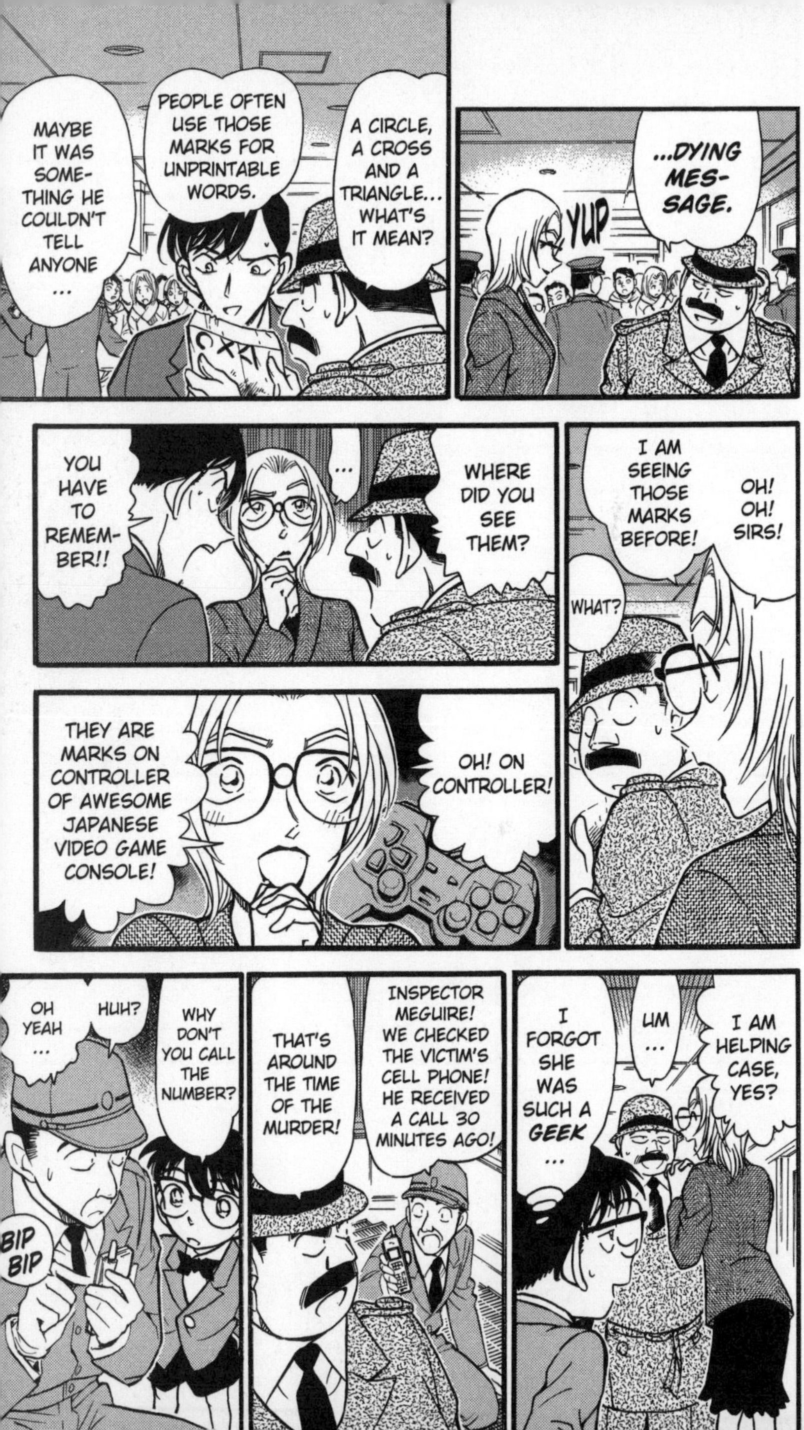
...DYING MES-SAGE.
YUP
A CIRCLE, A CROSS AND A TRIANGLE... WHAT'S IT MEAN?
PEOPLE OFTEN USE THOSE MARKS FOR UNPRINTABLE WORDS.
MAYBE IT WAS SOME-THING HE COULDN'T TELL ANYONE ...
OH! OH! SIRS!
I AM SEEING THOSE MARKS BEFORE!
WHAT?
WHERE DID YOU SEE THEM?
...
YOU HAVE TO REMEM-BER!!
OH! ON CONTROLLER!
THEY ARE MARKS ON CONTROLLER OF AWESOME JAPANESE VIDEO GAME CONSOLE!
I AM HELPING CASE, YES?
UM ...
I FORGOT SHE WAS SUCH A *GEEK* ...
INSPECTOR MEGUIRE! WE CHECKED THE VICTIM'S CELL PHONE! HE RECEIVED A CALL 30 MINUTES AGO!
THAT'S AROUND THE TIME OF THE MURDER!
WHY DON'T YOU CALL THE NUMBER?
HUH?
OH YEAH ...
BIP BIP

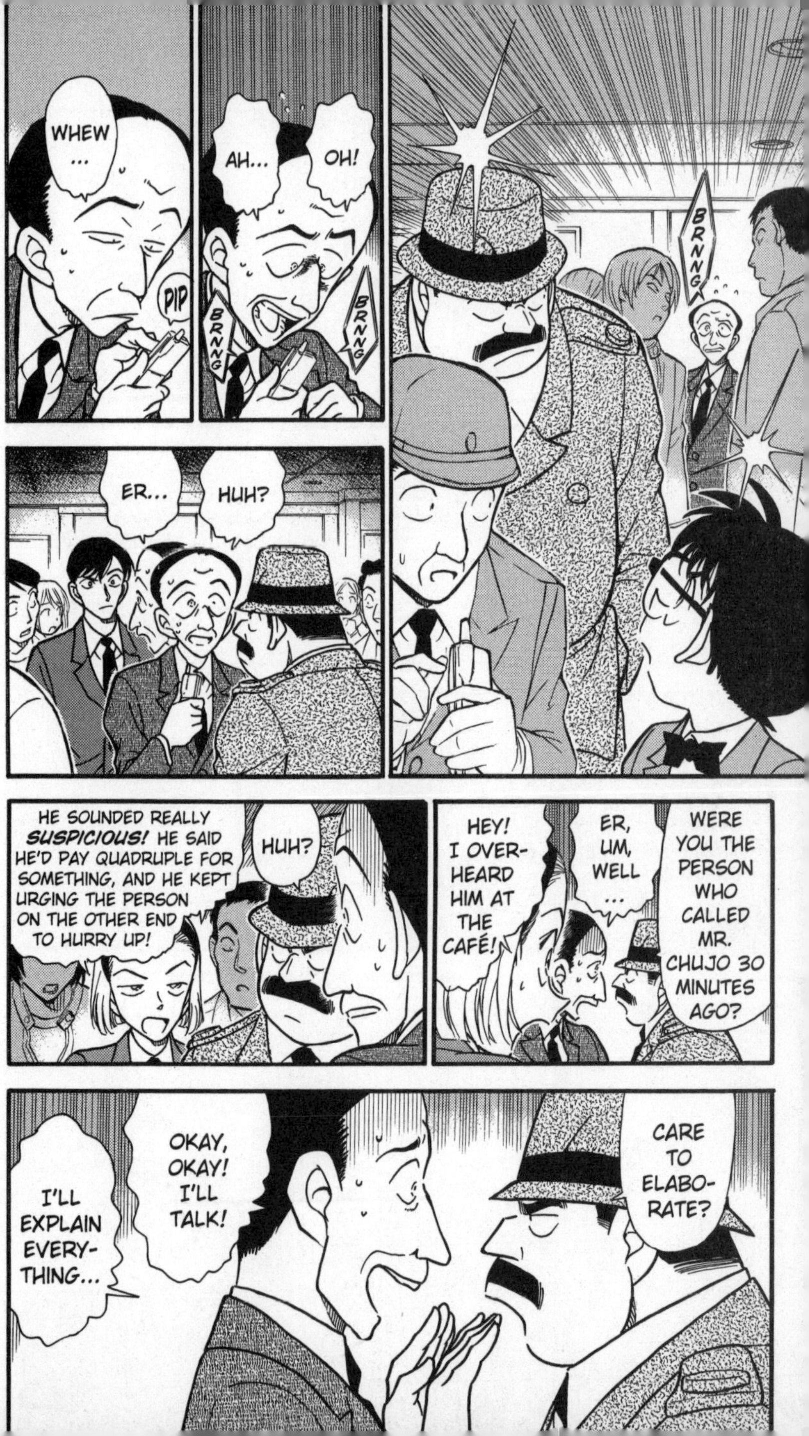
BRNNG
OH!
AH...
BRNNG
BRNNG
WHEW ...
PIP
HUH?
ER...
WERE YOU THE PERSON WHO CALLED MR. CHUJO 30 MINUTES AGO?
ER, UM, WELL ...
HEY! I OVERHEARD HIM AT THE CAFÉ!
HUH?
HE SOUNDED REALLY *SUSPICIOUS!* HE SAID HE'D PAY QUADRUPLE FOR SOMETHING, AND HE KEPT URGING THE PERSON ON THE OTHER END TO HURRY UP!
CARE TO ELABORATE?
OKAY, OKAY! I'LL TALK!
I'LL EXPLAIN EVERYTHING...

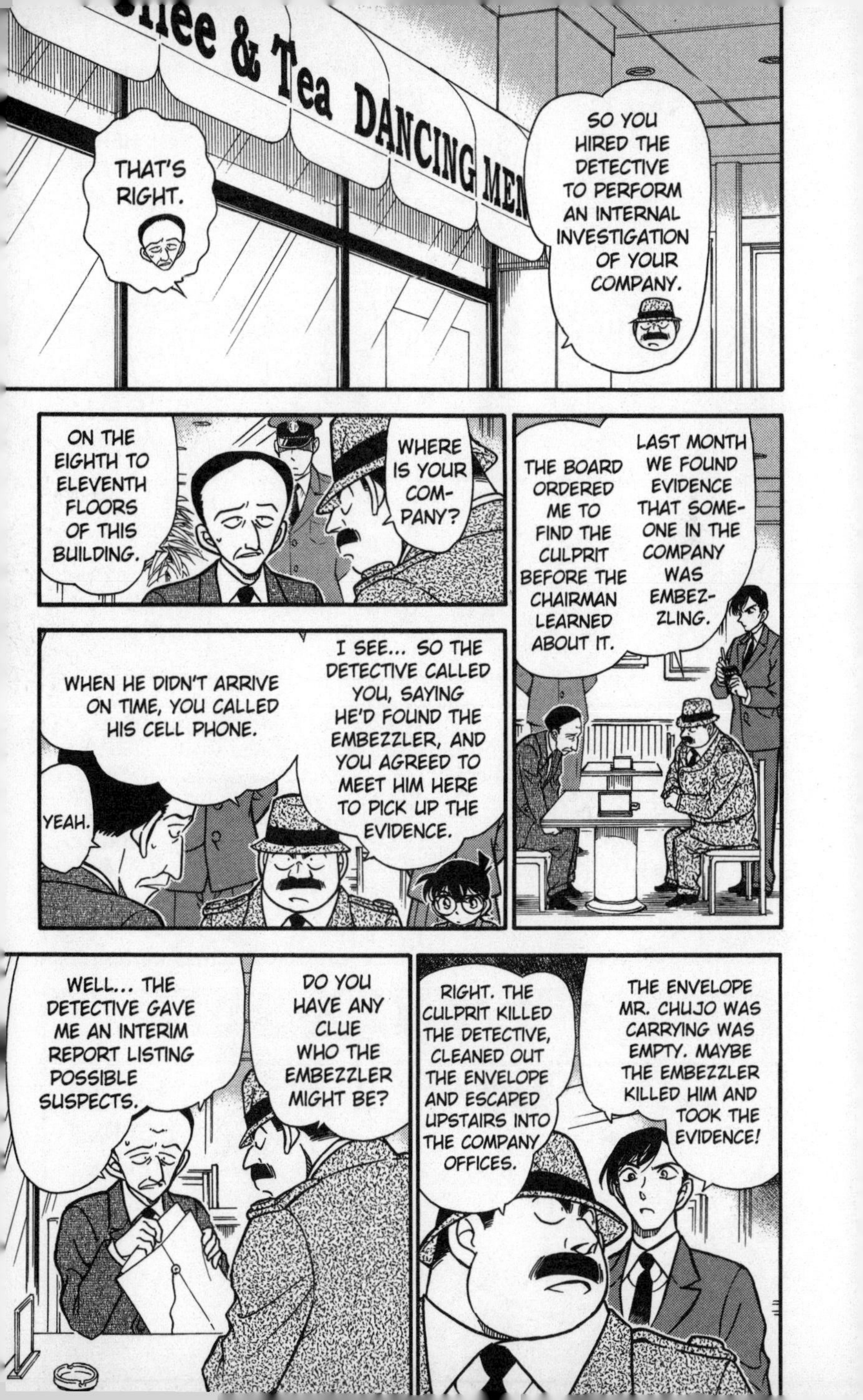
SO YOU HIRED THE DETECTIVE TO PERFORM AN INTERNAL INVESTIGATION OF YOUR COMPANY.
ffee & Tea DANCING ME
THAT'S RIGHT.
LAST MONTH WE FOUND EVIDENCE THAT SOME-ONE IN THE COMPANY WAS EMBEZ-ZLING.
THE BOARD ORDERED ME TO FIND THE CULPRIT BEFORE THE CHAIRMAN LEARNED ABOUT IT.
WHERE IS YOUR COM-PANY?
ON THE EIGHTH TO ELEVENTH FLOORS OF THIS BUILDING.
I SEE... SO THE DETECTIVE CALLED YOU, SAYING HE'D FOUND THE EMBEZZLER, AND YOU AGREED TO MEET HIM HERE TO PICK UP THE EVIDENCE.
WHEN HE DIDN'T ARRIVE ON TIME, YOU CALLED HIS CELL PHONE.
YEAH.
THE ENVELOPE MR. CHUJO WAS CARRYING WAS EMPTY. MAYBE THE EMBEZZLER KILLED HIM AND TOOK THE EVIDENCE!
RIGHT. THE CULPRIT KILLED THE DETECTIVE, CLEANED OUT THE ENVELOPE AND ESCAPED UPSTAIRS INTO THE COMPANY OFFICES.
DO YOU HAVE ANY CLUE WHO THE EMBEZZLER MIGHT BE?
WELL... THE DETECTIVE GAVE ME AN INTERIM REPORT LISTING POSSIBLE SUSPECTS.

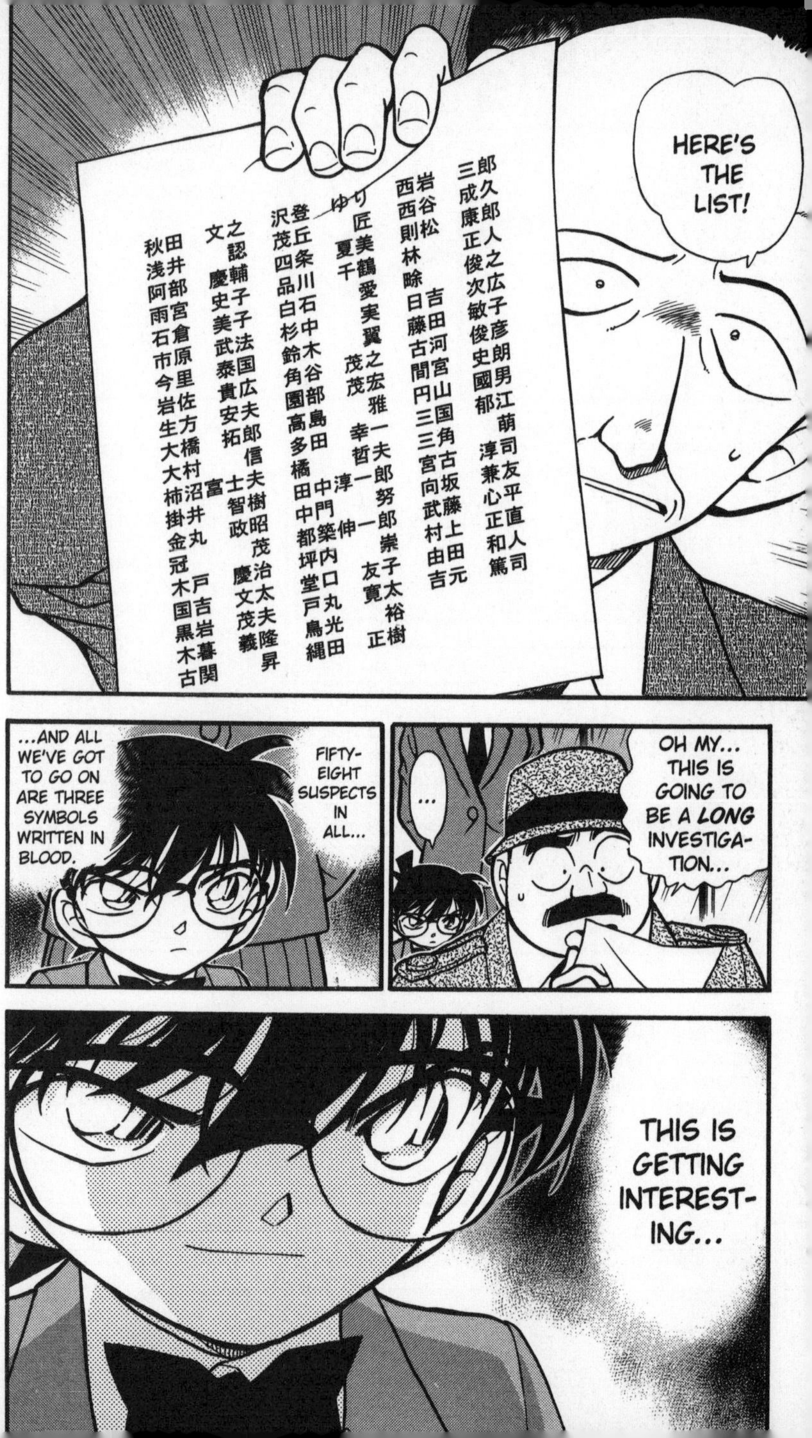
HERE'S THE LIST!
OH MY... THIS IS GOING TO BE A LONG INVESTIGATION...
...
FIFTY-EIGHT SUSPECTS IN ALL...
...AND ALL WE'VE GOT TO GO ON ARE THREE SYMBOLS WRITTEN IN BLOOD.
THIS IS GETTING INTERESTING...

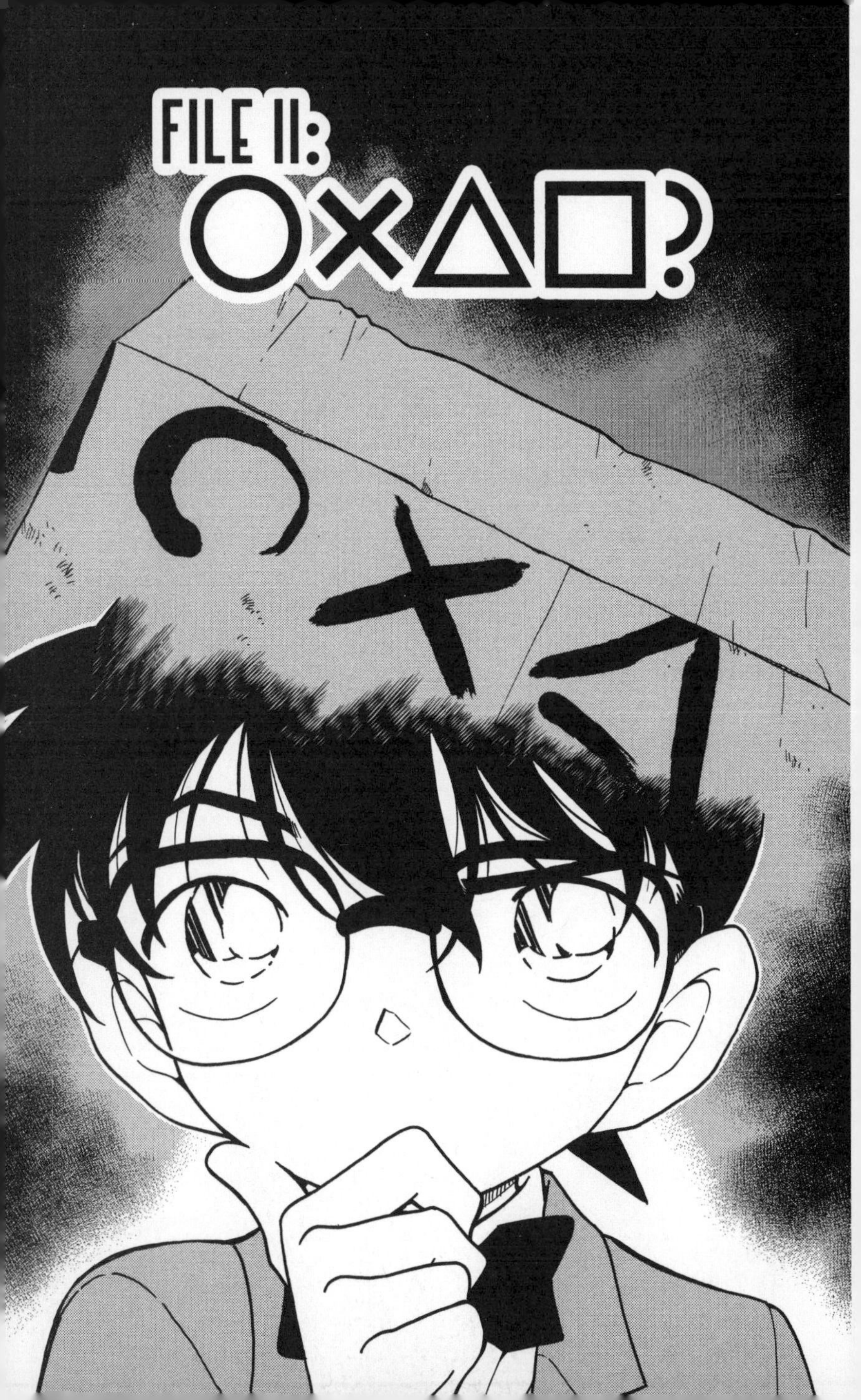
FILE 11:
○×△□?

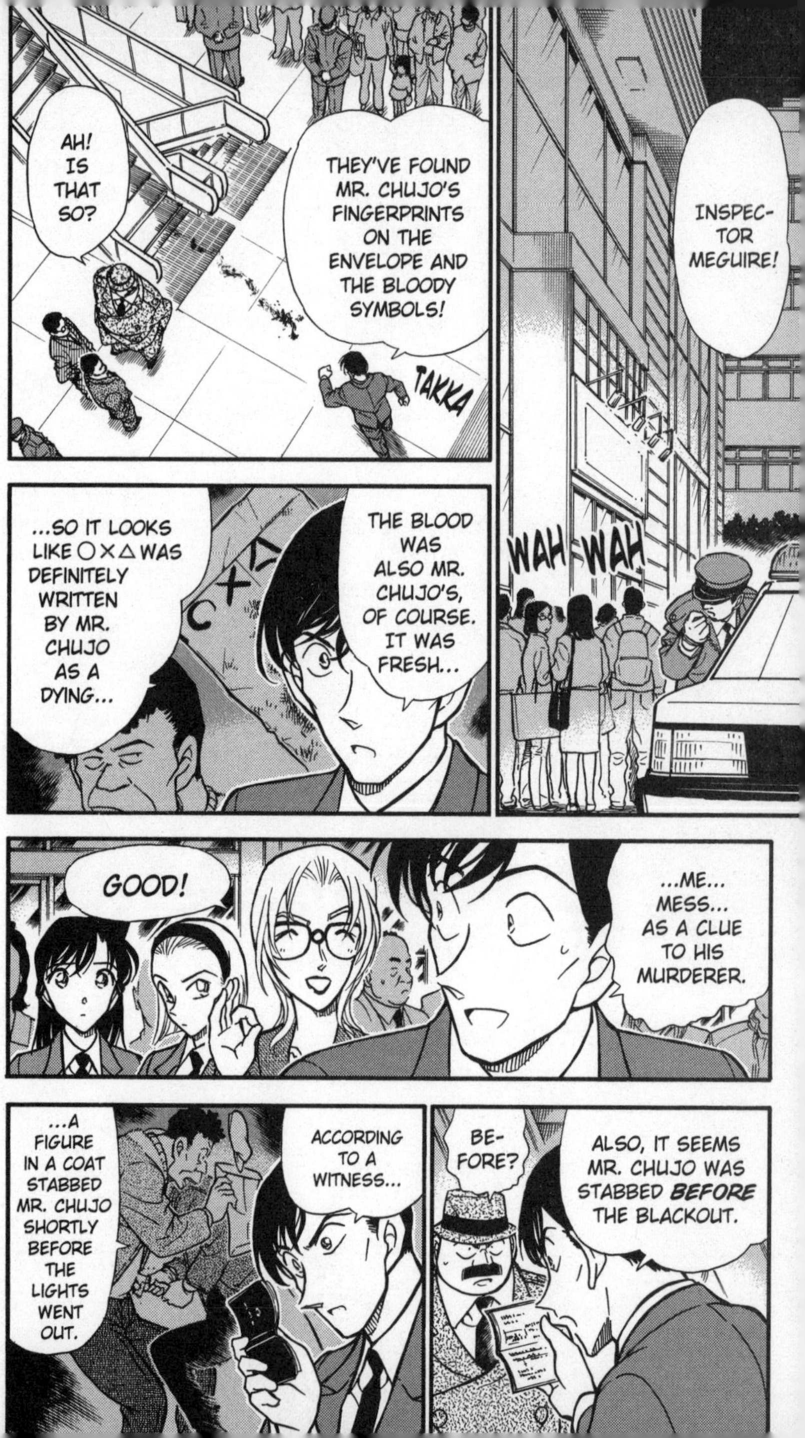
INSPECTOR MEGUIRE!
WAH WAH
THEY'VE FOUND MR. CHUJO'S FINGERPRINTS ON THE ENVELOPE AND THE BLOODY SYMBOLS!
TAKKA
AH! IS THAT SO?
THE BLOOD WAS ALSO MR. CHUJO'S, OF COURSE. IT WAS FRESH...
...SO IT LOOKS LIKE ○×△ WAS DEFINITELY WRITTEN BY MR. CHUJO AS A DYING...
...ME... MESS... AS A CLUE TO HIS MURDERER.
GOOD!
ALSO, IT SEEMS MR. CHUJO WAS STABBED BEFORE THE BLACKOUT.
BEFORE?
ACCORDING TO A WITNESS...
...A FIGURE IN A COAT STABBED MR. CHUJO SHORTLY BEFORE THE LIGHTS WENT OUT.

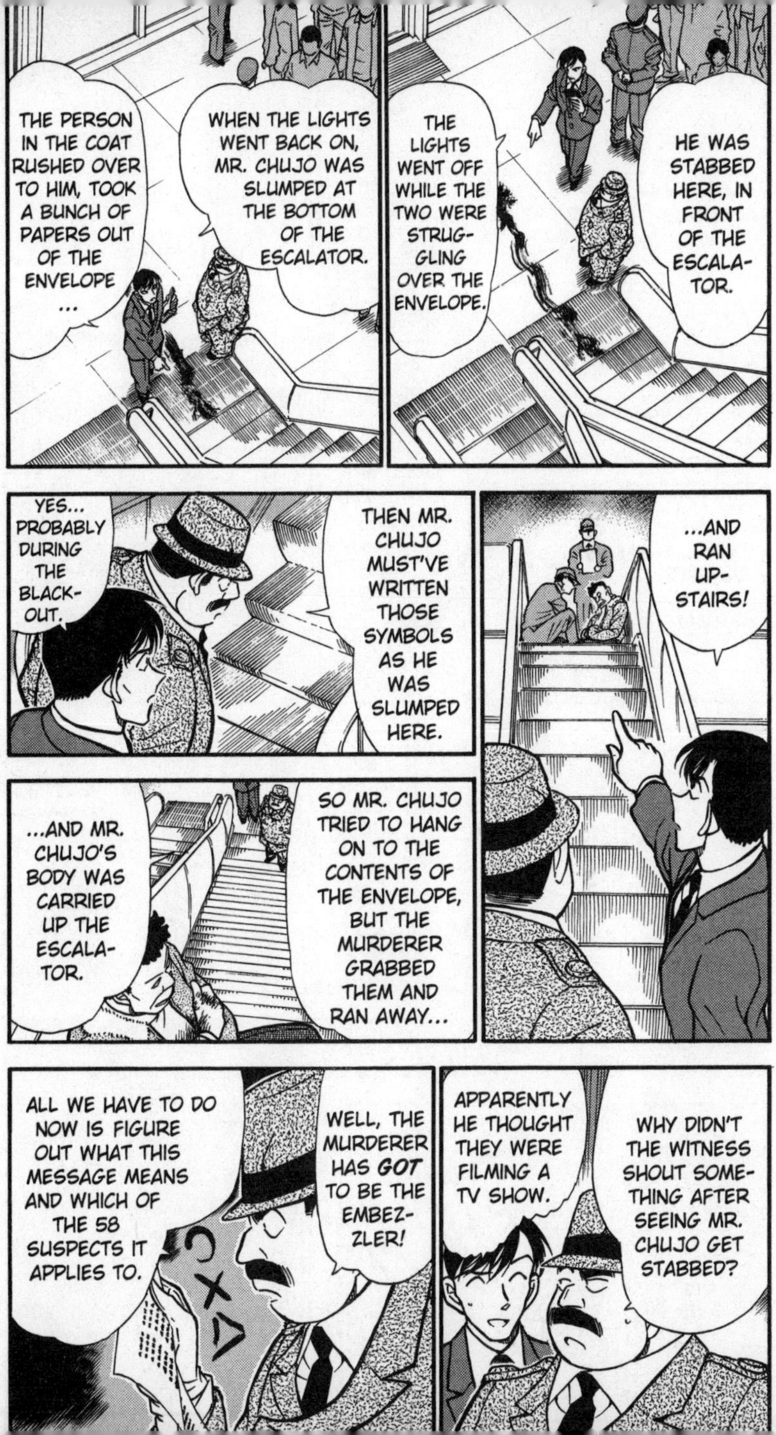
HE WAS STABBED HERE, IN FRONT OF THE ESCALATOR.
THE LIGHTS WENT OFF WHILE THE TWO WERE STRUGGLING OVER THE ENVELOPE.
WHEN THE LIGHTS WENT BACK ON, MR. CHUJO WAS SLUMPED AT THE BOTTOM OF THE ESCALATOR.
THE PERSON IN THE COAT RUSHED OVER TO HIM, TOOK A BUNCH OF PAPERS OUT OF THE ENVELOPE ...
...AND RAN UPSTAIRS!
THEN MR. CHUJO MUST'VE WRITTEN THOSE SYMBOLS AS HE WAS SLUMPED HERE.
YES... PROBABLY DURING THE BLACKOUT.
SO MR. CHUJO TRIED TO HANG ON TO THE CONTENTS OF THE ENVELOPE, BUT THE MURDERER GRABBED THEM AND RAN AWAY...
...AND MR. CHUJO'S BODY WAS CARRIED UP THE ESCALATOR.
WHY DIDN'T THE WITNESS SHOUT SOMETHING AFTER SEEING MR. CHUJO GET STABBED?
APPARENTLY HE THOUGHT THEY WERE FILMING A TV SHOW.
WELL, THE MURDERER HAS *GOT* TO BE THE EMBEZZLER!
ALL WE HAVE TO DO NOW IS FIGURE OUT WHAT THIS MESSAGE MEANS AND WHICH OF THE 58 SUSPECTS IT APPLIES TO.

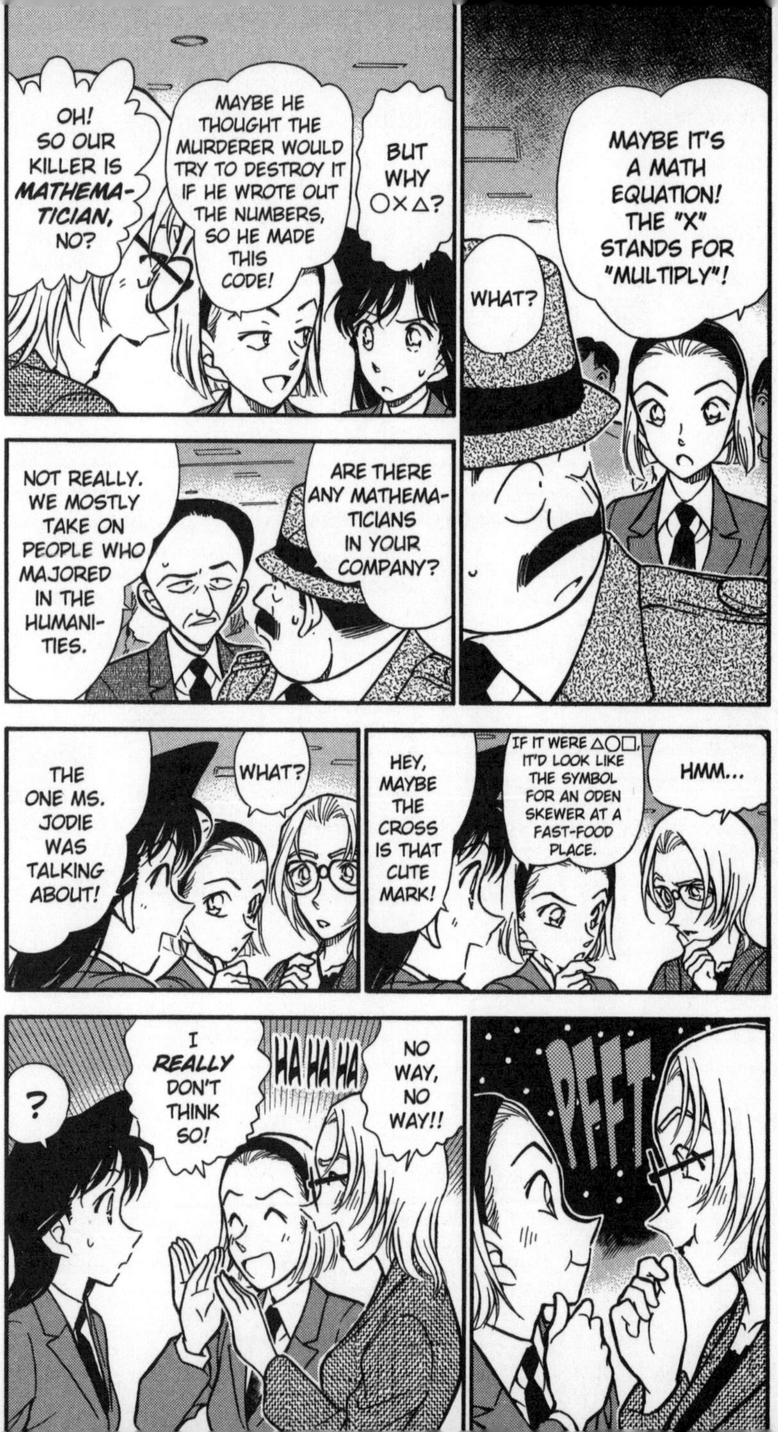
MAYBE IT'S A MATH EQUATION! THE "X" STANDS FOR "MULTIPLY"!
WHAT?
BUT WHY ○×△?
MAYBE HE THOUGHT THE MURDERER WOULD TRY TO DESTROY IT IF HE WROTE OUT THE NUMBERS, SO HE MADE THIS CODE!
OH! SO OUR KILLER IS *MATHEMATICIAN*, NO?
ARE THERE ANY MATHEMATICIANS IN YOUR COMPANY?
NOT REALLY. WE MOSTLY TAKE ON PEOPLE WHO MAJORED IN THE HUMANITIES.
HMM...
IF IT WERE △○□, IT'D LOOK LIKE THE SYMBOL FOR AN ODEN SKEWER AT A FAST-FOOD PLACE.
HEY, MAYBE THE CROSS IS THAT CUTE MARK!
WHAT?
THE ONE MS. JODIE WAS TALKING ABOUT!
PFFT
NO WAY, NO WAY!!
HA HA HA
I *REALLY* DON'T THINK SO!
?

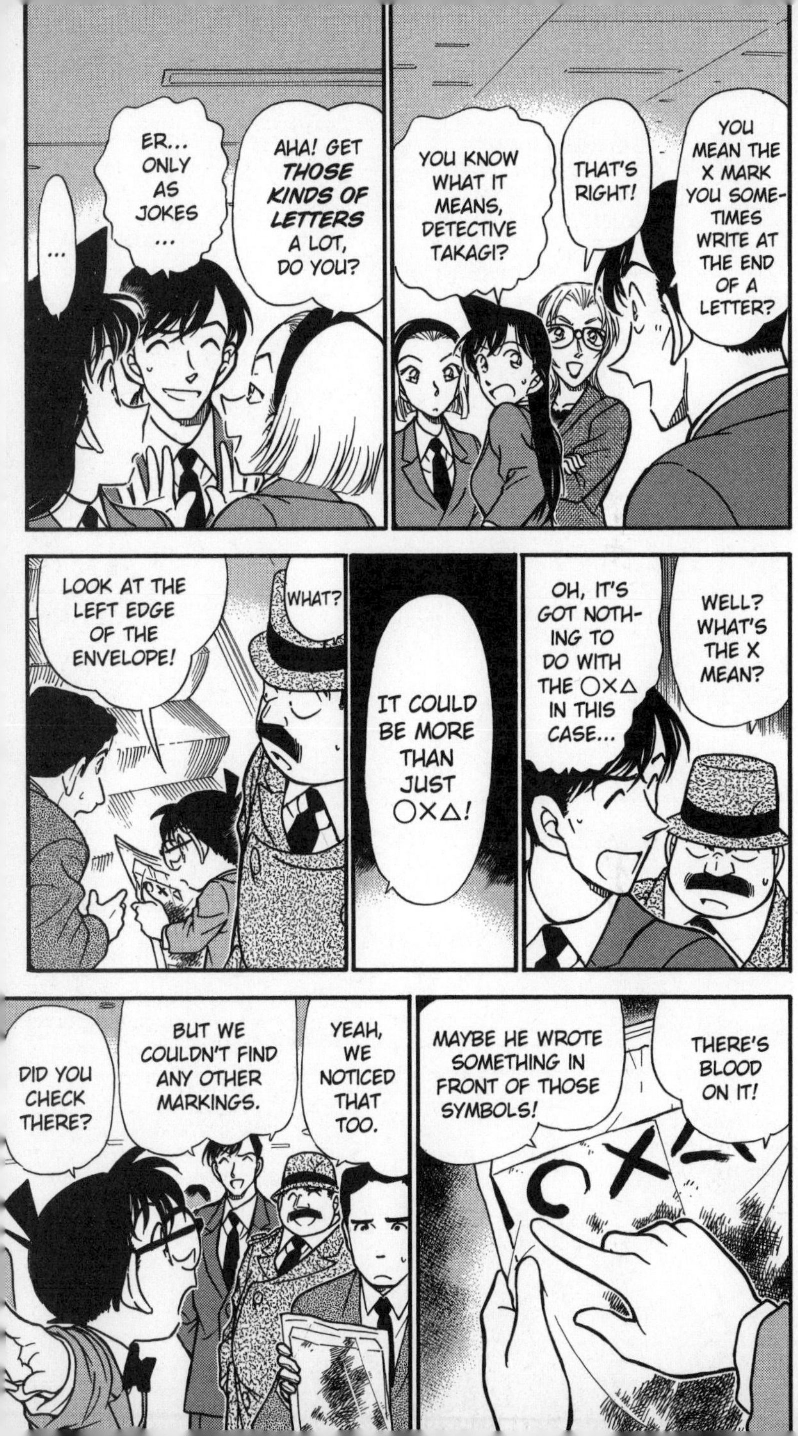
YOU MEAN THE X MARK YOU SOMETIMES WRITE AT THE END OF A LETTER?
THAT'S RIGHT!
YOU KNOW WHAT IT MEANS, DETECTIVE TAKAGI?
AHA! GET **THOSE KINDS OF LETTERS** A LOT, DO YOU?
ER... ONLY AS JOKES ...
...
WELL? WHAT'S THE X MEAN?
OH, IT'S GOT NOTHING TO DO WITH THE ○×△ IN THIS CASE...
IT COULD BE MORE THAN JUST ○×△!
WHAT?
LOOK AT THE LEFT EDGE OF THE ENVELOPE!
THERE'S BLOOD ON IT!
MAYBE HE WROTE SOMETHING IN FRONT OF THOSE SYMBOLS!
YEAH, WE NOTICED THAT TOO.
BUT WE COULDN'T FIND ANY OTHER MARKINGS.
DID YOU CHECK THERE?

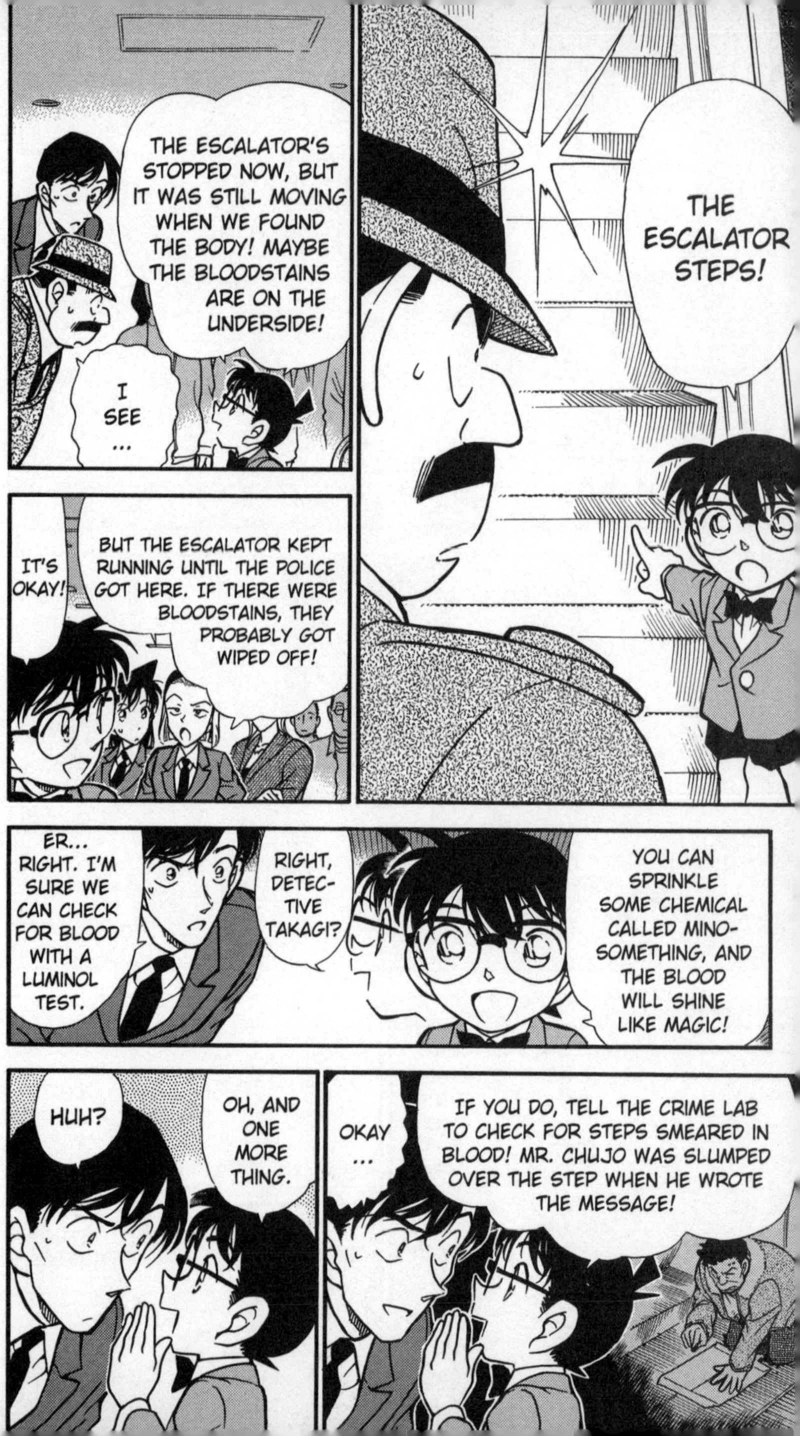
THE ESCALATOR STEPS!
THE ESCALATOR'S STOPPED NOW, BUT IT WAS STILL MOVING WHEN WE FOUND THE BODY! MAYBE THE BLOODSTAINS ARE ON THE UNDERSIDE!
I SEE ...
BUT THE ESCALATOR KEPT RUNNING UNTIL THE POLICE GOT HERE. IF THERE WERE BLOODSTAINS, THEY PROBABLY GOT WIPED OFF!
IT'S OKAY!
YOU CAN SPRINKLE SOME CHEMICAL CALLED MINO-SOMETHING, AND THE BLOOD WILL SHINE LIKE MAGIC!
RIGHT, DETEC-TIVE TAKAGI?
ER... RIGHT. I'M SURE WE CAN CHECK FOR BLOOD WITH A LUMINOL TEST.
IF YOU DO, TELL THE CRIME LAB TO CHECK FOR STEPS SMEARED IN BLOOD! MR. CHUJO WAS SLUMPED OVER THE STEP WHEN HE WROTE THE MESSAGE!
OKAY ...
OH, AND ONE MORE THING.
HUH?

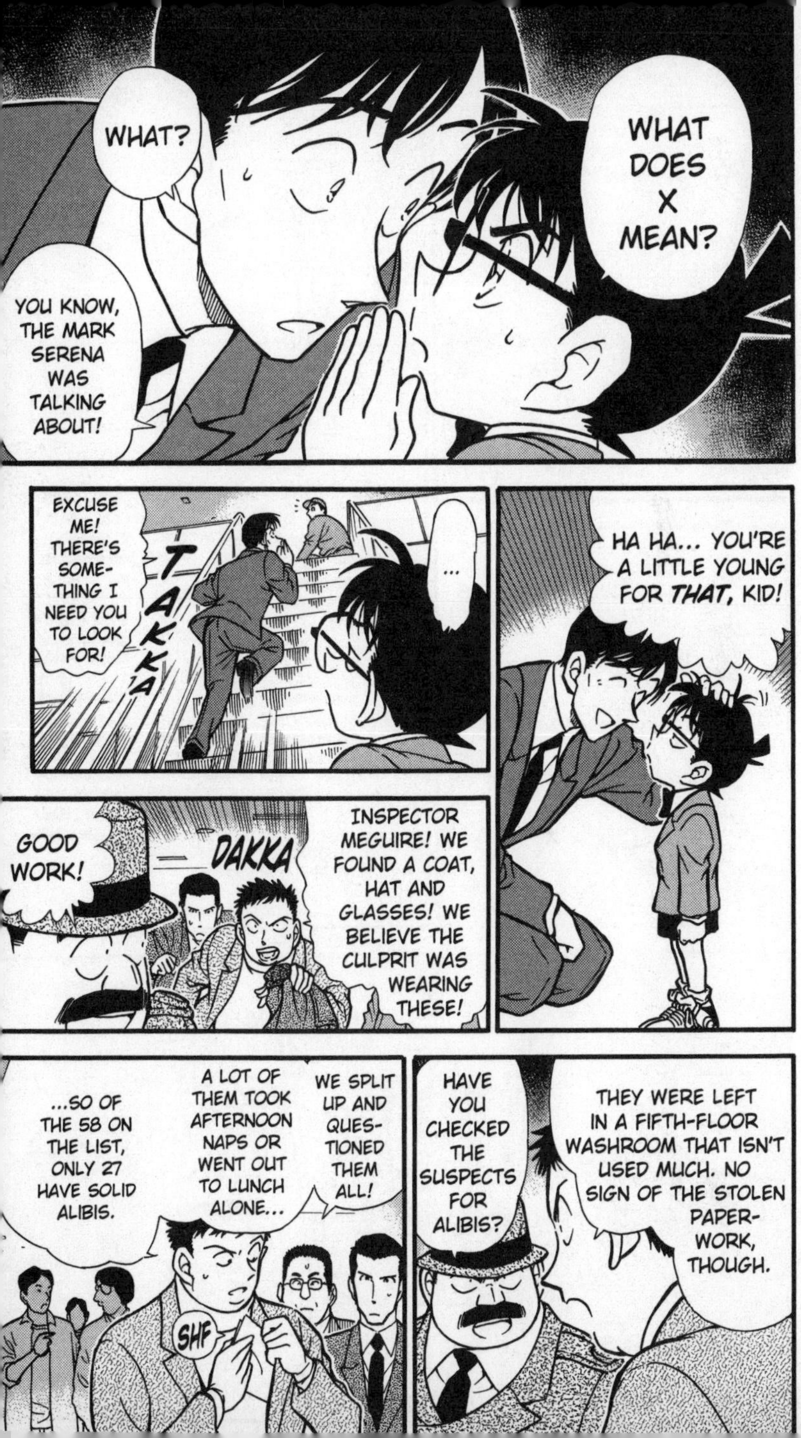
WHAT DOES X MEAN?
WHAT?
YOU KNOW, THE MARK SERENA WAS TALKING ABOUT!
HA HA... YOU'RE A LITTLE YOUNG FOR *THAT*, KID!
...
EXCUSE ME! THERE'S SOME-THING I NEED YOU TO LOOK FOR!
TAKKA
INSPECTOR MEGUIRE! WE FOUND A COAT, HAT AND GLASSES! WE BELIEVE THE CULPRIT WAS WEARING THESE!
DAKKA
GOOD WORK!
THEY WERE LEFT IN A FIFTH-FLOOR WASHROOM THAT ISN'T USED MUCH. NO SIGN OF THE STOLEN PAPER-WORK, THOUGH.
HAVE YOU CHECKED THE SUSPECTS FOR ALIBIS?
WE SPLIT UP AND QUES-TIONED THEM ALL!
A LOT OF THEM TOOK AFTERNOON NAPS OR WENT OUT TO LUNCH ALONE...
...SO OF THE 58 ON THE LIST, ONLY 27 HAVE SOLID ALIBIS.
SHF

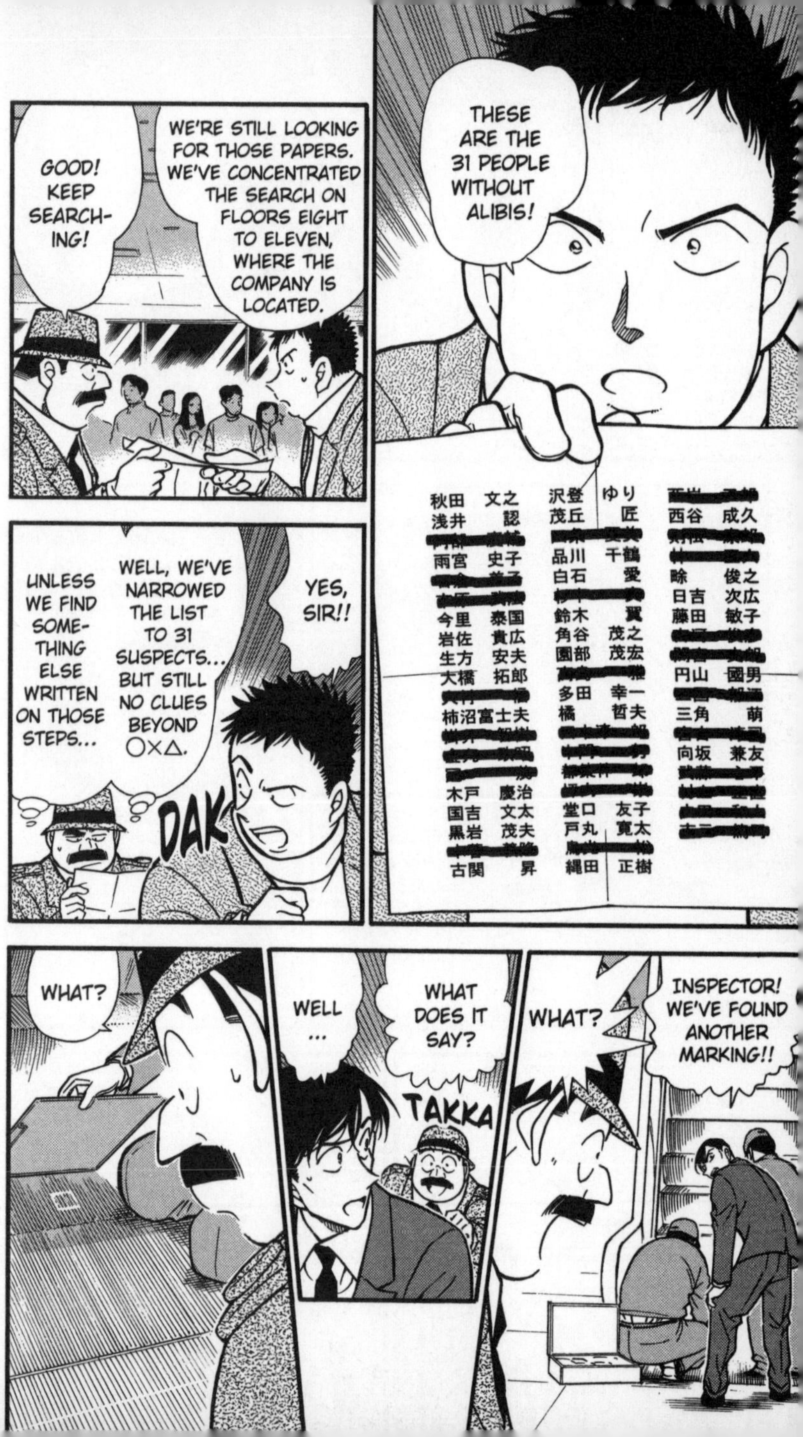
THESE ARE THE 31 PEOPLE WITHOUT ALIBIS!
秋田 文之
浅井 認
[redacted]
雨宮 史子
[redacted]
今里 泰国
岩佐 貴広
生方 安夫
大橋 拓郎
[redacted]
柿沼富士夫
[redacted]
木戸 慶治
国吉 文太
黒岩 茂夫
[redacted]
古関 昇
沢登 ゆり
茂丘 匠
[redacted]
品川 千鶴
白石 愛
[redacted]
鈴木 翼
角谷 茂之
園部 茂宏
[redacted]
多田 幸一
橘 哲夫
[redacted]
堂口 友子
戸丸 寛太
[redacted]
縄田 正樹
[redacted]
西谷 成久
[redacted]
畭 俊之
日吉 次広
藤田 敏子
[redacted]
円山 國男
[redacted]
三角 萌
[redacted]
向坂 兼友
[redacted]
WE'RE STILL LOOKING FOR THOSE PAPERS. WE'VE CONCENTRATED THE SEARCH ON FLOORS EIGHT TO ELEVEN, WHERE THE COMPANY IS LOCATED.
GOOD! KEEP SEARCH-ING!
YES, SIR!!
WELL, WE'VE NARROWED THE LIST TO 31 SUSPECTS... BUT STILL NO CLUES BEYOND ○×△.
DAK
UNLESS WE FIND SOME-THING ELSE WRITTEN ON THOSE STEPS...
INSPECTOR! WE'VE FOUND ANOTHER MARKING!!
WHAT?
WHAT DOES IT SAY?
TAKKA
WELL ...
WHAT?

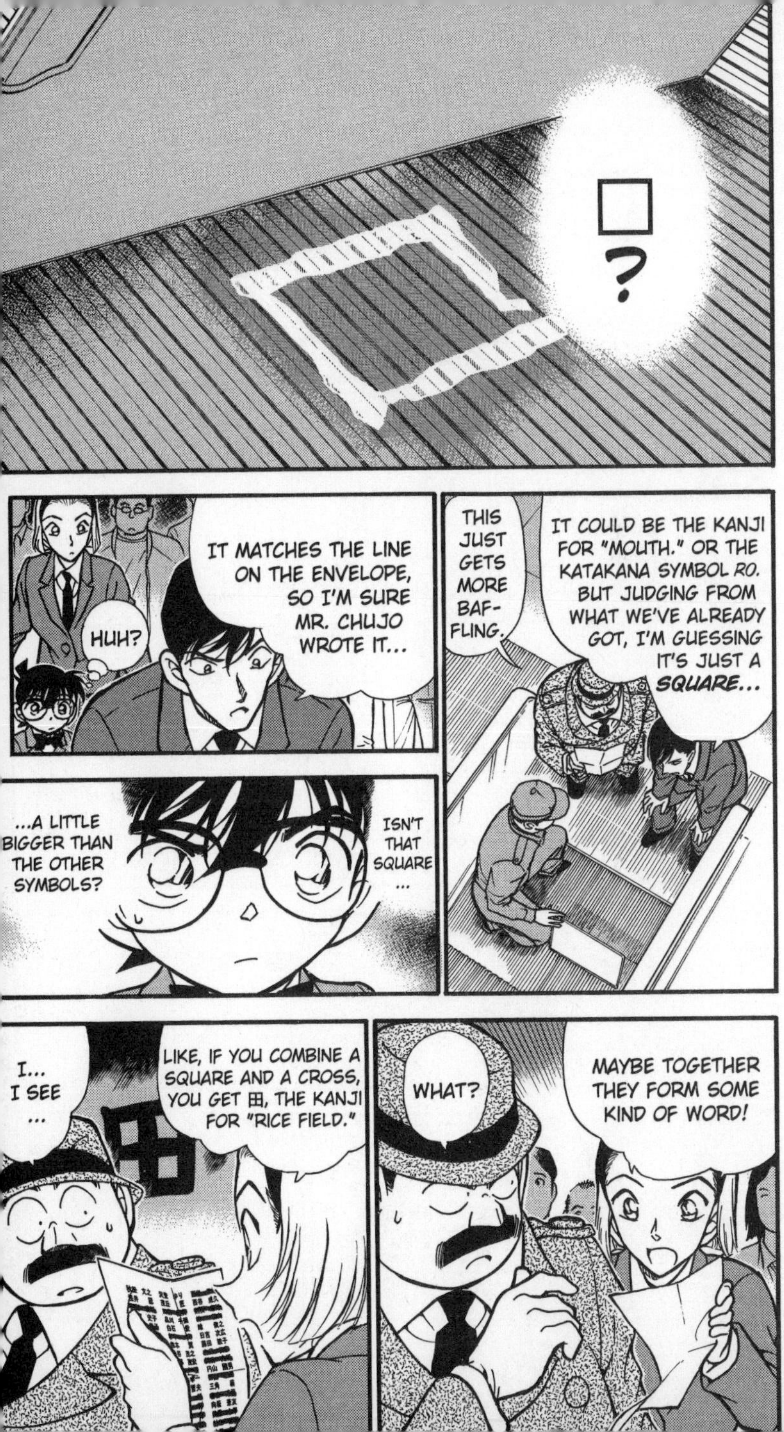
□?
IT COULD BE THE KANJI FOR "MOUTH," OR THE KATAKANA SYMBOL *RO*. BUT JUDGING FROM WHAT WE'VE ALREADY GOT, I'M GUESSING IT'S JUST A ***SQUARE...***
THIS JUST GETS MORE BAF-FLING.
IT MATCHES THE LINE ON THE ENVELOPE, SO I'M SURE MR. CHUJO WROTE IT...
HUH?
ISN'T THAT SQUARE...
...A LITTLE BIGGER THAN THE OTHER SYMBOLS?
MAYBE TOGETHER THEY FORM SOME KIND OF WORD!
WHAT?
LIKE, IF YOU COMBINE A SQUARE AND A CROSS, YOU GET 田, THE KANJI FOR "RICE FIELD."
I... I SEE...

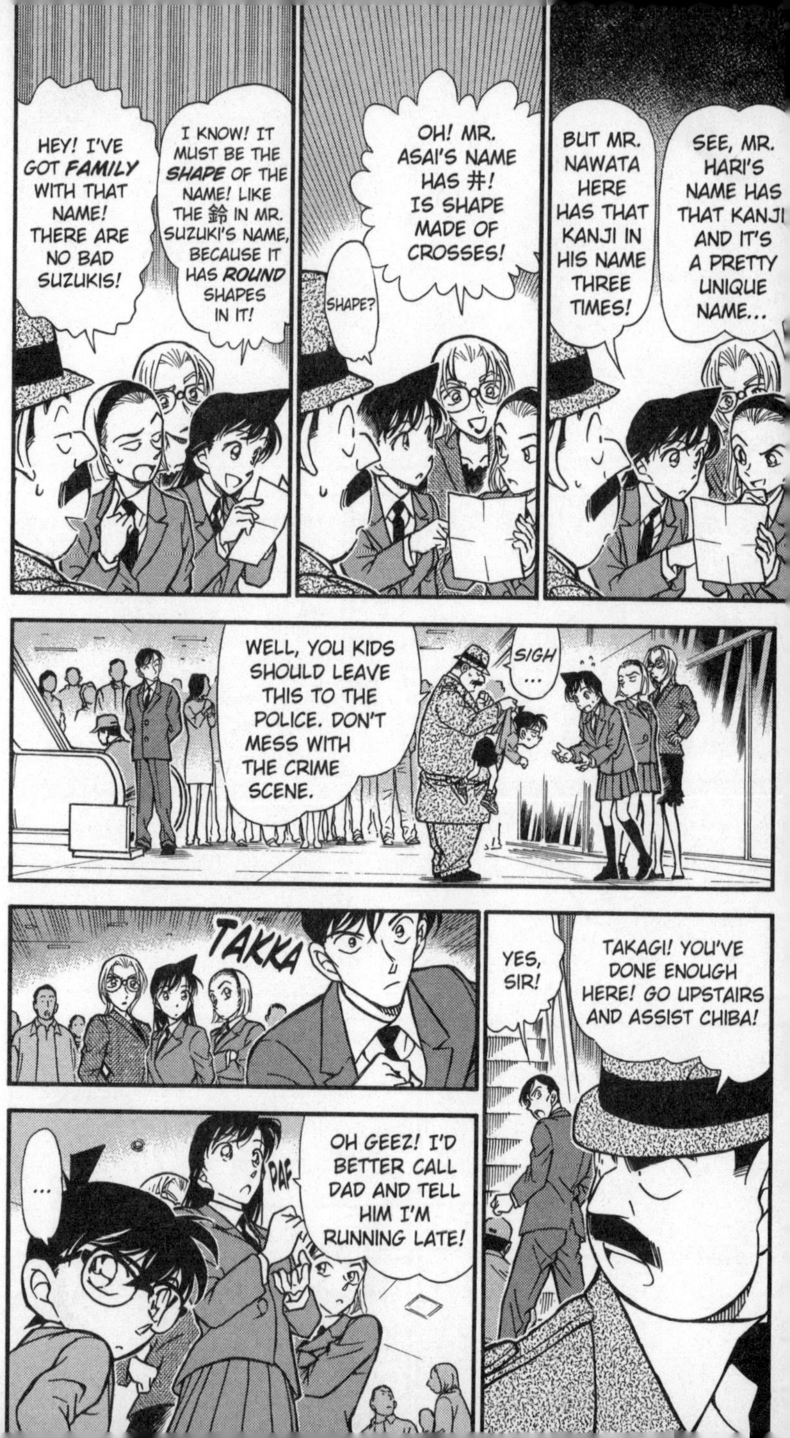
SEE, MR. HARI'S NAME HAS THAT KANJI AND IT'S A PRETTY UNIQUE NAME...
BUT MR. NAWATA HERE HAS THAT KANJI IN HIS NAME THREE TIMES!
OH! MR. ASAI'S NAME HAS 井! IS SHAPE MADE OF CROSSES!
SHAPE?
I KNOW! IT MUST BE THE SHAPE OF THE NAME! LIKE THE 鈴 IN MR. SUZUKI'S NAME, BECAUSE IT HAS ROUND SHAPES IN IT!
HEY! I'VE GOT FAMILY WITH THAT NAME! THERE ARE NO BAD SUZUKIS!
SIGH...
WELL, YOU KIDS SHOULD LEAVE THIS TO THE POLICE. DON'T MESS WITH THE CRIME SCENE.
TAKAGI! YOU'VE DONE ENOUGH HERE! GO UPSTAIRS AND ASSIST CHIBA!
YES, SIR!
TAKKA
PAF
OH GEEZ! I'D BETTER CALL DAD AND TELL HIM I'M RUNNING LATE!
...

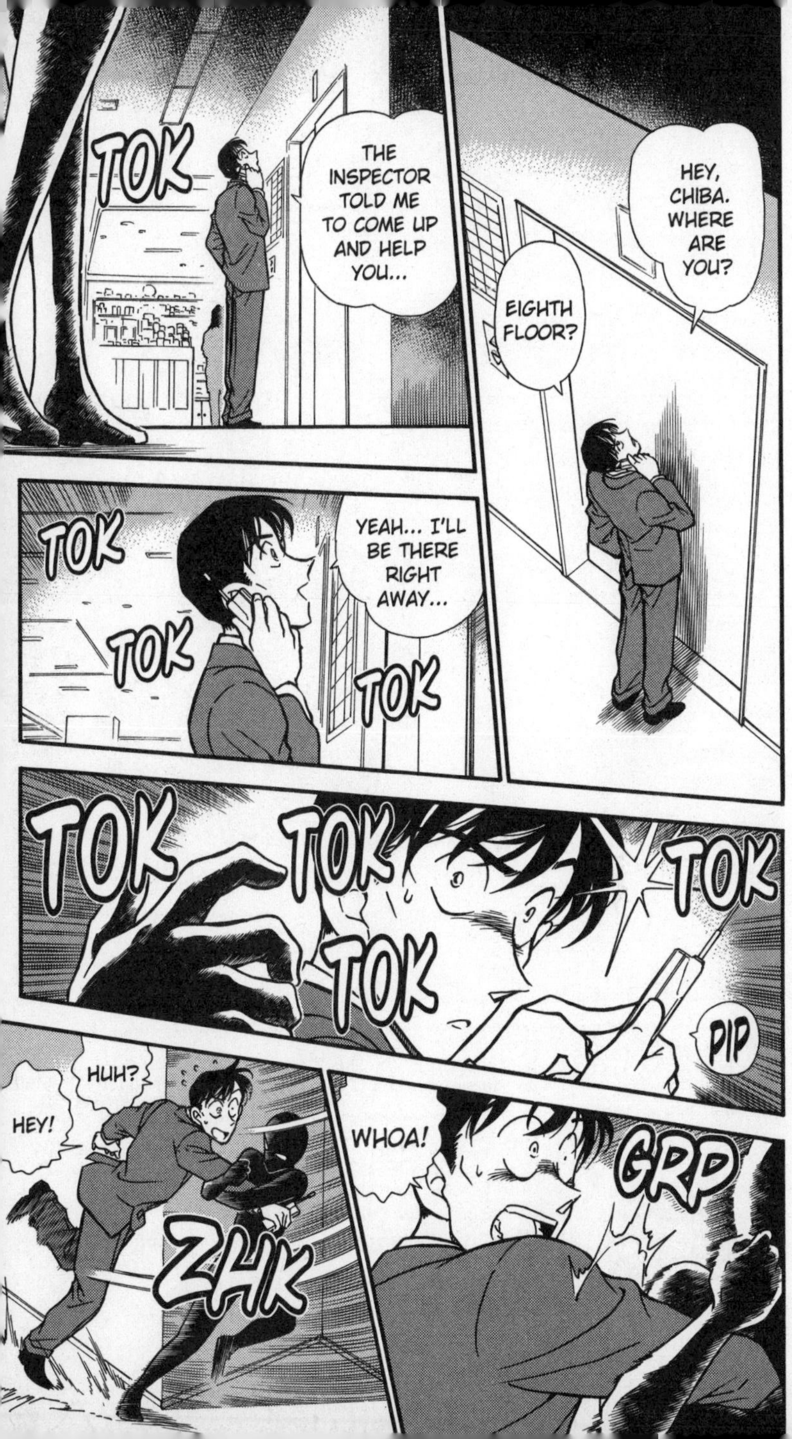
HEY, CHIBA. WHERE ARE YOU?
EIGHTH FLOOR?
THE INSPECTOR TOLD ME TO COME UP AND HELP YOU...
TOK
YEAH... I'LL BE THERE RIGHT AWAY...
TOK
TOK
TOK
TOK
TOK
TOK
TOK
PIP
GRP
WHOA!
HUH?
HEY!
ZHK

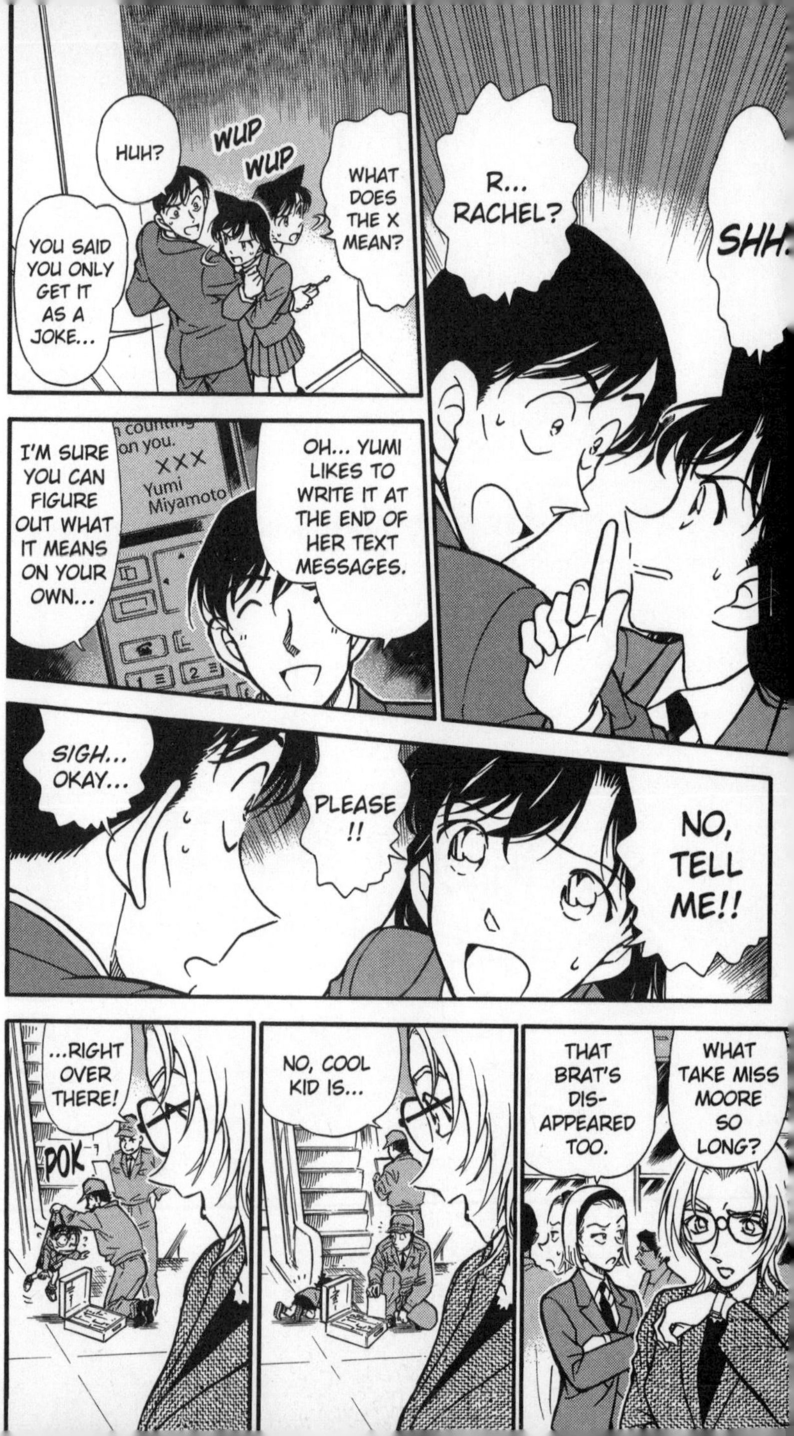
R... RACHEL?
SHH.
WHAT DOES THE X MEAN?
HUH?
WUP WUP
YOU SAID YOU ONLY GET IT AS A JOKE...
OH... YUMI LIKES TO WRITE IT AT THE END OF HER TEXT MESSAGES.
on you.
XXX
Yumi Miyamoto
I'M SURE YOU CAN FIGURE OUT WHAT IT MEANS ON YOUR OWN...
NO, TELL ME!!
PLEASE!!
SIGH... OKAY...
WHAT TAKE MISS MOORE SO LONG?
THAT BRAT'S DIS-APPEARED TOO.
NO, COOL KID IS...
...RIGHT OVER THERE!
POK

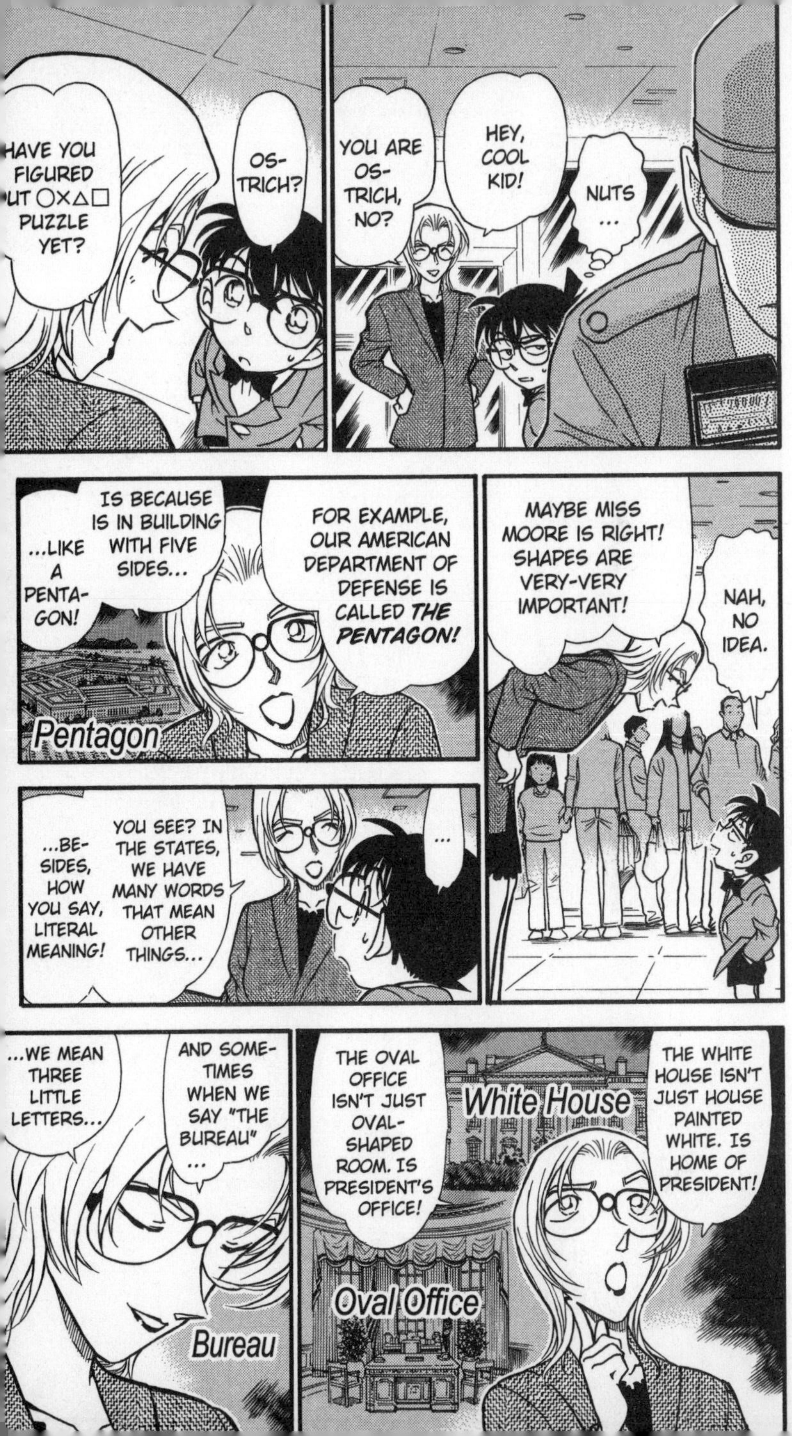
NUTS ...
HEY, COOL KID!
YOU ARE OS-TRICH, NO?
OS-TRICH?
HAVE YOU FIGURED UT ○×△□ PUZZLE YET?
NAH, NO IDEA.
MAYBE MISS MOORE IS RIGHT! SHAPES ARE VERY-VERY IMPORTANT!
FOR EXAMPLE, OUR AMERICAN DEPARTMENT OF DEFENSE IS CALLED *THE PENTAGON!*
IS BECAUSE IS IN BUILDING WITH FIVE SIDES...
...LIKE A PENTA-GON!
Pentagon
...
YOU SEE? IN THE STATES, WE HAVE MANY WORDS THAT MEAN OTHER THINGS...
...BE-SIDES, HOW YOU SAY, LITERAL MEANING!
THE WHITE HOUSE ISN'T JUST HOUSE PAINTED WHITE. IS HOME OF PRESIDENT!
White House
THE OVAL OFFICE ISN'T JUST OVAL-SHAPED ROOM. IS PRESIDENT'S OFFICE!
Oval Office
AND SOME-TIMES WHEN WE SAY "THE BUREAU" ...
...WE MEAN THREE LITTLE LETTERS...
Bureau

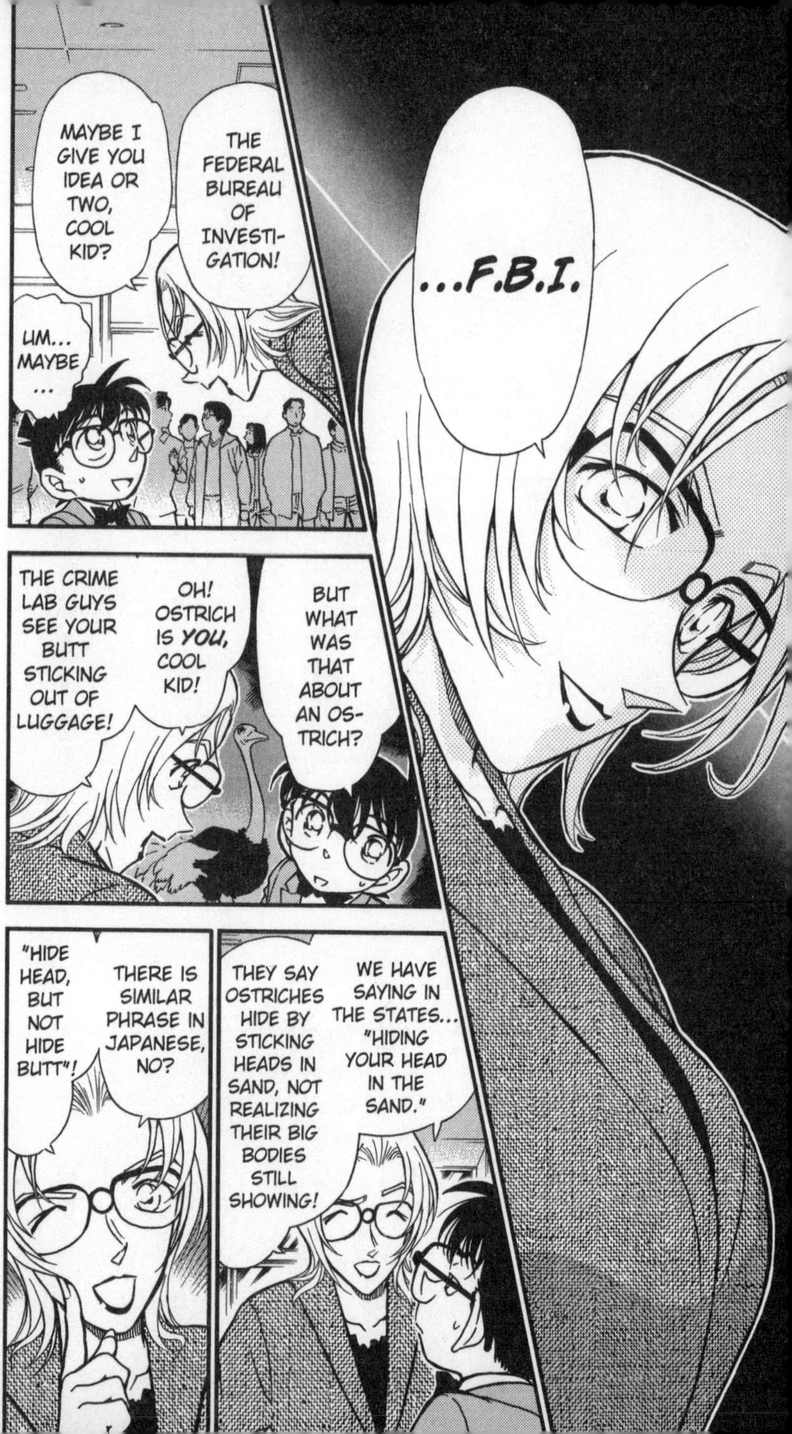
...F.B.I.
THE FEDERAL BUREAU OF INVESTIGATION!
MAYBE I GIVE YOU IDEA OR TWO, COOL KID?
UM... MAYBE ...
BUT WHAT WAS THAT ABOUT AN OSTRICH?
OH! OSTRICH IS *YOU*, COOL KID!
THE CRIME LAB GUYS SEE YOUR BUTT STICKING OUT OF LUGGAGE!
WE HAVE SAYING IN THE STATES... "HIDING YOUR HEAD IN THE SAND."
THEY SAY OSTRICHES HIDE BY STICKING HEADS IN SAND, NOT REALIZING THEIR BIG BODIES STILL SHOWING!
THERE IS SIMILAR PHRASE IN JAPANESE, NO?
"HIDE HEAD, BUT NOT HIDE BUTT"!

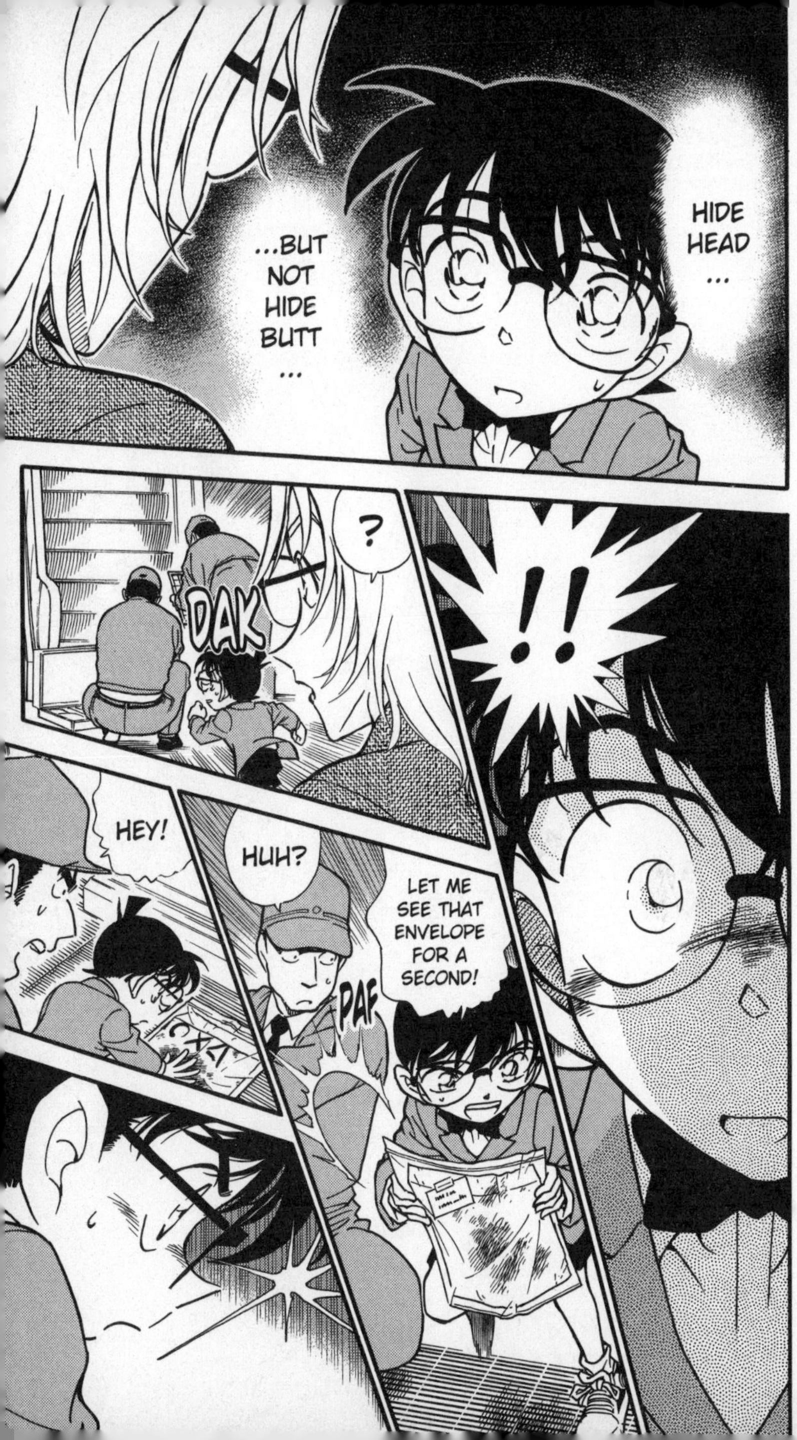
HIDE HEAD ...
...BUT NOT HIDE BUTT ...
!!
?
DAK
HUH?
LET ME SEE THAT ENVELOPE FOR A SECOND!
PAF
HEY!

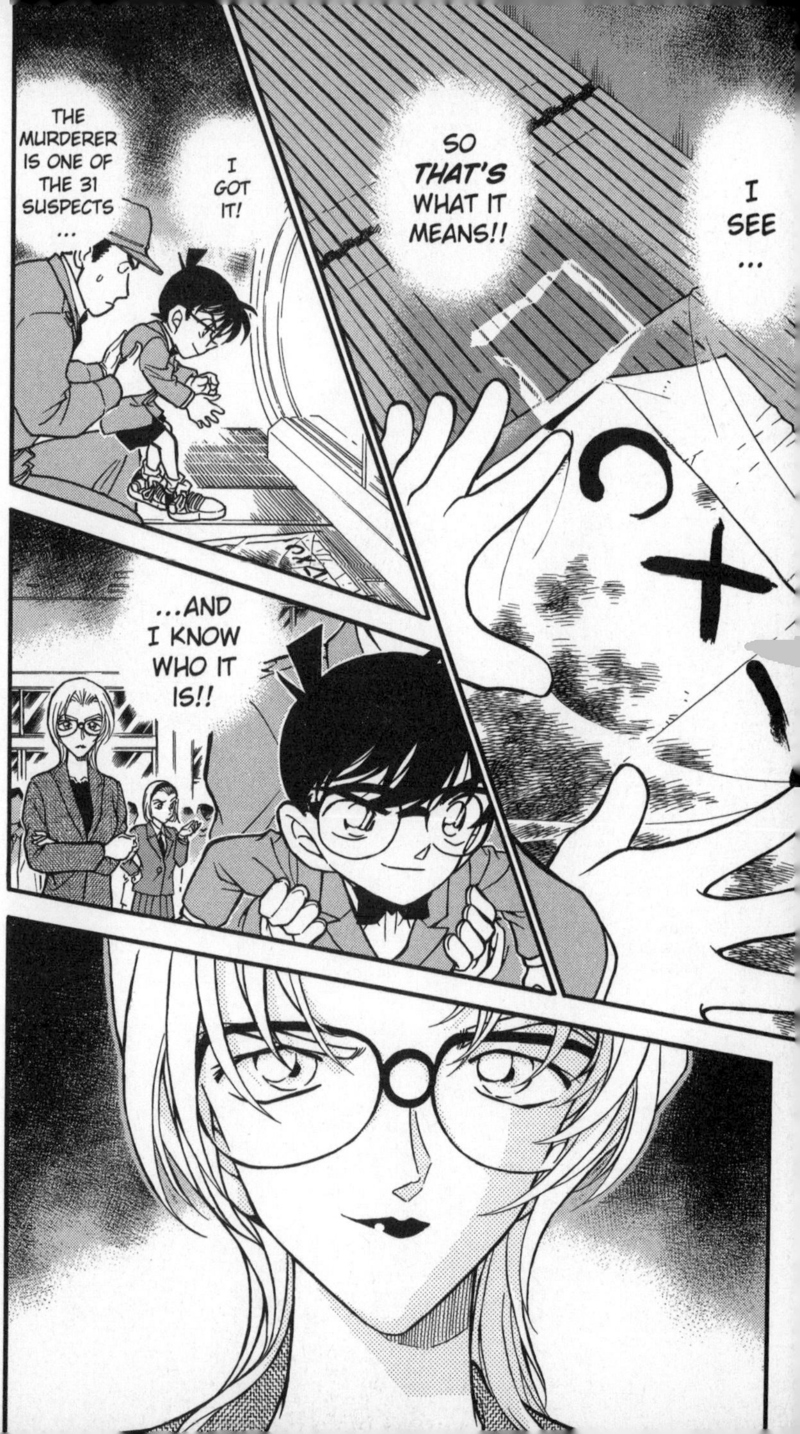
I SEE ...
SO *THAT'S* WHAT IT MEANS!!
I GOT IT!
THE MURDERER IS ONE OF THE 31 SUSPECTS ...
...AND I KNOW WHO IT IS!!

Hello, Aoyama here.

The last chapter in this volume includes 58 suspects! As it happens, 22 of them are the names of *Shonen Sunday* editors!!

It might be fun to try to deduce which names those are... but I guess there's no way for you to know. Heh...

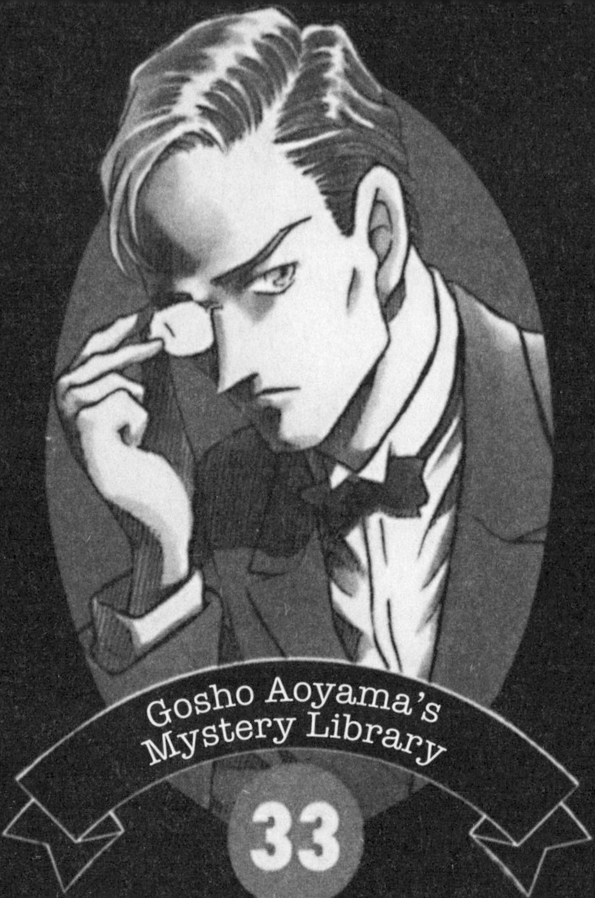
Gosho Aoyama's
Mystery Library
33

PHILO VANCE

Many master sleuths are so smart they can come off as annoying or offensive. Philo Vance is the epitome of this. He's a tall, well-built, handsome man with a European look, single and 34. He's very educated and has a wide variety of interests. His aunt left him a vast fortune, so he lives a life of leisure in a lavish condo in New York.

As a detective, Vance is less interested in physical evidence than in analyzing a criminal's psychology. He sarcastically tears through the no-nonsense investigations of his friend, District Attorney Markham, and solves the most puzzling cases with ease. His creator, S.S. Van Dine, is the author of the famous "Twenty Rules for Writing Detective Stories." His third rule is "There must be no love interest. The business in hand is to bring a criminal to the bar of justice, not to bring a lovelorn couple to the hymeneal altar." You should take these with a grain of salt... heh.

I recommend *The Bishop Murder Case.*

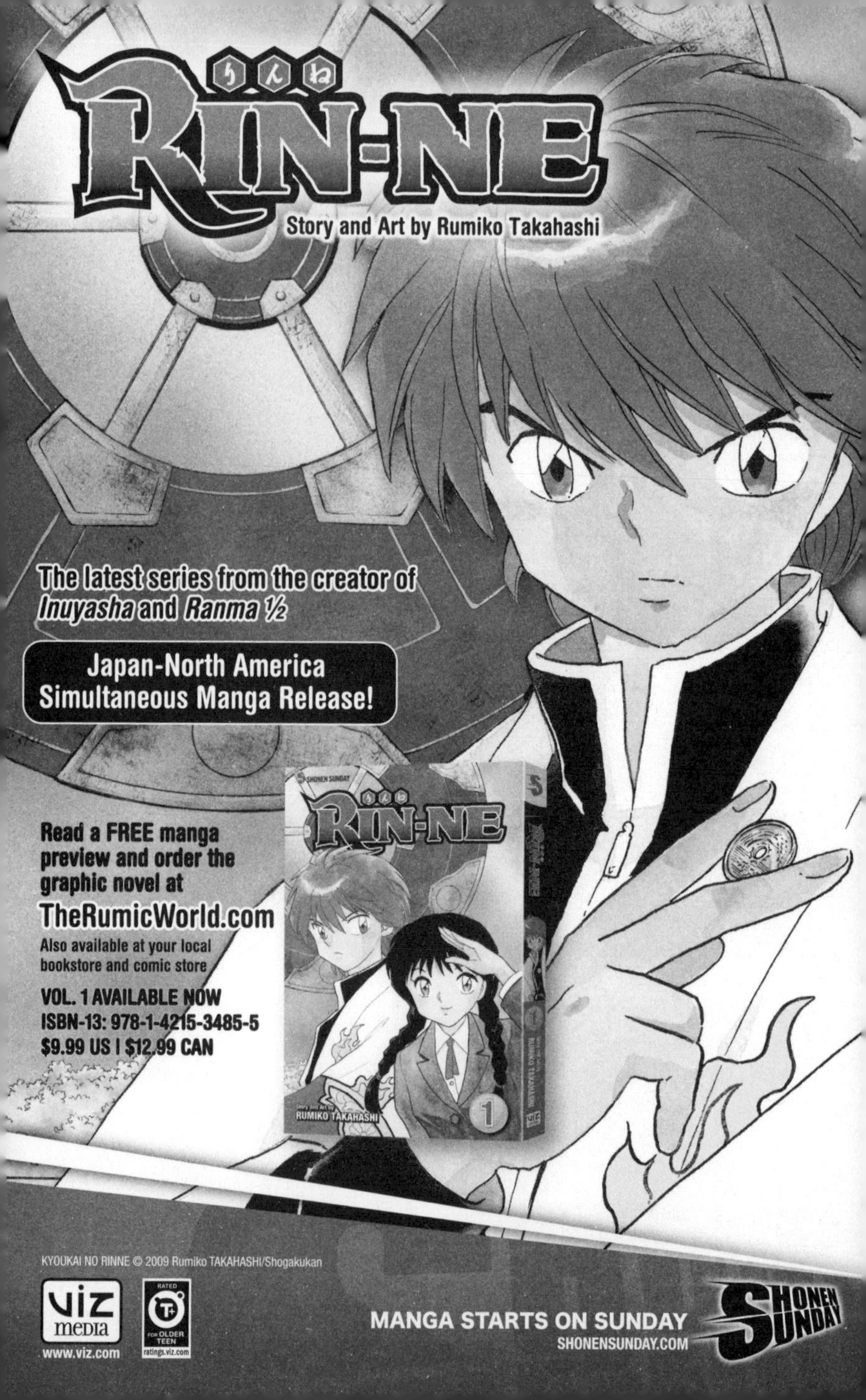

りんね
RIN-NE
Story and Art by Rumiko Takahashi
The latest series from the creator of
Inuyasha and *Ranma ½*
Japan-North America
Simultaneous Manga Release!
SHONEN SUNDAY
RIN-NE
Story and Art by
RUMIKO TAKAHASHI
1
Read a FREE manga
preview and order the
graphic novel at
TheRumicWorld.com
Also available at your local
bookstore and comic store
VOL. 1 AVAILABLE NOW
ISBN-13: 978-1-4215-3485-5
$9.99 US | $12.99 CAN
KYOUKAI NO RINNE © 2009 Rumiko TAKAHASHI/Shogakukan
viz media
www.viz.com
RATED T+ FOR OLDER TEEN
ratings.viz.com
MANGA STARTS ON SUNDAY
SHONENSUNDAY.COM
SHONEN SUNDAY

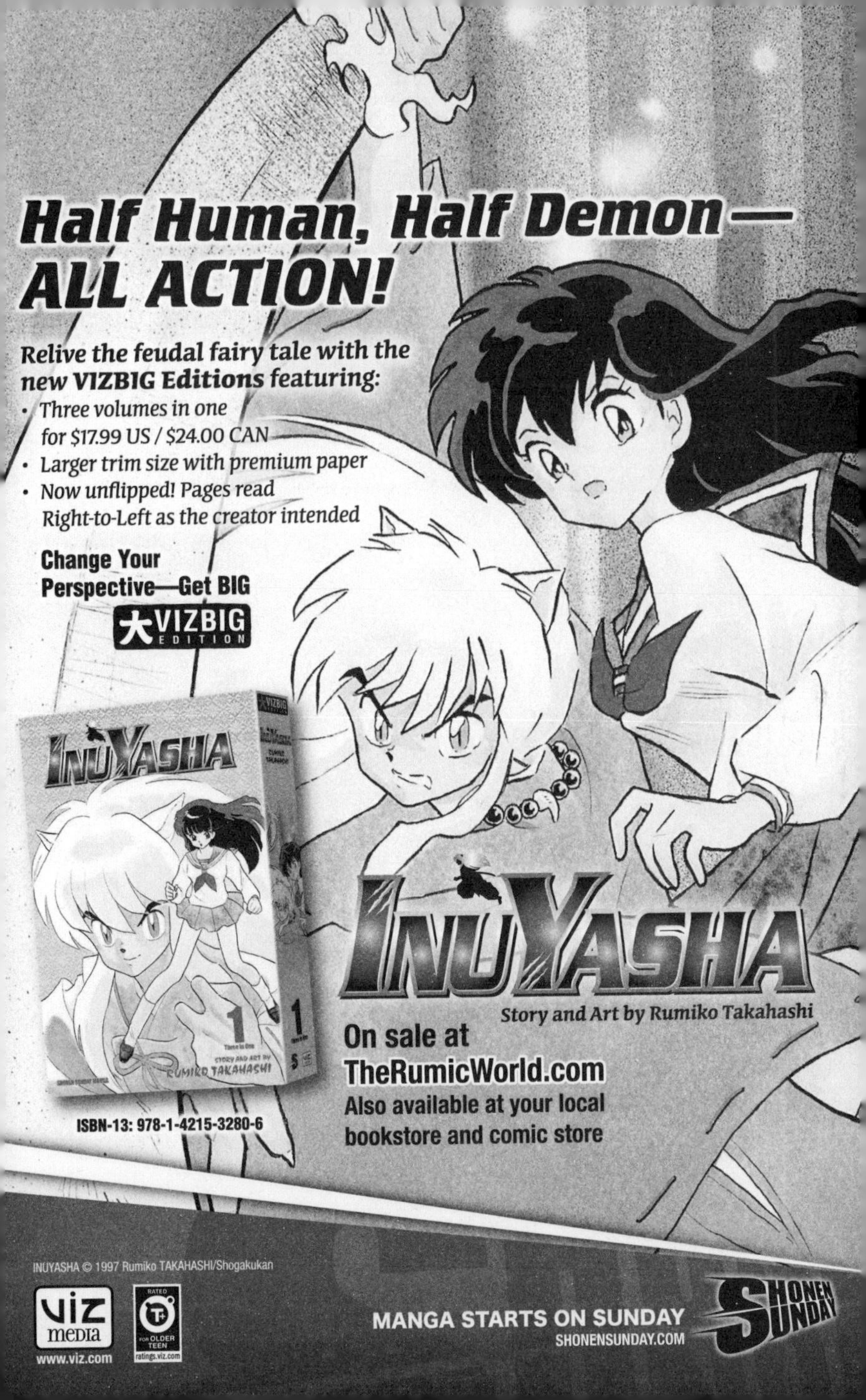
Half Human, Half Demon—
ALL ACTION!
Relive the feudal fairy tale with the new VIZBIG Editions featuring:
• Three volumes in one for $17.99 US / $24.00 CAN
• Larger trim size with premium paper
• Now unflipped! Pages read Right-to-Left as the creator intended
Change Your Perspective—Get BIG
大VIZBIG EDITION
INUYASHA
1
STORY AND ART BY RUMIKO TAKAHASHI
ISBN-13: 978-1-4215-3280-6
INUYASHA
Story and Art by Rumiko Takahashi
On sale at
TheRumicWorld.com
Also available at your local bookstore and comic store
INUYASHA © 1997 Rumiko TAKAHASHI/Shogakukan
viz media
www.viz.com
RATED T+ FOR OLDER TEEN
ratings.viz.com
MANGA STARTS ON SUNDAY
SHONENSUNDAY.COM
SHONEN SUNDAY

Hey! You're Reading in the Wrong Direction!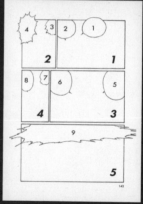

This is the **end** of this graphic novel!

To properly enjoy this VIZ graphic novel, please turn it around and begin reading from **right to left**. Unlike English, Japanese is read right to left, so Japanese comics are read in reverse order from the way English comics are typically read.

Follow the action this way

This book has been printed in the original Japanese format in order to preserve the orientation of the original artwork. Have fun with it!